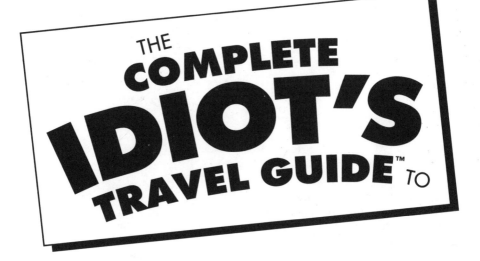

THE COMPLETE IDIOT'S TRAVEL GUIDE™ TO

Paris

p49

D0009588

by Suzanne Rowan Kelleher

Macmillan Travel   Alpha Books
Divisions of Macmillan Reference USA
A Pearson Education Macmillan Company
1633 Broadway, New York, NY 10019-6785

Macmillan Travel USA Alpha Books
Divisions of Macmillan General Reference
A Pearson Education Macmillan Company
1633 Broadway, New York, NY 10019-6785

ISBN 0-02-862834-9
ISSN 1520-5606

Editor: Kelly Regan
Production Editor: Robyn Burnett
Design by Glenn Larsen
Page Layout: Sean Monkhouse, Marie Kristine Parial-Leonardo
Proofreaders: Laura Goetz, Linda Quigley
Staff Cartographers: John Decamillis, Roberta Stockwell
Illustrations by Kevin Spear

Special Sales
Bulk purchases (10+ copies) of Frommer's and selected Macmillan travel guides are available to corporations, organizations, mail-order catalogs, institutions, and charities at special discounts, and can be customized to suit individual needs. For more information write to: Special Sales, Macmillan General Reference, 1633 Broadway, New York, NY 10019.

Manufactured in the United States of America

Contents

Maps

About the Author

Suzanne Rowan Kelleher is a Paris-based writer and the Europe Editor of *Travel Holiday* magazine. She has written about European travel and culture for *Esquire, Cigar Aficionado, Forbes Digital,* and other publications.

An Invitation to the Reader

In researching this book, we discovered many wonderful places—hotels, restaurants, shops, and more. We're sure you'll find others. Please tell us about them, so we can share the information with your fellow travelers in upcoming editions. If you were disappointed with a recommendation, we'd love to know that, too. Please write to:

Suzanne Kelleher
The Complete Idiot's Travel Guide to Paris
Macmillan Travel
1633 Broadway
New York, NY 10019

An Additional Note

Please be advised that travel information is subject to change at any time— and this is especially true of prices. We therefore suggest that you write or call ahead for confirmation when making your travel plans. The authors, editors, and publisher cannot be held responsible for the experiences of readers while traveling. Your safety is important to us, however, so we encourage you to stay alert and be aware of your surroundings. Keep a close eye on cameras, purses, and wallets, all favorite targets of thieves and pickpockets.

Introduction

Paris can make a visitor feel like a fish out of water. It's tangibly chic, palpably cosmopolitan, more than a shade reserved, and undeniably shrouded in a chilly indifference. What's more, it operates in a language than isn't yours. Don't let any of this intimidate you. The French capital is also perhaps the most civilized, energizing, romantic, elegant, user-friendly, and surprisingly easy-to-navigate city in the world. Come and partake, and you'll return home richer for the experience.

The Complete Idiot's Travel Guide to Paris is designed to walk you through each stage of your trip, replacing your question marks with confidence. It contains step-by-step, foolproof strategies on how to book your flight, find a great hotel, get around on public transportation, see the big sights, plan your days, track down great meals, and paint the town a magnificent shade of *rouge*.

Part 1 answers all your questions about planning: When to go? How to get there? Should I travel with a group or independently? How much will it cost? You'll find all the addresses, phone numbers, and Web sites you need to get more information.

Part 2 is all about hotels. It'll help you decide which neighborhood, which price level, and which amenities you want. A special feature of this book is the use of indexes for easy, at-a-glance references by neighborhood and price.

Part 3 helps you get oriented. It tells how Paris is organized, where main sights are located, and how to get around like a native. The neighborhoods are described in relation to their attractions.

Part 4 is all about food—from humble crêpe stands to Michelin-starred restaurants, and from cafes to wine bars to tearooms. Once again, specialized indexes help you narrow down your choices.

Part 5 tells you what there is to see and do, from museum-hopping to river tours to shopping. I've recommended some realistic and enjoyable itineraries, and I'll walk you through how to plan an itinerary of your own.

Part 6 belongs to the night. It covers music and the performing arts—and tells you how much they cost and where to get discount tickets. It also includes a chapter on the city's best watering holes, whether you want to have a drink or dance the night away.

Part 7 gets you out of town, with five great day-trip ideas. I'll tell you everything you need to know to get there, visit, and get back to Paris.

Extras

This book has several features you won't find in other guidebooks—helpers that help you find exactly the information you need, faster and easier.

As mentioned above, indexes in the hotel and dining chapters let you find establishments in the neighborhood you want, for the price you want. No flipping back and forth between pages for a hotel in your price bracket, no wasting time searching for a dinner spot.

Handy little tidbits of information fall under various sidebars:

Dollars & Sense

Here you'll find tips on managing your money, especially how to cut costs without jeopardizing the quality of your experience.

Time-Savers

Look here for hints on how to avoid lines and hassles and streamline the business of traveling.

Tourist Traps

These boxes warn you of rip-offs, shady dealings, and activities that just aren't worth the trouble. "Tourist Traps" also clues you in to some local quirks or unwritten rules that you might not be aware of—hints to help minimize breaches of etiquette and other such gaffes.

Bet You Didn't Know

Look here for interesting historical or trivial facts about the city.

Extra! Extra!

Check these boxes for news flashes, handy hints, and insider advice.

Sometimes the best way to get a handle on a topic is to write down what you want, and so you'll find worksheets throughout the book to help you line up pros and cons and make decisions.

A **kid-friendly icon** is used throughout the book to flag activities, attractions, restaurants, and hotels that are especially suited for families.

Appendices at the back of the book list important phone numbers and addresses covering every aspect of your trip, from reservations to emergencies to Internet access numbers. There's also a glossary of useful French phrases.

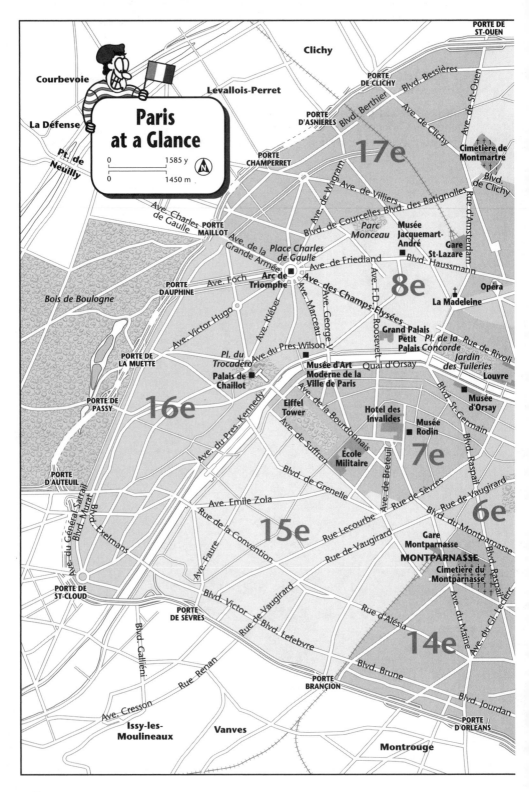

Paris at a Glance

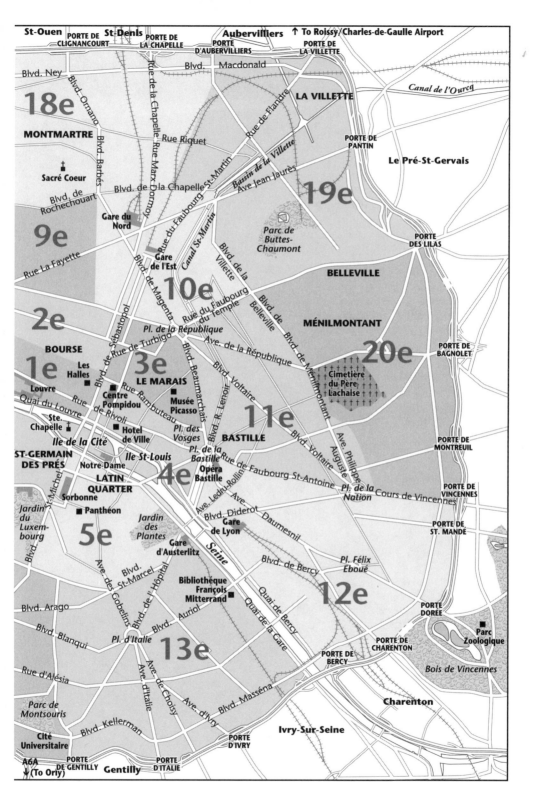

Part 1

Be Prepared: What You Need to Know Before You Go

Chances are that you've been looking forward to this trip to Paris for quite some time. You've probably set aside a significant wad of hard-earned cash, taken time off from work or school, and now want to make the most of your vacation. So where do you start?

Your trip will be far more rewarding if you do enough homework to help you optimize your two most precious resources: your time and your money. These first four chapters will help you through the advance preparations: getting your passport; choosing a tour package; scoring a deal on air travel; and finding information on the Web. I'll give you money-saving tips and answer all your last-minute questions (What should I pack? What's French for "aspirin"?). Soon enough, you'll be on the plane, armed with the info to make your trip run smoothly.

Chapter 1

How to Get Started

> ### In This Chapter
>
> ➤ Where to get information
>
> ➤ The best times of the year to visit
>
> ➤ The city's big annual events
>
> ➤ Special advice for families, seniors, disabled travelers, and gays and lesbians

When it comes to designing your trip, the best defense is a good offense. Better preparation means you'll have a chance at better deals. The key is arming yourself with information, so you won't waste valuable vacation time getting up to speed. And, as you'll find out in this chapter, you've got a lot of great resources at your disposal just waiting to be tapped.

Information, Please

If you've got a telephone—or much better, these days, access to the Internet—you can find a mountain of information to help you design an unforgettable trip.

Start with the **French Government Tourist Office**, 444 Madison Ave., New York, NY 10022. You can contact their "France On Call" hotline (☎ 202/659-7779) or Web site at **www.fgtousa.org** to order the "1999 Discovery Guide," an oversized packet stuffed with free maps, brochures, and itinerary ideas for every region of France.

Especially for Web-Footed Frog Lovers

There are Web sites galore on Paris. For a wealth of practical info as well as up-to-date events news, head to the **Maison de la France** at **www.franceguide.com**. The **Paris Tourist Office**'s site (**www.paris-promotion.fr**) is a good soup-to-nuts primer on essential Paris, with general data on everything from museums to nightlife to shopping to sports. The *Paris Free Voice*, an English-language free magazine published monthly in Paris, has recently launched a terrific Web site (**http://parisvoice.com**) with an events calendar and fun articles on everything from dining to current events. And don't forget to check out **Arthur Frommer's Budget Travel** Web site at **www.frommers.com** for an extensive archive of travel tips on Paris and other major destinations.

Sites That Dig Deeper

The Paris Pages (**www.paris.org**) and **Metropole** (**www.wfi.fr/metropole**) are both light on practical information, but excellent for their savvy columns and articles about Paris culture and history, written by English-speaking residents. **WebFrance International** at **www.wfi.fr** hosts a number of Paris-related pages—some factual, some just fun—and lets you subscribe to their free "in-sites newsletter."

If you want the latest scoop on Paris's most talked-about restaurants, check out recent reviews by the *International Herald Tribune*'s acclaimed food critic, Patricia Wells, at **www.iht.com/IHT/DINE/index.html**.

Participating in a walking tour, cooking class, or cultural workshop can be the highlight of your vacation. You'll find Web sites on these and other possibilities in chapters 12 and 14. Additional Paris-related Web sites are recommended throughout this book.

When Should You Go?

No matter which time of year you choose to visit, Paris has something to offer. Most residents think the city is at its most ideal in **spring** and **autumn,** when the weather is kind, the crowds reasonably sized, and Parisian life at a steady hum. Consider the pros and cons of each season, then decide what time of year is best for your visit.

Spring Is Great Because...

- ☺ What's not to like? Clear, fresh days and relatively short lines at the top sightseeing attractions.

- ☺ The gardens of Paris (as well as those at Versailles and at Claude Monet's home, Giverny) are at their blooming best in April and early May.

But Keep in Mind...

- ☹ The weather tends to be fickle, so you'll need to pack for every eventuality (think layers, and don't forget an umbrella).

3

Summer Is Great Because...

☺ Wonderfully long and sultry days—as in 6am sunrises and 10pm sunsets—afford additional hours to wander and discover.

☺ It's low season for hotels, so rates are generally cheaper and rooms easier to come by on short notice.

☺ July is one of the two big months for shopping sales, with discounts of 30 to 50 percent in most stores.

But Keep in Mind...

☹ It's high season for air travel, so landing a cheap flight can be difficult, especially at the last minute.

☹ The influx of tourists means long lines at museums and other sights.

☹ Most Parisians take their vacations in July or August, causing Paris's cultural calendar (big museum exhibitions, performing arts) to grind to a virtual standstill.

☹ While it's no longer true that the city shuts down in August, some shops and restaurants still close for the entire month.

Fall Is Great Because...

☺ The end of summer is known here as *la rentrée*, the postvacation return to work, school, and life's normal buzz. Any Parisian will tell you it's the city's most exciting time of year, when high-energy projects and scene-stealing new ventures take flight.

☺ Count on a wealth of important art exhibitions and a bevy of trendy new restaurants, shops, and cafes.

☺ Expect airfares to drop from their summertime high.

But Keep in Mind...

☹ 'Tis the season for business conventions and trade shows, making it hard to find a hotel at the last minute (so book ahead).

☹ Traditionally, autumn is a time for transportation strikes of varying intensities—some go virtually unnoticed by the average traveler, but others can be giant hassles.

Winter Is Great Because...

☺ The airlines and tour operators often offer exceptionally good deals on flights and fly-stay packages.

☺ Lines at museums and other sights can be mercifully short.

☺ January is a great shopping month due to ubiquitous semiannual sales.

But Keep in Mind...

☹ Because it seldom snows in Paris, winters sound mild, but residents know that winters are gray, dreary, and often bone-chillingly damp.

And then there are the wind tunnels that lash up the city's grand boulevards. Bring a warm, preferably rainproof, coat.

Hitting the Big Events

If you're passionate about a particular interest—perhaps art, opera, or tennis—you can time your trip to coincide with a seasonal event. Be aware that while summer is off-season for Paris's principal performing arts programs and major museum exhibitions, the city makes up for it in part by hosting a number of free outdoor concerts.

January
➤ **Chinese New Year,** around avenues d'Ivry and Choisy, 13e (Métro: Porte de Choisy or Porte d'Ivry). The city's vast Asian population rings in the New Year in Paris's Chinatown with fireworks and parades featuring dragons, lions, and Jackie Chan/Ninja Turtle wannabes. Late Jan./early Feb.

February
➤ Though light on big-name festivals, the shortest month ranks as one of Paris's richest for **big museum exhibitions** and **grand openings** in the performing arts. Consult a copy of *Pariscope* to find out what's on where.

March
➤ **Foire du Trône,** Bois de Vincennes, 12e (Métro: Porte Dorée). This annual funfair—billed as France's biggest—arrives complete with an enormous Ferris wheel, roller coasters, kiddie merry-go-rounds, jugglers, clowns, cotton candy, and enough arcade-style amusements to give Coney Island a run for its money. Two pm to midnight, late Mar. through late May.

April
➤ **Paris Marathon.** Third in size only to New York and London, this televised megarace begins at 9am on the Champs-Elysées. The winner crosses the finish line on avenue Foch a little more than 2 hours later, after taking in some of the city's most famous sights along its 26-plus-mile route. For more information, call ☎ **01/53-17-03-10**. A Sunday in early/mid Apr.

➤ **Les Grandes Eaux Musicales,** Gardens of Versailles. An exceptional chance to promenade through the palace gardens when all of the fountains are turned on, to the accompaniment of classical melodies by Mozart, Haydn, and French-born composers who were in favor during the *ancien régime*. (The music is recorded but sound quality is quite good.) Every Sunday from 3:30pm to 5pm, mid-Apr. through mid-Oct.

➤ **Bazart,** La Samaritaine department store, 19 rue de la Monnaie, 1e (Métro: Châtelet). Billed as the "hypermarket of contemporary art," this

5

annual art sale showcases thousands of original works by hot, young European artists in styles ranging from abstract to still life to surrealism. Don't worry if you've got more panache than cash; prices top out at around 900F (about $170). For more information, call ☎ **01/40-41-20-20.** Late Apr. through early Sept.

May

➤ **French Open Tennis Championships,** Stade Roland-Garros, 16e (Métro: Porte d'Auteuil). One of the sport's four Grand Slams, the French Open features 10 days of marquee-name tennis in the Bois de Boulogne–based stadium. Tickets are notoriously hard to come by, so start looking early. If you plan to stay at a posh hotel, enlist your concierge's help prior to your arrival and expect to pay through the nose. Late May/early June. For more information, call ☎ **01/47-43-48-00,** fax 01/47-43-04-94, or visit the Web site at **www. rolandgarros.org**.

June

➤ **Prix du Jockey Club** and the **Prix Diane-Hermès,** Hippodrome de Chantilly, Chantilly. Two of France's top horse events attract world-class thoroughbreds, international racing pundits, and big crowds of *le beau monde*. Catch a train from Gare du Nord, then a free shuttle bus from Chantilly station to the racetrack. First and second Sundays in June, respectively. Call ☎ **01/49-10-20-30** for information.

➤ **Fête de la Musique.** The summer solstice is marked with hundreds of free live concerts by local pop and rock bands in squares and cafes, and a classical orchestra at the Palais Royal. Once darkness falls, every Parisian under the age of 40 heads to the Place de la République for the grande finale—usually a big-name rock act. June 21.

➤ **Gay Pride Parade.** A week of concerts and partying culminates in a massive, colorful parade patterned after New York and San Francisco, full of exuberant floats and men in drag. It starts on the Left Bank at Place de l'Odéon and weaves its way over to the Right Bank before ending at Place de la Bastille. The evening is capped with partying in Marais wine bars and dancing at the Grand Bal de Gay, held at the Palais de Bercy, a huge culture and sports arena. Contact the Centre Gai et Lesbien, 3 rue Keller, 11e (☎ **01/43-57-21-47**) for more information. Late June.

July

➤ **French Independence Day.** July 14 is the commemoration of the 1789 storming of the Bastille prison, but the real party starts the night before at a dozen or so free *bals de pompiers* (firemens' balls) that get rolling after sundown. (Despite the name, dress is casual.) Ask your hotel manager to point you toward a participating firehouse, or simply go to the one at 7 rue de Sévigné, 4e (Métro: St. Paul). There's always live music and drinking until the wee hours, and a rare chance to see

Parisians dancing in the streets. The next day kicks off with a military parade down the Champs-Elysées and ends with fireworks over the Trocadéro. *One caveat:* Watch out for youths tossing firecrackers at your feet.

➤ **Tour de France.** As the famous cycling race comes to a Sunday finish in Paris, a 15-deep crowd gathers at the home stretch along the Champs-Elysées. Go several hours early to grab a viewing spot and catch a glimpse of the action. Late July.

August

➤ **Festival Musique en l'Ile.** The medieval churches of central Paris host a series of classical concerts, many of which feature music composed for 17th- to 19th-century masses. Venues include the St-Louis-en-l'Ile and St-Germain-des-Prés churches. For more information, call ☎ 01/44-62-70-90. Early Aug. through mid-Sept.

September

➤ **Festival d'Automne.** One of la rentrée's most satisfying cultural banquets, the Autumn Festival features excellent musical concerts, dance performances, and art exhibitions in diverse venues throughout the city. Its theater program regularly attracts such top-notch directors as Peter Sellers, Robert Wilson, and Werner Herzog. Call ☎ 01/53-45-17-00 or fax 01/53-45-17-01 for information. Mid-Sept through mid-Dec.

October

➤ **Prix de l'Arc de Triomphe,** Hippodrome de Longchamp, Bois de Boulogne, 16e (Métro: Porte d'Auteuil). Europe's most prestigious flat race attracts *le tout-Paris* and horseracing fans from all over the continent. Wear something chic; you won't be overdressed. For information, call ☎ 01/49-10-20-30. First Sunday in Oct.

November

➤ **Beaujolais Nouveau.** The arrival of the first wine of the Beaujolais vintage is heralded in virtually every wine bar and cafe in France with much ado and (often free) tastings. A generally festive night out. Third Thursday in Nov.

December

➤ **Christmas Festivities.** The Paris holiday season is much more low-key and less commercialized than what you'd find in London or New York. Don't expect Musak Christmas carols in every store and a bell-ringing Père Noël on every corner. Paris's Christmas is one of quiet understatement: A life-size crèche is set up under a tent in front of the Hôtel de Ville, and the trees that line the main boulevards are draped in twinkling white fairy lights. Especially beautiful are the Champs-Elysées, avenue Montaigne, and boulevard Haussmann. Arrive at Notre Dame by 11pm on the 24th if you want a seat for midnight mass.

Paris Average Temperature & Rainfall											
	Jan	Feb	Mar	Apr	May	June	July	Aug	Sept	Oct	Nov	Dec
Temp (°F/C)	38/4	39/5	46/9	51/11	58/15	64/18	66/20	67/21	62/17	53/12	54/12	40/5
Rain (inches)	3.2	2.9	2.7	3.2	3.5	3.3	3.7	3.3	3.3	3.0	3.5	3.1

Paris *En Famille:* Traveling with Your Kids

So you want to bring the kids? You've chosen your destination well. Paris is a fabulous city for children, as well as for parents who want to stimulate their kids' minds and spirits. Parisians also love children, but they have the nutty idea that kids are real people, not little aliens that need to be corralled into "child-friendly" areas of life. So consider your kids welcome in every restaurant, hotel, and museum in the city. There is one important disclaimer, however: Kids are welcome as long as they are well behaved. Perhaps because they are exposed to restaurants and museums from a very early age, French kids tend to behave appropriately (some might say eerily) adultlike in these settings. So be forewarned: Nothing provokes disapproving glances faster than a little kid pitching a screaming fit. You may feel more comfortable sticking to casual eateries such as those designated with the child icon in chapters 10 and 11.

Every parent will surely appreciate that Paris is a much safer place, statistically speaking, than any large American city. Violent crime is quite rare. Many Parisian kids walk to school unescorted, and milk cartons aren't plastered with pictures of missing children.

Despite all the good news, traveling with kids (like doing anything with kids) takes extra planning. How easy it is to visit Paris with your children in tow will depend largely on their respective ages, interests, and temperaments. A kid that is hard to entertain at home won't be any easier to entertain in a foreign city. But finding diversions for school-age children shouldn't be any more or less of a problem in Paris than in any other large city. The trick is keeping them involved and enthusiastic about your itineraries.

Strategies for Babies & Toddlers

An infant can be the easiest traveling companion of all, as long as you're aware of the lay of the land. Your biggest hassle will be getting around, since Paris's public transportation system isn't stroller-friendly. Unless you want to do most of your exploring on foot, it'll be far easier if you carry the little angel in a "snuggly" or sling. Strollers will do fine for toddlers who can be lifted out to board buses and climb up and down stairs in Métro stations.

Despite nonsmoking legislation, many restaurants and most cafes are smokier than what you might think is healthy for a child (or an adult, for that matter).

Requesting the nonsmoking section is the obvious strategy, but this can mean squat in a jam-packed cafe where every patron but you has an unfiltered Gaulois dangling from his or her lips. The best way to minimize your exposure is to dine outside on restaurant and cafe terraces, which means visiting during the warmer months.

And finally, if your kids are of the age where eating out in restaurants is just too much of a headache (not to mention the blow to your wallet), consider renting a studio or apartment with an equipped kitchenette. It needn't cost you any more than a hotel, and you'll save big on your food bill. For more on apartments and family-friendly hotels, see chapters 5 and 6.

Make Like a Boy Scout: Be Prepared

You and your children will enjoy the trip much more if everyone gets involved in the planning. Begin months ahead by introducing a book or two set in Paris. For kids under 8, try the *Madeline* series, *The Cows Are Going to Paris*, or *Madame Lagrande and Her So High, to the Sky, Uproarious Pompadour*. Preteens (especially boys) love *Stalked in the Catacombs* (in the "Daring Adventure" series), and no teen should leave Paris without having read Ernest Hemingway's *A Moveable Feast*. Ask your local bookseller for more recommendations, or visit **www.amazon.com** and access the "kids" rubric.

Your VCR can be another terrific tool for building vacation excitement. There's a mountain of movies that use Paris as a backdrop, starting with Disney's animated *Hunchback of Notre Dame* or *Anastasia* for small fries. Teens may be more likely to appreciate Woody Allen's *Everybody Says I Love You* or *French Kiss*, with Meg Ryan and Kevin Kline.

Take the time to pore over brochures with your child and decide which sights are at the top of everybody's must-do list. Try to develop itineraries that let each family member choose at least one of each day's activities.

Arriving & Finding Transportation

After a long flight, dealing with tired youngsters *and* airport-to-city transportation is probably not your idea of starting your Parisian vacation on the right foot. But before lining up for a taxi, be aware that Paris cabs will take a maximum of three passengers. If you really don't want to deal with buses or trains, consider one of the minivan shuttle services that will meet you at the airport and bring you right to your hotel's door, usually for less than what a cab would cost (see chapter 4 for details). If your kids are older and you're into saving money, see chapter 7 for the best public transit options into Paris.

Once in the city, the Métro is a speedy, safe, and easy mode of getting around. Bus travel is a more enjoyable way to get from A to B as long as you avoid rush-hour traffic, although many first-time visitors find deciphering the bus routes more trouble than it's worth. For the best no-brainer bus routes for sightseeing, see chapter 8.

Finding a Baby-Sitter

Only you can decide how much time you want to spend with your kids in Paris. If you want to enjoy a romantic *tête-à-tête* in a fancy Paris restaurant, however, you'll need to find an English-speaking baby-sitter.

A good place to begin is your hotel, preferably before you even arrive. Many (usually upscale) hotels have baby-sitting services or can recommend reliable sitters, though you should stress that their command of English must be excellent. For services that employ English-speaking sitters, see Appendix A.

Keeping the Kids Entertained

Museum fatigue. Long lines. Aching feet. If you're wincing at the mere thought, then just imagine how your kids might self-combust when faced with the real thing. Chances are that your child won't be as fascinated by Impressionist masterpieces or the Louvre's collection of Renaissance paintings as you are, so it's a good idea to plan a few kid-friendly outings to keep everyone in a good mood.

Look for the child icon throughout this book for places that kids find particularly fun and cool. Aside from the usual suspects—Disneyland Paris, a river cruise on a *bateau-mouche*, the Eiffel Tower, the Vincennes zoo, the catacombs—chapters 13 and 14 tell you about some less obvious places you'll want to work into your schedule.

If you have teenagers, they'll probably want to spend at least some time in the Bastille and/or Marais districts, both young and trendy neighborhoods bursting with hip fashion boutiques and cool discount music stores.

Travel Tips for Savvy Seniors

People over the age of 60 are traveling more than ever before. And why not? Being a senior citizen entitles you to some terrific travel bargains. If you're not a member of **AARP** (American Association of Retired Persons), 601 E St. NW, Washington, DC 20049 (☎ **202/434-AARP**), do yourself a favor and join. You'll get discounts on car rentals and hotels.

Mature Outlook, P.O. Box 9390, Des Moines, IA 50306-9519 (☎ **800/336-6330;** fax 847/286-5024), is a similar organization, offering discounts on car rentals and hotel chains (including the Best Western chain, which exists in Paris). The $20 annual membership fee also gets you $100 in Sears coupons and a bimonthly magazine. Membership is open to all Sears customers 18 and over, but the organization's primary focus is on the 50-and-over market.

In addition, most of the major North America–based airlines, including American, United, Continental, US Airways, and TWA, offer discount programs for senior travelers. Be sure to ask whenever you book a flight.

The Mature Traveler, a monthly 12-page newsletter on senior citizen travel, is a valuable resource. It is available by subscription ($30 a year) from GEM Publishing Group, Box 50400, Reno, NV 89513-0400. GEM also publishes *The Book of Deals*, a collection of more than 1,000 senior discounts on airlines, lodging, tours, and attractions around the country; it's available for $9.95 by calling ☎ **800/460-6676.** Another helpful publication is ***101 Tips for the Mature Traveler,*** available from Grand Circle Travel, 347 Congress St., Suite 3A, Boston, MA 02210 (☎ **800/221-2610** or 617/350-7500; fax 617/350-6206).

Elderhostel, 75 Federal St., Boston, MA 02110-1941 (☎ **877/426-8056;** www.elderhostel.org), arranges study programs for those age 55 and over (and a spouse or companion of any age) in the United States and in 77 countries around the world, including France. Most courses last about 3 weeks and many include airfare, accommodations in student dormitories or modest inns, meals, and tuition. Write or call for a free catalog, which lists upcoming courses and destinations.

Grand Circle Travel is also one of the literally hundreds of travel agencies specializing in vacations for seniors. But beware: many of them are of the tour bus variety, with free trips thrown in for those who organize groups of 20 or more. Seniors seeking more independent travel should probably consult a regular travel agent. **SAGA International Holidays,** 222 Berkeley St., Boston, MA 02116 (☎ **800/343-0273**), offers inclusive tours and cruises for those 50 and older.

And the deals won't stop once you get to Paris. Folks over 60 can get reduced admission at most museums and attractions, so be sure to bring a picture ID showing your birth date (a driver's license is best if you don't want to carry your passport around with you).

Access Paris: Advice for Travelers with Disabilities

Unfortunately, the very features that make Paris so easy on the eyes also make it tough for travelers with restricted mobility. The situation is improving, but very slowly and incompletely. New hotels with three stars or more are required by law to have at least one wheelchair-accessible guest room (usually on the ground floor), but most of the city's budget hotels occupy older buildings with corkscrew staircases and/or elevators the size of phone booths.

Moreover, the charm of Paris's older districts—skinny sidewalks, unevenly cobbled streets, and narrow entryways—becomes a nightmare if you've got a walker or wheelchair. Because of this, most equal-access restaurants and hotels are huddled on and around the *grands boulevards* (near the Arc de Triomphe and Opéra), where everything is bigger and wider. Major museums such as the Musée d'Orsay and the Louvre are accessible to wheelchairs, at least in part.

Sadly, Paris's public transportation system is shamefully unfriendly to folks with restricted mobility. Though a few Métro stations are equipped with elevators, the vast majority feature long tunnels and staircases. Escalators, where they exist, are guaranteed not to be running when you need them most. Buses have neither wheelchair lifts nor the ability to "kneel" closer to the curb to make the first step lower.

11

The good news is that there are more resources out there than ever before. The best English-language guide for travelers with disabilities is *Access in Paris,* which you can obtain from RADAR, Unit 12, City Forum, 250 City Rd., London EC1V 8AS (☎ **44-171-250-3222**). In addition, the **Paris Tourist Office** produces a guide for travelers with disabilities called *Tourism Pour Tout le Monde,* which costs 60F ($11).

Travelers with disabilities may also want to consider joining a tour that caters specifically to them. One of the best operators is **Flying Wheels Travel,** 143 West Bridge (P.O. Box 382), Owatonna, MN 55060 (☎ **800/535-6790**). It offers various escorted tours and cruises, as well as private tours in mini-vans with lifts.

Vision-impaired travelers should contact the **American Foundation for the Blind,** 11 Penn Plaza, Suite 300, New York, NY 10001 (☎ **800/232-5463**), for information on traveling with Seeing Eye dogs.

*A **World of Options,*** a 658-page book of resources for travelers with disabilities, covers everything from biking trips to scuba outfitters. It costs $45 and is available from **Mobility International USA,** P.O. Box 10767, Eugene, OR, 97440 (☎ **541/343-1284,** voice and TDD; www.miusa.org). For more personal assistance, call the **Travel Information Service** at ☎ **215/456-9603** or 215/456-9602 (for TTY).

You can join **The Society for the Advancement of Travel for the Handicapped** (SATH), 347 Fifth Ave., Suite 610, New York, NY 10016 (☎ **212/447-7284;** fax 212/725-8253; www.sath.org) for $45 annually, $30 for seniors and students, to gain access to its vast network of connections in the travel industry. It provides information sheets on destinations and referrals to tour operators that specialize in traveling with disabilities. Its quarterly magazine, *Open World for Disability and Mature Travel,* is full of good information and resources. A year's subscription is $13 ($21 outside the United States).

Out & About: Tips for Gay & Lesbian Travelers

Paris's reputation as a hospitable and tolerant city for gays and lesbians dates back to well before the outed Oscar Wilde came to live here in exile. And while the homosexual community is somewhat more discreet than in, say, New York or San Francisco, an exception is the *très* flamboyant Gay Pride Parade in late June.

Rest assured that any hotel receptionist in Paris will welcome a same-sex couple without so much as a raised eyebrow, and you'll find the same polite indifference in shops and restaurants. This book mentions particularly gay-friendly establishments in later chapters.

The best local source of information on gay and lesbian life is the **Centre Gai et Lesbien,** 3 rue Keller, 11e (☎ **01/43-57-21-47**). Once you're in town, you can also consult the following publications for the inside scoop on gay-friendly establishments and events:

➤ *Pariscope,* available at news kiosks for 3F, for its semiregular section in English called "A Week of Gay Outings."

➤ *3 Keller* and *Exit,* both published in French and distributed free in gay bars and bookstores, keep a finger on the pulse of the blink-and-you'll-miss-it gay club scene.

➤ *Le Guide Gai,* published in French by Gai Pied and available at news kiosks for 69F. (about $12)

Stretching roughly from the Hôtel de Ville to the Place de la Bastille, the Marais quarter is the city's gay district—Paris's Greenwich Village, if you will—though it probably won't hit you over the head until you notice the prevalence of rainbow decals in shop windows. The vast majority of visitors ramble up and down the neighborhood's streets without realizing that the quarter is home to dozens of gay nightclubs, cafes, and the city's don't-miss gay bookstore, **Les Mots à la Bouche,** 6 rue Ste-Croix-de-la-Bretonnerie, 4e (☎ **01/42-78-88-30**), which stocks both English- and French-language publications.

Chapter 2

Money Matters

In This Chapter

➤ Getting to know the currency

➤ Traveler's checks, cash, and paying with plastic

➤ What to do if you're robbed

➤ What your trip will *really* cost

➤ Tips on saving some dough

Get ready for sticker shock. How expensive is Paris? It can make New York look like a gigantic blow-out sale. The single biggest reason for souped-up prices is the 20.6% French value-added tax, known as the TVA. That's right, one-fifth of everything you buy in Paris goes straight to the French government.

But don't worry, there are plenty of ways to keep your travel costs down and still have a fabulous trip. That's what this chapter is all about.

Let's Get Franc

The basic unit of currency is the **French franc** (written F or FF), which is divided into 100 centimes. Bills come in 500F, 200F, 100F, 50F, and 20F denominations; there are 20F, 10F, 5F, and 1F coins as well as 50, 20, 10, and 5 centime coins.

It's very easy for visitors to confuse the franc coins with the centime coins. Always remember that coins with any silver on them are worth more than what the French call the "yellow pieces." The silver ones add up to real money quickly, so think twice before emptying your pockets to panhandlers or buskers without first knowing what you've got on you.

Unless you're very good with numbers or have a pocket calculator on hand, it's a good idea to make a "cheat sheet" of currency equivalents. The back of a business card or a similarly sized paper is ideal because you can carry it in your pocket for at-a-glance conversions. At press time, the exchange rate was 5.6 francs to 1 U.S. dollar, so your chart might look like this:

Tourist Traps

You'll find yourself constantly weighed down with tons of loose change. Spend it as quickly you get it for two reasons. The first: Even a small handful is usually worth quite a tidy sum. And the second? At the end of your trip, bureaux de change will only change back notes, not coins. So spend 'em or be stuck with 'em.

$150 = 840F	$20 = 112F
$100 = 560F	$10 = 56F
$75 = 420F	$5 = 28F
$50 = 280F	$1 = 5.6F

Note that when writing sums of money, the French use commas where we use periods, and vice versa. For example, 1,200.58 francs is written as 1.200,58F.

Meet the Euro

The currency in the European Union is called the euro, a monetary unit that will eventually make it possible to travel anywhere in Europe without ever changing currencies. While you're in Paris, you may notice that sales bills sometimes show the total in both francs and euros. For the time being, however, the euro is a theoretical currency—it exists on paper but isn't used in local commerce. The French still run their lives in francs, the Germans in deutsche marks, the Italians in lire, and so on. But not for long: The switch from theory to practice will begin in January 2002.

Should You Carry Traveler's Checks?

Traveler's checks are something of an anachronism from the days when people used to write personal checks all the time instead of going to the cash machine or using credit cards. In those days, travelers could not be sure of finding a place that would cash a check for them on vacation. And because traveler's checks could be replaced if lost or stolen, they were a sound alternative to filling your wallet with cash at the beginning of a trip.

But these days, traveler's checks are less necessary because most cities have banks with 24-hour ATMs. Traveler's checks are also a lot more hassle than ATMs because it's increasingly difficult to find a place that will cash them. But the most compelling reason not to use them is that they don't deliver the bang for your buck that ATMs do.

Still, if you've always used traveler's checks and feel more comfortable with the tried-and-true, you can get them at almost any bank. **American Express** offers checks in denominations of $10, $20, $50, $100, $500, and $1,000. You'll pay a service charge ranging from 1% to 4%, though AAA members can obtain checks without a fee at most AAA offices. You can also get American Express traveler's checks over the phone by calling ☎ **800/221-7282;** Amex gold and platinum cardholders who call this number are exempt from the 1% fee.

Visa also offers traveler's checks, available at Citibank locations across the country and at several other banks. The service charge ranges between 1.5% and 2%; checks come in denominations of $20, $50, $100, $500, and $1,000. **MasterCard** also offers traveler's checks. Call ☎ **800/223-9920** for a location near you.

Dollars & Sense

Repeat this until it sticks: The best way to get cash is with your bank card. This is because Cirrus and Plus let you take advantage of their high-volume whole-sale exchange rate, which leaves all other players—traveler's checks, *bureaux de change*, and credit cards—in the dust.

Show Me the Money: Using ATMs in Paris

Whatever you do in Paris, you'll need a ready supply of cash. The good news is that it's easy to get. You'll find **ATMs** at every major French bank and outside most French post offices (look for the yellow-and-blue "La Poste" signs), and virtually every cash machine is plugged into both the Cirrus and Plus networks. Even better, French ATMs will walk you through the transaction in English. Contact Cirrus (☎ **800/424-7787;** www.mastercard.com/atm/) or

Plus (☎ **800/843-7587;** www.visa.com/atms) for the names of French banks that will accept your card. You'll get a list that's a mile long.

One caveat: It's absolutely vital to realize that not all plastic is created equal. Using your Visa or MasterCard to get cash from an ATM will be treated as a cash advance, and you'll pay through the nose for the privilege. Use your credit card to make withdrawals only in emergencies.

Parlez-Vous ATM?

Foreign ATMs are almost exactly like the ones you're used to seeing at home. One difference is that ATMs in Paris won't let you transfer funds between your checking and savings accounts, so make sure there's enough cash in your primary checking account before you leave home. French ATMs also won't let you retrieve your account balance, so keep track of your withdrawals as you go.

Virtually all French bank cards are issued with personal identification numbers (PINs) of four digits, but thanks to cutting-edge technology, nearly all French ATMs now accept PINs of up to six digits. One hiccup, however, is that French ATMs typically don't have alphanumeric keypads. So to withdraw cash using your bank card, your PIN has to be made up of *just numbers*. If your PIN features only letters (DAVE) or a combination of letters and numbers (STAN37), use a telephone dial to figure out the numeric equivalent.

Finally, remember that each time you withdraw cash, your bank will slap you with a fee of between $3 and $5 (check how much your bank charges before leaving home). Rather than taking out small denominations again and again, it makes sense to take out larger amounts every two or three days. Not only will this keep you from racking up fees, but you won't have to waste precious vacation time in front of a machine. The per-transaction limit usually hovers somewhere between 2,000F and 3,000F ($360 and $540), depending on the bank you visit.

Credit Cards: Le Plastique, C'est Fantastique

Credit cards are invaluable when traveling. They are a safe way to carry money and provide a convenient record of all your travel expenses when you arrive home. In France, you can use plastic to pay for practically anything that costs a minimum of 100F ($18). In the months leading up to your departure, you may want to diminish your Visa and MasterCard balances to give yourself a cushion while you're in France.

You can also get cash advances from your Visa and MasterCard at any bank, but it'll cost you. You'll start paying interest on the advance the moment you receive the cash, and you won't receive frequent-flyer miles on an airline credit card. At nearly any French bank, you won't even need to go to a teller; you can get a cash advance at the ATM if you know your PIN. If you've forgotten your PIN or didn't even know you had one, call the phone number on the back of your credit card and ask the bank to send it to you. It usually takes 5 to 7 business days, though some banks will do it over the phone if you recite your mother's maiden name or some other security clearance.

Not All Plastic Is Created Equal

The credit/debit card carried by virtually every French person with a bank account is called Carte Bleue—the Gallic equivalent of Visa—and MasterCard is also universally accepted. But most small restaurants, shops, and budget hotels accept *neither* American Express nor Diner's Club. Keep this all in mind if you're planning to finance your trip on credit, so you can decide in advance which card to use for your flight, hotel, dining, and so on.

For cash advances on your American Express card, go to the Amex office at 11 rue Scribe, 9e, Métro: Opéra (☎ **01/47-77-79-50**).

Stop, Thief! What to Do If Your Loot Gets Stolen

The best way to avoid disaster is simply to be prepared for it. Every credit card company has an emergency overseas number that you can call if your card is stolen—this is *not* the 800 number, which is inaccessible from the French phone system (You can, however, access US-based 800-numbers if you use one of the long-distance calling cards, mentioned in chapter 7). The issuing bank's emergency number is usually on the back of the credit card. But that doesn't help you once the card gets stolen, now does it? So it's a good idea to prepare a list of emergency numbers and pack it separately from your wallet or handbag. (While you're at it, carrying photocopies of your passport and important prescriptions is smart advice, too). If you opt to carry traveler's checks, be sure to keep a record of their serial numbers.

Your credit card company may be able to wire you a cash advance immediately, and in many places, it can get you an emergency replacement card in a day or two. If you don't know the U.S.-based number, the France-based emergency numbers are: **American Express** (☎ **01/47-77-72-00;** for traveler's checks, call ☎ **08/00-90-86-00**); **MasterCard** (☎ **08/00-90-13-87**); **Visa** (☎ **04/42-77-11-90**); and **Diner's Club** (☎ **01/47-62-75-00**).

OK, So What'll This Trip *Really* Cost?

Budgeting a trip to Paris is different from planning one to San Francisco, London, or Rome. It's rare that a city is cheap or expensive across the board; one might have fabulous, cheap restaurants but an outrageously expensive hotel scene, or vice versa. Paris tends to be reasonable for accommodation but pricey for dining. The budget worksheets at the end of this chapter will help you figure out where your money will go.

Lodging

Landing affordable accommodation isn't a huge problem in Paris. Determining how much to budget for a hotel should depend on your finances and how much time you plan to spend in your room. If you'd be happy with a clean but functionally furnished hotel room with a private bathroom and cable TV, it'll run you about 350 to 450F ($65 to $80). Just keep in mind that this is budget land, and harbor no illusions of grandeur—your room will be no frills where decor is concerned, but it'll be livable and perfectly inoffensive to the average traveler's sensibilities. If you're willing to part with 800F ($143), you can get a room oozing that much-coveted but intangible "Parisian charm." And naturally, the more you're willing to spend, the better the service and more luxurious the accommodations become.

Restaurants

Unfortunately, it's alarmingly easy to eat your way through what you might save on your hotel bill. Options range from inexpensive to astronomical, and cover dozens of cuisines. If you don't mind throwing your gastronomic net wide to include international cuisines (American, Greek, Japanese, Indian), fast-food joints, and sandwich shops, you can eat out in Paris for very little (more on this in chapter 11). But since dining *à la française* is such a highlight for so many travelers, let's focus on local fare.

There's no way around it: Eating out is expensive if you want French chow. So what does an "average" Parisian dining experience cost? Your typical three-course dinner in a deservedly popular neighborhood bistro runs about 175F to 200F ($31 to $36) per head. Having said this, you can find restaurants serving satisfying two-course meals for as little as 120F ($21) if you know where to look, and chapter 10 points out some gems.

Tourist Traps

Cafes are the cheapest species in the French food chain but may leave you feeling ripped off. A *croque-monsieur* and *frites* (toasted ham and cheese sandwich with fries) can routinely set you back $15 to $20. It's unfortunate how many tourists go the cafe route hoping to save a few francs and return home convinced that French food is tragically overrated. You'll probably be happier springing for a full bistro meal, at least once in a while.

Transportation

Paris is a relatively small city, and it's blessed with one of the most efficient and reasonably priced transit systems in the world. The Métro can get you across town in less than half an hour, and the cost is negligible if you purchase one of several discount tickets available. (See chapter 8 for options and prices).

You really, really don't want a car in Paris. Parking is a nightmare, traffic is hell, labyrinthine one-way streets are everywhere, and the French are statistically the worst drivers in Europe. 'Nuff said. If you want to rent a car to tour other parts of France or to make a day trip outside the city, do it on your way out of town.

Sightseeing

Entry fees to museums and other sights can quickly add up, especially if you're a culture vulture. After referring to chapters 12 through 14, make a list of "must-dos" to get a feel for how much money you need to earmark for sightseeing.

Shopping

This is the most elastic part of your budget, since you can buy nothing at all or enough to fill a dozen suitcases. Paris is a tempting shopping mecca, and don't forget that Paris's semiannual sales are held in January and July. But steer clear of most items you can buy at home (they'll almost certainly cost less without the French tax). If you live outside the European Union, you might be able to reclaim part of the sales tax, but only if certain requirements are met. See chapter 15 for details.

Entertainment

The price of your evening entertainment will depend on your finances and stamina level. See the chart below for a general idea of what tickets and cover fees cost around town. Note that nightclubs and bars of all sorts charge a small fortune for alcoholic beverages, so budget big if you plan to paint the town *rouge*.

What Things Cost in Paris	
1 Métro or bus ride (not discount ticket)	$1.40
Café crème	$2.50
Ticket to opera at Opéra Bastille	$11–$113
Ticket to ballet at Palais Garnier	$9–$71
Movie ticket (many are shown in English)	$9
Dinner cruise on a *bateau-mouche*	$89–$116
Ticket to top of Eiffel Tower	$10
Dinner and show at the Moulin Rouge	$134
Cover charge at New Morning jazz club	$21–$32
Cover charge at Le Queen dance club	$9

Tipping

In restaurants and cafes, a 15% service charge is included in the price of the meal. While technically unnecessary, it's still customary to leave a small tip (10F for a moderately priced meal) for the waiter if you're satisfied with your meal. Don't tip a bartender with each round of drinks; leave 5F to 10F at the end of the night if you'd like to show your appreciation. In a hotel, tip the bellhop, room service waiter, or porter 5F per luggage item or service performed. Taxi drivers should be tipped 10% of the fare. Ushers in movie theaters, as well as in opera and dance houses, should be tipped 5F if you are shown to your seat.

What's with All Those Dollar Signs?

In the accommodation and dining chapters, you'll notice one or more dollar symbols preceding each hotel and restaurant listing. These symbols are keyed to a scale at the beginning of the chapter and aim to help you gauge the price bracket at a glance. For example, a hotel prefaced by "$$" will cost between $89 and $143 a night, and one marked "$$$" will cost $143 to $214.

What If I'm Worried I Can't Afford It?

Terrified at the prospect of getting stranded penniless in Paris? Don't be. You won't get caught short of funds as long as you've planned your budget to include those "hidden extras" many travelers forget about. That's what the worksheet at the end of the chapter is for. If the final total is too high, think about where you can cut back as painlessly as possible. Scattered throughout this book are "Dollars & Sense" boxes, which offer tips on how to trim your costs. Here are some good starting points:

1. **Go in the off-season.** If you can travel at nonpeak times (for Paris that means winter), you'll find airfares are far lower than they are during peak months.

2. **Travel on off days of the week.** Airfares vary depending on the day of the week. If you can travel on a Tuesday, Wednesday, or Thursday, you may find cheaper flights to your destination. When you inquire about airfares, ask if you can obtain a cheaper rate by flying on a different day.

3. **Try a package tour.** You can book airfare, hotel, ground transportation, and even some sightseeing just by making one call to a travel agent or packager, and it will cost a lot less than if you tried to put the trip together yourself. (See chapter 3 for more on packages.)

4. **Rent an apartment with a kitchen and do your own cooking.** Many apartments are available for short-term rental. It may not feel like as much of a vacation if you have to do your own cooking and dishes, but you'll save a lot of money by not eating in restaurants three times a day. Even if you only make breakfast and an occasional bag

lunch in the kitchen, you'll still save in the long run. And you'll never be shocked by a hefty room service bill. (See chapter 6 for more on apartments.)

5. **Always ask for discount rates.** Membership in AAA, frequent-flyer plans, trade unions, AARP, or other groups may qualify you for discounted rates on car rentals, plane tickets, hotel rooms, even meals. Ask about everything; you could be pleasantly surprised.

6. **Ask if your kids can stay in your room with you.** Even if you have to pay $15 for a rollaway bed, you'll save hundreds by not taking two rooms.

7. **Try expensive restaurants at lunch instead of dinner.** Lunch tabs are usually a fraction of what dinner would cost at most top restaurants, and the menu often features many of the same specialties.

8. **Walk a lot.** A good pair of walking shoes can save you a lot of money on taxis and other local transportation. And as a bonus, you'll get to know Paris more intimately.

9. **Buy discount passes for travel and museums.** You can save a lot on transportation and attractions if you buy passes that allow you unlimited access for a certain number of days. (See chapters 8 and 13 for details.)

10. **Skip the souvenirs.** Your photographs and memories should be the best mementos of your trip. If you're worried about money, you can do without the T-shirts, key chains, and other trinkets. For where to buy nice but inexpensive keepsakes, see chapter 15.

Budget Worksheet: You Can Afford This Trip

Expense	Amount
Airfare (x no. of people traveling)	
Lodging (x no. of nights)	
Breakfast may be included in your room rate (x no. of nights)	
Lunch (x no. of nights)	
Dinner (x no. of nights)	
Babysitting	
Attractions (admision charges to museums, theme parks, tours, theaters, nightclubs, etc.)	
Night life (admission to theater, concerts, shows, nightclubs, etc)	
Transportation (cabs, subway, buses, etc.)	
Shopping	
Souvenirs (T-shirts, postcards, small gifts)	
Tips (think 15% of your meal total plus $1 a bag every time a bellhop moves your luggage)	
Transportation to and from the airport in your hometown, plus long-term airport parking (x no. of nights)	
Grand Total	

Chapter 3

How Will I Get There?

> ### In This Chapter
>
> ➤ Travel agents and escorted tours demystified
>
> ➤ To package tour or not to package tour
>
> ➤ How to win the airfare war
>
> ➤ Which airport should you fly into?
>
> ➤ How to make your flight more pleasant

Now that you've gathered your research and had a crash course in French currency, the next step is booking your trip. How you go about this will depend on what kind of traveler you are. Should you enlist a travel agent's help? What about taking an escorted group tour? Can you save money with a package deal? Or are you better off purchasing each part of your trip separately? This chapter will give you a good idea of which method will work best for you.

Travel Agent: Friend or Foe?

Any travel agent worth his salt can help you find a bargain airfare, hotel, or rental car. A good travel agent will also know how to balance price with value—in other words, how to stop you from ruining your vacation by trying to save a few bucks. The very best travel agents can tell you how much time you should budget in a destination, find a cheap flight that doesn't require an awkward layover, get you a better hotel room for the same money you would have spent otherwise, and even give restaurant recommendations.

To make sure you get the most out of your travel agent, do a little homework up front. Read up about your destination (you've already made a sound decision by buying this book) and pick out some accommodations and attractions you think you'd like. If you have access to the Internet, check airfare prices on the Web in advance (see "Winning the Airfare Wars" later in this chapter for more information on how to do that), so you can do a little prodding. Let the travel agent know you've got a good feel for what's out there and what it costs, then ask him if he knows of any special deals or discounts. Because your travel agent has access to more resources than even the most complete Web travel site, he should be able to get you a better price than you could on your own. And he or she can issue your tickets and vouchers right on the spot. If the travel agent can't get you into the hotel of your choice, he should be able to recommend a good alternative.

Extra! Extra!

Travel agents work on commission. The good news is that *you* don't pay the commission; the airlines, hotels, resorts, and tour companies do. The bad news is that too many travel agents will try to persuade you to book the vacations that net them the highest commissions.

In the past two years, some airlines and resorts have started limiting or eliminating travel agent commissions altogether. The immediate result has been that travel agents won't book these services unless the customer specifically requests them. But some travel industry analysts predict that if other airlines and accommodations follow suit, travel agents may have to start charging customers for their services. When that day arrives, the best agents will be even harder to find.

Group Travel vs. Independent Travel

The first thing you need to decide is whether you want to travel independently or in a group. An escorted group tour is the most inclusive kind of travel. Nearly everything is spelled out in advance: your flights, your hotel, your meals, your sightseeing itineraries, and your costs. As such, it's the least independent way to travel. Some folks just adore it, and some fervently despise it.

What kind of traveler are you? Do you like listening to a tour guide tell you about a city's important sights, or would you rather discover them—and lesser-known attractions—on your own? Do you like avoiding the stress of getting from A to B in unfamiliar places, or do you fancy sussing out a foreign city on your own? Is meeting new people one of your goals, or do you positively cringe at the thought of sharing hard-earned holiday time with a bunch of strangers? How you answer these kinds of questions gives you a clue as to whether you'd enjoy an escorted tour.

25

If It's Tuesday, This Must Be Montmartre

Many travelers find escorted tours extremely liberating. No hassles with public transportation, no deciphering maps, no rifling through endless museum literature. There's also comfort in knowing what you're getting: costs are straightforward, itineraries are preset, and you know you'll see the top sights in the minimum amount of time. These are all reasons why escorted tours are so popular with senior citizens.

Other folks absolutely can't stand the "mass market" mentality of tours. They hate feeling like they're being herded from one sight to the next and miss the individuality that independent travel affords. Instead, they prefer to plan out their own itineraries and relish the adventure of discovering a city on their own. Folks under 40 may find escorted tours are full of people their parents' age.

Buyer Beware

If you do choose an escorted tour, ask a lot of questions before you buy:

1. **What is the cancellation policy?** Do you have to put down a deposit? Can the tour company cancel the trip if they don't get enough people? How late can you cancel if you are unable to go? When do you pay? Do you get a refund if you cancel? What if they cancel?

2. **How jam-packed is the schedule?** Do they try to fit 25 hours into a 24-hour day, or is there ample free time for cafe-hopping and shopping? If you don't enjoy getting up at 7am and not returning to your hotel until 6pm, certain escorted tours may not be for you.

3. **How big is the group?** The smaller the group, the more flexible the itinerary and the less time you'll spend waiting for people to get on and off the bus. Tour operators may be evasive about this because they may not know the exact size of the group until everybody has made their reservations, but they should be able to give you a rough estimate. Some tours have a minimum group size and may cancel the tour if they don't book enough people.

4. **What will be the average age of your fellow travelers?** Will the group be made up mostly of couples or of singles? It may not be possible to know in advance, but some tours consistently attract the same type of traveler, and this can influence how much you enjoy your trip.

5. **What is included?** Don't assume anything. You may have to pay to get yourself to and from the airport. Or lunch may be included in an excursion but drinks might cost extra. How much choice do you have? Can you opt out of certain activities, or does the leader leave once a day, with no exceptions? Are all your meals planned in advance? Can you choose your entree at dinner, or does everybody get the same chicken cutlet?

Lastly, if you choose an escorted tour, think strongly about **purchasing travel insurance,** especially if the tour operator asks you to pay up front. But NEVER buy insurance directly from the tour operator. If they don't fulfill their obligation to provide the vacation you've paid for, there's no reason to think they'll fulfill their insurance obligations either. Get travel insurance through an independent agency. (See "What about Travel Insurance?" in chapter 4.)

Take Me to Your Leader

If you do decide to take an escorted tour, there are several different levels to choose from. The top of the line is **Abercrombie & Kent** (☎ **800/ 323-7308**), a specialist in customized, luxurious, detail-minded tours. Hotels and restaurants are top class and comfort is a priority. Because A&K keeps group size really low, itineraries can be much more tailored to individual interests. The "sky's the limit" describes both their philosophy and their prices.

A 1997 survey of American travel agents found that **Brendan Tours** (☎ **818/785-9696;** fax 818/902-9876; e-mail info@brendantours.com) provided "the best overall value for first-class tours." A recently advertised eight-day tour of Paris, including airfare and hotel, started at $779.

Globus, 5301 South Federal Circle, Littleton, CO 80123 (☎ **800/221-0090** or 303/797-2800), has seven decades of experience in first-class, land-only "independent city stays." This means that a Paris-based "host" is there to answer your questions but doesn't show you around the city, except on a designated day. A recent eight-day package for $639 included hotel, local transportation, museum passes, and a one-day city tour. **Cosmos** is Globus's downscale sister, offering cheaper, but similar, land-only tours. You can reach both companies at their Web site **www.globusandcosmos.com**.

Bet You Didn't Know

Many people confuse **escorted tours** with **package tours,** but they are like apples and oranges. On an escorted tour, every detail of your trip is pre-arranged: flights, hotels, meals, sightseeing, transportation, and so on. Package tours bundle various elements of the trip—perhaps your flights and hotel or your flights and a rental car, for example. But once you arrive at your destination, your time is your own. You are still an independent traveler.

The Pros & Cons of Package Tours

Packages are a happy medium between hooking up with a group and going it alone. They are enormously popular because they save you a ton of money. A package that bundles your flights and accommodation, for example, will nearly always be much cheaper than the individual elements would cost separately. And like escorted tours, packages let you pay the lion's share of your costs up front.

So what's the hitch? Packages are able to remain cheap by imposing what are often strict limitations. You might only be able fly on certain days of the week, for example, and you'll probably be given only a few hotels to choose from.

Not All Packages Are Created Equal

Remember that price isn't the only indicator of value. Packages come in all shapes, sizes, and colors, so it pays to shop around and ask lots of questions. Will you be flying with a "brand name" airline or a charter? When you come across a package that's unbeatably inexpensive, be particularly suspicious about the quality and location of hotels. If the ambiance of your hotel is important to you, ask for brochures with photos. And find out *exactly* where the hotels are located, with street addresses that you can check against a map. You may be happier with a higher-quality, more expensive package. Don't forget to ask what little extras (breakfast, airport-to-hotel transportation, museum passes, department store discounts), if any, are included. Will you be responsible for taxes and service charges? The more discriminating you are now, the happier you'll be when you get to Paris.

A Pile of Packages

If money is most certainly an object, it's hard to beat the deals offered by **New Frontiers**, 12 East 33rd St., New York, NY 10016 (☎ **800/366-6387** or from New York 212/779-0600; fax 212/770-1007); another branch is at 5757 West Century Blvd., Suite 650, Los Angeles, CA 90045 (☎ **800/677-0720** or from L.A. 310/670-7318; fax 310/670-7707). A recent trip including round-trip airfare and seven nights in a moderate-class hotel was offered for $599 (leaving from New York, Washington, D.C., or Chicago). Meanwhile, the West Coast office was touting a five-night trip (leaving from Los Angeles or Oakland) for $519. Already bought your plane tickets? Consider a land-only package; a recent deal for $199 included five nights in a moderate hotel plus a boatload of free passes for transportation, museums, Seine cruises, and more. This is an excellent try-here-first resource; you can peruse the latest deals on the Web at **www.newfrontiers.com**.

American Express cardholders can check out the offerings by **American Express Vacations** (☎ **800/446-6234;** www.americanexpress.com), a pro at bundling flights on big-name carriers with accommodation in mid-priced hotels. A recent six-night "Go Go Worldwide Vacations Paris" deal included round-trip airfare on American Airlines, accommodation (choice of three hotels), breakfast, and minivan shuttles to and from the airport. Prices started at $889.

The other hotbed for Paris packages is the airlines, especially if you feel more comfortable flying with major carriers. Almost every airline that flies to Paris offers money-saving air-hotel packages, especially in winter. Try **Air France**

(☎ 800/237-2747); **British Airways Holidays** (☎ 800/247-9297); **Continental Vacations** (☎ 800/634-5555); **Delta Vacations** (☎ 800/872-7786); **United Vacations** (☎ 800/328-6877); and **US Airways Vacations** (☎ 800/455-0123). For Web sites for these and other airlines, see Appendix B.

Winning the Airfare Wars

Airfares represent capitalism at its purest. Passengers within the same cabin on an airplane rarely pay the same fare. Rather, they pay what the market will bear. As a leisure traveler, you should never, *ever* pay full fare. The top price is for business travelers who need unrestricted flexibility. They buy their tickets a few days or hours in advance, need to be able to change itineraries at the drop of a hat, and want to be back home with their families for the weekend. Flying unrestricted coach class from New York to Paris on a major carrier will cost around $1,500 if go during the summer high season. In the middle of winter the unrestricted fares cost in the ballpark of $1,200.

Most leisure travelers will snag a great fare by buying a ticket with restrictions. Book your tickets at least 14 days in advance, travel midweek (Tuesday to Thursday is cheapest) and stay over one Saturday night. Do all three, and you can nab the airline's lowest available fare, typically around $650 in summer and $400 in winter. That's a huge savings over the full unrestricted fare.

At least once a year, the airlines hold some fantastic sales. This tends to happen during the winter, but it's been known to happen at other times of the year. There are advance-purchase requirements and date-of-travel restrictions, but fares can be as low as $200 (round-trip!).

The cardinal rule is to never, ever buy an airline ticket before checking the going rate. And the easiest way to do this is by surfing the Web's travel sites (see below).

Dollars & Sense

Consolidators, a.k.a. bucket shops, are an excellent place to shop for dirt-cheap fares. They work with major carriers and/or charter flights and their prices are often lower than what even a travel agent can offer—and certainly less than what you'd get on your own. Look for their ads in the Sunday travel section of your local newspaper. Among the more reliable consolidators are **Cheap Tickets** (☎ 800/377-1000; www.cheaptickets.com) and **Payless Travel** (☎ 202/822-8018; www.paylesstickets.com). At presstime, using Payless, a round-trip New York–Paris fare cost $328 on a major carrier and $319 on a charter during the fall season.

Surfing *Le Web*

It gets easier all the time to find and book plane tickets on the Internet, as the number of on-line travel agents explodes at a fever pitch. There are too many companies to mention here, but some of the most respected ones are **Travelocity** (www.travelocity.com), **Microsoft Expedia** (www.expedia.com), **Travel Web** (www.travelweb.com), and **Yahoo's Flifo Global** (http://travel.yahoo.com/travel). For each of them, the drill is basically the same: You enter your departure city, destination, and travel dates, and the site generates a list of flights, noting the lowest fare. If you tell Travelocity your desired destinations, it will even give you a "heads up" e-mail every time the fares dip.

A relatively new development on the Internet scene is the arrival of on-line travel auctions, where you can bid for plane tickets as you would items in a conventional auction. Bidding occasionally starts as low as one dollar. One of the leading players is **TravelBids** at **www.travelbids.com**.

Another very interesting player to emerge in the on-line travel scene is **www.priceline.com**. Brilliant in its simplicity, Priceline solves a dilemma for both the passenger and the airline. You offer what you are willing to pay for a plane ticket. The airline then either accepts or rejects your bid. When it works, it's a win-win situation. You get a great fare, and the airline gets rid of what would otherwise have been an empty seat.

Great last-minute deals for weekend getaways are also available directly from the airlines through a free e-mail service called **E-savers.** Each week, the airline sends you a list of discounted flights, typically departing the upcoming Friday or Saturday, and returning the following Monday or Tuesday. E-saver fares from the United States to Paris have been as low as $249. To sign up for E-saver notifications, you can go to each individual airline's Web site; you'll find a comprehensive list in Appendix B. Or you can subscribe to the **Smarter Living** newsletter (see "Time Savers" box on this page).

Time-Savers

If the thought of all that comparison shopping gives you a headache, then head right for Smarter Living (www.smarterliving.com). Sign up for their newsletter service, and every week you'll get a customized e-mail summarizing the discount fares available from your departure city. They track more than 15 different airlines, so it's a worthwhile time saver.

Which Airport: Charles–de–Gaulle or Orly?

Most likely you'll be getting to Paris by plane. The city's two main international airports are **Charles-de-Gaulle** (a.k.a. Roissy because it's located in the northern suburb of that name) and **Orly,** located south of the city. In terms of convenience and speed, it really doesn't matter whether you land at CDG or Orly. Both are well served by taxis, shuttle buses, and the local commuter train known as the RER. And in any case, the choice of airport is probably not yours to make. If you're coming from North America on a scheduled, noncharter flight, you'll almost certainly be arriving at Charles-de-Gaulle in the early morning (an exception is American Airlines, which flies into Orly). See chapter 7 for advice on how to get from the airport to your hotel.

Tips for Making Your Flight More Pleasant

➤ **Fly midweek** whenever possible. Not only will your ticket be cheaper, but you've also got a much better chance of winding up with a free seat beside you. Some midweek flights between the United States and Paris are only half full, allowing passengers to have entire rows to themselves. On a 7-hour flight, that can be a little slice of heaven.

➤ **Bulkhead seats** (the seats in the front row of each airplane cabin) usually have the most leg room. They have some drawbacks, however. Because there's no seat in front of you, there's no place to put your carry-on luggage, except in the overhead bin. If you're in the center section of the plane, the in-flight movie will be two feet from your face—an unenviable position regardless of whether you want to watch the flick or not. And airlines tend to put passengers with young children in the bulkhead row so the kids can sleep on the floor. This is terrific if you have kids, but a nightmare if you have a headache.

➤ **Emergency-exit row seats** also have extra leg room. They are assigned at the airport, usually to folks with no obvious mobility problems. Airlines like assigning these rows to young, trim passengers, since they should be able to vacate their row quickly in an emergency. When you check in, ask whether you can be seated in one of these rows. In the unlikely event of an emergency, you'll be expected to open the emergency-exit door and help direct traffic.

➤ Request a seat toward the **front of the plane.** The minute the captain turns off the "Fasten Seat Belts" sign after landing, people jump up out of their seats and clog up the aisles for ten minutes while the ground crew puts the gangway in place. The closer to the front of the plane you are, the less hurry-up-and-waiting you'll have to do. Why do you think they put first class in the front?

➤ **Stay hydrated** during the flight by drinking plenty of water and avoiding alcohol. Airplane cabins are notoriously dry places. Take a hotel-size (the free one you get in a hotel room) bottle of moisturizer or lotion to refresh your face and hands and, if you're taking an overnight flight, don't forget to pack a toothbrush. Remove your contact lenses before you get on board and wear glasses instead. (If vanity must win the day, at least bring eye drops.)

➤ If you have special dietary needs, don't forget to **order a special meal** when you book your tickets—it'll be too late if you wait until you're in-flight. Most airlines offer vegetarian meals, macrobiotic meals, kosher meals, meals for the lactose intolerant, and the like. The low-sodium option is a good bet for combating dehydration. Some people without special dietary needs order these special meals anyway because they are generally better quality than the mass-produced dinners served to the rest of the passengers.

➤ **Wear comfortable clothes** and dress in layers; the supposedly controlled climate in airplane cabins is anything but predictable. You'll be glad to have a sweater or jacket that can be put on or taken off as needed.

➤ The best way to combat jet leg is to **get acclimated to local time** as quickly as possible. Stay up as long as you can on the day of your arrival, then try to wake up at a normal time the second day. Drink plenty of water for several days after your arrival to hydrate yourself from the flight.

➤ And if you're **flying with kids,** don't forget chewing gum (good for making ears pop when the air pressure changes), a few favorite toys to keep them entertained, plus extra bottles, pacifiers, and diapers if needed.

Other Ways to Get There

As noted in chapter 1, bringing a car into Paris is more trouble than it's worth. Traffic, parking, one-way streets and Parisian drivers all conspire to make driving a giant headache, especially for out-of-towners. But if you can't be dissuaded from renting a car, you'll save big if you book it from home using a rental car company's toll-free number. If you wait until you arrive in France, that same company will quote you a much higher rate. Be aware that most French cars have a stick shift. Renting a car with automatic transmission will cost considerably more.

From London by Train

Many people combine Paris and London on the same trip. If you're coming from London, the best way to Paris is on the **Eurostar** train (☎ **08/ 36-35-35-39,** or in England 44/345-881881; www.eurostar.com). This train has revolutionized getting between the two capitals, and it's absolutely fabulous. You'll board the train at London's Waterloo station and arrive at Gare du Nord 3 hours later. There are no hassles with getting to and from the airports, and you go straight from central London to central Paris. From the *gare*, you can get to anywhere in the city via the RER, Métro, or taxi. Fares vary greatly depending on when you travel (weekdays are the most expensive unless you're staying over a Saturday night), but it's possible to pay as little as $100. There always seem to be great last-minute promotions, so there's no urgency to book these tickets until you get to Europe. You can also get a discount if you travel with at least one other passenger.

Worksheet: Fare Game—Choosing an Airline

Arranging and booking flights are a complicated business—that's why a whole industry has grown up to handle it for you. If you're searching for a deal, though, it helps to leave a trail of bread crumbs through the maze so you can easily find your way to your destination and back. You can use this worksheet to do just that.

There's a chance that you won't be able to get a direct flight, especially if you're looking to save money, so we've included space for you to map out any connections you'll have to make. If a connection is involved in the fares you're quoted, make sure to ask how much of a layover you'll have between flights, 'cause nobody likes hanging around the airport for 8 to 10 hours. Be sure to mark the layover times in the appropriate spot on the worksheet, so you can compare them easily when you go back over everything to make a decision.

1 Schedule & Flight Information Worksheets

Travel Agency: _____ **Phone #:** _____

Agent's Name: _____ **Quoted Fare:** _____

Departure Schedule & Flight Information

Airline: _____ Airport: _____

Flight #: _____ Date: _____ Time: _____am/pm

Arrives in _____ Time: _____ am/pm

Connecting Flight (if any)

Amount of time between flights: _____ hours/mins.

Airline:_____ Flight #:_____ Time: _____am/pm

Arrives in _____ Time: _____ am/pm

Return Trip Schedule & Flight Information

Airline:_____ Airport: _____

Flight #: _____ Date: _____ Time: _____am/pm

Arrives in _____ Time: _____ am/pm

Connecting Flight (if any)

Amount of time between flights: _____ hours/mins.

Airline:_____ Flight #:_____ Time: _____am/pm

Arrives in _____ Time: _____ am/pm

2 Schedule & Flight Information Worksheets

Travel Agency: _____ **Phone #:** _____

Agent's Name: _____ **Quoted Fare:** _____

Departure Schedule & Flight Information

Airline: _____ Airport: _____

Flight #: _____ Date: _____ Time: _____am/pm

Arrives in _____ Time: _____ am/pm

Connecting Flight (if any)

Amount of time between flights: _____ hours/mins.

Airline:_____ Flight #:_____ Time: _____am/pm

Arrives in _____ Time: _____ am/pm

Return Trip Schedule & Flight Information

Airline:_____ Airport: _____

Flight #: _____ Date: _____ Time: _____am/pm

Arrives in _____ Time: _____ am/pm

Connecting Flight (if any)

Amount of time between flights: _____ hours/mins.

Airline:_____ Flight #:_____ Time: _____am/pm

Arrives in _____ Time: _____ am/pm

Tying Up Those Loose Ends

In This Chapter

➤ The lowdown on getting a passport and getting through customs

➤ What transportation and events should you book ahead?

➤ What about travel insurance?

➤ What if you get sick away from home?

➤ Packing strategies and what *not* to bring

So the trip is planned, and you're raring to go. But wasn't there something else to do? Right... The passport. Insurance.

You Aren't Who You Say You Are Without a Passport

You'll need a passport if you're going to Paris. Getting one is easy, but it takes some time to complete the process. If you're applying for your first passport, you can do it in person at one of 13 passport offices throughout the United States, or at many federal, state, or probate courts, or major post offices (not all accept applications; call the number below to find the ones that do). You need to bring proof of citizenship, which means an original certified birth certificate (not a photocopy). It's wise to bring along your driver's license, state or military ID, and any other picture IDs. You'll also need two *identical* passport-sized photos (2"× 2"). You can get these taken at just about any corner photo shop; just be sure to tell the photographer that you need the photo for a passport. You *cannot* use the strip photos from one of those photo vending machines.

For people over 15, an American passport is valid for 10 years and costs $60 ($45 plus a $15 handling fee); for kids 15 and under it's valid for 5 years and costs $40 total. If you're over 15, you can renew your passport by mail and waive the $15 handling fee.

The average passport takes 3 weeks to process, but it can take longer in busy periods (especially spring). It helps speed things along if you note on the application that your departure date is within the next 3 weeks. To **expedite** your passport—you'll get it in 5 business days—visit an agency directly and pay the additional $35 rush fee. For more information, and to find your regional passport office, call the **National Passport Information Center** (☎ **900/225-5674**) or get on the Web (**http://travel.state.gov**).

It's required by French law to carry a piece of legal, picture ID with you at all times. If your hotel room has a safe, it's better to leave your passport locked away and go about town with only your driver's license. **If your passport gets lost or stolen** while you're in Paris, go to the American Consulate at 2 rue St-Florentin, 8e (☎ **01/43-12-22-22**) just off the place de la Concorde.

Tips for Safeguarding Your Passport

Always have a photocopy of the inside page of your passport (with photo) packed separately from your wallet, handbag, or day bag. If your passport gets stolen, this photocopy will help the consulate officers speed up the replacement process. If you're traveling in a group, never have one person carry all the passports. If, God forbid, they all were to get stolen, it'd be much more difficult for any of you to get new passports issued. At least one of you will need to prove his identity in order to identify the others at the consulate.

I *Do* Declare! Getting Through Customs

Keep the sales receipts of everything you buy in Paris. Upon your arrival back home, be prepared to show customs officials what you've bought. You can bring home $400 worth of goods into the United States without paying duty, providing that you've been out of the country at least 48 hours and haven't used the exemption in the past 30 days. The list of items you're allowed to import duty-free includes 2 liters of wine, 1 liter of spirits, 200 cigarettes or (but not both) 50 non-Cuban cigars, and 50 milliliters of perfume. Antiques and works of art are exempt from the $400 limit.

What Transportation Should You Book Ahead?

Your first transportation dilemma will be how to get from the airport to your hotel. Not only do you *not* need a car in Paris, but you would be crazy to rent one. Traffic and parking are constant problems, and French drivers are notorious for tailgating, passing on the right, and cheating on left turns. Do yourself a favor and pocket the money you would have spent on the rental car.

Time-Savers

The **U.S. State Department's Bureau of Consular Affairs** maintains a Web site (http://travel.state.gov) that tells you more than you ever wanted to know about passports (including a downlaodable application), customs and other aspects of travel in which the goverment has a say.

See chapter 7 for the pros and cons of commuter trains, shuttle buses, and taxis—none of which has to be pre-booked. One service that does need to be reserved ahead, however, is the **Airport Shuttle.** You can book either by calling an English-speaking sales rep (☎ **01/ 45-38-55-72;** fax 01/43-21-35-67), or through the Web site at **www. paris-anglo.com/clients/ashuttle. html**. The service is a great alternative to a taxi. A minivan meets you at the airport and takes you right to your hotel's front door for 89F ($16) per person, with no extra charge for baggage. Passengers traveling alone are charged 120F ($21). Consider that a cab from Charles-de-Gaulle airport to central Paris costs 200 to 240F ($36 to $43) and will take a maximum of three passengers. So...

In a nutshell: The Airport Shuttle is cheaper than a taxi if you've got one, two, or more than three travelers in your party. If you've got exactly three in your party, a taxi will be less expensive.

What About Travel Insurance?

There are three kinds of travel insurance: trip cancellation insurance, medical, and lost luggage. Trip cancellation insurance is a good idea if you've paid a large portion of your vacation expenses up front, as you would with an escorted tour or a package.

But the other two types of insurance don't make sense for most travelers. Your existing health insurance should cover you if you get sick while on vacation (though you should check to see whether you are fully covered when out of the United States). Most insurance providers will make you pay the bills up front at the time of care, and you'll get a refund after you've returned and filed all the paperwork. Members of **Blue Cross/Blue Shield** can use their cards at select hospitals just as they would at home, which means lower out-of-pocket costs (☎ **800/810-BLUE** or www.bluecares.com/ blue/bluecard/wwn for a list of participating hospitals).

Your homeowner's insurance should reimburse you for stolen luggage if you have off-premises theft coverage. Check your existing policies before you buy any additional coverage. Some credit cards (particularly gold and platinum cards) offer automatic insurance against death or dismemberment in case of an airplane crash, as well as for lost luggage (as long as you've paid for your flight with that card). If you still feel you need more insurance, try one of the companies listed below. But don't pay for more insurance than you need. Trip cancellation insurance typically costs approximately 6% to 8% of the total value of your vacation. So a trip that costs $3,000 can be insured for as little as $180—a small price to pay for peace of mind. Among the reputable issuers of travel insurance are **Access America,** 6600 W. Broad St., Richmond, VA 23230 (☎ 800/284-8300); **Mutual of Omaha,** Mutual of Omaha Plaza, Omaha, NE 68175 (☎ 800/228-9792); **Travel Guard International,** 1145 Clark St., Stevens Point, WI 54481 (☎ 800/826-1300); **Travel Insured International, Inc.,** P.O. Box 280568, East Hartford, CT 06128 (☎ 800/243-3174).

Ahhh–choo! What If I Get Sick Away from Home?

There's nothing worse than getting sick in a foreign country and not being able to get the medical care you need. If this happens to you in Paris, you'll need a doctor or pharmacist who speaks your language.

If you're taking prescription medication, be sure to pack enough to get you through your trip. Keep all medicines in their original vials, in case you're stopped by customs officers. It's always a good idea to bring along a photocopy of prescriptions, with the name of active ingredients clearly noted. These terms are universal and a French pharmacist could find an equivalent product should lose your medicine.

Finding a Doctor Who Can Help You

The **American Consulate (☎ 01/43-12-22-22)** publishes a list of English-speaking doctors and will even fax it to your hotel on request, but it doesn't go so far as to actually recommend them or vouch for their language skills. Apart from that, below you'll find a list of doctors who are frequented by English-speaking expats (though I have not visited them personally):

General Practitioner: Dr. Nancy Salzman, 36 rue du Colisée, 8e (☎ 01/45-63-18-43); Dr. Francis Slattery, 32 rue de Vignon, 9e (☎ 01/47-42-02-34)

Pediatrician: Dr. Pierre Bitoun, 8 rue de Jarente, 4e (☎ 01/42-77-74-37)

OB/GYN: Dr. Tatiane Oppenheim, 17 boulevard du Temple, 3e (☎ 01/48-87-22-63); Dr. Diane Winaver, 109 rue de l'Université, 7e (☎ 01/45-51-82-32)

Yes, You Can Drink the Water

The tap water in Paris has been purified and is perfectly safe to drink. Still, if you've got a particularly sensitive stomach, the change in diet can give you tummy trouble. See below for recommended remedies available in French pharmacies.

Dentist: Dr. Gérard Benmoussa, 18 rue Duphot, 1er (☎ **01/40-20-03-00**); Dr. Edouard Cohen, 20 rue de la Paix, 2e (☎ **01/42-61-65-64**). The **American Hospital**, 63 boulevard Victor Hugo in Neuilly-sur-Seine (☎ **01/46-41-25-41**) has a 24-hour English/French dental clinic.

Chiropractor: Chiropractic Center, 76 avenue des Champs-Elysées, 8e (☎ **01/42-56-06-57**)

If a Hospital's What You Need...

It's a good idea to travel with your health insurance card in your wallet, just in case you need to get in touch with your provider. If you can't find a doctor who'll see you right away, there are two hospitals, both located on the fringe of the city, with a good percentage of English-speaking doctors. They are the **American Hospital** (see above) and the **Hertford British Hospital,** 3 rue Barbès in Levallois-Perret (☎ **01/46-39-22-22**). You can get to either hospital in 15 to 45 minutes by cab, depending on where you start. If time is of the essence, try the emergency room at the nearest hospital (ask your hotel manager for assistance).

What's French for "Sneeze"? A Guide to Pharmacy Speak

For most common ailments, you'll be able to get the relief you need from a pharmacist. (See Appendix A for a list of English-speaking pharmacies). Your favorite over-the-counter remedy may not be available in France. Instead of playing a game of charades with the pharmacist, here's a guide to some popular French brands and their rough American equivalents:

Headache: Doliprane (paracetemol, similar to Tylenol), Advil (ibuprofen), Novacetol (stronger combination painkiller)
Runny Nose: Vick's Rhume, Laroscorbine (1000mg of vitamin C)
Cough: Broncorinol Expectorant
Upset Stomach: Digedryl (similar to Alka-Seltzer)
Diarrhea: Diaralac
Blisters: *Pansements* (generic term for Band-Aids)
Allery Relief: Primalan (safe for children)
🌟*Kids* **Diaper Rash:** Eryplast, Mitosyl
🌟*Kids* **Cold:** Camphopneumine (suppository)
🌟*Kids* **Cough:** Rhinathiol

Making Reservations & Getting Tickets Ahead of Time

One wonderful reason for visiting Paris is its buzzing cultural and entertainment scene. You'll need to book early for highbrow events such as the hottest opera and ballet performances, classical musical concerts, and some museum exhibitions. You'll also need to reserve ahead if you want to dine at the most sought-after restaurants (see chapter 10 for those that require early booking). The most popular walking tours and cultural courses also should be booked in advance (see chapters 12 and 14). Waiting until you've arrived in Paris may mean you get shut out.

What's on Where? Searching from Home

For information on major cultural events, begin with the sources mentioned in chapter 1. In particular, the French Government Tourist Office (☎ 202/659-7779) and the Web sites for the **Paris Tourist Office (www.paris-promotion.fr)** and the **Maison de la France (www.franceguide.com)** are excellent starting places.

The most comprehensive Web site for highbrow arts is **Culture Kiosque (www.culturekiosque.com)**. Within this umbrella site, you'll find excellent magazine-style sites about opera, dance, and major museum exhibitions—all replete with schedules of upcoming events, reviews of ongoing productions, and phone numbers for ordering tickets. A free monthly magazine published in Paris, the *Paris Free Voice* (http://parisvoice.com) features an events calendar and reviews of current opera, dance, and theater offerings.

To find out what pop, rock, and jazz concerts will be held in the coming month, visit **Musi-Cal** at **http://concerts.calendar.com**. Just click "Browse Concerts by Location" and search under Europe and then Paris. A good Web site for jazz fans is **Jazz en France** at **www.jazzfrance.com**. Although written in French, this weekly updated site is easy for English-speakers to navigate. Just click on "Cette Semaine" to find out who's playing at various clubs during the current week, or "La Semaine Prochaine" for next week's shows. A terrific English-language resource is **JazzNet**, one of the on-line magazines that can be accessed through the Culture Kiosque site, above. JazzNet features a calendar of upcoming jazz club dates in Paris.

Once in Paris...

The Bible of what's happening in the city, *Pariscope,* comes out every Wednesday and can be picked up for 3F (54¢) from any Paris newsagent. Look for the English-language "Time Out" section for the lowdown on the current week's events. Make this your first purchase once you get into town—or better yet, buy a copy at the airport.

Also look for the English-language freebie *Where Paris,* a bimonthly magazine distributed at many of the city's four-star hotels.

Time-Savers: Getting Those Tickets in Hand

To secure hard-to-get tickets to music, dance, and opera performances, here are three strategies you can try from home:

1. **Call the Box Office.** To purchase tickets to most performances, you can call the venue's box office directly and pay over the phone with your credit card. It's probably easier to have the tickets sent to your hotel (alert the manager or concierge if you decide to do this) or have them held at the box office for you. See chapters 18 and 19 for phone numbers to specific venues.

2. **Contact Your Hotel's Concierge.** If you're staying at a hotel with a staff concierge, phone or fax ahead and ask him to obtain tickets for the productions you want to see. Do this as early as possible, but don't make him recite the entire gamut of price/seating possibilities. Just specify your preferred date (with a back-up or two) along with the maximum amount you're willing to pay, and ask him to get the best seats he can for that sum. Expect to pay a premium for hard-to-land tickets, and don't forget to tip him for his efforts (slipped discreetly into an envelope, which you present to him upon receipt of your tickets).

3. **Try a Ticket Broker.** The ticket broker is the true middleman. The agency receives an allotment of tickets from various theaters, opera houses, sports arenas, and concert halls and then resells them to travelers for a commission (typically 20% of the ticket price). Using a broker not only saves you the hassle of tracking down tickets yourself, but it can get you into sold-out shows; even if the box office is cleaned out, the broker may still have tickets. One of the most respected international ticket agencies is Keith Prowse, 234 West 44th St., Suite 1000, New York, NY 10036 (☎ 800/669-7469, or in New York 212/398-1430; fax 212/302-4251). Prowse almost always has excellent seats to upcoming musical concerts, ballets, operas, and some sports events. You can also prepurchase city tours, museum passes, and transportation discounts here. Peruse the possibilities on-line at www.keithprowse.com.

Packing Strategies

Start by taking everything you think you'll need and laying it out on the bed. Then get rid of half of it because (a) you don't want to lug around more than is absolutely necessary; and (b) Paris hotels have small rooms and notoriously tiny closets. The bottom line is that you won't have space for much.

The trick to packing light is bringing items that make the transition from day to night with just a slight modification—perhaps by adding a jacket or scarf, by taking off a sweater, or by wearing your hair up instead of down. If you bring a capsule wardrobe—separates in neutral colors that can easily be mixed and matched to make several outfits—you'll never be without something to wear and you'll always look smart.

Limit yourself to two pairs of shoes. No exceptions. You'll need one pair of comfortable walking shoes, preferably not sneakers. Paris is more formal than any North American city, and your daily wanderings will take you places where sneakers just don't cut it. You'll feel a lot more comfortable if you feel neither overdressed nor underdressed. The look to aim for is smart casual.

The same holds true in the evening. Think a notch dressier than what you'd wear at home. Even at neighborhood bistros, most men wear sports jackets and women wear skirts or smart pant suits.

Ziploc bags are one of the world's greatest travel accessories. The small bags make fantastic toiletry cases for things that leak. If you've got small kids, always have a few large Ziplocs in your carry-on bag. Put a moist washcloth in one (great for cleaning up little messes), and keep the others empty for storing things that are wet and messy, such as half-eaten snacks or soiled clothing. To save space, buy travel-size plastic bottles (available at drugstores) and fill them with shampoo, suntan lotion, moisturizer, and other liquid beauty essentials.

Dollars & Sense

Don't forget to bring your camera and enough film to last your entire trip. Film is quite expensive in Paris.

Now for a few packing tips: Start by filling your shoes with small items like socks and underwear, then pack them in your suitcase. Fit the rest of your small items around them. Pack breakable items between several layers of clothes. You know those plastic sheaths in which your shirts and blouses return from the dry cleaner? They are fabulous for protecting items that wrinkle easily, like button-down cotton shirts. And sorry, but there's no way to pack anything made of linen without it looking like you slept in it.

To Carry on or Not to Carry on?

Even if your main suitcase conforms to the airline's carry-on specifications, it's easier to rid yourself of it at check-in. Only a tiny percentage of all luggage gets lost, and the overwhelming majority is returned to their owners within two days. Be sure to label your bags with identification tags indicating both your name and the name, address, and phone number of your hotel in Paris (change this to your home address for the return flight). Keep photocopies of vital documents (passports, prescriptions, credit card emergency numbers, and the like) in your main suitcase, and the originals in your carry-on bag.

You're allowed two pieces of carry-on luggage, both of which must fit in the overhead compartment or the seat in front of you. Pack your carry-ons with things you'll need in-flight. Think about bringing a snack, since the airline's meal is often delayed until over an hour after takeoff. Pack a bottle of water, a toothbrush and toothpaste, moisturizer, thick socks, a sweatshirt, and anything else that will keep you hydrated, warm, and comfortable. What you bring for your in-flight entertainment (books, magazines, a GameBoy, playing cards, a Walkman) is up to you. Don't forget a set of Walkman headphones if you want to watch the in-flight movie (sometimes the airline runs out of them).

Your Cell Phone: Leave Home Without It

The European cell phone system works on the GSM norm, which means that your North American–based cell phone probably won't function here. If you can't live without being armed with a phone at all times, see Appendix A for companies that provide short-term cellular rentals.

Paris Unplugged: Electronics *Not* to Bring

American current runs on 110V, 60 cycles. Europe runs on 210–220V and 50 cycles. You can't plug an American appliance into a European outlet without frying your appliance, blowing a fuse, or maybe even starting an electrical fire. To protect you from such dangers, American plugs have flat prongs, but French sockets have round holes. Believe it or not, there are grown adults who still haven't mastered the round-peg-square-hole concept from kindergarten and still try to cram their flat-pronged plugs into French sockets.

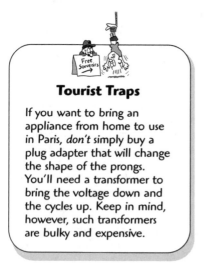

Tourist Traps

If you want to bring an appliance from home to use in Paris, *don't* simply buy a plug adapter that will change the shape of the prongs. You'll need a transformer to bring the voltage down and the cycles up. Keep in mind, however, such transformers are bulky and expensive.

If you must bring an appliance, be sure it's made specifically for travelers and runs on dual voltage, which means that it has a built-in transformer. When you book your hotel, ask if bathrooms are equipped with hair dryers—most Parisian hotels have them these days. The one appliance that does come in handy is a travel iron, since many hotels won't lend irons to guests. Most travel irons come with a set of international plug adapters. If yours doesn't, airport shops are great for just this sort of globe-trotter gizmo.

Packing Checklist: Don't Forget the Following

☐ This book

☐ Camera and film and/or camcorder

☐ Shoes (one walking pair for days and a dressier pair for evenings)

☐ Smart casual pants and/or skirts

☐ Shirts and/or sweaters

☐ Outerwear: coat, small umbrella

☐ Sports jacket (tie optional) for men, skirt or pants suit for women

☐ Socks and underwear

☐ Sleepwear

☐ Workout clothes, if you plan to get in some exercise

☐ Toiletries: shampoo, soap, deodorant, razor, shaving cream, makeup, contact lens necessities, perfume, toothpaste, toothbrush, hair brush

☐ Accessories: belts, scarves, hair ties and barrettes, jewelry

☐ Medications (pack these in your carry-on) and vitamins

☐ Battery-operated alarm clock

☐ Address book (for sending postcards)

☐ Travel iron that works on 220V (most hotels don't lend them)

Part 2

Finding the Hotel That's Right for You

Hotels in Paris are perhaps not as pricey as you had imagined. The average three-star establishment charges 900 to 1100F ($160 to $196) for a double room, including tax, which makes Paris less expensive than New York and London. Yet these figures only tell part of the story because they only speak of averages. There are great little hotels in this city for every budget.

Chapter 5 starts off with neighborhood-by-neighborhood descriptions to help you decide what kind of surroundings you want. Then it's time for a reality check: Just what can you expect from a Parisian hotel in terms of space, service, and price? And after a few hints on how to land a better room, hop to chapter 6 to see my choices for the best hotels in the city.

Pillow Talk: The Lowdown on the Paris Hotel Scene

In This Chapter

➤ How to choose the neighborhood you'll stay in

➤ How to choose your hotel

➤ How to snag a great room

➤ A great alternative for families

Okay, let's get down to the business of bedtime. To find the hotel that's right for you, you'll need to weigh five variables: price, location, room size, amenities, and the least tangible but perhaps most desired of them all: a charming, très Parisian ambiance. You can put these variables in the order that suits you. If the first variable, price, poses no problem for you, then you can have it all: great location, huge room, super perks, and sumptuous surroundings. Most travelers, however, will have to make some compromises.

Compromises don't always have to be painful, though. You won't miss top-drawer services like a concierge and twice-daily maid service if you're only going to use your hotel room as a place to sleep. And you won't miss having a restaurant on the premises if you plan to try out the great bistros, cafes, and other eateries recommended in chapters 10 and 11. (Hotel restaurants tend to be pricey, anyway.) Perhaps your biggest priority is being within walking distance of all the main sights. Or maybe all you really want is heaps of je ne sais quoi. In other words, a room that's clean, comfortable, and unabashedly Parisian in character.

Of the five factors you need to consider—price, location, room size, amenities, ambiance—you should already know your limitations on the first, since you worked out your budget on the worksheet in chapter 2. So now it's on to the second consideration: location.

Location, Location, Location

You're coming to Paris to see the city, and you'll need a hotel that puts you in the middle of everything. Not a short Métro ride away, but smack dab in the center. Toss aside any book that recommends a well-run little hotel next to the Gare du Nord or an adorable pension near Place d'Italie. They may well be well-run and adorable, but they're not for you.

You want to be able to walk out the door of your hotel and be within walking distance of at least two major sights. The river should be a short stroll away. Therefore, you absolutely need a hotel in one of the first eight districts. Period. The next chapter has already done the hard work for you, since every single one of the 40 recommended hotels is located in *arrondissements* one through eight. Pick one of them, and you're guaranteed a decent address.

With the field narrowed to central Paris, you next have to decide which neighborhood you want. The city is made up of a patchwork of districts, and each has a distinctive style and character. The kind of Paris experience you will have depends greatly on which neighborhood you choose. Here's a run-through:

Right Bank

Louvre (1er)

You can't get more central than the 1st *arrondissement*, smack in the heart of Paris's museums and monuments. Many of the city's most important sights are within a five-minute walk of each other—the Louvre, Tuileries Gardens, Musée de l'Orangerie, Place de la Concorde, Palais Royal, Place Vendôme—and there's also *haute couture* shopping nearby on rue du Faubourg St-Honoré. Well connected by Métro and buses, this area makes for an ideal hotel location in terms of convenience, though it's more crowded with tourists and less atmospheric than the nearby Marais.

In a Nutshell:

☺ You'll be close to the Louvre and other major sights.

☺ The rest of Paris is easily accessible.

But...

☹ You may meet more tourists than French folks.

☹ The area isn't known for its cheap hotels, so you may have to sacrifice ambiance if you're on a budget.

Opéra (2e)

The Opéra district, dominated by the Opéra Garnier, is convenient to boulevard Haussmann's big-name department stores (Galéries Lafayette, Printemps) and to most Right Bank sights. But the Bourse (Paris stock exchange) and *grands boulevards* make the area more business-oriented, and there's also fewer glimpses of essential Parisian daily life (such as outdoor food markets and neighborhood shops) than in the more residential districts.

In a Nutshell:

☺ If you're a ballet and opera fan, you're in the right place.

☺ You'll be close to the big department stores.

But...

☻ It's not an atmospheric neighborhood for strolling and hanging out.

☻ You'll see fewer slices of French life than in residential neighborhoods.

Marais (3e, 4e)

This captivating district was built atop a reclaimed marsh (indeed, the word *marais* means marsh) and is Paris's answer to Greenwich Village. Its labyrinthine cobblestone lanes are lined with Renaissance mansions that were residences of the *noblesse*, which today house hip boutiques, congenial bistros, and wonderful wine bars. Major sights include the Picasso Museum, Place des Vosges, and Pompidou Center (closed through 1999). The city's most eclectic area, the Marais is a hub of both the gay and the Jewish communities. It's also the only neighborhood in which most shops and restaurants stay open on Sunday.

In a Nutshell:

☺ Only St-Germain-de-Prés rivals it for ambiance.

☺ The neighborhood isn't dead on Sunday.

But...

☻ If you're a light sleeper, it may be too animated.

☻ Narrow sidewalks and cobblestones are tough if you've got limited mobility.

The Islands (1er, 4e)

Paris has two islands, which lay side-by-side in the Seine: Ile de la Cité and Ile St-Louis. While the Ile de la Cité is a trove of top sights—Notre Dame, Sainte-Chapelle, the Conciergerie—tiny Ile St-Louis oozes an aristocratic brand of romance. The tiny island is all atmosphere, with its gorgeous town houses, leafy courtyards, and tiny one-of-a-kind boutiques and antiques dealers. The location is superb, with the Marais directly across the river on one side, and the Latin Quarter on the other. Most Parisians would give their eye teeth to live here.

In a Nutshell:
☺ It's a picture-postcard island idyll.

☺ You'll be practically on top of Notre Dame, and the Latin Quarter and Marais are within walking distance.

But...
☹ The islands often get overrun with visitors.

☹ Lots of tourists mean higher prices at cafes, shops, restaurants, etc.

Champs-Elysées (8e)
If you're into designer shopping, this is the place. The stately 8th district is best known for its swanky *Triangle d'Or* ("Golden Triangle"), formed by the Champs-Elysées, avenue George V, and avenue Montaigne. All three, but especially the avenue Montaigne, feature haute couture designer shopping at its very hautest. And on the other side of the Champs, the rue du Faubourg St-Honoré is also chock-a-block with designer shops. The Champs-Elysées itself is a mixed bag of movie theaters, touristy cafes, luxury shops, and chain stores, but it's been moving distinctly upscale in recent years. Major sights include the Arc de Triomphe and the Grand Palais, and the area bristles with tangible excitement day and night.

In a Nutshell:
☺ It's tops for designer shopping.

☺ You're never at a loss for something to do or see.

But...
☹ Budget hotels are scarce.

☹ The neighborhood's commercial-driven personality can be impersonal.

Left Bank
Latin Quarter (5e)
The intellectual and free-thinking pocket of Paris that Hemingway so adored still overflows with university students and smoky jazz clubs, and remains a hub of bohemian Paris. It's also home to myriad cheap bistros and Greek kebab joints, which makes the neighborhood more downscale but perhaps more democratic than many in Paris. Sights include the Panthéon, Musée de Cluny, and Luxemburg Gardens.

In a Nutshell:
☺ You'll be close to the Luxemburg Gardens.

☺ Students and tourists keep restaurant prices down.

But...

- ☹ It's harder to find a great restaurant among the mediocre, high-priced eateries.

- ☹ Room size is often tighter than in other neighborhoods.

St-Germain-des-Prés (6e)

For many travelers, St-Germain-des-Prés is a byword for everything there is to love about the Left Bank—the best sidewalk cafes, to-die-for boutiques, and immensely strollable streets that seem plucked from a picture postcard. It's home to publishing houses, antiques dealers, and lucky residents like actresses Isabelle Adjani and Catherine Deneuve. But urbane chic comes at a price, and so the most romantic area of the city is also one of the most expensive. Nearby main attractions include the Luxemburg Gardens, fabled cafes (Café Flore, Les Deux Magots), the Musée d'Orsay, and last but not least by a long shot, super shopping.

In a Nutshell:

- ☺ You'll be in the middle of the Left Bank's best cafes and shops.

- ☺ You'll be near the Luxemburg Gardens.

But...

- ☹ Establishments of all kinds are pricier than those in nearby Latin Quarter.

- ☹ There are comparatively few major sightseeing attractions at your doorstep.

Eiffel Tower & Invalides (7e)

The smart 7th district is the conservative yin to St-Germain-des-Prés's chic yang. Here you find stately French government buildings (including the National Assembly and the Prime Minister's residence), traditional bourgeois shops, and some of the most magnificent mansions in Paris. Travelers know it as the home of the Eiffel Tower, Les Invalides, and the Musée d'Orsay. Overall, it makes a great base if you want to be central but still favor peace and quiet at night. On the other hand, it can feel rather staid if you want to go out on the town. Also, the Métro stations are scattered a bit farther apart than in other neighborhoods, which makes it slightly less convenient.

In a Nutshell:

- ☺ You'll be near the Eiffel Tower and Musée d'Orsay.

- ☺ You'll be surrounded by some of Paris's wealthiest residents.

But...

- ☹ Nightlife is practically nonexistent.

☹ The mood is noticeably more sober than in nearby St-Germain.

☹ Métro stations are farther apart than those in other neighborhoods.

The Price Is Right

The **rack rate** is the full rate you'd pay if you called a hotel and booked a room with no discount. At chain hotels (such as Hyatt and Marriott) and at other luxury hotels you can often get a good deal by simply asking for a discounted rate. Your odds improve drastically if you're staying for more than just a few nights.

Here's some advice to keep in mind when trying to save money on a room:

➤ Whenever there's a **toll-free 800 number** and a local number, it's best to call both to see if you get quoted a lower rate from one of them. It's surprising how often this works.

➤ Ask about **corporate discounts** at the hotel chains.

➤ If you're interested in staying at one of the top-end properties, a **travel agent** may be able to negotiate a better price than you could get by yourself. (That's because the hotel gives the agent a discount in exchange for steering business toward that hotel.)

Dollars & Sense

Keep in mind that bartering for a cheaper room isn't the norm in Paris. Most establishments are small and privately owned; they're not as likely to be willing to negotiate as the chains are. To be fair, they can't afford to be.

➤ Always ask if the hotel offers any **weekend specials,** which typically require that you stay two nights (either Friday and Saturday or Saturday and Sunday). In Paris, this kind of deal is prevalent from September through March at hotels at every price level.

➤ *Forfaits* (for-feh) are discounts that require you to stay a certain number of nights—perhaps a minimum of three or five. Sometimes there's something else thrown in—like a bottle of champagne—to sweeten the deal. If you're going to be in Paris for more than 2 days, always ask if there's a *forfait* and then pick the hotel with the best deal.

➤ Visit during the **summer low season.** That's no typo. Room rates tend to be lower in late July and August, which, though big tourist months, is considered low season by Paris hoteliers. November and December are also low season. October, on the other hand, is light on tourists but heavy on conventioneers, making it difficult to find a room.

Great Expectations vs. Reality Check

If this is your first visit to Europe, your expectations about what a hotel room should look like are probably based on what you've seen in North America. This is as good a time as any for a reality check.

Time-Savers

Remember back in chapter 4 when you were advised to pack light? I really meant it: Not only will your room be too small to accommodate many large suitcases, but your closet will be pint-size, too. You can count on it.

Let's start with room size. Think small. (Remember the old joke about the room so small you had to step outside to change your mind?) Parisian doubles are never big enough to hold two queen-size beds, as you see so often in the states. There probably won't be enough space around the bed to put more than a desk and perhaps a chest of drawers. Welcome to Europe; the story is the same in London, Rome, and most other continental capitals.

If you're going to enjoy your stay in Paris, you simply must take a deep breath, accept it, and get over it. More than one visitor has stomped out of a Paris hotel after seeing his tiny room, only to discover that rooms at the more expensive hotel down the block are exactly the same size. On the bright side, what Paris hotels lack in space they often make up for in character.

Bet You Didn't Know

Why are hotel rooms in Paris so small? Chalk it up to architecture. Paris is eye candy from the exterior because many buildings date back two, three, or sometimes even four centuries. And in those eras, rooms were simply built to smaller dimensions. Short of gutting the building and starting over, there's not much a hotelier can do about it

What You Get for Your Money

Prices for the hotels recommended in chapter 6 are designated with dollar signs—the more you see, the more expensive the hotel. The number of dollar signs corresponds to the hotel's rack rates, from the cheapest double room in low season to the most expensive in high season. It runs like this:

$	Under 600F (Under $107)
$$	600–1000F ($107–$179)
$$$	1000–1500F ($179–$268)
$$$$	1500–2100F ($268–$375)
$$$$$	2100F and up (over $375)

The most noticeable difference between hotels in the budget bracket and the most expensive hotels is better amenities and services, followed by a more-luxurious decor.

Don't waste time trying to figure out which of these hotels are dumps; the places recommended in this book are all decent and reputable. Naturally, the luxury level in a 2000F room is substantially higher than in a 500F one.

$. The low end of the scale represents the true budget hotels. Don't expect a lot of space or extras: You won't get room service, and though you'll have a TV, it may only receive French channels. But there will be a clean, private bathroom with shower or tub, and the room will offer a basic level of comfort. Even at this level, the decor can evoke true Parisian charm—though it may be slightly dated or old-fashioned.

$$. Moving up one level, the rooms are roughly the same size as those in the first category. The decor is a big step up, however, and the overall comfort is substantially higher. While there won't be a concierge, the front desk will be happy to help you make dinner reservations if you ask. Some creature comforts—air conditioning, satellite TV, and in-room hair dryers—can be expected. Don't think of this as another budget category—the loving care that hoteliers put into their properties is visible here, even if they can't afford to offer real luxury. And that's why this category holds so many real bargains.

$$$. The middle-range hotels offer rooms that are slightly larger than those in the first two categories. The decor tends to be more luxurious—often featuring at least some antique furnishings—and there are more amenities (better toiletries, perhaps more English-language channels on TV). At this level there won't be a restaurant, but there's usually limited room service available. There also won't be a concierge, but the front desk will prove very helpful when tapped to make reservations for dinner or entertainment.

$$$$. Hotels at this level feel like luxury hotels, though not the sky's-the-limit kind. This is where room size starts to make a noticeable jump. There will be a concierge and 24-hour room service, and decor will be palpably more luxurious—with antiques and quality fabrics being ubiquitous. There will probably be a restaurant or other in-house facilities. Probably no fitness center, but then, those are rare in Paris at every price level.

$$$$$. Here you get much more than just a place to stay: You get an experience. Service will be irreproachable, decor will feature quality down to the smallest details, and rooms will be large compared to those in the rest of the city. The hotel's restaurant will serve excellent (though probably pricey) fare,

55

and you may even get a fitness center. These hotels do everything with just a little more style than their less-expensive counterparts.

Let's Face It, Size Matters

With rooms as small as they are in Paris, every extra inch helps. Try these strategies for landing more elbow room:

➤ **Book a suite** in a cheaper hotel. If you were planning to spend $200 on a double room, you're looking at hotels in the $$$ category. Opting for a suite in a hotel from the $$ category will almost always buy you more space for the same price.

➤ **Book a twin.** A room with two twin beds (*chambre à deux lits*) is usually slightly larger than one with one double bed (*chambre à grand lit*).

➤ **Ask for a corner room.** They're often larger, quieter, and have more windows than other rooms. Best of all, they don't always cost significantly more.

➤ **Specify the 2nd through 5th floors.** The architecture of Paris is noticeably uniform. Many, many hotels were converted from putty-colored town houses, each comprising seven stories topped with a mansard roof. Back in the olden days, Parisians lived and received guests on floors two through five, and rooms here were built slightly larger.

➤ **Request a balcony.** The largest rooms in the house have balconies, without exception.

Dollars & Sense: Tax Facts

The good news is that the 20.6% French **value-added tax** is already figured into the rate. Rest assured there won't be any major surprises at the end of your stay, as can happen in most European countries. A nominal **room tax** of 7F ($1.25) per night, however, will be added to your bill.

Budget Hotels: What Else Do You Need to Know?

While air conditioning remains uncommon in budget properties, it's now ubiquitous in moderate- and high-priced hotels. But even if you're on a shoestring budget, don't think about foregoing your summer trip. Consider that very few Parisians have air-conditioned apartments due to the very moderate climate. Aside from a few balmy weeks in August, nighttime temperatures rarely get hot enough to be uncomfortable. You can assume that all the hotels listed in chapter 6 have air-conditioned rooms except when otherwise mentioned.

What Is That Thing in My Bathroom?

There's also a chance that your hotel bathroom will contain a device called a **bidet,** which is a low basin with a faucet that was originally conceived for giving oneself a sponge bath. Nowadays a bidet is handy for washing out clothing, soaking delicates, and bathing babies, among other things.

Likewise, every hotel recommended in this book offers rooms with private bathrooms equipped with a shower (*douche*), a tub (*baignoire*), or both. Sometimes you run across a tub that has only a handheld shower, and necessary to make matters infinitely worse, there's no shower curtain. This can be a major drag because the only way to take a shower without soaking the bathroom is to do it while sitting or kneeling. The irrational aversion to shower curtains is just one of those quirky European things (also common in Italy and Spain) that nobody can ever explain satisfactorily.

Book 'Em, Danno

Some things to keep in mind when you're ready to make your reservations:

➤ When possible, try to **book at least a month ahead.** As previously stated, most Paris hotels are small establishments with fewer than 30 rooms, and they fill up very quickly.

➤ It's common practice to **pay a deposit** when you reserve a room in France, particularly if the hotel is small and family run. During peak periods, some hotels may even ask for **total prepayment.** But before you fork over your credit card number, inquire whether there is a **cancellation policy.** (Typically, you forfeit your deposit if you call off your trip.) Always **request a faxed or e-mailed confirmation** that specifies the type of room, the rate, your time of arrival, and the amount of the prepaid deposit.

➤ In Paris, as in other major cities around the world, hotels are **routinely overbooked.** Booking by credit card does not automatically hold your room if you arrive significantly later than expected or after 6pm. Hotels in Paris usually ask when you expect to arrive; always pad several hours just to be safe. (If you're coming from the United States, you'll undoubtedly arrive in the early morning and your room probably won't be ready until noon, anyway.) If you've made your reservation very far in advance, it's always smart to confirm within 24 hours of your arrival. And it goes without saying that you should alert the hotel in the event of a major delay.

➤ **Request a nonsmoking room** if you don't smoke and hate the tell-tale smell of tobacco in the drapes and upholsteries. Many hotels, beginning at the mid-priced ($$$) level, offer them.

➤ If you're a light sleeper, **ask for a room overlooking the courtyard** instead of the street. Even double-glazed windows can't completely drown out city traffic.

➤ If you aren't happy with your room when you arrive, **tell the hotel manager.** If he has another room, he'll usually be more than happy to accommodate you, within reason. This might mean switching rooms midway through your stay.

Tourist Traps

Those little extras have a way of adding up quickly. Beware of the big three hotel rip-offs:

➤ Virtually every Parisian hotel **charges extra for breakfast.** (The Relais St-Germain and L'Abbaye St-Germain, both recommended in chapter 6, are notable exceptions). In France, breakfast is not a fortifying meal. At a moderately priced hotel, you can expect to pay 45F to 55F per person for a classic Continental breakfast. This means that for roughly $18 a couple, you'll get coffee (or tea or hot chocolate) with rolls and/or croissants. Partake of the hotel breakfast on every morning of your stay and you'll end up with a healthy surcharge on your bill. You'll probably be happier, and wealthier, if you take your coffee and croissant in a neighborhood cafe.

There are exceptions; some hotels make a genuine effort to prepare a delightful and more satisfying breakfast. Try it once and if you aren't satisfied, go to a cafe or a bakery on subsequent mornings. While the hotel cannot automatically add the breakfast charge to your bill, it's a good idea to let the staff know if you're going to skip breakfast or eat out.

➤ You'll be charged for anything you consume from the **minibar,** and at a price that's three times higher than in a local store. Resist temptation, or bring in your own refreshments and snacks from supermarkets.

➤ Making **phone calls,** even local calls, from your hotel room will always incur a hefty surcharge. If you want to keep costs low, use public phones for local calls and a calling card for long-distance communications. (See chapter 7 for detailed tips on mastering the French phone system.)

A Family Affair: The Aparthotel

Bringing the kids with you to Paris? Staying in a hotel might be less appealing than staying in an apartment. And better than both might be an **aparthotel,** which as the name implies is a hybrid between an apartment and a hotel. For many families, aparthotels offer the best of both worlds—the autonomy of an apartment with some of the amenities of a hotel. Like hotels, they have 24-hour reception desks, satellite TV, housekeeping services, and sometimes even fitness rooms. And like apartments, they have equipped kitchenettes and Laundromats. For a family of four, a one-bedroom apartment is a savvy, good-value alternative to two double rooms in a cheap hotel. And if you use your kitchenette to prepare even half of your own meals in Paris, you'll reap huge savings on your dining bill.

Accommodations that are particularly good for families are designated in the next chapter with a "kid-friendly" icon. These include a quartet of the best aparthotels in Paris.

Strategies for Travelers with Disabilities

New hotels with three stars or more must, by law, have at least one wheelchair-accessible guest room (usually on the ground floor). Unfortunately, most of the city's budget hotels occupy older buildings with corkscrew staircases and/or elevators the size of phone booths.

The best English-language guide for disabled travelers is *Access in Paris,* which you can obtain from RADAR, Unit 12, City Forum, 250 City Rd., London EC1V 8AS (☎ **44–171/250–3222**). In addition, the **Paris Tourist Office** (see address and phone number, below) produces a guide called *Tourisme Pour Tout le Monde,* which costs 60F ($11).

Oops! What If You Didn't Book Ahead?

If you arrive in Paris without a hotel reservation, you have two choices: Pick up the phone and start dialing, or let the multilingual staff at the **Paris Tourist Office** do it for you. You must go in person, and you'll be charged between 8F and 55F ($1.50 and $10), depending on the category of the hotel you choose. The main branch is at 127 avenue des Champs-Elysées, 8e, Métro: Charles-de-Gaulle-Etoile (☎ **01/49-52-53-54;** 24-hour recording in English ☎ **01/49-52-53-56**), and is open every day from 9am to 8pm. Smaller branches are located on the Right Bank inside the Gare du Nord (10e), Gare de l'Est (10e), and Gare de Lyon (12e). And there are Left Bank branches at the Eiffel Tower (7e), and in Gare d'Austerlitz (13e) and Gare Montparnasse (14e).

Chapter 6

Paris Hotels from A to Z

> **In This Chapter**
>
> ➤ Quick indexes by location and price
>
> ➤ Reviews of the best hotels in central Paris
>
> ➤ Top picks for romantics, families, business travelers, and more
>
> ➤ A worksheet to help you make your choice

Okay, it's time make one of your most important decisions: Where are you going to snooze? The chapter kicks off with indexes that break down the Idiot's list of top 40 hotels in Paris by neighborhood and by price. Reviews of individual hotels come next, giving you all the information you need to make an informed choice.

The reviews are arranged alphabetically for easy reference. Listed immediately beneath the name of each hotel is its neighborhood and price category—the more dollar signs you see, the heftier the price tag. The number of dollar signs corresponds to the hotel's rack rates, from the cheapest double room in low season to the most expensive in high season.

Of the some 2,200 hotels in Paris, only 40 receive the Idiot's seal of approval. What gives? Well, to be perfectly honest, you really don't need to know about zillions of great hotels. You just need to find one that's right for you, plus a couple of back-ups should your top choice be booked solid. In compiling the Idiot's top 40, the first step was to consider the average visitor's wish list. For most travelers, location, location, location is of utmost concern when choosing a hotel. And so the first criterion was simple yet ruthless: If the hotel isn't located within Paris's central eight *arrondissements*, it's not recommended in this book.

Another big concern is price. Don't you just hate guidebooks that recommend slews of extremely expensive hotels and forget about the average Joe? Sure, there are wealthy folks who can afford to stay in Paris's palace hotels. And we're truly happy for you if you're lucky enough to fall into that category. Staying at the Ritz, Crillon, or Plaza Athénée is a magical experience, where every detail of decor and service attains near perfection—as it should, considering the hefty price tag. Even the worst room will empty your wallet a minimum of 3000F, or a cool $540. The most expensive category ($$$$$) in this book contains hotels that cost over 2100F ($375) per night, which is very expensive by almost everybody's standards but still far below the palaces' rates. Moreover, a full half of the hotels in the Idiot's top 40 rent double rooms under $200, and a half dozen of those do it for under $100.

Finally, care was taken so that the Idiot's top 40 represented a variety of neighborhoods (since everyone's got a favorite) and offered a nice range of styles (conservative, eccentric, familial, trendy—whatever your cup of tea). The overall aim was to make sure there was something for everyone, regardless of budget, taste, or travel style.

Kids Hotels that are especially good for families are designated with this "kid-friendly" icon. And the chapter is interrupted periodically with handy roundups for those of you with special considerations in mind—the best hotels for romantic interludes, the best for gay travelers, the best for dining, and so on.

Hint: At the end of this chapter, you'll find a worksheet to help you rank your preferences. As you read through the reviews, keep track of the ones that appeal to you by putting a little check mark in the margin beside them. It'll save you a lot of time later.

Quick Picks: Paris's Hotels at a Glance
Hotel Index by Location

Right Bank

Louvre (1er)

Britannique $$

Costes $$$$$

Louvre Forum $

Orion Les Halles $$

Orion Louvre $$

Régina $$$$–$$$$$

Relais du Louvre $$

Timhôtel Louvre $

Opéra (2e)

Citadines Paris Opéra
Aparthotel $$

Le Marais (3e, 4e)

Caron de Beaumarchais $$

Pavillon de la Reine $$$$

7ème Art $–$$

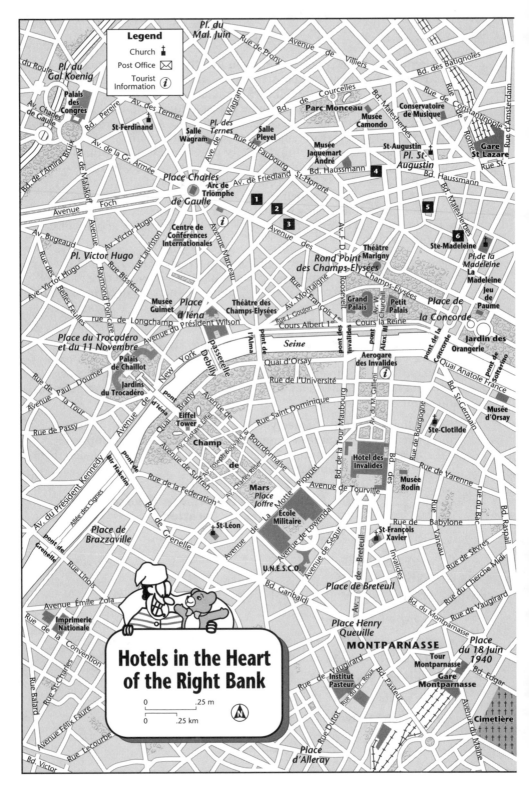

Hotels in the Heart of the Right Bank

0 .25 m
0 .25 km

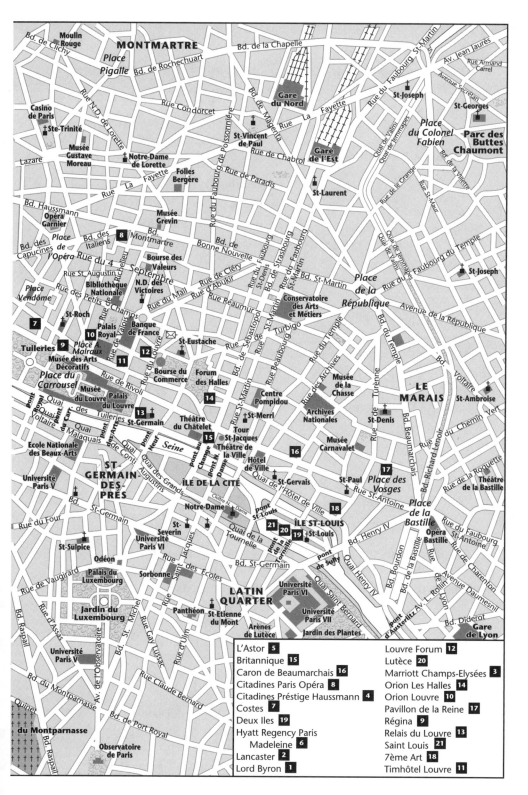

The Islands (1er, 4e)

Deux Iles $$

Lutèce $$

Saint Louis $$

Champs-Elysées (8e)

L'Astor $$$$$

Citadines Préstige Haussmann
Aparthotel $$$

Hyatt Regency
Paris Madeleine $$$$–$$$$$

Lancaster $$$$$

Lord Byron $$

Paris Marriott
Champs-Elysées $$$$$

Left Bank
Latin Quarter (5e)

Familia $

Jardin du Luxembourg $$

St-Germain-des-Prés (6e)

L'Abbaye Saint-Germain
$$$–$$$$

Atelier Montparnasse $$

d'Aubusson $$$

Clos Médicis $$

Fleurie $$–$$$

Globe $

Relais Christine $$$$

Relais Saint-Germain $$$$

Saints-Pères $$–$$$

Eiffel Tower & Invalides (7e)

Champ de Mars $

Duc de Saint-Simon $$$

Grand Hôtel l'Evèque $

Lenox Saint-Germain $$–$$$

Montalembert $$$$–$$$$$

Quai Voltaire $$

Le Tourville $$–$$$

de l'Université $$

Hotel Index by Price Category

$

Champ de Mars (Eiffel Tower
& Invalides)

Familia (Latin Quarter)

Globe (St-Germain-des-Prés)

Grand Hôtel L'Evèque (Eiffel
Tower & Invalides)

Louvre Forum (Louvre)

Timhôtel Louvre (Louvre)

$–$$

7ème Art (Le Marais)

$$

Atelier Montparnasse
(St-Germain-des-Prés)

Britannique (Louvre)

Caron de Beaumarchais
(Le Marais)

Citadines Paris Opéra Aparthotel
(Opéra)

Clos Médicis (St-Germain-
des-Prés)

Deux Iles (The Islands)

Jardin du Luxembourg
(Latin Quarter)

Lord Byron (Champs-Elysées)

Lutèce (The Islands)

Orion Les Halles (Louvre)

Orion Louvre (Louvre)

Quai Voltaire (Eiffel Tower & Invalides)

Relais du Louvre (Louvre)

Saint-Louis (The Islands)

de l'Université (Eiffel Tower & Invalides)

$$–$$$

Fleurie (St-Germain-des-Prés)

Lenox Saint-Germain (Eiffel Tower & Invalides)

Saints-Pères (St-Germain-des-Prés)

Le Tourville (Eiffel Tower & Invalides)

$$$

d'Aubusson (St-Germain-des-Prés)

Citadines Préstige Haussmann Aparthotel (Champs-Elysées)

Duc de Saint-Simon (Eiffel Tower & Invalides)

$$$–$$$$

L'Abbaye Saint-Germain (St-Germain-des-Prés)

$$$$

Pavillon de la Reine (Le Marais)

Relais Christine (St-Germain-des-Prés)

Relais Saint-Germain (St-Germain-des-Prés)

$$$$–$$$$$

Hyatt Regency Paris Madeleine (Champs-Elysées)

Montalembert (Eiffel Tower & Invalides)

Régina (Louvre)

$$$$$

L'Astor (Champs-Elysées)

Costes (Louvre)

Lancaster (Champs-Elysées)

Paris Marriott Champs-Elysées (Champs-Elysées)

Favorite Paris Hotels

L'Abbaye Saint-Germain
$$$–$$$$. St-Germain-des-Prés (6e).

Transformed from an 18th-century convent into one of the Left Bank's most charming and intimate hotels, L'Abbaye is a popular *pied-à-terre* for travelers who have a taste for chic surroundings but a budget where the sky just ain't the limit. Some of the 46 rooms have their original oak ceiling beams, and all are appointed with 19th-century-style furnishings and damask upholsteries. Walls are bathed in ocher or apricot and doorjambs stained a dusky green, giving an overall effect of sophistication and restfulness. Even the standard rooms are a good size for Paris, and the duplex suites are downright spacious. Of the first-floor quarters that open onto a vine-clad courtyard, No. 3 was a favorite of the late Italian actor Marcello Mastroianni. Rooms are air-conditioned, and a rarity in Paris, Continental breakfast is included in the rates. There's no restaurant, but the public areas include a trio of salons and a bar.

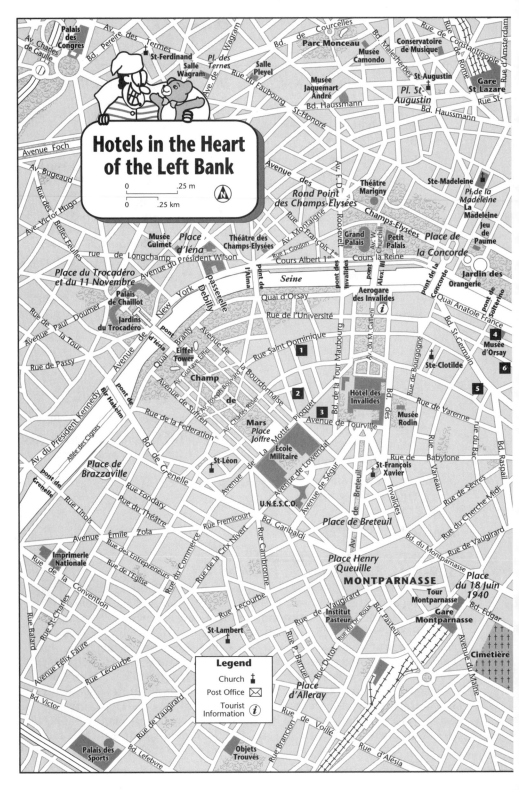

Hotels in the Heart of the Left Bank

0   .25 m
0   .25 km

Legend

Church ✝
Post Office ✉
Tourist Information ⓘ

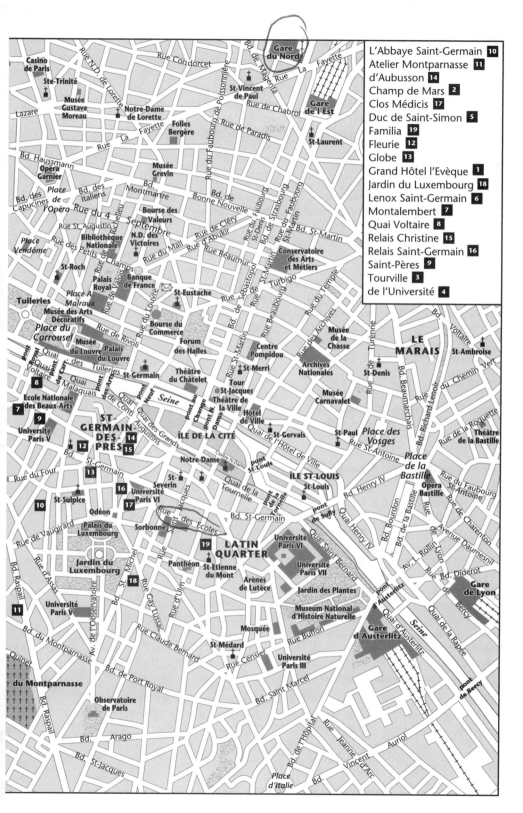

L'Abbaye Saint-Germain **10**
Atelier Montparnasse **11**
d'Aubusson **14**
Champ de Mars **2**
Clos Médicis **17**
Duc de Saint-Simon **5**
Familia **19**
Fleurie **12**
Globe **13**
Grand Hôtel l'Evèque **1**
Jardin du Luxembourg **18**
Lenox Saint-Germain **6**
Montalembert **7**
Quai Voltaire **8**
Relais Christine **15**
Relais Saint-Germain **16**
Saint-Pères **9**
Tourville **3**
de l'Université **4**

10 rue Cassette, 6e. ☎ *01/45-44-38-11.* *Fax 01/45-48-07-86. E-mail: hotel.abbaye@wanadoo.fr. Web site: www.hotel-abbaye.4in.com.* **Métro:** *St-Sulpice, then 1 block south on rue de Rennes to rue Cassette.* **Rates:** *1050–1650F ($188–$295) double, 1950F ($348) suite. AE, MC, V.*

L'Astor
$$$$$. Champs-Elysées (8e).
Part of the elite Westin-Demeure group, L'Astor is a bastion of refinement that feels much more intimate than its 138 rooms suggest. Rooms are done up in the elegantly sober Regency style, with weighty marble fireplaces, mahogany furnishings, and heavy fabrics. Standard rooms are a good size for Paris; the deluxe rooms are very spacious and have sofas and armchairs. Several of the four suites have walk-out balconies with superb vistas. Everything the upscale traveler needs is here: a business center, a health club, express laundry service, and superb room service from the hotel's one-star restaurant. One of L'Astor's main claims to fame is that Joël Robuchon, who was heralded as France's greatest three-star chef before he went into semiretirement in 1996, supervises the kitchen here. There's also a cozy bar and a small, neoclassic-inspired library.

11 rue d'Astorg, 8e (7-minute walk to the Champs-Elysées). ☎ *800/WESTIN1 in the U.S.,* *01/53-05-05-05.* *Fax 01/53-05-05-30. E-mail: hotelastor@ aol.com.* **Métro:** *St-Augustin, then cross boulevard Malesherbes to rue de la Boétie, and turn left on rue d'Astorg.* **Rates:** *2070–2700F ($370–$482) double, 3100F ($554) suite. AE, DC, MC, V.*

Atelier Montparnasse
$$. St-Germain-des-Prés (6e).
It's no wonder that the word *artist* pops up so often in this intimate hotel's guest register. For starters, it's within spitting distance of three famous cafes— Le Select, La Coupole, and Le Dôme—that were the stamping grounds of Picasso, Matisse, and other artists in the 1920s. Secondly, the art deco– inspired lobby doubles as a gallery for paintings by local artists. Rooms are decorated in warm pastels, with art nouveau–style bedside lamps and some of the most memorable bathrooms in Paris. The walls behind each tub feature mosaic reproductions of masterpieces by Chagall, Picasso, Matisse, Gauguin, and their contemporaries. Another of the hotel's real delights is the cheerful owner, Marie-José Tible, who is always happy to recommend her favorite bistros and boutiques. All the rooms are priced at 800F ($143), except for a considerably larger junior suite with a wicker sitting area at 1100F ($196). One bummer: no air-conditioning.

49 rue Vavin, 6e (on the fringe of St-Germain and Montparnasse). ☎ *01/46-33-60-00.* *Fax 01/40-51-04-21.* **Métro:** *Vavin, then head toward Le Select cafe and turn right on rue Vavin.* **Rates:** *800–1100F ($143–$196) double. AE, DC, MC, V.*

d'Aubusson
$$$. St-Germain-des-Prés (6e).
Since this 50-room hotel opened in 1997, it's been among the best mid-priced addresses in St-Germain-des-Prés. The quality of the decor is superb; note the original Aubusson tapestries, Versailles-style parquet floors, chiseled stone fireplace in the lobby, and the restored antiques throughout the hotel. Even the smallest rooms are larger than what you normally find at this price level, and all are bathed in rich blues, greens, and burgundies. Ask for one of the 10 rooms with canopied beds and oak ceiling beams. When the weather is warm, you can enjoy breakfast or an aperitif in the paved courtyard.

33 rue Dauphine, 6e (1 block from the Seine). ☎ **01/43-29-43-43.** *Fax 01/ 43-29-12-62.* **Métro:** *Odéon, then rue de l'Ancienne Comédie to rue Dauphine.* ***Rates:*** *1,050–2,050F ($188–$366) double. AE, MC, V.*

Britannique
$$. Louvre (1er).
This three-star hotel, smack in central Paris and just a block from the Seine, is a terrific bargain. Though the least-expensive quarters are small, all the rooms are well decorated with warm colors and tasteful fabrics. Furthermore, the rooms are comfortable and soundproof (though not air-conditioned), and the satellite TV channels feature English-language programs. There's an old-fashioned French ambiance here, despite a top-quality, British style of service.

Best for Travelers with Disabilities

Hyatt Regency Paris Madeleine	$$$$–$$$$$
Orion Louvre	$$
Paris Marriott Champs-Elysées	$$$$$

20 av. Victoria, 1er. ☎ **01/42-33-74-59.** *Fax 01/42-33-82-65. E-mail: mailbox@hotel-britannique.fr. Web site: www.hotel-britannique.fr.* **Métro:** *Châtelet, exit at Place du Châtelet, which bisects avenue Victoria.* ***Rates:*** *620–950F ($111–$170) double. AE, DC, MC, V.*

Caron de Beaumarchais
$$. Le Marais (4e).
Nearly every detail in this 19-room hotel is a tribute to the era leading up to the French Revolution, when the Marais was the hub of dances, duels, and other high-society doings. Each butter-yellow room reflects the taste of the 18th-century French *noblesse*, from the gilded mirrors and original engravings to rough-hewn ceiling beams and wire-covered cabinets. The accommodations overlooking the interior courtyard are snug but cozy in the best sense of the word, and the top-floor rooms (Nos. 60 and 61) are also pint-sized but boast oak ceiling beams and wonderful balcony views across Right Bank rooftops. For more space, ask for a street-side room on floors two through five. There's air-conditioning, satellite TV, and an eager-to-please staff.

12 rue Vieille-du-Temple, 4e. ☎ **01/42-72-34-12.** *Fax 01/42-72-34-63. Web site: www.carondebeaumarchais.com.* **Métro:** *Hôtel-de-Ville, then west on rue de Rivoli 5 blocks, then turn left.* **Rates:** *730–810F ($130–$145) double. AE, DC, MC, V.*

Champ de Mars
$. Eiffel Tower & Invalides (7e).

Just a stone's throw from the Eiffel Tower, this small place (just 20 rooms) has a cheerful blue-and-yellow country-house style. Rooms are small but comfortable (as long as you don't have lots of luggage) and are equipped with satellite TV with CNN. In the summer, the best rooms are the two ground-floor quarters that open onto the leafy courtyard and stay cool despite a lack of air-conditioning. Considering the location and prettier-than-average decor for this price range, this is a bargain that's hard to beat.

7 rue du Champ de Mars, 7e. ☎ **01/45-51-52-30.** *Fax 01/45-51-64-36. E-mail: stg@club-internet.fr.* **Métro:** *Ecole Militaire.* **Rates:** *380–440F ($68–$79) double. AE, DC, MC, V.*

Best for Dining

L'Astor	$$$$$
Costes	$$$$$
Hyatt Regency Paris Paris Madeleine	$$$$–$$$$$
Montalembert	$$$$–$$$$$
Paris Marriott Champs-Elysées	$$$$$

Kids Citadines Paris Opéra Aparthotel
$$. Opéra (2e).

Blending the autonomy of a private apartment with many of the services of a hotel, Citadines is a major player in the French aparthotel market (see chapter 5 for more information). And of Citadines' half-dozen Paris properties, the Opéra location is the most central. Whether you book a studio or one-bedroom apartment (duplexes also available), you'll have a fully equipped kitchenette at your disposal. For a family of four, a one-bedroom apartment is a savvy alternative to renting two rooms in a cheap hotel. Decor is inoffensive but unimaginative, but that's outweighed by the long list of amenities and services: 24-hour reception, satellite TV, air-conditioning, baby-equipment rental, dry cleaning, Laundromat, housekeeping—and there's even a bar and a fitness center.

18 rue Favart, 2e (6 blocks from the Opéra Garnier). Citadines central reservations: ☎ **01/41-05-79-79.** *Fax 01/47-59-04-70. Web site: www.citadines.fr.* **Métro:** *Richelieu-Drouot, then 2 blocks on bd. des Italiens and turn left.* **Rates:** *790–845F ($141–$151) 2-person studios, 1230–1630F ($220–$291) 1-bedroom apartment (sleeps 4). Ask about special rates for stays of 7 nights or more. AE, MC, V.*

Kids Citadines Préstige Haussmann Aparthotel
$$$. Champs-Elysées (8e).

This is one of Citadines' "Préstige" properties, which means that its studios and apartments are more expensive but also considerably more spacious and luxe. They boast a much more refined decor than do Citadines's other properties (see the Opéra location, above), featuring furnishings of precious woods and granite bathrooms. And you still get the same roster of services and amenities offered at all Citadines properties.

129 bd. Haussmann (10-minute walk from the Champs-Elysées). Citadines central reservations: ☎ *01/41-05-79-79. Fax 01/47-59-04-70. Web site: www. citadines.fr.* **Métro:** *Miromesnil, then av. Percier to bd. Haussmann.* **Rates:** *1055–1180F ($188–$211) 2-person studios, 1385–1795F ($247–$321) 1-bedroom apartments (sleeps 4). Ask about special rates for stays of 7 nights or more. AE, MC, V.*

Clos Médicis
$$. St-Germain-des-Prés (6e).

This classy little hotel a few blocks from the Luxembourg Gardens blends contemporary touches with the warm colors of Provence. The furnishings are a pleasing hodgepodge of painted rustic-style tables, wrought-iron items, and sleekly modern pieces. Rooms are compact, but the comfort level is boosted by air-conditioning, crisp terry robes, and in-room modem lines. Other pluses include a verdant garden with lattices and exposed stone walls and a multilingual staff.

56 rue Monsieur-le-Prince, 6e. ☎ *01/43-29-10-80. Fax 01/43-54-26-90. E-mail: clos-medicis@compuserve.com.* **Métro:** *Odéon, then head through the Carrefour de l'Odéon to rue Monsieur-le-Prince.* **Rates:** *790–990F ($141–$177) double, 1200F ($214) duplex. AE, DC, MC, V.*

Costes
$$$$$. Louvre (1er).

The ultrahip brother team of Jean-Louis and Louis Costes is behind some of the city's most voguish restaurants, and this 86-room townhouse—their first foray into the hotel scene—has quickly become a style icon. Since its opening in 1996, the Costes has been the darling of show biz and fashion folk, not to mention a frequent backdrop for international decorating magazines. The look conjures up the palaces of Napoléon III, with every room a sumptuous *mélange* of garnet and bronze, laden with enough swags, damask, and brocade to blanket the Tuileries Gardens. Beyond the usual suspects of luxe services (concierge, room service, dry cleaning, laundry, baby-sitting), there's a gym, a sauna, and an indoor pool. The restaurant, which overlooks an Italianate inner courtyard, serves expensive but delicious modern French fare, and it positively teems with European film stars.

239 rue St-Honoré, 1er (between the Tuileries Gardens and Place Vendôme). ☎ *01/ 42-44-50-50. Fax 01/42-44-50-01.* **Métro:** *Tuileries or Concorde.* **Rates:**

2250–3000F ($402–$536) double, 3500F ($625) duplex, 5250F ($938) suite. AE, DC, MC, V.

Deux Iles
$$. The Islands (4e).
This much-restored 17th-century town house is a favorite of travelers seeking an intimate ambiance (just 17 rooms), loads of traditional French charm, and a decent level of comfort. Rooms are compact but winningly old-fashioned, with exposed oak ceiling beams and classic floral upholsteries. Ask for one overlooking the little leafy courtyard. Yet perhaps this hotel's most compelling selling point is its superb location on the magical Ile St-Louis.

59 rue St-Louis-en-l'Ile, 4e. ☎ *01/43-26-13-35. Fax 01/43-29-60-25.* **Métro:** *Pont-Marie, then cross the bridge to the Ile St-Louis.* **Rates:** *860F ($154) double. AE, MC, V.*

Duc de Saint-Simon
$$$. Eiffel Tower & Invalides (7e).
Set on a quiet little residential street between Invalides and St-Germain-des-Prés, this small villa has a tiny front garden, an 1830s decor with *trompe l'oeil* paneling, a frescoed elevator, and a courtyard abloom with climbing wisteria. Rooms are tastefully and individually appointed with antiques and smart fabrics, and crisp terry bathrobes are provided for guests. The service is pitch-perfect at every turn, including a do-anything concierge. One small disappointment: There are no in-room televisions, but the staff is happy to provide one for you upon request.

14 rue de St-Simon, 7e. ☎ *01/44-39-20-20. Fax 01/45-48-68-25. E-mail: Duc. desaintsimon@wannadoo.fr.* **Métro:** *Rue-du-Bac, then rue Paul-Louis Courier 1 block to rue de St-Simon.* **Rates:** *1350–1475F ($241–$263) double, 1900F ($339) suite. AE, MC, V.*

Familia
$. Latin Quarter (5e).
This family-run budget hotel has been enthusiastically penned into many a traveler's journal. Every year, Eric Gaucheron and his parents make improvements to their property and seldom increase their prices. About half of the 30 rooms are graced with sepia frescoes depicting Parisian landmarks (Notre Dame, the Place des Vosges), painted by an artist from the Ecole des Beaux-Arts. Most rooms are done up in warm shades of apricot, deep claret, or rich gold, and seven have balconies with delightful views over the Latin Quarter. All rooms have cable TV (including CNN) and private bathrooms with tub or shower. Insist on one of the more expensive rooms, like No. 33, which faces the street and has beautifully rich fabrics. Or better yet, request one of the four rooms with a walk-out balcony—Nos. 22, 23, 52, and 53. (A balcony is particularly welcome in August, as the hotel isn't air-conditioned). Steer way clear of the least-expensive corner doubles, which are minuscule.

11 rue des Ecoles, 5e (2 blocks from the Seine). ☎ *01/43-54-55-27. Fax 01/43-29-61-77.* **Métro:** *Jussieu, then 1 block on rue Jussieu to rue des Ecoles. Or Maubert-Mutualité, then 1 block on rue Monge to rue des Ecoles.* **Rates:** *390–580F ($70–$104) double. AE, MC, V.*

Kids Fleurie
$$–$$$. St-Germain-des-Prés (6e).

Just off Place de l'Odéon on a colorful little side street, the Fleurie is a dapper little family-run place (29 rooms) with pretty pastel rooms that feel reassuringly traditional thanks to Oriental rugs and a smattering of antiques. The marble bathrooms have been modernized and feature heated towel racks. Families should book at least six weeks in advance for one of the *chambres familiales*—connecting rooms with two large beds. Children 12 and under stay free in parents' room.

Best for Families

Citadines Paris Opéra Aparthotel	$$
Citadines Préstige Haussmann Aparthotel	$$$
Fleurie	$$–$$$
Orion Les Halles	$$
Orion Louvre	$$
Relais du Louvre	$$
Relais Saint-Germain	$$$$

32–34 rue Grégoire-de-Tours, 6e. ☎ *01/53-73-70-00. Fax 01/53-73-70-20. E-mail: bonjour@hotel-de-fleurie.tm.fr. Web site: www.hotel-de-fleurie.tm.fr.* **Métro:** *Odéon, then 1 block west on bd. St-Germain to rue Grégoire-de-Tours.* **Rates:** *900–1200F ($162–$216) double, 1600F ($261–$281) family room. AE, DC, MC, V.*

Globe
$. St-Germain-des-Prés (6e).

This budget hotel has an eccentric yet appealing mix of styles. Gothic wrought-iron doors lead to florid hallways, and a suit of armor surveys guests in the salon. The 15 rooms are individually decorated, be it in bamboo ("The Tahiti Room") or more-conventional woods and fabrics. Tip #1: The rooms with a tub are almost twice as large as those with a shower stall, and well worth the extra expense. The largest and most desirable rooms are Nos. 1, 12 (both with canopy beds), 14, 15, and 16. Tip #2: Don't bring heavy luggage—there's no elevator, just a narrow, winding staircase. Tip #3 (summer only): Book a room on one of the lower floors. There's no air-conditioning and the uppermost floors can get quite hot.

15 rue des Quatre-Vents, 6e. ☎ *01/46-33-62-69. Fax 01/46-33-62-69.* **Métro:** *Odéon, then cross the Carrefour de l'Odéon to rue des Quatre-Vents.* **Rates:** *480–590F ($86–$105) double. MC, V.*

Grand Hôtel L'Evèque
$. Eiffel Tower & Invalides (7e).

Located on Paris's most chichi market street, right under the Eiffel Tower, this 1930s-era hotel retains a faint art deco feel. The pastel rooms are snug, with just enough space to be comfortable, but double-insulated windows ensure a quiet stay. The hotel was most recently renovated in early 1998 and tends to be perpetually loaded with English-speaking clients, many of whom have seen it recommended on Rick Steve's travel show. There's no air-conditioning but, overall, this is a good budget find in a great neighborhood.

29 rue Cler, 7e (3 blocks from the Eiffel Tower). ☎ **01/47-05-49-15.** *Fax 01/45-50-49-36.* **Métro:** *Ecole Militaire, then 1 block on av. de la Motte Picquet, then left on rue Cler.* **Rates:** *380–450F ($68–$80) double, 550F ($98) triple. AE, MC, V.*

Best Views

Paris Marriott Champs-Elysées	$$$$$
Quai Voltaire	$$
Régina	$$$$–$$$$$

Hyatt Regency Paris Madeleine
$$$$–$$$$$. Champs-Elysées (8e).
The 86-room Hyatt opened in the summer of 1997 and became an overnight sensation with business and leisure travelers alike. The elegant Haussmannesque building near the Place de la Concorde feels more like a boutique hotel than an international business chain, thanks to stylized details like cherry paneling and mismatched bedside tables. Standard rooms are a good size for Paris and have satellite TV with CNN and up-to-date gadgetry like voice mail and in-room data ports. Streetside rooms on the seventh and eighth floors have views of the Eiffel Tower, though rooms overlooking the inner courtyard are about 400F ($71) less expensive.

24 bd. Malesherbes, 8e (5-minute walk from Place de la Concorde). ☎ **800/223-1234** *in the U.S., or 01/55-27-12-34. Fax 01/55-27-12-10. Web site: www.hyatt. com.* **Métro:** *Madeleine. Bd. Malesherbes is on the opposite side of Place de la Madeleine.* **Rates:** *1950–2800F ($348–$500) double. AE, DC, MC, V.*

Jardin du Luxembourg
$$. Latin Quarter (5e).
This friendly little 25-room place just a block from the Luxemburg Gardens is one of the best moderately priced deals in the city. Rooms are compact (common for the Latin Quarter) but well arranged to optimize space. The decor is a step above most hotels at this price level, featuring rustic furnishings and a stylish Provençal color scheme of ocher, indigo, and terra-cotta. Some have balconies with views that skip across rooftops; the best (No. 25) has dormer windows and a glimpse of the Eiffel Tower.

5 impasse Royer-Collard, 5e (1 block east of the Luxemburg Gardens). ☎ **01/40-46-08-88.** *Fax 01/40-46-02-28.* **Métro:** *RER Luxembourg, exit at Place E. Rostand. Take rue Gay Lussac to the first intersection, then impasse Royer-Collard (not rue Royer-Collard, which is perpendicular).* **Rates:** *795–840F ($142–$150) double. AE, DC, MC, V.*

Lancaster
$$$$$. Champs-Elysées (8e).

In 1996 hotel style guru Grace Leo-Andrieu (also the creative force behind the Montalembert, below) transformed the historic Lancaster into one of the city's top luxury hotels. The new decor seamlessly blends Louis XV and XVI furnishings with pieces from some of Europe's hottest interior designers. The overall effect is timeless elegance. Every detail speaks of quality, from the specially commissioned line of scented bath products to the D. Porthault linens to the in-room data ports and VCRs. The service is impeccable.

Best Trendy Hotels

Costes	$$$$$
Lancaster	$$$$$
Montalembert	$$$$–$$$$$

7 rue du Berri, 8e (less than a block from the Champs-Elysées). ☎ **800-63SAVOY** in the U.S. or 01/40-76-40-76. Fax 01/40-76-40-00. E-mail: pippaona@hotel-lancaster.fr. Web site: www.hotel-lancaster.fr. **Métro:** George V, then 1 block down Champs-Elysées and left on rue du Berri. **Rates:** 2350–2750F ($420–$491) double, 3000F ($536) junior suite, 4500–6500F ($804–$1161) suite. AE, DC, MC, V.

Lenox Saint-Germain
$$–$$$. Eiffel Tower & Invalides (7e).

The Lenox is a favorite for travelers seeking reasonably priced accommodations near St-Germain-des-Prés. In 1910 T. S. Eliot spent a summer here "on the old man's money" when the hotel was just a basic pension. Today this much-improved establishment offers a helpful staff and comfortable rooms done up in an English country-house style with chintzes and sturdy, traditional furnishings. Double rooms vary greatly in size, from compact to quite spacious, and this is reflected in the price range. Many returning guests request the attic duplex with its tiny balcony and skylight.

9 rue de l'Université, 7e. ☎ **01/42-96-10-95.** *Fax 01/42-61-52-83.* **Métro:** Rue-du-Bac. **Rates:** 680–1,100F ($121–$196) double, 1,500F ($268) duplex suite. AE, DC, MC, V.

Lord Byron
$$. Champs-Elysées (8e).

Just off the Champs-Elysées on a narrow street lined with handsome town houses, Lord Byron is one of the best-value hotels in this upscale neighborhood. Correct, unassuming, and a bit staid, it's exactly what repeat clients want and expect: a sense of luxury, peacefulness, and understatement. Rooms are furnished with fine antique reproductions, traditional French fabrics, and framed prints of the French landscape. Service is discreet and helpful.

5 rue de Chateaubriand, 8e. ☎ **01/43-59-89-98.** *Fax 01/42-89-46-04. Web site: www.leisureplan.com.* **Métro:** George V, then rue Washington 1 block and turn left. **Rates:** 870–970F ($155–$173) double, from 1340F ($239) suite. AE, DC, MC, V.

Louvre Forum
$. Louvre (1er).
This friendly bargain hotel has a brilliant address just a stone's throw from the Louvre. What's more, it was entirely renovated in early 1999 and prices haven't budged one franc. Everything is tasteful (if a bit timid) and brand new, from the bathrooms to the carpeting to the armoires. And there's satellite TV to boot, though no air-conditioning.

25 rue du Bouloi, 1er. ☎ **01/42-36-54-19.** *Fax 01/42-33-66-31.* **Métro:** *Louvre-Rivoli, then 2 blocks on rue du Louvre, left on rue du Colonel Driant, and right on rue du Bouloi.* **Rates:** *490–540F ($88–$96). AE, DC, MC, V.*

Love Your Laptop?

If you need to send e-mail or surf the Web, you may need one of these local access numbers: America Online (☎ 08/36-06-13-10) and Compuserve (☎ 01/41-30-20-10). The following hotels feature in-room data ports:

L'Astor	$$$$$
Costes	$$$$$
Clos Médicis	$$
Fleurie	$$–$$$
Hyatt Regency Paris Madeleine	$$$$–$$$$$
Lancaster	$$$$$
Montalembert	$$$$–$$$$$
Paris Marriott Champs-Elysées	$$$$$

Lutèce
$$. The Islands (4e).
This homey hotel evokes a Breton country house, with its old fireplace and wanton placement of antiques. Rooms are smallish but prettily decorated with old-fashioned floral upholsteries, and many have exposed ceiling beams. The hotel has the same owners as the Deux Iles and is similar in style and amenities. The two hotels also share the same fabulous street on Ile St-Louis.

65 rue St-Louis-en-l'Ile, 4e. ☎ **01/43-26-23-52.** *Fax 01/43-29-60-25.* **Métro:** *Pont-Marie, then cross bridge and continue 1 block to rue St-Louis-en-l'Ile.* **Rates:** *860F ($154) double, 990F ($179) triple. AE, MC, V.*

Montalembert
$$$$–$$$$$. Eiffel Tower & Invalides (7e).
Paris's most original and stylish boutique hotel is the brainchild of hotelier Grace Leo-Andrieu and the hyperhip architect Christian Liaigre. Whether decorated with traditional Louis-Philippe elegance or contemporary sleekness, the rooms all convey chic luxury through simple lines. Elements designed especially for the hotel include bold navy-and-white striped duvets, Frette linens, Cascais marble bathrooms, cast-bronze door handles, and a signature line of toiletries. There's satellite TV and a VCR in every room, 24-hour room service, and free access to a nearby health club. The hotel's restaurant is one of the Left Bank's trendiest eating spots.

3 rue de Montalembert, 7e. ☎ **800/447-7462** *in the U.S. and Canada, or 01/45-49-68-68. Fax 01/45-49-69-49. E-mail: welcome@hotel-montalembert.fr. Web site:*

www.montalembert.com. **Métro:** *Rue-du-Bac, then head toward the Seine on rue du Bac and take second right.* **Rates:** *1750–2300F ($313–$411) double, 2850F ($509) junior suite, 4400F ($786) suite. Ask about special packages for stays longer than 3 nights. AE, DC, MC, V.*

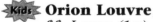 Orion Les Halles
$$. Louvre (1er).

Based on the same aparthotel concept as Citadines (see above), Orion is another great name for travelers who want a hybrid between a private apartment and a hotel. Of Orion's handful of Paris properties, this is the second only to the Orion Louvre (see below), which is brand new and slightly better located. Studios and one-bedroom apartments have fully equipped kitchenettes. Like at Citadines, decor is bland and chainlike but there's a long list of amenities and services: 24-hour reception, satellite TV, air-conditioning, baby equipment rental, Laundromat, and housekeeping. This makes a good fallback if the Louvre property is booked.

4 rue des Innocents, 1er (100 yards from the Forum des Halles). ☎ **800/ 755-8266** *or 212/688-9489. Fax 212/688-9467. E-mail: sales@apartmenthotels. com. Web site: www.apartmenthotels.com.* **Métro:** *Les Halles.* **Rates:** *$150–$169 (rates quoted in dollars) 2-person studios, $218–$230 4-person apartments. AE, MC, V.*

Orion Louvre
$$. Louvre (1er).

This brand new property is the best Orion has to offer in Paris. The lineup of amenities and services is the same as at Les Halles, above, but this address is in a more upscale and prettier neighborhood. Several studios and apartments are equipped for travelers with disabilities.

8 rue de Richelieu, 1er (1 block north of Louvre). ☎ **800/755-8266** *or 212/ 688-9489. Fax 212/688-9467. E-mail: sales@apartmenthotels.com. Web site: www.apartmenthotels.com.* **Métro:** *Palais-Royal or Pyramides.* **Rates:** *$155–$175 (rates quoted in dollars) 2-person studio, $235–$280 4-person apartment. AE, MC, V.*

Paris Marriott Champs-Elysées
$$$$$. Champs-Elysées (8e).

Take a fantastic location, an impressive atrium lobby, and a chic, 19th-century decor, and you've got the makings of the Paris Marriott. Ebony furnishings and antique prints are a few of the touches that set this apart from the typical chain property. State-of-the-art soundproofing shuts out the cacophonic Champs to encourage a good night's sleep, and there's a slew of terrific services for business travelers (in-room data ports, business center, fax machines on request). Service is professional and efficient.

70 av. des Champs-Elysées, 8e. ☎ **800/MARRIOTT** *in the U.S., or 01/ 53-93-55-00. Fax 01/53-93-55-01. Web site: www.marriott.com.* **Métro:** *George V.* **Rates:** *2500–2800F ($446–$500) double, 3600F ($643) studio, 5300F ($946) junior suite. AE, DC, MC, V.*

Best for Romantic Interludes

L'Abbaye Saint-Germain
$$$–$$$$
Caron de Beaumarchais $$
Pavillon de la Reine $$$$
Relais Christine $$$$
Relais Saint-Germain $$$$

Pavillon de la Reine
$$$$. Le Marais (3e).

Though built in 1986, this cream-colored Renaissance-style villa was constructed from centuries-old plans and blends in perfectly with the rest of the sumptuous Marais. It's one of the most romantic hotels in this romantic city. You enter through a *porte-cochère* (arched stage-coach doorway) on the Place des Vosges, which opens onto a small formal garden. The history of the neighborhood is harkened with Louis XIII furnishings, rich fabrics, and stone fireplaces. Each room is unique; some are duplexes with sleeping lofts above cozy salons. All have weathered beams, reproductions of famous oil paintings, and marble baths. The hotel has an "honesty bar" and a limited 24-hour room-service menu.

28 place des Vosges, 3e. ☎ **800/447-7462** *in the U.S. or 01/40-29-19-19. Fax 01/40-29-19-20. E-mail: pavillon@club-internet.fr.* **Métro:** *St-Paul.* **Rates:** *1900–2100F ($339–$375) double, 2350–2700F ($420–$482) duplex, 2950–3900F ($527–$696) suite. AE, DC, MC, V.*

Quai Voltaire
$$. Eiffel Tower & Invalides (7e).

Built in the 1600s as an abbey, then transformed into a hotel in 1856, the Quai Voltaire is best known for its long line of illustrious guests, including Wilde, Baudelaire, and Wagner, who occupied rooms 47, 56, and 55, respectively. Camille Pissarro painted Le Pont Royal from the window of his room on the fourth floor. Rooms are small and the pastel decor is slightly dated, but they are clean and comfortable. Most overlook the bookstalls and boats of the Seine. You can have drinks in the bar or small salon, and simple meals (like omelettes and salads) can be provided.

19 quai Voltaire, 7e. ☎ **01/42-61-50-91.** *Fax 01/42-61-62-26.* **Métro:** *Musée d'Orsay.* **Rates:** *670–720F ($120–$129) double, 870F ($155) triple. MC, V.*

Régina
$$$$–$$$$$. Louvre (1er).

The management of this art nouveau gem poured a lot of francs into a 1995 renovation that upgraded the rooms, spruced and buffed the sublime belle epoque lounge, and added that Paris rarity: a health center. Now the Régina ranks among the city's top drawer hotels, at prices that are more than reasonable considering its location and level of luxury. Rooms and public areas feature antique furnishings, Oriental carpets, and 18th-century etchings and paintings, and fountains play in a lovely flagstone-paved courtyard. Request a room overlooking the Tuileries for views that stretch as far away as the Eiffel Tower. There's an excellent restaurant on the premises (closed Sundays) and a roster of amenities and services that provide what you'd expect and more from a four-star property, including concierge, 24-hour room service, twice-daily maid service, laundry/dry cleaning, in-room massage, exercise room, and sauna.

2 place des Pyramides, 1er (facing the Tuileries Gardens and Louvre). ☎ *01/ 42-60-31-10. Fax 01/40-15-95-16. E-mail: helene@reginotel.com. Web site: www.reginotel.com.* **Métro:** *Tuileries, then 1 block east on rue de Rivoli.* **Rates:** *1650–2250F ($295–$402) double, from 2800F ($500) suite. AE, DC, MC, V.*

Relais Christine
$$$$. St-Germain-des-Prés (6e).

On a narrow cobblestone street in the heart of St-Germain, in what was a 16th-century monastic cloister, this very popular hotel oozes luxurious romance at every turn. You enter from the street through a private courtyard to an elegant reception area filled with baroque sculptures and Renaissance antiques. Rooms are spacious (particularly the duplexes) and sumptuously evoke old Paris with mahogany Louis XIII–style furnishings and acres of rich fabrics. The best rooms feature original oak ceiling beams and overlook the little garden courtyard. Breakfast is served in an erstwhile stone chapel. There's no restaurant, but 24-hour room service is provided, as well as laundry service.

3 rue Christine, 6e (between the Seine and bd. St-Germain). ☎ **800/447-7462** *in the U.S. or 01/40-51-60-80. Fax 01/40-51-60-81. E-mail: relaisch@club-internet.fr.* **Métro:** *Odéon, then 1 short block on rue de l'Ancienne Comédie, 2 short blocks on rue Dauphine, turn right on rue Christine.* **Rates:** *1800–2100F ($306–$342) double, 2700–4200F ($482–$750) duplex suite. AE, DC, MC, V.*

🌟Kids Relais du Louvre
$$. Louvre (1er).

This little 20-room place has an awful lot going for it. It's located right beside the Louvre and around the corner from the Pont Neuf, which leads to the Ile de la Cité. Rooms are smallish but clean, bright, airy, and well equipped with mod cons like cable TV and hair dryers. The new penthouse apartment, which sleeps four and features an equipped kitchen, is a good deal for families.

19 rue des Prêtres St-Germain l'Auxerrois, 1er (between the Louvre and Ile de la Cité). ☎ **01/40-41-96-42.** *Fax 01/40-41-96-44. E-mail: le-relais-du-louvre@ dial.oleane.com.* **Métro:** *Pont-Neuf, then 25 yards down rue de l'Arbre Sec and turn left.* **Rates:** *850–980F ($152–$175) double, 2200F ($393) 4-person penthouse apartment. AE, MC, V.*

🌟Kids Relais Saint-Germain
$$$$. St-Germain-des-Prés (6e).

Looking for a hotel that has it all? Never mind the unbeatable location in the heart of St-Germain-des-Prés. Rooms here are nearly twice the size of what you normally find in this price bracket, with the doubles feeling like junior suites due to their separate sitting areas. Yet location and room size pales against the sublime decor. The interior-designer owners used their exquisite taste to fill the hotel with treasures they've unearthed at the city's *brocantes* (secondhand dealers)—an Empire canopied bed here, an antique rolltop desk there, and gorgeous French fabrics everywhere. Four rooms feature kitchenettes (wonderful for families), and two suites have terraces. There's a concierge, plus laundry and twice-daily maid service, and newspapers are brought to your room upon request. And atypically in Paris, the rates include breakfast.

9 carrefour de l'Odéon, 6e. ☎ *01/43-29-12-05. Fax 01/46-33-45-30.* **Métro:** *Odéon. The hotel is just off Place de l'Odéon.* **Rates:** *1600–1850F ($286–$330) double, 2100F ($375) suite. AE, DC, MC, V.*

Best for Gay Travelers

Caron de Beaumarchais $$
Costes $$$$$
Montalembert $$$$–$$$$$

Saint-Louis
$$. The Islands (4e).
Guy Record and his wife, Andrée, promote a charming family atmosphere at their antiques-filled, 17th-century town house hotel, which was given a top-to-bottom sprucing in 1998. The place offers incredible value considering its prime location on the highly desirable Ile St-Louis. Rooms are smallish and rather old-fashioned with traditional fabrics and furnishings. The most evocative are the cozy top-floor quarters under the mansard roof, which charm with inclined walls, dormer windows, thick moldings, and tiny balconies from which to survey the rooftops of Old Paris. The one time of year to avoid the top floor is August, as the hotel isn't air-conditioned and the lower floors remain cooler.

75 rue St-Louis-en-l'Ile, 4e. ☎ *01/46-34-04-80. Fax 01/46-34-02-13. Web site: www.paris-hotel.tm.fr/saint-louis_marais.* **Métro:** *Pont-Marie, then cross bridge and continue 1 block to rue St-Louis-en-l'Ile.* **Rates:** *775–875F ($138–$156) double. MC, V.*

Saints-Pères
$$–$$$. St-Germain-des-Prés (6e).
This hotel has long lured travelers who adore Paris and, more specifically, adore traditional Left Bank hotels. It's located a stone's throw from the triumvirate of celebrated St-Germain cafes—the Deux-Magots, Flore, and Lipp. Designed in the 17th century by Louis XIV's architect, the place proudly shows off its age with antique furnishings, old paintings, tapestries, and gilt mirrors. The most sought-after room is the *chambre à la fresque,* which has a 17th-century painted ceiling. The late Edna St. Vincent Millay enjoyed the camellia-filled garden, where breakfast is served in fine weather.

65 rue des Sts-Pères, 6e. ☎ **01/45-44-50-00.** *Fax 01/45-44-90-83. E-mail: hotelst.peres@wanadoo.fr.* **Métro:** *St-Germain-des-Prés, then past the Café aux Deux-Magots and take second right.* **Rates:** *800–1250F ($143–$223) double; 1700F ($304) suite. AE, MC, V.*

7ème Art
$–$$. Le Marais (4e).
The clientele at this hip Marais budget hotel is young, trendy, and mainly American. The name—"seventh art," what the French call filmmaking, clues you in that the theme here is vintage Hollywood. Images of James Cagney, Marilyn Monroe, Charlie Chaplin, and James Dean are posted in both the public areas and rooms, which are small and Spartanly furnished, but clean, quiet, and blessed with cable TV. There's a washing machine and dryer available to guests, and an exercise room will be added as of spring 1999. There's neither air-conditioning nor an elevator, though, so travel light and think about booking on one of the lower floors.

20 rue St-Paul, 4e. ☎ **01/44-54-85-00.** *Fax 01/42-77-69-10.* **Métro:** *St-Paul.* **Rates:** *420–670F ($75–$120) double. AE, DC, MC, V.*

Timhôtel Louvre
$. Louvre (1er).
Timhôtel is one of the better French budget hotel chains catering to business travelers on small expense accounts. What sets this particular property apart from the pack is its brilliant location near the Louvre. The decor is unimaginative and chainlike but inoffensive, and rooms are clean and comfortable, with modern bathrooms and cable TV. There's no air-conditioning, so stick to the lower floors during summer hot spells. Breakfast is provided rather anonymously from a self-service cafeteria.

4 rue Croix des Petits-Champs, 1er. ☎ **01/42-60-34-86.** *Fax 01/42-60-10-39. E-mail: pascalgauthier@compuserve.com.* **Métro:** *Palais-Royal.* **Rates:** *580F ($104) double. AE, MC, V.*

Le Tourville
$$–$$$. Eiffel Tower & Invalides (7e).
This intimate little gem is less expensive than most other four-star hotels and has a terrific location in the swanky seventh district, almost directly behind Les Invalides and a short walk from the Eiffel Tower. Rooms are done up in pastels or ochers, with crisp white damask upholsteries, antique bureaus and lamps, and fabulously mismatched old mirrors. Most doubles are priced at 690F ($123) in low season, but four superior rooms with walk-out, vine-clad terraces come in at 1090F ($196). The junior suites are more spacious and boast whirlpool baths. You couldn't hope for a more helpful staff.

16 av. de Tourville, 7e (100 yards from the Hôtel des Invalides). ☎ **800/528-3549** *in the U.S., or 01/47-05-62-62. Fax 01/47-05-43-90. E-mail: hotel@tourville.com. Web site: www.hoteltourville.com.* **Métro:** *Ecole-Militaire.* **Rates:** *690–1090F*

Hotel Preferences Worksheet

Hotel	Location	Price per night

Advantages	Disadvantages	Your Ranking (1–10)

($123–$195) standard double, 1090–1390F ($195–$248) superior double with terrace, 1690–1990F ($301–$355) junior suite. AE, DC, MC, V.

de l'Université
$$. Eiffel Tower & Invalides (7e).

This hotel enjoys a smart location in a visibly well-heeled neighborhood. Its owner, Madame Bergmann, transformed this 300-year-old town house into an affordable and personable hotel and filled it with fine antiques. All the rooms have different sizes and features. No. 54 is a favorite, with a rattan bed, period pieces, and a marble bath. No. 35, which opens onto a pretty courtyard and has a fireplace, is another charmer. The triple has a small terrace overlooking the surrounding rooftops.

22 rue de l'Université, 7e. ☎ **01/42-61-09-39.** *Fax 01/42-60-40-84. Web site: www.paris-hotel.tm.fr/fr/saintgermain.04/univerisite.html.* **Métro:** *St-Germain-des-Prés.* **Rates:** *850–950F ($152–$170) double, 1300F ($232) triple. AE, MC, V.*

Too Many Hotels, Too Hard to Choose?

For some of you the decision will be easy. Maybe you wouldn't be happy staying anywhere but the Marais. Or maybe you plan to log in days at the Louvre, so a hotel that's a two-minute walk away is just the ticket. Or perhaps you have business near the Champs-Elysées and need to stay in the neighborhood. If so, you're ahead of the game.

For the rest of you, there's a chart on the two preceding pages to help you land the hotel that's right for you. First ask yourself a few questions: Which neighborhood sounds most appealing? How much can you afford to spend? What sort of ambiance are you looking for? Now go back to those hotels you thought looked pretty good, then jot down their names and vital statistics in the worksheet. Get everything lined up so you can compare pros and cons, then step back and see how the various hotels stack up against each other. Rank them in the column on the right so that you can have your preferences ready when you make reservations. If there's no room at the inn of your choice, just move on to your second pick.

Part 3

Learning Your Way Around Paris

Like any old European city, Paris is made up largely of a mishmash of streets of random lengths and widths, with seemingly no set pattern. For many North Americans, this is a big part of what gives Europe its charm. But its apparent lack of logic can also be intimidating for first-time visitors trying to get their bearings.

Don't worry—learning your way around is nowhere near as difficult as it looks. Despite initial appearances, there is a system behind the way Paris is organized, and once you learn what to look for you'll hit a comfort zone. You'll be able to discern subtle differences between neighborhoods, and know the important land-marks in each one. Next, I'll run through a few tips that will get you ready to navigate the Métro. And before you know it, you'll have the air of someone who knows where she's going, and other travelers will be asking you for directions.

Chapter 7

Getting Your Bearings

> **In This Chapter**
>
> ➤ Getting into Paris from the airports
>
> ➤ The city, neighborhood by neighborhood
>
> ➤ Where to learn more once you're there

It begins as soon as your plane lands at the airport—all the sights and sounds are unmistakably French. The smell of strong coffee and croissants wafts out of the airport cafe. A lot of people are smoking. Luggage carts are free! People are dressed more formally than at home.

As all this sinks in, you start to realize that there are just as many similarities as differences between Paris and home. So the sooner you stop feeling like a fish out of water, the sooner you'll relax and start having fun. But first, you need to get from the airport to your hotel.

You've Just Arrived—Now What?

More people visit Paris than any other foreign capital in the world, and con-sequently both of Paris's two international airports, **Charles-de-Gaulle** (a.k.a. Roissy or CDG) and **Orly,** are impressively user-friendly. For every-thing you ever wanted to know about CDG and Orly—including departure and arrival timetables, duty-free shopping, and services—visit **@Paris** on the Web at **www.smartweb.fr/aero/index.html**.

If You're Arriving at Charles-de-Gaulle International Airport

Virtually every flight on a major airline originating from North America lands at **Charles-de-Gaulle** in the early morning. CDG has two terminals. **Terminal One** is older, smaller, and bilevel; **Terminal Two** is divided into Halls **2A, 2B, 2C, 2D,** and the spanking new, futuristic **2F.** Both terminals are well signposted in both French and English to direct you toward baggage claim, customs, and transportation to the city. Information desks are also on hand if you have any questions.

Regardless of the terminal, you'll need French francs to get from the airport into Paris. Pass up the bureaux de change and get cash from an ATM if you want to get the best possible exchange rate. ATMs are located in the arrivals hall of each terminal.

Grabbing a Cab

A taxi from Charles-de-Gaulle into Paris costs from 200 to 240F ($36 to $43). If your high-school French is dodgy, it's a good idea to make sure your cab driver is clear about where you're heading. Write down the name of your hotel, its street, and its postal code and show it to the driver. It may seem strange, but the postal code is the most important morsel of information (see "Paris Orientation," below, for why that's true); it's a five-digit number starting with "75," such as 75006 or 75004. Cabs charge 6F ($1) for each piece of luggage carried in the trunk, so bring small bags into the back seat with you.

Here's where you'll find the taxi ranks:

CDG 1: Porte 16, arrivals level

CDG 2A and 2C: Hall A, Porte 7

CDG 2B and 2D: Hall D, Porte 7

CDG 2F: Porte 1, arrivals level

My Baby Takes the Morning Train

If you're not overloaded with baggage and want to keep down your expenses, the best way into Paris is *probably* the RER B commuter train. (For cases when a bus is better, see below). This is how most Parisians get back home from the

Which Airport? Which Terminal?

Below is a list of the major airlines servicing Paris and the airport terminals they fly into (CDG = Charles de Gaulle).

Airline	Terminal
Aer Lingus	CDG 1
Air Canada	CDG 2A
Air France	CDG 2A, B, C, D, F
American Airlines	Orly Sud
Brit Air	CDG 2D
British Airways	CDG 1
British Midland	CDG 1
Continental	CDG 2C
Delta	CDG 2C
Northwest	CDG 1
TWA	CDG 1
United Airlines	CDG 1
US Airways	CDG 1

airport, since it's easy, cheap, and convenient. The line operates from 5am to midnight Monday to Friday, and from 7am to 9pm on weekends. Trains run every 15 minutes during most of the day and twice as often during peak periods. The trip from the airport into central Paris takes about 30 minutes.

Dollars & Sense

Regardless of whether you fly into Charles-de-Gaulle or Orly, the door-to-door **Airport Shuttle** (☎ **01/45-38-55-72**; fax 01/43-21-35-67) is a great alternative to a taxi. The service aims to be hassle-free: A minivan meets you at the airport and drops you off on your hotel's doorstep for 89F ($16) per person, with no extra baggage charge. Single passengers are charged 120F ($21). Consider that cabs take a maximum of three passengers, then do the math. From Charles-de-Gaulle airport, the Airport Shuttle is cheaper than a taxi if you've got one, two, or more than three travelers in your party. If you've got exactly three in your party, a taxi is better. You need to book in advance; the easiest way is from the Web site at **www.paris-anglo.com/clients/ashuttle.html**.

If you land in **CDG 1,** exit the terminal at Porte 28 on the arrivals level. A free shuttle bus (marked "RER" over the driver) will pick you up right outside the door and bring you to the train station. If you land in **CDG 2,** there's no need to take a shuttle bus, since the terminal is linked to the RER by a walkway. Look for the round RER logo or ask an airport employee. (*Note:* It's pronounced "air-uh-air" in French).

At the RER ticket counter, ask for the **"RER plus Métro"** ticket, which costs 47F ($8). This will get you into to the Métro system once you get to Paris. You probably won't run into ticket inspectors on the RER, but whatever you do, hang onto your ticket. If you're aboard the rare train that does have an inspection, you'll be fined 100F ($18) if you can't produce your ticket. And in any case, you'll need the ticket later to get out of the RER system and into the Métro system (see chapter 8 for how to navigate on the Métro). You can get off on the **Right Bank** at the Gare du Nord or Châtelet, or on the **Left Bank** at Luxembourg, Port-Royal, or Denfert-Rochereau.

A Trio of Buses
A bus is better than the RER if *and only if:*

➤ You're not heading into town during weekday rush hour; and

➤ Your hotel is located near one of the drop-off points. This way, once in Paris, it won't cost much to take a cab the rest of the way to your hotel.

How Will I Know Which Bus to Take?

1. If you're staying on the **Right Bank,** in the **8e, 16e,** or **17e arrondissements:** An **Air France coach** stops at Porte Maillot before ending up at the "Etoile," the name for the huge traffic round-about at the Arc de Triomphe. The bus runs every 12 minutes from 5:40am to 11pm and costs 60F ($11) one-way. In light traffic (such as a weekend morning), it takes about 40 minutes to get from the airport into the city. Pick up this coach from:

   CDG 1: Porte 34, arrivals level

   CDG 2A and 2C: Porte 5

   CDG 2B and 2D: Porte 6

   CDG 2F: Porte G, arrivals level

2. If you're staying on the Right Bank near the Bastille (11e or 12e) or on the Left Bank in Montparnasse (14e): A different Air France coach stops at Gare de Lyon before ending up at the Montparnasse Tower. The bus runs every 30 minutes from 7am and 9pm and costs 70F ($13) one-way. In light traffic, it takes about 50 minutes to get from the airport into the city. Catch this coach from:

   CDG 1: Porte 26, arrivals level

   CDG 2A and 2C: Hall C, Porte 2

   CDG 2B and 2D: Hall B, Porte 1

   CDG 2F: Porte G, arrivals level

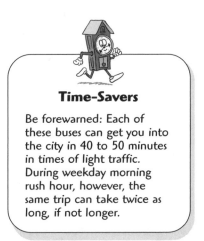

Time-Savers

Be forewarned: Each of these buses can get you into the city in 40 to 50 minutes in times of light traffic. During weekday morning rush hour, however, the same trip can take twice as long, if not longer.

3. If your hotel is on the Right Bank near the Opera (2e or 9e), take the Roissybus. This coach leaves every 15 minutes between 6am and 11pm and costs 45F ($8). The drop-off point is on rue Scribe, a block from the opera house. In light traffic, it takes about 45 minutes to get into town. Pick up this coach from:

   CDG 1: Porte 30, arrivals level

   CDG 2A and 2C: Hall A, Porte 10

   CDG 2B and 2D: Hall D, Porte 12

   CDG 2F: Porte H, arrivals level

If You're Flying into Orly

Orly airport has two terminals—**Ouest** (West) and **Sud** (South)—but all international flights land at Orly Sud. English speakers will find the terminal easy to navigate, and there's a tourist information desk where you can pick up city maps and other visitor essentials.

Dollars & Sense

Before leaving Orly airport, don't forget to get cash. Using an ATM in the arrivals hall will get you the best possible exchange rate, so give the bureau de change a pass.

Taking a Taxi

A cab from Orly into Paris costs 160 to 200F ($29 to $36) and takes anywhere from 25 minutes to an hour, depending on traffic. You'll find the taxi rank just outside Porte H. The same advice holds true here: Write down your hotel's name and address, including postal code, for your cab driver. And remember that cabs charge 6F ($1) for each piece of luggage that's put in the trunk, so keep your small bags in the back seat with you.

From the Plane to the Train

The cheapest way into town is to take the **RER C line.** You can catch a free shuttle bus from Porte H, Platform 1 to the **Rungis** station, from where RER C trains leave every 15 minutes. A one-way fare is 32F ($6) and the trip into the city takes 30 minutes, making various stops along the Seine on the Left Bank. Cheap, yes. But more hassle than the Air France bus, below.

If you're staying on the **Right Bank,** your best bet is the **Orlyval/RER B** combination. The Orlyval monorail leaves from Porte E on the ground floor and runs every 7 minutes to **Antony** station, where you board the **RER B** train into Paris. When you switch from the Orlyval to the RER, simply look on the platform for the round RER logo. The total fare into Paris is 57F ($10), and the trip takes about 45 minutes. Once in Paris, the train stops at **Denfert-Rochereau, Port-Royal, Luxembourg,** and **St-Michel** on the Left Bank, then crosses to the Right Bank and stops at **Châtelet** and **Gare du Nord.** See chapter 8 for how to get around by Métro.

When the Bus Is Best

If you're staying on the **Left Bank** near Les Invalides (**7e**), take the **Air France coach.** It leaves from Porte F, Platform 5, every 12 minutes between 5:45am and 11pm, and takes you to the Gare des Invalides. A one-way fare costs 70F ($13) and travel time is anywhere from 35 minutes in light traffic to over an hour in rush hour.

Paris Orientation: You'll Never Get Lost in This Town Again!

Paris may not be laid out on a grid like New York, but learning your way around isn't as tough as you may think. There is a method to the madness, and once you crack the code you'll be getting around like a native in no time. You'll never be lost in Paris if you:

1. Know Where the River Is

No other city in the world defines itself by its river the way Paris defines itself by the Seine (rhymes with "men," not "main"). The river determined how the city's history unfolded, how streets are numbered, how directions are given, and how neighborhoods are characterized.

Paris is divided by the Seine into the **Rive Droite** (Right Bank) on the north side and the **Rive Gauche** (Left Bank) on the south. The Right Bank is where you find Haussmann's *grands boulevards*, wide avenues such as the Champs-Elysées, stately facades, the Bourse (Paris stock exchange), and the Louvre. Tucked away in the midst of all the grandeur is the charmingly labyrinthine Marais, and to the north is Montmartre with its village atmosphere and steep cobblestone streets. To the east, the area around the Bastille is one of the trendiest pockets of Paris and a hub of youth culture.

If you're on the same side of the river as the Eiffel Tower, the Hôtel des Invalides, the Luxemburg Gardens, and the Latin Quarter, you're on the Left Bank. While the Right Bank traditionally meant business and haute couture fashion, the Left Bank was the city's intellectual and artistic heart. Even today, the Left Bank is still smaller, funkier, and more romantic than the Right. **St-Germain-des-Prés** and the **Latin Quarter** remain favorite neighborhoods for residents and tourists alike. The cafes of St-Germain, where Sartre and de Beauvoir once debated existentialism, are still a magnet for intellectuals, pseudo and otherwise. In recent years, big-name international designers have invaded the Left Bank, blurring the line of specialty between the two sides of the river.

2. Know What District You're in

Paris is divided into 20 numbered **arrondissements,** or municipal districts. Each has its own town hall, outdoor markets, police and fire stations, and central post office. The *arrondissements* are not only the key to how the city is organized but also, perhaps more important, how Parisians themselves think of their hometown. While visitors tend to speak of neighborhoods, residents talk about *arrondissements*. A Parisian who lives in the Latin Quarter and works near the Champs-Elysées would likely say that he lives in the 5th and works in the 8th. The faster you start to think of Paris this way, the faster you'll feel oriented.

Extra! Extra!

The first nine districts are central Paris, where you'll likely spend most of your time. It makes a lot of sense to choose a hotel here, too. The outer 11 *arrondissements* are mainly residential and, while they all have their respective charms, make less convenient bases for visitors.

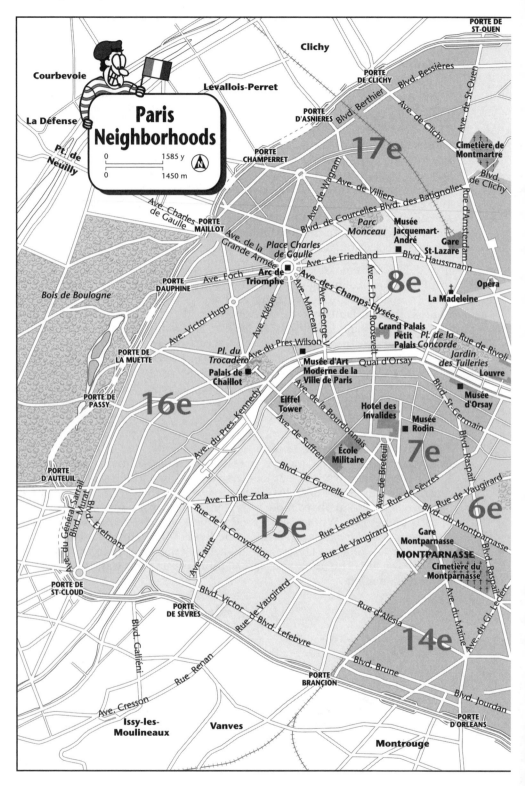

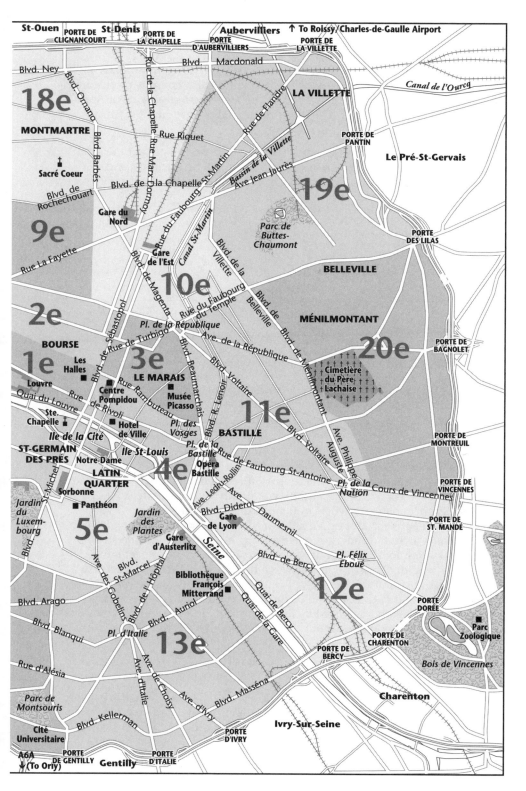

The layout of these districts follows a pattern (see "Paris Neighborhoods" map, above). The first *arrondissement* is dead-center Paris, comprising the area around the Louvre. From there, the rest of the *arrondissements* spiral outward, clockwise, in ascending order. The lower the *arrondissement* number, the more central the location.

As you're walking around in the city, you'll see blue street signs on the sides of corner buildings. Above the name of the street will be the *arrondissement* number. Keep tabs on what district you're in at all times. It will also tell you which side of the river you're on:

> **Right Bank:** 1er–4e, 8e–12e, 16e—20e

> **Left Bank:** 5e–7e, 13e–15e

Bet You Didn't Know

If you know the address of a hotel, restaurant, or shop, you can tell where it's located by its postal code. All Paris postal codes have five digits and begin with "75." The last two digits designate the *arrondissement*. For example, 75004 is the 4th district, 75019 is the 19th district, and so on.

3. Know Where Your *Plan de Paris* Is

The street maps handed out by the tourist office are maddeningly vague and destined to drive you crazy. Because they plot only the larger streets, it's hard to judge distances between where you are and where you're going. If you plan to stay in Paris for more than a day or two, invest in a detailed *plan de Paris* and carry it at all times. It'll make finding even the tiniest side street a breeze, and you'll look and feel like a real Parisian. Every news agent and bookshop (look for "Presse" signs) carries a half dozen different pocket-size *plans de Paris*—three of the best are *Paris Classique-l'Indispensable, Paris Par Arrondissement,* and *Paris Eclair*. All of them have alphabetized street-name indexes and are clearly organized by *arrondissement*. Buying one will cost you about 35F ($6), but you'll get more than your money's worth over the duration of your visit.

Paris by Neighborhood

The next step in familiarizing yourself with Paris is to get an idea of what the city's main *quartiers* are like. Each has its own personality, and you'll invariably prefer spending more time in some and less in others.

THE RIGHT BANK

Louvre (1er)

It's hard to get more central than smack in the heart of the city's monuments and museums. Well connected by Métro and buses, this area makes for an ideal hotel location in terms of convenience, though it's more commercialized and less atmospheric than the nearby Marais. **What's Nearby:** Louvre, Tuileries Gardens, Musée de l'Orangerie, Place de la Concorde, Palais Royal, Place Vendôme, haute couture shopping on rue St. Honoré.

Opéra (2e, 9e)

Also central, but more business oriented with the Bourse (Paris stock exchange) just a stone's throw away. The *grands boulevards* make the area teem with traffic, and this area delivers few glimpses of essential Parisian daily life. **What's Nearby:** Palais Garnier, Boulevard Haussmann's department stores (Galéries Lafayette, Printemps).

Marais (3e, 4e)

The prettiest and most enchanting of all Right Bank neighborhoods is Paris's answer to Greenwich Village. This enclave of 17th- and 18th-century mansions is home to hip boutiques, congenial bistros, and wonderful wine bars. One of the most eclectic residential areas, the Marais is a hub of both the gay and the Jewish communities. It's also one of the only neighborhoods in which shops stay open on Sunday. **What's Nearby:** Picasso Museum, Place des Vosges, Pompidou Center (closed through 1999).

Bet You Didn't Know

When it comes to prime real estate, the 2nd district has the edge—or so says Parker Brothers. In the French version of Monopoly, **Rue de la Paix,** a street packed with jewelers and deluxe fashion boutiques, is the most expensive property. And the second most pricey? The **Champs-Elysées,** in the 8th *arrondissement.*

The Islands (1er, 4e)

Paris has two islands, side by side in the Seine: the **Ile de la Cité** and the **Ile St-Louis.** Acre for acre, the Ile de la Cité is perhaps the richest place in Paris for sightseeing, as it contains **Notre Dame, Sainte-Chapelle,** and the **Conciergerie,** as well as administrative buildings such as the main police *préfecture* and the Palais de Justice. Just across a 30-yard footbridge, the tiny Ile St-Louis is all atmosphere, with its aristocratic town houses, shady courtyards, elfin antiques shops, and **Berthillon,** the city's most famous ice cream parlor (see chapter 11, "Light Bites and Munchies"). Marie Curie lived at 36 quai de Béthune, near Pont de la Tournelle.

Champs-Elysées (8e)
The district is known for its swanky *Triangle d'Or* ("Golden Triangle"), formed by the Champs-Elysées, avenue George V, and avenue Montaigne. All three, but especially the avenue Montaigne, feature haute-couture designer shopping at its very hautest. These days, the Champs-Elysées is a mixed bag of movie theaters, touristy cafes, luxury shops, and chain stores—but it still bristles with excitement day and night. **What's Nearby:** Arc de Triomphe, embarkment for the *Bateaux-Mouches*, Grand Palais.

Bastille-Oberkampf-Menilmontant (11e)
As the hub of Paris' youth scene, the 11th district's triumvirate of Bastille-Oberkampf-Menilmontant is one of the few areas that pulses with bars and clubs until the wee hours. Low rents in the once blue-collar area have attracted artists and young entrepreneurs, and the district is now a trove of funky shops from up-and-coming designers, trendy cafés, and ultracool nightclubs. A must for fashionable young things and clubgoers, but prone to make anyone over 35 feel positively ancient. **What's Nearby:** Opéra Bastille, Place de la Bastille's lively café and nightclub scene, Place de la République, Père Lachaise cemetery.

Montmartre (18e)
One of Paris's most famous districts, Montmartre still manages to retain its village character and artistic bonhomie. Wonderfully atmospheric, brimming with nostalgia, and definitely worth a visit, but too far from the main sights to be considered central (count on 20 minutes by Métro). **What's Nearby:** Sacré Coeur Basilica, Place du Tertre (artists displaying paintings), Moulin Rouge cabaret.

THE LEFT BANK
Latin Quarter (5e)
Fear not, romantics: The intellectual and free-thinking pocket of Paris that Hemingway so adored still overflows with university students and smoky jazz clubs, serving up a satisfying taste of bohemian Paris. **What's Nearby:** Panthéon, Musée de Cluny, Luxemburg Gardens.

St-Germain-des-Prés (6e)
Central location, sidewalk cafes, to-die-for boutiques—St-Germain has it all. This picturesque bastion of urbane chic is one of the most romantic areas of the city and home to lucky residents like Catherine Deneuve. **What's Nearby:** St-Germain-des-Prés Church, Luxemburg Gardens, fabled cafes (Café Flore, Les Deux-Magots), Musée d'Orsay, and super boutique shopping.

Eiffel Tower & Invalides (7e)
The smart 7th district is known for its stately French government buildings (including the National Assembly and the Prime Minister's residence),

bourgeois shops, and some of the most magnificent homes in Paris. It makes a great base if you're looking for peace and quiet at night, but is rather staid if you want to go out on the town. **What's Nearby:** Eiffel Tower, Les Invalides, Ecole-Militaire, Musée d'Orsay.

Montparnasse (14e)

This was the stomping ground of the Lost Generation of writers (Gertrude Stein, James Joyce, Henry Miller) and painters (Picasso, Matisse, Gauguin) in the 1920s, but their ghosts have long since fled. **What's Nearby:** Famed brasseries La Coupole, Le Dôme, Le Select.

Where to Get More Info Once You're There

The main branch of the **Paris Tourist Office** is at 127 avenue des Champs-Elysées, 8e (☎ **01/49-52-53-54;** 24-hour recording in English ☎ **01/49-52-53-56;** Métro: Charles-de-Gaulle-Etoile), and is open every day from 9am to 8pm. The multilingual staff has a ready supply of events programs, store discount vouchers, and enough leaflets advertising day trips and other outings to sink a barge on the Seine. This is a great place to pop into when you're in the Champs neighborhood.

Smaller branches are located on the Right Bank in the Gare du Nord (10e), Gare de l'Est (10e), and Gare de Lyon (12e). There are Left Bank branches at the Eiffel Tower (7e), Gare d'Austerlitz (13e), and Gare Montparnasse (14e).

Mastering *Le Système Téléphonique:* How to Make a Phone Call

All French telephone numbers have 10 digits. Numbers in Paris and Ile de France start with **01,** and the rest of the country is divided into four regional zones (from **02** to **05**). Cell phone numbers start with **06.** Numbers that begin with 08/ are "national" numbers, which means you're charged only for a local call regardless of where you're calling from in France. Some national numbers are toll-free; those phone numbers begin with **08/00.**

If you want to call France from North America, dial **011,** followed by France's country code (**33**), and then last nine digits of the 10-digit number. For example, to reach 01-22-33-44-55, you'd dial 011-33-1-22-33-44-55.

To phone abroad from France, dial **00,** then the country code (**1** for the U.S. and Canada, **44** for the UK, **353** for Ireland), followed by the number. For collect calls from France to the United States, dial 00-00-11. To speak with an international operator, dial 00-33-12 plus the country code of the number you want to dial.

Avoid dialing a transatlantic phone call direct from your hotel room; you risk being socked with a hefty surcharge—sometimes as high as 400%—for the privilege. The cheapest way to call internationally from France is with a long-distance calling card. If you go through one of the major companies—MCI, AT&T, and Sprint—you'll pay up to 50% less than what France Télécom charges.

If you don't already have a card with one of these companies, get one before leaving home. It costs nothing to open an account and there's no monthly minimum charge, so you'll be billed only for the calls you make. All three companies offer a menu of programs tailored to specific needs, so be sure to request the card best suited to making multiple calls from Europe to the US. Once in France, you can make calls by dialing the toll-free access numbers: **MCI, ☎ 08-00-99-00-19; AT&T, ☎ 08-00-99-00-11;** and Sprint, **☎ 08-00-99-00-87.**

Like in virtually every European country, the public phones in France use microchip-bearing phonecards (*télécartes*) the size of credit cards, which you can buy at airports, post offices, tobacconists, Métro ticket windows, and many newsagents. Lift the receiver and wait until a LED display prompts you to "*introduire votre carte*" (insert your card). Insert your card arrow first, then wait a moment. Once the number of units is displayed, you can begin dialing. *Télécartes* are the cheapest way to make local and long-distance calls within France.

Chapter 8

Getting Around the City of Light

Now that you've gotten safely into Paris, it's time to start exploring. How you get around will depend on how much ground you need to cover in a given time frame, but you'll probably end up using several modes of transportation before your trip is over. This chapter will give you pointers on how to master the public transportation system, how to find a cab when you need one most, and what to watch out for while strolling to your heart's content.

That's the Ticket

The city transport system (RATP) consists of the Métro (subway), buses, and the RER suburban railway. It has an English-language hotline at ☎ **08/36-68-41-14** and a Web site (in French) at **www.ratp.fr**. The Métro and buses accept the same magnetized paper ticket.

Don't buy your ticket on the bus because you'll only be able to buy individual tickets. Go instead to the ticket window in any Métro station and ask for one of the discount cards described below. While you're there, get a free pocket-size Métro map (*plan de Métro*) from the teller if you don't want to use the one in this book.

Tourist Traps

Hang on to your ticket for the entire journey (longer if it's a discount pass), since ticket inspectors often make spot controls on buses and in the Métro system. You'll recognize the RATP inspectors by their green suits and green-and-burgundy-striped ties. They tend to travel in packs like wolves. If you're stopped and can't come up with your ticket, you'll be fined 100F ($18) on the spot, no exceptions. (They tend to be humorless, so just cough up the dough and get on with your day).

So Which Ticket Should I Buy?

A single Métro or bus ticket costs **8F ($1.40)** and is valid for one journey. But buying tickets one at a time is an expensive way of getting around. If you're like most visitors, you'll be on and off the Métro so often that buying a block of tickets or a discount pass will save big money in the long run.

Always buy travel cards for zones 1 and 2—the cheapest option—which lets you go anywhere within the city limits. If you're only in town for a day or two, a ***carnet*** (kar-*nay*) of 10 tickets costs 52F ($9). If you'll be packing a lot into a single day, an even better option is the **Mobilis** pass for 30F ($6), which gives you unlimited access to the Métro, buses, and RER for 1 day.

If you'll be in town for 3 days or more, buy a weekly pass, called a ***carte hebdomadaire.*** It costs 80F ($14) and is valid only from Monday to Sunday, so the earlier in the week you buy it, the better. Unless you're going to travel outside the city a few times on the RER, the weekly pass is a better value than the **Paris Visite** pass. Along with unlimited travel in Paris and to the near suburbs, the Paris Visite includes discounts on entry to some tourist attractions. A 3-day pass costs 120F ($21) and a 5-day pass costs 170F ($30).

Extra! Extra!

You're minding your own business on the Métro, when suddenly you look up and notice...Whoa, there's no driver! Time to call Mulder and Scully? Naw, you've just experienced the **Méteor,** the city's first automated subway. Line 14 travels twice as fast as other Métro lines and is a cool look into the 21st century. In central Paris, it links Madeleine, Pyramides, Châtelet, and the Gare de Lyon.

Métro Stations: But Are They Art?

As if you needed convincing that Paris is an art-loving town, just check out these Métro stations. **Louvre-Rivoli** (line 1) is a mock museum with replicas of Egyptian mummies and medieval doorways from the Louvre's collections. **Varenne** (line 13) displays reproductions from the Musée Rodin. **Concorde** (lines 1, 8, 12) is lined with tiles that spell out the Declaration of the Rights of Man. **Arts et Métiers** (lines 3, 11) features a dramatic copper-lined tunnel with porthole exhibits of engineering inventions. **Assemblée Nationale** (line 12) hints at the proximity of the French parliament with giant political heads. **Bastille** (lines 1, 5, 8) is decorated with scenes depicting the storming of the eponymous prison.

Meet the Métro

Paris's *Métropolitain* has been around since the turn of the century and is used by some five and a half million passengers every day. So essential is the Métro to daily life here that a much-quoted ad for public transportation reads simply *"Métro, Boulot, Métro, Resto, Métro, Disco, Métro, Dodo"* ("Métro, Work, Métro, Restaurant, Métro, Disco, Métro, Sleep"). In other words, the average Joe tends to spend a lot of time on the Métro. And no wonder: It runs from 5:30am to 12:45am and is an efficient, clean, reliable, quick, cheap, and safe means of getting around. Don't be afraid to use it. Occasionally it's noisy and overcrowded (at its worst on weekdays between 6pm and 8pm), but overall it's one of the world's best underground systems.

Once you get beyond the ticket booths, you enter the Métro system through a turnstile with two ticket slots. Insert your ticket into the nearer slot, magnetic strip facing down. The ticket will pop out of the second slot. Remove it and then push through the turnstile.

Your Training Wheels: Four Steps to Mastering the Métro

The best way to feel comfortable using the Métro is to take a test run. Let's walk through a hypothetical scenario: You've just spent the morning at the Louvre and now want to go shopping in St-Germain-des-Prés. Here's a step-by-step guide to getting there. But first, get out your map. Free pocket-size maps are available at Métro ticket counters, or you can tear out the full-color map at the front of this book.

1. **Know Where You Are and Where You're Going.** Look on your map for the Métro stops at your starting point and at your destination. In this scenario, you're starting at Palais Royal–Musée du Louvre and going to St-Germain-des-Prés.

2. **Know Which Métro Line You Want.** Each station is connected to the rest of the system by one or more Métro lines. The number of each line is shown at both termini. The Louvre stop is on Line 1 and the St-Germain stop is on Line 4. This means you'll need to take Line 1 and then change trains where it intersects Line 4.

Stop the Train, I Want to Get Off!

Unlike many subway doors, those on Métro cars don't open automatically at each station. On older trains, you need to lift the door handle. On newer trains, push the release button. You'll hear a single buzz before the train takes off for the next stop.

3. **Know Which Direction You're Going.** Trace Line 1 past the intersection with Line 4 and continue until you reach the terminus, Château de Vincennes. This is the direction you want to go. At the Louvre stop, you'll see signs for Line 1. (The circle with the "M" inside is the Métro logo; the second circle has a "1" for Line 1.) The next step is to choose between the two possible directions: La Défense or Château de Vincennes. In this case, you'd follow signs to the Château de Vincennes platform.

4. **Know Where and How to Transfer.** You need to change trains where Line 1 intersects Line 4, at Châtelet. As you disembark the Line 1 train, look along the platform for the bright orange *"Correspondance"* (Connections) sign, and the white sign that shows a circle with a "4" inside, indicating Line 4.

Uh-Oh, Where's My Wallet?

Paris is a relatively safe city and violent crime is rare. Still, **purse snatchers** and **pickpockets** are as prevalent as in any large city. Men should never carry their wallets in their back pockets. Women should wear shoulder bags crossed over the chest and neck. Be especially attentive in museum lines, around crowded tourist attractions, and on the Métro and crowded buses. **Métro line 1,** which links many tourist sights, is a particular favorite of pickpockets.

Now trace Line 4 on your map from Châtelet past St-Germain-des-Prés to the terminus, Porte d'Orléans. This is the direction you want, so follow signs to the Porte d'Orléans platform. When you get off Line 4 at St-Germain-des-Prés, follow the blue "Sortie" (Exit) signs out of the station.

For more on how to use the Métro, visit **@Paris** on the Web at **www. smartweb.fr/guide/transports.htm**.

Getting Around by Bus

The beauty of buses is that they let you see a lot more Paris. The downside is that they are much slower than the Métro because they can get bogged down in traffic. Buses run Monday to Saturday from 6:30am to 8:30pm, but some have a reduced service on Sundays.

Up until a few years ago, the bus was more expensive than the Métro. Each bus route was divided into zones and you needed several tickets to get across town. But a few years ago the transit system did away with the zones, and you now only need one ticket to travel anywhere in the city.

The Best Bus Routes for Sightseeing

Some bus routes are particularly good for travelers because they take a scenic route and link many attractions. Try these three routes for easy jump-on, jump-off sightseeing itineraries (for information on the specific attractions listed below, see chapters 13 and 14):

Bus 69: Eiffel Tower, Invalides, Louvre, Hôtel de Ville, Place des Vosges (St. Paul), Bastille, Père Lachaise Cemetery

Bus 80: Boulevard Haussmann's department stores (St. Augustin), Champs-Elysées, Avenue Montaigne haute-couture shopping, Bateaux Mouches (Alma-Marceau), Eiffel Tower

Bus 96: St-Germain-des-Prés, Musée de Cluny, Hôtel de Ville, Place des Vosges (St. Paul)

Using the buses is more complicated than using the Métro, but if you're willing to invest some effort you'll get a better feel for Paris by bus. Determining which bus goes where can be tricky. By using the bus maps distributed by the tourist office and the transit system, you can see the routes but not where the specific stops are. The main stops are written on the sides of the buses (you have to look quickly) with the terminus shown on the front above the driver. There are also large bus maps on the back of every bus shelter. Inside the shelters are smaller maps showing the specific route of each bus that stops there. But the very best bus guides are the little pocket-size *plans de Paris* mentioned in chapter 7 (and again in Appendix A). They have bus maps and detailed listings of each stop on every route.

Board at the front of the bus, and insert your ticket in the slot of the little gray box. The machine will punch it and spit it back out. (Punch only single-trip tickets. If you have a discount pass, just flash it by the driver.) If you want to get off at the next stop, push one of the red buttons on the safety poles and the *"arrêt demandé"* (stop requested) sign will light up. Once the bus comes to a complete stop, push the exit button and the doors will open.

Yo! Monsieur Cab Driver!

There are three ways to get a cab in Paris: Hail it, pick it up at a taxi rank, or call for it to come and collect you. Metered-cab rates vary with the area and time of day. From 7am to 7pm, rates begin with a 13F get-in fee ($2.30) and then go up 3.5F (63¢) per kilometer after that. After 7pm and on Sundays, the rate jumps to 5.8F ($1) per kilometer. Most journeys within central Paris cost 40 to 70F ($7 to $12). Cabs charge 6F ($1) for each piece of luggage that you put in the trunk, so keep your bags in the back seat with you whenever possible.

The surest way to catch a cab is to find a taxi rank and join the line. Ranks are found on major avenue and boulevards; ask your hotel manager for directions to the nearest one. You can hail a cab on the street as long as you're not within 50 meters (165 feet) of a taxi rank. Parisian cabs tend to be white sedans. If the light on the taxi's roof is lit, the cab is occupied. The standard tip for cabbies is 10 percent of the fare.

Phoning for a cab is more expensive because the meter starts running as soon as you make the call. That means you pay for the time it takes the cab to arrive, perhaps 10 minutes or more. Still, these cab services can be handy for late-night and early-morning trips. Several call-up taxi services are listed in Appendix A.

Here's the Scoop on Parisian Dog Poop

A warning: Parisians love dogs, but they don't love cleaning up after them. There's no "pooper-scooper" law, and even if there were, most Parisians feel that cleaning up what their dogs do outdoors is beneath them. The city's solution is to hire grown men dressed in bright green coveralls to drive little green motorized cars with giant vacuum hoses to suck up the God-knows-how-many tons of the stuff off the sidewalks. This helps, but you still need to watch your step.

Paris on Foot

Paris is one of the prettiest cities in the world for strolling, and getting around on foot is probably the best way to really appreciate the city's character. The best walking neighborhoods are St-Germain-des-Prés on the Left Bank and the Marais on the Right Bank, both of which are chock-a-block with romantic little courtyards, wonderful boutiques, and convivial cafes and watering holes.

A word to the wise: Take special care when crossing streets, even when you have the right of way. The number-one rule of the road in France (in practice if not in law) is that whoever is coming from the right side has the right of way. This means that drivers often make right turns without looking, even when faced with pedestrians at crosswalks. And don't *ever* attempt to cross a traffic circle if you're not on a crosswalk. The larger roundabouts, such as the one at the Arc de Triomphe, have pedestrian tunnels.

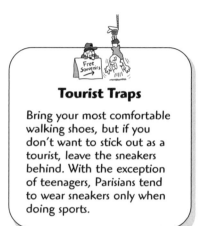

Tourist Traps

Bring your most comfortable walking shoes, but if you don't want to stick out as a tourist, leave the sneakers behind. With the exception of teenagers, Parisians tend to wear sneakers only when doing sports.

Part 4

Where & What to Eat in Paris

The French national passion for excellent cuisine makes dining one of the great pleasures of any trip. Yet, while there's no excuse for not eating well in Paris, it still requires a vigilant eye. Long gone are the days when you could walk into just about any neighborhood brasserie and have a truly incredible meal. Mediocrity has become as prevalent in Paris as it is everywhere else, and there's no shortage of pricey eateries churning out food that's pas grand-chose (no big deal)—although many of these cater almost exclusively to tourists.

This section aims to teach you how to eat like a local—that is, how to be discriminating and get the most for your money. Chapter 9 will give you the lay of the gastronomic landscape and tips on how to get the most out of your dining experiences. Chapter 10 will point you toward some of the best restaurants in town when you want a leisurely meal of two or three courses.

In France, lunch and dinner both tend to be full-course meals with meat, vegetables, bread, cheese, dessert, wine, and coffee. If you're looking for the sort of light lunch spots that North Americans are used to, you'll find recommendations in chapter 11, along with suggestions for snacks and picnic provisions. Bon Appetit!

Chapter 9

The Lowdown on the Paris Dining Scene

In This Chapter

➤ The latest restaurant trends

➤ Where to eat (and where not to)

➤ Anatomy of a French meal

➤ Dining no-nos

➤ Understanding the menu lingo

Of course we've all eaten out in restaurants and know how to order a meal. But dining out in a French restaurant is slightly different from in America and other English-speaking countries. The language, the menu, and the local dining etiquette all conspire to make visitors feel intimidated. This chapter is designed to make you feel more comfortable about eating in Paris restaurants, and thus enjoy your dining experience. It'll tell you the difference between a bistro, a brasserie, and a cafe; offer hints about how not to pay more than you should; and, critically, help you make sense of the menu.

Parisians take dining out very seriously. They are forever in search of the perfect meal and make a pastime of sharing *les bonnes adresses* (the right addresses) with their friends. Knowing *les bonnes adresses* is very important and a sure sign of being *branché*, or cool (it literally means "plugged-in").

What's Hot in Paris Right Now

In the early 1990s, the Paris dining scene was all about the **baby bistro.** To attract diners during the recession, the city's top celebrity chefs began opening restaurants that offered dishes that were not only simpler than what was served at their deluxe establishments, but infinitely more affordable. So after creating the menu and overseeing the decor of his new place, the chef turned the stove over to a gifted protégé and *voilà*—a baby bistro was born. Within a few years, half a dozen of Paris's top chefs had opened fleets of baby bistros, with varying degrees of success. Some of the best are still going strong.

In the wake of the baby bistros have come the **young upstarts.** This time around, it isn't celebrity chefs but their gifted young apprentices who are spawning new restaurants. Dozens of impeccably trained chefs in their 20s and 30s have cut the umbilical cord with their famous chef-bosses and set up their very own ventures. Some of the best in the pack—Alain Antibard at L'Affriolé, Gilles Ajuelos at La Bastide Odéon, Flora Mikula at Les Olivades, and Yves Camdeborde at La Régalade—are recommended in chapter 10. The good news is that this young breed of chef knows how to cook and has the confidence to deliver a satisfying meal without performing the expense-inducing culinary acrobatics. The hallmark is well-prepared, home-style food in an intimate setting and at affordable prices—a trend we all can welcome.

What Should I Wear?

Only the most expensive restaurants enforce dress codes, and in theory you can dress up or down as you like. Realize, however, that Parisians still value style, even when dressing informally. Relaxed dressing doesn't mean sloppy jeans and sneakers. The look to aim for is smart casual. You won't go wrong if you dress in neutral colors—think black, beige, cream, navy, and chocolate. Go a notch dressier than what you'd wear at home. Even at neighborhood bistros, most men wear sports jackets and women wear skirts or smart pants suits.

Chefs Who Make Michelin Starry-Eyed

If you're a hard-core foodie, you have probably come to Paris armed with the *Michelin Red Guide to France*. This little book is the Bible of French gastronomy and can literally make or break a chef's career. Naturally, an accolade as important as a Michelin star tends to be reflected in the bill. Dining at Michelin-starred restaurants is extremely expensive, with dinners at three-star places easily costing $200 per head.

Why so much? Dining on *haute cuisine* is the gastronomic equivalent of dressing in *haute couture*. You're paying for the chef's reputation and artistry, his superbly trained staff, the sumptuous surroundings, the premium ingredients, and the incredibly work-intensive nature of the cooking. Since most top chefs create their daily menus around what's available at the market that very morning, the produce is fresh as can be; every leaf of lettuce, every filet of salmon, every ounce of beef has been hand chosen. Parisians confine their trips to deluxe establishments to special occasions, and you should do the same.

This guide recommends only a handful of Michelin-starred restaurants because, quite frankly, they are beyond the budget of the average traveler. Still, if you're in the mood to splurge, dining in one of these foodie temples is an unforgettable experience.

Bet You Didn't Know

The sentimental favorite among Michelin-starred chefs is **Pierre Gagnaire,** a.k.a. the Comeback Kid. After his three-star restaurant in the economically struggling town of St-Etienne was forced into receivership in 1996, he relocated to Paris, opened a brand new restaurant, and promptly won back his trio of stars. He is especially known for his knack of pulling off daring combinations of flavors and textures.

If three stars is too rich for your wallet, consider trying a one- or two-star establishment. A few years ago, chef Christian Constant surprised *le tout Paris* by leaving the prestigious Les Ambassadeurs in the Hôtel Crillon to open an infinitely more down-to-earth place that was all his own. The result is the one-star **Violon d'Ingres.** What's to love about this intimate restaurant, apart from the sublime cuisine? How about the way Monsieur Constant comes out of the kitchen to greet you at the end of a meal, inviting you to return as if this were his private home?

Surveying the Landscape: Bistros, Brasseries, and Cafes

Eateries go by various names in France, and in theory at least, these labels give you some clue to how much a meal will cost. From most expensive to least expensive, the lineup generally goes like this: restaurant, bistro, brasserie, cafe. The key word is *generally*. Never rely on the name of an establishment as a price indicator; some of the city's most expensive eateries call themselves Cafe Such-and-Such. Furthermore, the awnings above quintessential cafes often read something like "Restaurant Cafe Brasserie St Jean" or some other combination of labels. The only way to be sure of price is to read the menu, which by law must be posted outside the eatery.

➤ **Restaurants** tend to enforce strict meal times. As of noon, most have their tables set for lunch, though the rush of diners won't arrive until 12:30 to 1pm. Generally, you must be seated for lunch no later than

2pm, or 2:30pm at the very latest, if you want a full meal. Between 3pm and 7pm, it's pretty much impossible to have a sit-down meal in a Paris restaurant or bistro. During this swing shift, your best bet is to head to a cafe, tea room, or wine bar. Dining at 7pm would be considered a very early dinner in Paris; most Parisians wouldn't think about sitting down before 8pm. But starting too late—10pm is getting dangerous—can also leave you without too many options.

In the city's top restaurants, the *menu dégustation* (sampler menu) is almost always worth trying, since it's made up of small portions of the chef's signature dishes. It offers tremendous bang for your buck because you have the opportunity to try more variety.

➤ **Bistros** tend to keep the same strict meal times as restaurants. They are small, often family-run establishments serving a limited but excellent menu of home-style favorites. Think crush of elbows and the sounds of corks popping, glasses clinking and people having a good time. Bistros are where Parisians come to dine the most often, and with good reason. Most of the eateries recommended in chapter 10 are bistros that offer good cooking at reasonable prices.

➤ **Brasseries** literally means "breweries." Some are open 24 hours a day, but many keep similar hours to restaurants and bistros. The classic brasserie is a large, bustling affair with an immense selection of dishes on the menu. As you might suspect, beer is also in ready supply. Quintessential brasserie fare includes Alsatian specialties like *choucroute garnie* (sauerkraut with pork sausages), shellfish platters, and a large selection of grilled meat dishes.

Bet You Didn't Know

If you like **beer**, it's worth paying a bit more for the imported **German, Dutch,** or **Danish** brands, which are much better than the French brews. If you insist on a French brand, order a draught beer, or *bière à pression* (bee-yare ah preh-see-yohn), which is of better quality.

➤ **Cafes** typically open from about 8am to 1am. They serve drinks and food all day from a short menu that often includes salads, sandwiches, mussels, and French fries. At meal times, there are also rib-sticking dishes such as steak and fries or *blanquette* of veal. Cafes are best for light fare in between and after standard meal times.

Dollars & Sense

Some **cafes** offer lunch menus for under 80F, and these can be super deals. But the quality of food is extremely variable, particularly in large cafes on major boulevards. It's difficult to tell from the exterior whether a cafe serves good food. Too often, you end up paying a lot for a lousy sandwich and fries. Consider that for just a few francs more, you could enjoy a full three-course meal at one of the less expensive bistros recommended in chapter 10.

Parisians use cafes the way Brits use pubs—as extensions of their living rooms. They are places where you meet friends before heading to the cinema or a party, read your newspaper, write in your journal, or—the favorite Parisian pastime—just hang out and people watch. Regardless of whether you order a cup of coffee or the most expensive cognac in the house, nobody will pressure or hurry you to leave your perch. If you wish to stay until the place closes, that's your affair.

Coffee, of course, is the chief drink. It comes black in a small cup, unless you specifically order a *café crème* or *café au lait* (coffee with steamed milk). Tea (*thé*, pronounced tay) is also fairly popular, but is generally not of a high quality. On the other hand, French hot chocolate (*chocolat chaud*, pronounced shock-o-*lah* shoh), is absolutely superb and made from real ground chocolate, not a chemical compound.

➤ **Tea rooms,** or *salons de thé,* usually open mid-morning and close by early evening. Some serve light lunches, but most are at their best in the afternoon for desserts with coffee or tea.

➤ **Wine bars** are informal watering holes where, from mid-morning into mid- to late-evening, you can order wine by the glass and munch on snacks such as tartines (open-face sandwiches), olives, and cheese. Some offer simple lunch menus, but, like cafes and tearooms, they are generally better for light bites. Some of the city's best cafes, tearooms, and wine bars are recommended in chapter 11.

Anatomy of a French Meal

In France, the value of a meal is determined not by how *much*, but by how *well* you eat. And eating well means enjoying quality food at a leisurely pace. The typical dinner in a French restaurant or bistro requires at least 2 hours, comprising an opening dish, a main dish, a cheese course and/or a dessert, followed by coffee. And there's wine, of course. Because the meal has so many elements, portions are smaller than their American counterparts. At the end of the meal, you should feel pleasantly full, not belt-looseningly stuffed.

Classic French Dishes to Try

Bouillabaisse: A favorite from Provence, this tomato-based seafood stew is made with mussels, shellfish, and the catch of the day. A great *bouillabaisse* is hard to find, but you won't be disappointed at Le Petit Niçois (see chapter 10).

Cassoulet: A quintessential dish from Southwestern France, this stalwart is made by alternating layers of white beans with pork in a casserole. It's topped with bread crumbs, then baked until brown and crusty.

Coq au Vin: Chicken stewed in red wine and mushrooms.

Hachis Parmentier: The Gallic equivalent of shepherd's pie, this dish consists of ground beef and mashed potatoes, topped with a *Béchamel* sauce and served in a casserole.

Pot-au-feu: Beef and vegetable stew, like your French *grand-mère* used to make. If you had one, that is.

Tarte Tatin: An upside-down caramelized apple pie.

Getting the Order Right

After you've been seated, your waiter may ask if you want an aperitif. The traditional before-dinner drink is a *kir* (white wine with crème de cassis), but variations include the *kir royale*, in which champagne is substituted for the wine. It's become fashionable in recent years to order a glass of champagne as an aperitif. (*Note:* Unless it is included in the fixed-price menu, you'll be charged extra, so feel free to decline.)

Next, tell your waiter whether you'll take *le menu* (a.k.a. *la formule*, the fixed-price menu) or choose *à la carte* (from the main menu). You'll then place your order for your appetizer, main dish, and wine. The waiter will return to take your dessert and coffee order after you've finished the main course.

When the *Menu* Isn't the Menu

The word *menu* is a good example what the French call a *faux ami* (literally, a false friend)—a term for tricky words that are spelled similarly in two languages but mean two different things. In French, *le menu* (also called *la formule*) refers specifically to the fixed-price deal. If you want to see the restaurant's regular menu, ask for *la carte*. Likewise, in French an *entrée* listed on a French *carte* is an appetizer, *not* the main course (think of it as the "entry" into your meal).

Dollars & Sense

Meals at a set price are up to 30% cheaper than ordering the same dishes *à la carte*. What's the trade-off? Your options are more limited than if you order from the main menu. Review the prix-fixe option carefully to determine what you're getting for that price. Does it come with wine, and if so, how much—a glass or a half bottle? Is dessert or coffee included?

Wine lists usually contain only French vintages, with red wine far more popular than white. Even if you think you don't like red wine, you might be surprised to find you like French reds. The top restaurants sell wine by the bottle, but bistros are usually more flexible. Check the menu for mention of a house wine (*vin de maison*, pronounced "van de may-zohn"). It's usually of decent quality and reasonably priced. You can usually order *un quart* (25 centiliters, pronounced "uhn kar"), which fills two glasses, for the same price as it would cost to buy a single glass. Ordering *un demi* (a half liter, pronounced "uhn duh-mee") would allow two people to have two glasses of wine each.

You will also be asked if you'd like water (*de l'eau*) with your meal. Mineral water is very popular in France and is available *plate* (still) and *gazeuse* (fizzy). You'll be charged extra if you order mineral water, but you can have tap water for free. Many Parisians drink the city's excellent-quality tap water with their meals. Signal that you want tap water by requesting a carafe of water, or *une carafe d'eau* (oon kah-raff doe). Note that the waiter will almost always bring mineral water unless otherwise requested. Whichever you choose, don't expect ice cubes. The French believe that the meal's flavors are undermined when something is too hot or too cold. Very little ice is consumed in France, be it in restaurants or in private homes. And soft drinks are generally considered between-meal refreshments, and never an accompaniment to the meal.

Lastly, Europeans rarely eat butter (*du beurre*) with their bread, so if you want it, you'll have to ask for it. But first, taste the bread without butter. You might find that it's so good, you don't need the butter.

Timing Is Everything

At first, you may think the service is dreadfully slow. Your main dish doesn't materialize immediately after your appetizer has been cleared. And after you've finished the main dish, the waiter doesn't buzz over to take your dessert order. The quick meal has never been understood in France. The waiter assumes that you are there to enjoy the company of your companions, and service is timed to allow breathers between courses.

Time-Savers

When French pollsters have asked what motivates restaurateurs, the over-whelming response has been bringing pleasure to customers. For most of them, making money is secondary. Waiters don't work for tips, and the chef isn't interested in cranking out your meal so he can turn your table over to some-body else. Hurrying customers through their meals is just not part of the dining mentality. So relax and enjoy. You may discover that good service has little to do with speed, and that you've been rushing through meals all your life.

Hey, Where's My Coffee?

After ordering dessert and coffee, you may be surprised when the waiter returns with only the dessert. In France, coffee is served after dessert. The French never drink coffee during the meal, and, unless you specifically order it with milk (*café au lait* or *café crème*), the coffee will be served black and in a small demitasse cup. If you want a big cup of coffee with milk, ask for *un grand café crème*.

To Tip or Not to Tip?

Only after you've finished your coffee and are ready to leave is it time to request the bill, or *la note*. It won't arrive automatically because the house assumes you'll take a few moments to relax before departing. Since a 15% service charge is almost always included, it's not necessary to leave a hefty tip. It's considered good form, however, to leave a small token sum—10F for a moderately priced meal—for the waiter to show that you enjoyed your meal.

Dining Dos and Don'ts

➤ Do avoid large cafes on the major boulevards, and be wary of cafes in well-touristed areas. You'll often pay a high price for thoughtlessly pre-pared, mediocre food and insincere service.

➤ Do **read the menu** posted outside the establishment before entering. This gives you a good idea of how much your meal will cost.

➤ Do **book in advance.** It's almost always a good idea to make a same-day reservation for even a modest neighborhood bistro. Some top restaurants require several weeks' notice. The vast majority of French restaurants are very small establishments with limited seating, and tables are scrupulously saved for folks who book.

➤ Do ask to be seated in the ***non-fumeur*** (**nonsmoking**) section if you prefer it.

➤ Do **call if you'll be more than 20 minutes late.** Reservations are carefully honored in France, and showing up late is considered bad form. Most bistros are small, independently run establishments that depend on customers honoring their reservations.

➤ **Don't ask if you can make substitutions** and recompose the *menu* or *formule*. It marks you as an uneducated tourist and is taboo.

➤ Do **know what you're ordering.** (See "A Glossary of French Food Terms," below). It's not cool to order something, act disgusted when you figure out what it is, and try to send it back to the kitchen. Sending something back signifies that there's something wrong with the dish, which would not necessarily be the case.

➤ Do **go overboard with politeness.** As in all human interactions in France, peppering your speech with plenty of Ps and Qs is a sign of being well bred. Using these five phrases will greatly improve the way you're treated in France: "*Bonjour/Bonsoir*" (bohn-*jhoor*/ bohn-*swahr*; hello/good evening); "*Excusez-moi*" (ek-*scoo*-zay mwah; excuse me); "*S'il vous plaît*" (see voo *play*; please); "*Merci*" (mair-*see*; thank you); and "*Au revoir*" (o ruh-*vwahr*; good-bye).

➤ **Don't speak too loudly.** If Americans have a hang-up with personal space, the French have one with noise. It's considered rude to interfere with the private conversations of others. So from childhood, they learn never to speak so loudly that neighboring diners can overhear.

➤ **Don't call "Garçon"** to get your waiter's attention; a low-key "S'il vous plaît, Monsieur" is infinitely more polite and thus more effective. All waitresses, on the other hand, are addressed as "Mademoiselle," regardless of age or marital status.

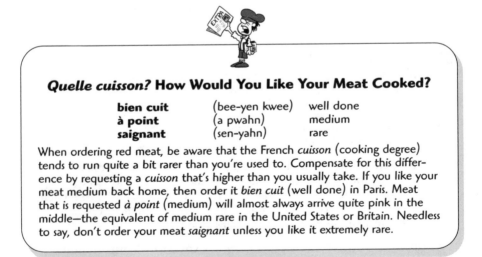

Quelle cuisson? How Would You Like Your Meat Cooked?

bien cuit	(bee-yen kwee)	well done
à point	(a pwahn)	medium
saignant	(sen-yahn)	rare

When ordering red meat, be aware that the French *cuisson* (cooking degree) tends to run quite a bit rarer than you're used to. Compensate for this difference by requesting a *cuisson* that's higher than you usually take. If you like your meat medium back home, then order it *bien cuit* (well done) in Paris. Meat that is requested *à point* (medium) will almost always arrive quite pink in the middle—the equivalent of medium rare in the United States or Britain. Needless to say, don't order your meat *saignant* unless you like it extremely rare.

A Glossary of French Food Terms

Here are some basic terms you'll run across when dining out:

General Terms

Compris Included

Déjeuner Lunch

Dîner Dinner

Petit Déjeuner Breakfast

Supplément Extra charge

Les Entrées (Appetizers)

Crudités Assorted raw vegetables

Foie Gras Goose liver

Saumon fumé Smoked salmon

Potage/Soupe (Soup)

Soupe à l'oignon Onion soup

Soupe au pistou Vegetable soup with pesto

Velouté de... Cream of...

Vichyssoise Cold leek and potato cream soup

Salade (Salad)

...Composée/Mixte Mixed Salad

...à Chèvre Croutons... with goat cheese and croutons

...Niçoise... with potato, tuna, and anchovies

Les Plats (Main Courses)

Viande (Meat)

Agneau Lamb

Bifteck/Steack Steak

Boeuf Beef

Charcuterie Cold cuts

Châteaubriand Double filet steak

Contrefilet Porterhouse steak

Côte de boeuf T-bone steak

Daube Braised meat

Entrecôte Rib-eye steak

Epaule Shoulder

Escalope Cutlet

Faux-filet Sirloin steak

Filet mignon Beef tenderloin

Gigot Leg (of lamb, usually)

Jambon Ham

Médaillon Tenderloin steak

Merguez Spicy sausage

Porc Pork

Saucisses Sausage

Tournedos Tenderloins of T-bone steak

Veau Veal

Volaille (Game)

Blanc de volaille Chicken breast

Caille Quail

Canard Duck

Cerf/Chevreuil Venison

Dinde Turkey

Magret de canard Duck breast

Oie Goose

Pintade Guinea fowl

Poulet Chicken

117

Fruits de Mer/Poissons (Seafood/Fish)

Bar Bass

Coquilles Scallops

Crevettes Shrimp

Daurade Sea bream

Homard Lobster

Huîtres Oysters

Langoustine Prawn

Morue/Cabillaud Cod

Moules Mussels

Rascasse Scorpionfish

Raie Skate

Rouget Red mullet

Saumon Salmon

Thon Tuna

Truite Trout

Les Légumes (Vegetables)

Artichaut Artichoke

Asperge Asparagus

Aubergine Eggplant

Champignons/Cèpes Mushrooms
Truffes/Girolles

Choucroute Sauerkraut

Choufleur Cauliflower

Choux Cabbage

Choux de Bruxelles Brussels sprouts

Courgette Zucchini

Epinard Spinach

Frites/Pommes frites French fries

Haricots Beans

Haricots verts String beans

Oignons Onions

Petits pois Peas

Poireaux Leeks

Poivron rouge Red pepper

Poivron vert Green pepper

Pomme de terre Potato

Riz Rice

Tomate Tomato

Les Fruits (Fruits)

Abricot Apricot

Ananas Pineapple

Banane Banana

Cerise Cherry

Citron Lemon

Citron vert Lime

Pomme Apple

Prune Plum

Pruneau Prune

Fraise Strawberry

Framboise Raspberry

Myrtille Blueberry

Pamplemousse Grapefruit

Pêche Peach

Poire Pear

Raisin Grape

Raisin sec Raisin

Les Desserts (Desserts)

Clafoutis Thick batter filled with
fruit

Charlotte Molded cream ringed with
biscuit

Crème brûlée Creamy custard with
caramel topping

Fromage blanc Smooth cream cheese

Gâteau Cake

Glace Ice cream

Marquise Light, mousselikecake

Mousse au chocolat Chocolate mousse

Tarte aux... ...Pie

Tarte Tatin Caramelized upside-down apple pie

Vacherin Cake of layered meringue, fruit, and ice cream

How Dishes Are Prepared:

à l'ail with garlic

au four baked

Béarnaise Hollandaise with tarragon, vinegar, shallots

Béchamel white sauce made with onions and nutmeg

Beurre blanc white sauce made with butter, white wine, and shallots

Bordelaise brown meat stock made with red wine, mushrooms, shallots, and beef marrow

bouilli boiled

Bourguignon brown meat stock flavored with red wine, mushrooms, and onions

confit meat (usually duckor goose) cooked in its own fat

consommé clear broth

coulis any nonflour sauce, purée, or juice

en croûte in a pastry case

cru raw

diable brown sauce flavored with cayenne pepper, white wine, and shallots

estouffade meat that has been marinated, fried, and braised

farci stuffed

feuilleté in puff pastry

forestière with mushrooms

fumé smoked

gratiné topped with browned bread crumbs or cheese

grillé grilled

Hollandaise white sauce of butter, egg yolks, and lemon juice

Lyonnais with onions

marinière steamed in garlicky wine stock

meunière fish rolled in flour and sautéed

en papillote cooked in parchment and openedat the table (usually fish)

parmentier with potato

Provençal tomato-based sauce, with garlic, olives, and onions

rôti roasted

terrine paté cooked in an earthenware dish

I Just Ate *WHAT??* A Vocabulary for Adventurous Eaters

Andouillette	Tripe sausage	*Gésiers*	Gizzards
Boudin	Blood sausage	*Langue*	Tongue
Carpaccio	Thinly sliced, cured (but raw) beef	*Lapin*	Rabbit
		Lièvre	Hare
		Pieds de cochon	Pig's feet
Cervelles	Brains	*Ris de veau*	Veal sweetbreads
Cheval	Horse meat	*Rognons*	Kidneys
Cuisses de grenouilles	Frogs' legs	*Steack Tartare*	Raw minced steak
Escargots	Snails	*Tête de veau*	Calf's head
Foie	Liver		

Chapter 10

Restaurants from A to Z

In This Chapter

➤ Restaurant indexes by location, price, and cuisine

➤ Reviews of the best eating spots in town

➤ Top spots for families, romantics, and night owls

Finally the moment you've been waiting for: Time to loosen your belts and pick up your forks. Plucked from the vast sea of restaurants in Paris, here are 45 tried-and-tested winners. Each delivers the sort of memorable dining experience most of us come to Paris hoping to find.

This chapter is dedicated to restaurants best appreciated at a leisurely meal that lingers over several courses. When you're in the mood for just a single course or a light bite, turn to the chapter 11 for cafes, tearooms, burger joints, sandwich bars, and bakeries.

With so many great dining spots in town, you might be wondering how the list was whittled down to just 45. Each of the establishments recommended below possesses all the ingredients of a great dining spot: fantastic cooking, reasonable prices, and great atmosphere. In other words, the same criteria that Parisians use when deciding where to eat. The list concentrates on moderately priced bistros with big local followings, from modest neighborhood joints to downright fashionable hot spots. Also included are some bargain eateries and, for special occasions, several of the city's most splurge-worthy restaurants where you can sample *haute cuisine*.

With very few exceptions, these restaurants are conveniently located—not only in central Paris, but in neighborhoods where you'll most likely be spending most of your time. This is not to imply that there aren't great restaurants in the outlying districts, only that you'll find it more convenient to dine near your hotel and major sights.

This chapter kicks off with indexes to help you choose a restaurant according to location, budget, and type of cuisine. Then come the individual reviews. Restaurants are listed alphabetically for easy reference, followed by price range, neighborhood, and type of cuisine. Throughout the chapter you'll also find specialized listings for night owls, families, and romantic couples. Price ranges reflect the cost of a three-course meal for one person ordered *à la carte* featuring an appetizer, main dish, dessert, and coffee:

$	Under 125F ($22)
$$	125–200F ($22–$36)
$$$	200–300F ($36–$53)
$$$$	300–500F ($53–$89)
$$$$$	Over 500F ($89)

Dollars & Sense

Use the dollar icons to get a ballpark idea of how much a meal will cost at dinnertime—but don't make that your only criteria for choosing a restaurant. Most establishments offer fixed-price menus (also called *formules*) that are significantly cheaper than their à la carte options. Going the prix-fixe route very often may bring the cost down one whole price category. I've noted at the end of each review when a restaurant offers set menus. And if you're dying to try out a place that's above your budget, keep in mind that meals tend to be far less expensive at lunchtime.

Quick Picks: Paris Restaurants at a Glance
Restaurant Index by Location

Right Bank

Louvre (1er)

Café de Vendôme $$$

Gros Minet $$

Macéo $$$

L'Ostréa $$

Restaurant du Palais-Royal $$$

Willi's Wine Bar $$

Yvan Sur Seine $$

Opéra (2e, 9e)

Chartier $

Chez Georges $$$

Le Marais (3e, 4e)

L'Alisier $$$

L'Ambroisie $$$$$

Bofinger $$$

Le Coude Fou $$

Le Réconfort $$

Trumilou $

The Islands (1er, 4e)

Le Vieux Bistro $$$

Champs-Elysées (8e)

Androuët $$$

L'Appart' $$$

Michel Rostang $$$$$

Pierre Gagnaire $$$$$

Tante Louise $$$

Bastille (11e)

Astier $$

Au C'Amelot $$

L'Ebauchoir $$

Au Trou Gascon $$$$

Montmartre (18e)

Le Maquis $$

Le Moulin à Vins $

Left Bank

Latin Quarter (5e)

Chez Alexandre $

Les Fêtes Galantes $$

St-Germain-des-Prés (6e)

Alcazar $$$$

La Bastide Odéon $$$

Le Bouillon Racine $$

Les Brezolles $$$

La Closerie des Lilas $$$

L'Epi Dupin $$$

L'O à la Bouche $$

Polidor $

Eiffel Tower & Invalides (7e)

L'Affriolé $$$

Le Bamboche $$$

Au Bon Accueil $$

La Fontaine de Mars $$$

Les Olivades $$$

Le Petit Niçois $$

Le Violon d'Ingres $$$$

Montparnasse (14e)

Le Régalade $$

Restaurant Index by Price Category

$

Chartier (Opéra)

Chez Alexandre (Latin Quarter)

Le Moulin à Vins (Montmartre)

Polidor (St-Germain-des-Prés)

Trumilou (Le Marais)

$$

Astier (Bastille)

Au Bon Accueil (Eiffel Tower & Invalides)

Le Bouillon Racine (St-Germain-des-Prés)

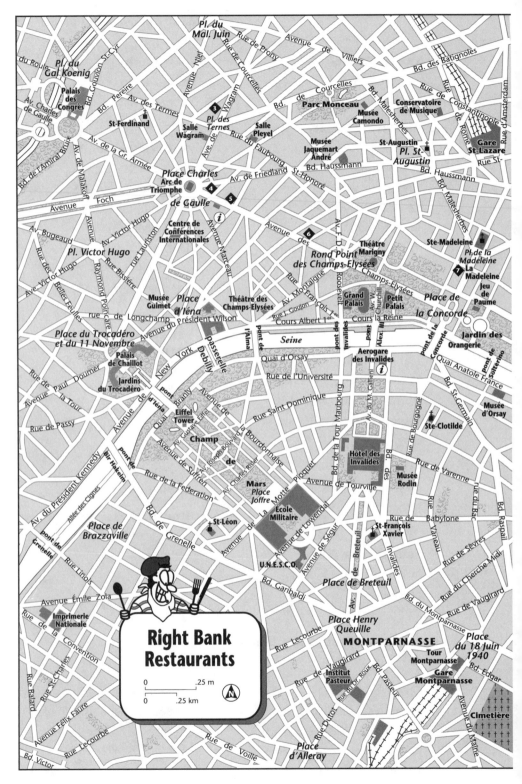

Right Bank
Restaurants

0   .25 m
0   .25 km

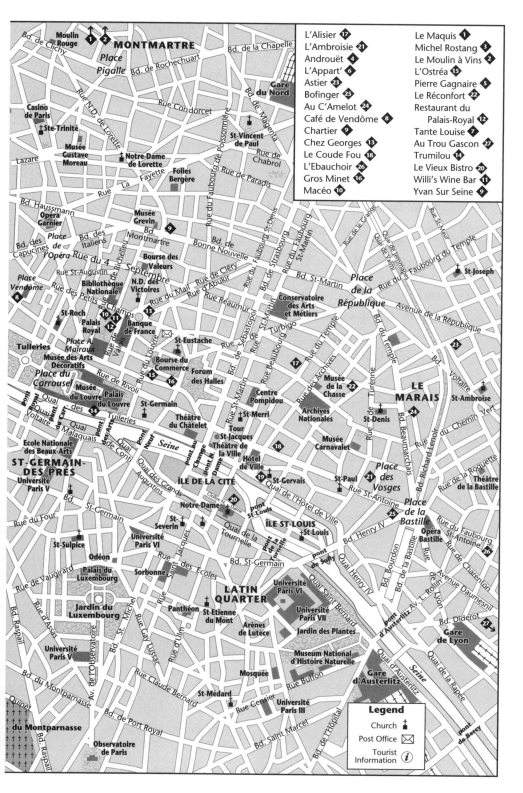

L'Alisier ⑰
L'Ambroisie ㉑
Androuët ④
L'Appart' ⑥
Astier ㉓
Bofinger ㉕
Au C'Amelot ㉔
Café de Vendôme ⑧
Chartier ⑨
Chez Georges ⑬
Le Coude Fou ⑱
L'Ebauchoir ㉖
Gros Minet ⑯
Macéo ⑩

Le Maquis ❶
Michel Rostang ❸
Le Moulin à Vins ❷
L'Ostréa ⑮
Pierre Gagnaire ❺
Le Réconfort ㉒
Restaurant du
    Palais-Royal ⑫
Tante Louise ❼
Au Trou Gascon ㉗
Trumilou ⑭
Le Vieux Bistro ⑳
Willi's Wine Bar ⑪
Yvan Sur Seine ⑨

Legend

Church †
Post Office ✉
Tourist
Information ⓘ

125

Au C'Amelot (Bastille)

Le Coude Fou (Le Marais)

L'Ebauchoir (Bastille)

Les Fêtes Galantes (Latin Quarter)

Gros Minet (Louvre)

Le Maquis (Montmartre)

L'O à la Bouche (St-Germain-des-Prés)

L'Ostréa (Louvre)

Le Petit Niçois (Eiffel Tower & Invalides)

Le Réconfort (Le Marais)

La Régalade (Montparnasse)

Willi's Wine Bar (Louvre)

Yvan Sur Seine (Louvre)

$$$

L'Affriolé (Eiffel Tower & Invalides)

L'Alisier (Le Marais)

Androuët (Champs-Elysées)

L'Appart' (Champs-Elysées)

Le Bamboche (St-Germain-des-Prés)

La Bastide Odéon (St-Germain-des-Prés)

Bofinger (Le Marais)

Les Brezolles (St-Germain-des-Prés)

Café de Vendôme (Louvre)

Chez Georges (Opéra)

La Closerie des Lilas (St-Germain-des-Prés)

L'Epi Dupin (St-Germain-des-Prés)

La Fontaine de Mars (Eiffel Tower & Invalides)

Macéo (Louvre)

Les Olivades (Eiffel Tower & Invalides)

Restaurant du Palais-Royal (Louvre)

Tante Louise (Champs-Elysées)

Le Vieux Bistro (The Islands)

$$$$

Alcazar (St-Germain-des-Prés)

Au Trou Gascon (Bastille)

Le Violon d'Ingres (Eiffel Tower & Invalides)

$$$$$

L'Ambroisie (Le Marais)

Michel Rostang (Champs-Elysées)

Pierre Gagnaire (Champs-Elysées)

Restaurant Index by Cuisine

Belgian

Le Bouillon Racine ($$, St-Germain-des-Prés)

Cheese

Androuët ($$$, Champs-Elysées)

Haute Cuisine

L'Ambroisie ($$$$$, Le Marais)

Michel Rostang ($$$$$, Champs-Elysées)

Pierre Gagnaire ($$$$$, Champs-Elysées)

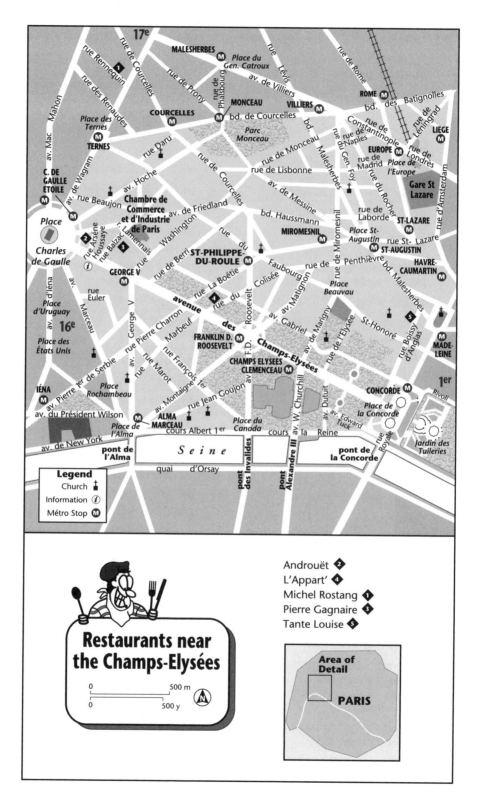

Restaurants near
the Champs-Elysées

Androuët ❷
L'Appart' ❹
Michel Rostang ❶
Pierre Gagnaire ❸
Tante Louise ❺

Area of
Detail

PARIS

127

Modern Bistro

L'Affriolé ($$$, Eiffel Tower & Invalides)

Alcazar ($$$$, St-Germain-des-Prés)

L'Appart' ($$$, Champs-Elysées)

Les Brezolles ($$$, St-Germain-des-Prés)

Café de Vendôme ($$$, Louvre)

L'O à la Bouche ($$, St-Germain-des-Prés)

Le Réconfort ($$, Le Marais)

Restaurant du Palais-Royal ($$$, Louvre)

Le Violon d'Ingres ($$$$, Eiffel Tower & Invalides)

Regional French
Alsatian (Brasserie)

Bofinger ($$$, Le Marais)

Chartier ($, Opéra)

La Closerie des Lilas ($$$, St-Germain-des-Prés)

Burgundian

Tante Louise ($$$, Champs-Elysées)

Lyonnais

Le Vieux Bistro ($$, The Islands)

Northern French

Le Bamboche ($$$, Eiffel Tower & Invalides)

Provençal

La Bastide Odéon ($$$, St-Germain-des-Prés)

Les Olivades ($$$, Eiffel Tower & Invalides)

Le Petit Niçois ($$, Eiffel Tower & Invalides)

Seafood

Le Bamboche ($$$, Eiffel Tower & Invalides)

L'Ostréa ($$, Louvre)

Le Petit Niçois ($$, Eiffel Tower & Invalides)

Southwestern French

La Fontaine de Mars ($$$, Eiffel Tower & Invalides)

La Régalade ($$, Montparnasse)

Au Trou Gascon ($$$$, Bastille)

Traditional Bistro

L'Alisier ($$$, Le Marais)

Astier ($$, Bastille)

Au Bon Accueil ($$, Eiffel Tower & Invalides)

Au C'Amelot ($$, Bastille)

Chez Alexandre ($, Latin Quarter)

Chez Georges ($$$, Opéra)

Le Coude Fou ($$, Le Marais)

L'Ebauchoir ($$, Bastille)

L'Epi Dupin ($$$, St-Germain-des-Prés)

Les Fêtes Galantes ($$, Latin Quarter)

Gros Minet ($$, Louvre)

Le Maquis ($$, Montmartre)

Polidor ($, St-Germain-des-Prés)

Trumilou ($, Le Marais)

Le Vieux Bistro ($$$, The Islands)

Yvan Sur Seine ($$, Louvre)

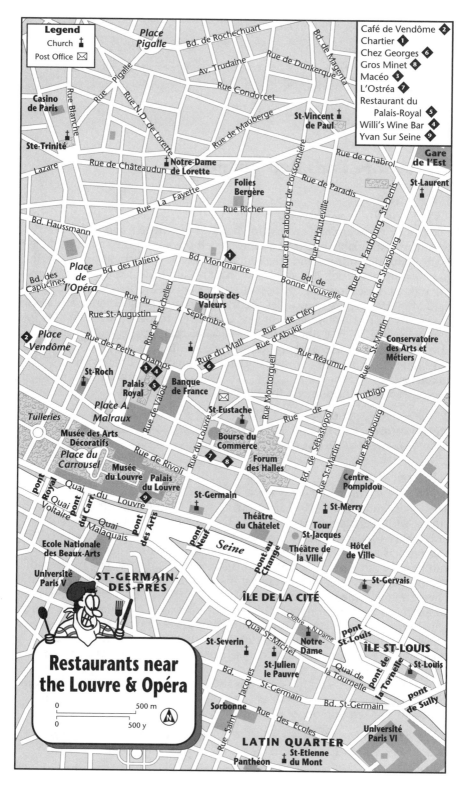

Restaurants near the Louvre & Opéra

Wine Bistro

Macéo ($$$, Louvre)

Le Moulin à Vins
($, Montmartre)

Willi's Wine Bar ($$, Louvre)

My Favorite Paris Restaurants

L'Affriolé
$$$. Eiffel Tower & Invalides (7e). MODERN BISTRO.
The French word *affrioler* means "to charm or to seduce," and that's exactly what this fashionable bistro has done since it opened in the summer of 1996. If the 1930s bistro front and checked tablecloths hint at traditionalism, chef Alain Antibard quickly lets you know that this ain't no average bistro. Having trained under some of the best chefs in France, Antibard knows that behind every culinary genius lies the freshest possible ingredients. His daily-changing, four-course *formule* consists of a starter (choices might include foie gras, lobster salad, or a quiche made with cèpe mushrooms and Laguiole cheese), a main course (perhaps jarret of glazed and roasted pork or scallops with lime juice), a cheese course, and a dessert (crêpes stuffed with quince marmalade or apricot bonbons). If you're not feeling particularly hungry, you can order a two-course menu for 120F ($22).

17 rue Malar, 7e (☎ 01/44-18-31-33). **Métro:** *RER Pont de l'Alma.*
Reservations: *4 days ahead.* **Prix-Fixe Menus:** *120F ($22) and 180F ($32).*
MC, V. **Open:** *Mon–Fri lunch and dinner, Sat dinner only. Closed 3 weeks in Aug.*

Alcazar
$$$$. St-Germain-des-Prés (6e). MODERN BISTRO.
This smart and stylish 200-seater from Terence Conran has hit Paris by storm, with French cuisine influenced by the Euro-Asian fusion that Londoners and New Yorkers can't get enough of. For his first foray into Paris, Conran has plucked Guillaume Lutard (formerly of three-star Taillevent) to run the kitchen. Lutard executes a mixed menu of brasserie fare (platters of shellfish and oysters), Mediterranean-inspired dishes (puff pastry with goat cheese and sundried tomatoes), and Pan-Asian staples like chicken and duckling infused with the unmistakable tang of soy sauce. Arugula, rocket, couscous, and artichokes appear often enough to make sure the trendy message is hammered home, but the foundation is clearly French. The food is quite good and the service enthusiastic, but the sheer size of the dining room means that noise can be deafening, so come for the buzz rather than for a romantic *tête-à-tête*. Another option is the upstairs piano bar, where you can order wine by the glass, as well as small plates of sushi, oysters, caviar, foie gras, and smoked salmon.

62 rue Mazarine, 6e (☎ 01-53-10-19-99). **Métro:** *Odéon.* **Reservations:**
2 days ahead. **Prix-Fixe Menus:** *None. AE, DC, MC, V.* **Open:** *Daily lunch and dinner, until 1am.*

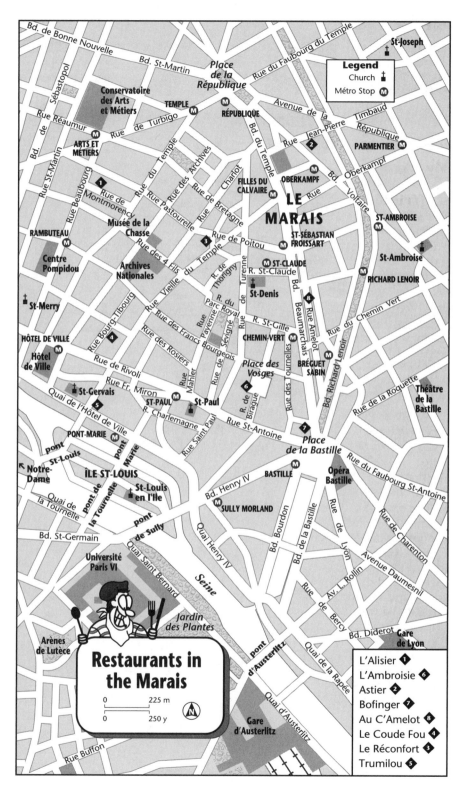

Restaurants in the Marais

0   225 m
0   250 y

L'Alisier ❶
L'Ambroisie ❻
Astier ❷
Bofinger ❼
Au C'Amelot ❽
Le Coude Fou ❹
Le Réconfort ❸
Trumilou ❺

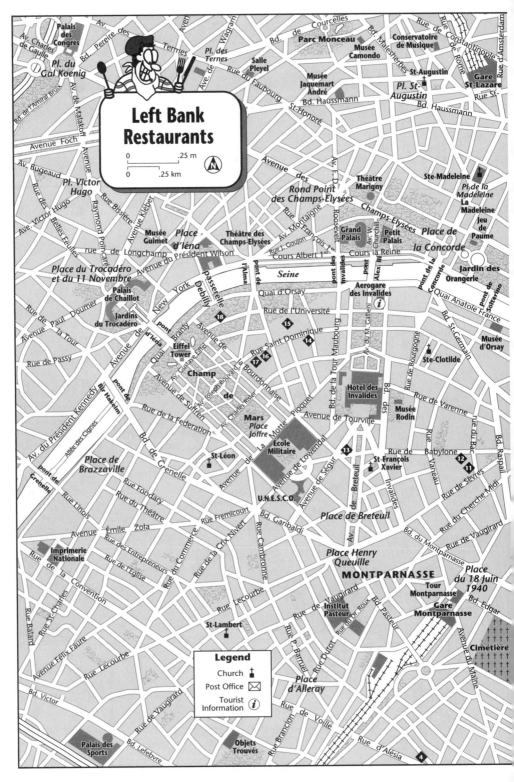

Left Bank
Restaurants

0   .25 m

0   .25 km

Legend

Church ✝
Post Office ✉
Tourist
Information ⓘ

L'Affriolé **15**
Alcazar **10**
Le Bamboche **12**
La Bastide Odéon **8**
Le Bon Accueil **18**
Le Bouillon Racine **7**
Les Brezolles **9**
Chez Alexandre **1**
La Closerie des Lilas **3**
L'Epi Dupin **11**
Les Fêtes Galantes **2**
La Fontaine de Mars **16**
L'O à la Bouche **5**
Les Olivades **13**
Le Petit Niçois **14**
Polidor **6**
La Régalade **4**
Le Violon d'Ingrès **17**

L'Alisier
$$$. Le Marais (3e). TRADITIONAL BISTRO.

Ensconced in a small Marais hideaway unlikely to be stumbled upon by the casual passerby, young chef Jean-Luc Dodeman changes his inventive set-price menus on a weekly basis and, twice a month, builds spectacular meals around wines from one of France's regions. Rather than offering a lengthy à la carte menu, the chef offers two set-price daily *formules:* a two-course lunch for 140F ($25) and a four-course dinner for 195F ($35). Dishes are artful and elegant, such as shrimp ravioli in lemongrass sauce or sumptuous roast lamb in a thyme butter sauce. Ask to be seated in the cozy ground-floor dining room, which resembles a country inn. The upstairs room is more spacious but less evocative.

26 rue de Montmorency, 3e (☎ 01/42-72-31-04). **Métro:** *Rambuteau. Head 3 blocks north on rue Beaubourg, and turn right.* **Reservations:** *3 days ahead.* **Prix-Fixe Menus:** *Lunch 140F ($25); dinner 195F ($35). MC, V.* **Open:** *Mon–Fri lunch and dinner. Closed Aug.*

L'Ambroisie
$$$$$. Le Marais (4e). HAUTE CUISINE.

French Prez Jacques Chirac and his wife, Bernadette, took Bill and Hillary Clinton to this atmospheric three-star restaurant during a visit from the Americans. Here in this gorgeous 17th-century mansion on the place des Vosges, Bernard Pacaud has made a name for himself with his imaginative and vividly flavorful, yet elegantly simple, dishes. The decor in the two high-ceilinged salons evokes an Italian palazzo, and tables spill onto the terrace in fine summer weather. Specialties include fricassée of lobster in wine sauce, roasted free-range chicken with black truffles, and an award-winning *tarte fine,* a chocolate pie served with bitter chocolate and mocha ice cream. This place was put on Earth for marriage proposals, anniversaries, and other special and romantic events.

9 place des Vosges, 4e (☎ 01/42-78-51-45). **Métro:** *St Paul.* **Reservations:** *4 weeks ahead. Jacket and tie advised.* **Prix-Fixe Menus:** *None. AE, DC, MC, V.* **Open:** *Tues–Sat lunch and dinner.*

Kids Androuët
$$$. Champs-Elysées (8e). CHEESE.

Don't think of Androuët as a novelty restaurant; this temple of cheese consistently rates highly with the most revered French gastronomic guides and there's nothing else like it in Europe. In this contemporary dining room, the specialty is cheese-oriented dishes such as fondues, raclettes, green salads with warm goat cheese, and beef with Roquefort sauce. But many aficionados simply opt for a bottle of good wine and the 300F ($54) sampler plate—six platters of different kinds of cheese dishes (triple creams, goat cheeses, *choucroute* with Muenster sauce, and the like)—which arrives at your table accompanied by freshly baked, delectable bread from the celebrated baker J. L. Poujaran; you can sample randomly and to your heart's content.

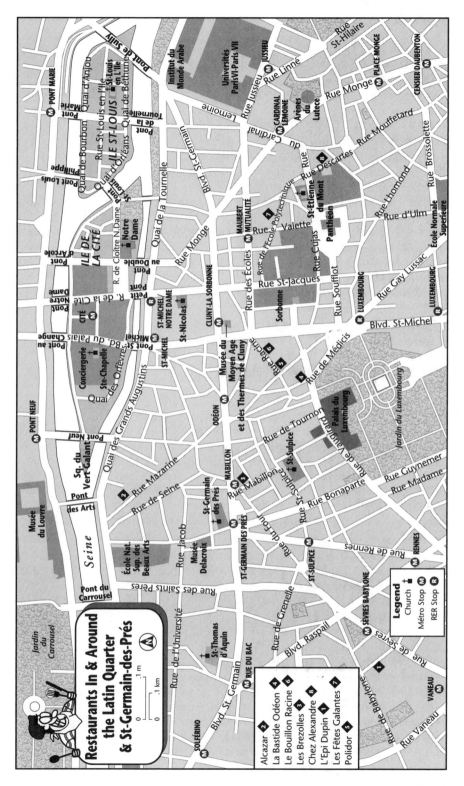

Restaurants In & Around the Latin Quarter & St-Germain-des-Prés

Legend
Church ✝
Métro Stop Ⓜ
RER Stop Ⓡ

Alcazar ❷
La Bastide Odéon ❹
Le Bouillon Racine ❻
Les Brezolles ❸
Chez Alexandre ❽
L'Epi Dupin ❼
Les Fêtes Galantes ❼
Polidor ❺

0 .1 km
0 .1 m

6 rue Arsène Houssaye, 8e (☎ 01/42-89-95-00). **Métro:** *Charles de Gaulle-Etoile.* **Reservations:** *2 days ahead.* **Prix-Fixe Menus:** *Lunch 210F ($37); dinner 230F ($41) and 300F ($54). AE, DC, MC, V.* **Open:** *Mon–Fri lunch and dinner, Sat dinner only.*

L'Appart'
$$$. Champs-Elysées (8e). MODERN BISTRO.

This classy three-room eatery less than a block from the Champs-Elysées is decked out to evoke a chic Parisian *appartement*: The salon boasts mismatched mirrors, oil paintings, and wainscoting; the boudoir is done up in romantic upholsteries; and the cozy bar/library has floor-to-ceiling bookshelves. The excellent cuisine takes its cue from different regions of France and pays equal time to meat (roast lamb with basil, veal grilled in balsamic vinaigrette) and fish (sole *en papillote* with herbs, prawn ravioli). Two-person tables are placed very close together, but larger groups are allotted more elbow room. The downstairs bar is a very fashionable rendezvous point before dinner.

9 rue du Colisée, 8e (☎ 01/53-75-16-34). **Métro:** *Franklin D. Roosevelt.* **Reservations:** *2 days ahead.* **Prix-Fixe Menus:** *175F ($31). AE, MC, V.* **Open:** *Daily lunch and dinner.*

Astier
$$. Bastille-Oberkampf (11e). TRADITIONAL BISTRO.

Since its founding "sometime during the administration of Charles de Gaulle," no one has tried to glamorize this much-loved old-fashioned bistro, understanding that hearty, well-prepared food always keeps the crowds coming. The 135F ($24) set menu offers at least 10 different choices for each of four courses (appetizer, main dish, cheese tray, and dessert). Starters might include chicken-liver terrine or eggs with truffled foie-gras, followed by main dishes such as roasted rabbit with mustard sauce, *racasse* (scorpionfish) with fresh spinach, breast of duckling served with a foie-gras cream sauce, and an ever-wide selection of steaks and chops. Great wine list.

44 rue Jean-Pierre Timbaud, 11e (☎ 01/43-57-16-35). **Métro:** *Parmentier.* **Reservations:** *1 day ahead.* **Prix-Fixe Menus:** *Lunch 110F ($20); dinner 135F ($24). MC, V.* **Open:** *Mon–Fri lunch and dinner.*

Le Bamboche
$$$. Eiffel Tower & Invalides (7e). NORTHERN FRENCH/ SEAFOOD.

On the fringe between Invalides and St-Germain-des-Prés, David van Laer's restaurant offers masterful cooking for prices well below what you'd expect to pay for this quality. The seafood-heavy, Northern French menu changes according to market availability, but might feature raw crayfish served with *rémoulade* sauce and a galette of Parmesan; a delectable squid and pepper salad; a *papillote* of scallops and foie gras with a confit of turnips; or young guinea fowl with pears and fresh truffles. Dessert often includes a can't-miss hot chocolate soufflé, which you must order at the beginning of your meal.

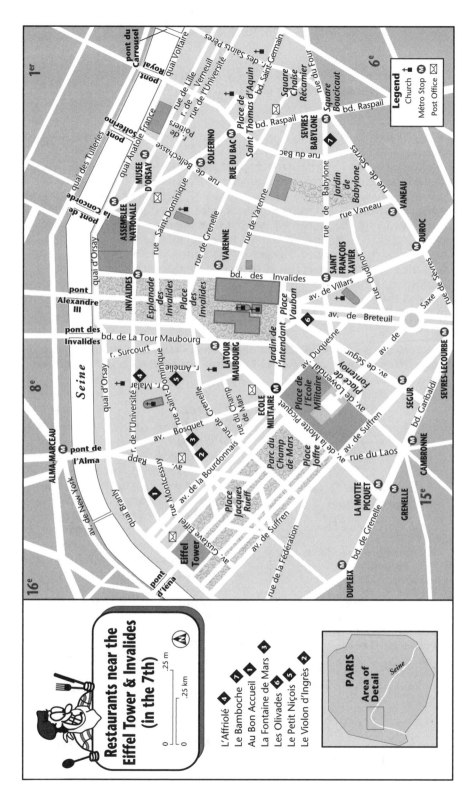

Restaurants near the
Eiffel Tower & Invalides
(in the 7th)

L'Affriolé 4
Le Bamboche 7
Au Bon Accueil 1
La Fontaine de Mars 3
Les Olivades 6
Le Petit Niçois 5
Le Violon d'Ingrès 2

PARIS
Area of Detail
Seine

Legend
Church
Métro Stop
Post Office

15 rue de Babylone, 7e (☎ 01/45-49-14-40). **Métro:** *Sèvres-Babylone.*
Reservations: *4 days ahead.* **Prix-Fixe Menus:** *190F ($34). AE, MC, V.*
Open: *Mon–Fri lunch and dinner.*

La Bastide Odéon
$$$. St-Germain-des-Prés (6e). PROVENÇAL.

Located just across from the Luxembourg Gardens, this is deservedly one of
the most successful Provençal restaurants in the city. The dining room's
decor points due south, with butter-yellow walls, beamed-ceilings, heavy oak
tables, and artfully arranged bouquets of dried flowers. Chef Gilles Ajuelos,
who trained with the renowned two-star chef Michel Rostang (see his sepa-
rate listing, below), prepares a market-driven menu that is chock-full of dishes
that are modern, light, and thoughtfully executed. The best first courses are
often the simplest, such as tagliatelle in pesto sauce with wild mushrooms
or grilled eggplant layered with herbs and oil. Main courses might include
roast cod with capers or duckling with pepper sauce. Winners among desserts
are the rhubarb tart and warm almond pie served with prune and Armagnac
ice cream.

7 rue Corneille, 6e (☎ 01/43-26-03-65). **Métro:** *Odéon or RER Luxembourg.*
Reservations: *1 week ahead.* **Prix-Fixe Menus:** *180F ($32). MC, V.* **Open:**
Tues–Sat lunch and dinner.

Restaurants Open on Sundays

L'Appart' (Champs-Elysées, $$$)
Bofinger (Le Marais, $$$)
Café de Vendôme
(Louvre, $$$)
Chartier (Opéra, $)
La Closerie des Lilas
(St-Germain-des-Prés, $$$)
Le Coude Fou (Le Marais, $$)
Polidor (St-Germain-
des-Prés, $)
Trumilou (Le Marais, $)
Le Vieux Bistro (The Islands,
$$$)

Bofinger
*$$$. Le Marais (3e, 4e). ALSATIAN
(BRASSERIE).*

Open since 1864, Bofinger is not only
one of Paris's gastronomic institutions,
but it's as classic an Alsatian brasserie as
you'll find west of Strasbourg. All the
hallmark brasserie fixtures are here:
white-aproned waiters, good beer on tap,
and a fine belle époque interior of
stained glass and shiny brass. In the summer, you can dine out on the terrace
when weather permits. The fare is also
quintessential Alsatian: classic brasserie
shellfish, steaks, good saddle of lamb,
onion soup, *choucroute* (sauerkraut)
served with sausage, bacon, or pork
chops, and daily specials that often
include an excellent cassoulet. Bofinger's
sole downfall is service that can be indif-
ferent to the point of being rude.

*5 rue de la Bastille, 4e (☎ 01/42-
78-51-45).* **Métro:** *Bastille.* **Reservations:**
4 days ahead. **Prix-Fixe Menus:** *169F ($30). AE, DC, MC, V.* **Open:** *Daily
lunch and dinner.*

Au Bon Accueil
$$. Eiffel Tower & Invalides (7e). TRADITIONAL BISTRO.
A friendly atmosphere and Jacques Lacipière's delicious, superb-value, set-price menu has made this simple bistro wildly popular with the well-heeled set. The menu changes according to what Lacipière finds at the Rungis market that morning, and you won't go wrong whether you prefer meat (filet of beef bordelaise, veal mignon) or fish (skate terrine, turbot in an herbal vinaigrette). The classic French desserts are excellent, and the service is friendly and well informed.

14 rue de Monttessuy, 7e (☎ 01/47-05-46-11). Métro: RER Pont de l'Alma. Reservations: 3 days ahead. Prix-Fixe Menus: Lunch 120F ($22); dinner 145F ($26). MC, V. Open: Mon–Fri lunch and dinner, Sat dinner only. Closed Aug.

Le Bouillon Racine
$$. St-Germain-des-Prés (6e). BELGIAN.
An exceptionally pretty setting and very good Belgian food from chef Olivier Simon at reasonable prices has made this restaurant a success story. The stunning art nouveau decor—beveled mirrors, mosaic floor, rosebud chandeliers, floral tiles, and stained-glass insets—creates the sort of *fin-de-siècle* atmosphere you usually only find in upscale brasseries and palace hotels. Start with shrimp-stuffed tomatoes, then try the *waterzoi* (a delicate chicken and vegetable stew), shrimp croquettes, Ardennes ham mousse, or lamb roasted in blond beer. Speaking of beer, the list of brews is fabulous, as is the bread, from the baker J. L. Poujaran.

3 rue Racine, 6e (☎ 01/44-32-15-60). Métro: Odéon. Reservations: 1 day ahead. Prix-Fixe Menus: 78F ($14) and 108F ($19). MC, V. Open: Mon–Sat lunch and dinner.

Les Brezolles
$$$. St-Germain-des-Prés (6e). MODERN BISTRO.
This chic little coffee-and-cream dining room in St-Germain-des-Prés has become a bona fide hit with stylish Left Bankers. Chef Jean-Paul Duquesnoy is no culinary neophyte, having already run a successful two-star restaurant before setting up this less-expensive bistro. On a typical menu, starters might include zucchini flowers stuffed with crab mousse or a very good terrine of chicken. The list of main courses is often heavy on the fish (salmon steak with new potatoes and apples, grilled tuna steak, or roast cod with eggplant-stuffed cannelloni) while always featuring a few meat dishes (veal shank with chestnuts, roast lamb with rosemary). Desserts are elegant and scrumptious, like the caramelized pastry puff that comes filled with rice pudding and apricot coulis.

5 rue Mabillon, 6e (☎ 01/43-26-73-70). Métro: Mabillon. Reservations: 3 days ahead. Prix-Fixe Menus: Lunch 160F ($29); dinner 195F ($35). MC, V. Open: Tues–Sat lunch and dinner, Mon dinner only.

Café de Vendôme
$$$. Louvre (1er). MODERN BISTRO.

What's not to love? Start with an exceptionally brilliant address on the gorgeous place Vendôme just a few paces from the Ritz hotel and Europe's finest jewelry boutiques. Add an elegant decor, smart service, and terrific food, and you have the recipe for one of the brightest stars to emerge from 1998's *rentrée* season. Chef Gérard Salle, formerly of the Plaza Athenée hotel's restaurant, has a creative touch with classics like gnocchi in dill cream sauce, fennel-infused tomato tart, and roast Pauillac lamb with a patina of cumin. More crowd-pleasers: yummy desserts, dinner service until 11:30pm, and affordably priced wines by the glass.

*1 place Vendôme, 1er (☎ 01/55-04-55-55). **Métro:** Concorde or Tuileries. **Reservations:** 3 days ahead. **Prix-Fixe Menus:** 190F ($34). AE, DC, MC, V. **Open:** Daily lunch and dinner.*

Au C'Amelot
$$. Bastille (11e). TRADITIONAL BISTRO.

Nothing fancy, no surprises, just good, straight forward, family-style cooking—that's what you'll find at this winningly unpretentious, tiny place (just 10 tables) not far from the place de la Bastille. The decor can best be described as shabby chic, right down to the dated chandeliers and mix-and-match china. But behind the stove lurks Didier Varnier, a protégé of Michelin-starred chef Christian Constant (see review of Le Violon d'Ingres, below), whose meals are bargain-priced at 120F ($22) for five courses. Selections change daily but might feature deliciously crusty bread slathered with paté and served with thinly sliced sausage, a homemade soup, a main dish of fish (codfish with marinated cabbage) or fowl (guinea hen with roast potatoes), a luscious cheese course, and hot-out-of-the-oven apple tart like your grandma used to bake.

*50 rue Amelot, 11e (☎ 01/43-55-54-04). **Métro:** Bastille. **Reservations:** 4 days ahead. **Prix-Fixe Menus:** 120F ($22). No credit cards. **Open:** Mon–Fri lunch and dinner.*

Kids Chartier
$. Opéra (2e, 9e). ALSATIAN (BRASSERIE).

Established in 1896, this budget favorite has long offered great-value cooking in a superb belle epoque setting. Though many items on the menu are strictly for the adventurous, there's also beef bourguignon, *pot-au-feu*, pavé of rump steak, and at least five kinds of fish. Prices are low enough that you can choose three courses à la carte and still have change from 100F ($18), a fact that as many as 320 happy diners at a time can appreciate.

*7 rue de Faubourg Montmartre, 9e (☎ 01/47-70-86-29). **Métro:** Rue Montmartre. **Reservations:** Not necessary. **Prix-Fixe Menu:** 83F ($15). MC, V. **Open:** Daily lunch and dinner.*

Kids **Chez Alexandre**
$. Latin Quarter (5e). TRADITIONAL BISTRO.
This tiny restaurant near the rue Mouffetard market is a huge step up from the mediocrity that pervades most of the Latin Quarter's budget eateries. The lunch *formule* offers 10 choices for each of three courses and is priced at an unbeatable 49F ($9). Best of all, the quality of this down-home bistro fare is very good. Start with a salad of greens topped with warm goat cheese, then enjoy tarragon chicken, grilled steak in shallot-and-wine sauce, or duckling in mandarine sauce. The dessert list is a roster of French classics, like crème brûlée and *fondant* of chocolate.

39 rue Descartes, 5e (☎ 01/40-46-82-20). **Métro:** *Cardinal Lemoin or Place Monge.* **Reservations:** *Not necessary.* **Prix-Fixe Menus:** *Lunch 49F ($9); dinner 75F ($13). MC, V.* **Open:** *Mon–Sat lunch and dinner.*

Chez Georges
$$$. Opéra (2e, 9e). TRADITIONAL BISTRO.
This bistro is something of a local landmark, opened in 1964 and run by three generations of the Broillet family. At lunch it's packed with traders from the nearby stock exchange, who come for the excellent comfort food, the convivial atmosphere, and the quintessential bistro decor, right down to the closely packed tables and worn tile floors. Start with celery *rémoulade*, herb-flavored herring, or a salad of greens topped with warm bacon and a soft-cooked egg. You can follow with *pot-au-feu* (beef-and-veggie stew), a classic cassoulet, duck with cèpe mushrooms, beef braised in red wine, steak with béarnaise sauce, or a delectable filet of sole in white wine-and-cream sauce. Desserts include excellent profiteroles and *tarte Tatin*.

1 rue du Mail, 2e (☎ 01/42-60-07-11). **Métro:** *Bourse.* **Reservations:** *4 days ahead.* **Prix-Fixe Menus:** *None. AE, MC, V.* **Open:** *Mon–Sat lunch and dinner. Closed 3 weeks in Aug.*

La Closerie des Lilas
$$$. St-Germain-de-Prés (6e). ALSATIAN (BRASSERIE).
This old literary haunt on the border of St-Germain-des-Prés and Montparnasse remains one of the city's most historic and romantic sites for a meal. In their day, customers included Gertrude Stein, Henry James, Chateaubriand, Picasso, Hemingway, Apollinaire, Lenin and Trotsky (at the chess board), and Whistler, who would expound on the "gentle art" of making enemies. The clientele may not be sprinkled with celebrities these days, but it's just as Left Bank chic as ever. Seating is divided between the pricey restaurant and the brasserie. Request a table in the brasserie, where you can dine much less expensively on such quintessential fare as excellent oysters (in season), grilled meats, and *choucroute* dishes.

171 bd. du Montparnasse, 6e (☎ 01/40-51-34-50). **Métro:** *Port-Royal or Vavin.* **Reservations:** *4 days ahead for the restaurant; 2 days ahead for the brasserie.* **Prix-Fixe Menus:** *Lunch 250F ($45) in the restaurant. AE, DC, MC, V.* **Open:** *Daily lunch and dinner.*

141

Le Coude Fou
$$. Le Marais (4e). TRADITIONAL BISTRO.
This cheerful little wine bistro-cum-restaurant in the Marais has amusing murals on the walls, a blackboard menu of well-priced wines, and a faithful clientele of artsy regulars who return again and again for the consistently excellent food. Start with the balsamic vinaigrette-doused roasted eggplant, the warm goat cheese salad, or the excellent *salade coude fou* (greens topped with foie gras, grapes, and pine nuts). Main dishes include grilled tuna steak with herb butter, luscious lamb chops in garlicky cream, grilled steak Auvergnat with blue cheese sauce, and a meltaway liver grilled in balsamic vinaigrette. Desserts are delectable, from the chocolate roulade cake to the apple tart to the sorbets, and the service is always upbeat and helpful.

12 rue Bourg-Tibourg, 4e (☎ 01/42-77-15-16). **Métro:** *Hôtel-de-Ville.* **Reservations:** *1 day ahead.* **Prix-Fixe Menus:** *169F ($30). MC, V.* **Open:** *Daily lunch and dinner.*

L'Ebauchoir
$$. Bastille (11e). TRADITIONAL BISTRO.
Tucked into the part of the Bastille district rarely visited by tourists, this neighborhood favorite is well worth seeking out. It has all the hallmarks of a bygone era—lace curtains, worn tile floors, huge gilt mirrors, contented diners seated elbow-to-elbow—plus lots of good ol' down-to-earth cooking. There's always a duly enthusiastic crowd of local artisans, young couples, intellectuals, and the occasional well-known actor or director, and everyone gets the same friendly service and first come, first served seating. If there are no tables available when you arrive, you'll be invited to have a glass of wine at the bar. The menu is handwritten on blackboards that get passed between tables and the kitchen dishes up the kind of satisfying comfort food that gives bistros a good name. Start with warm foie gras served on a bed of greens or garlicky escargot-filled ravioli, then move on to grilled rib steak Bordelaise *à la moëlle* (its red wine sauce is enriched with marrow) that comes served with potatoes au gratin. Desserts are a disappointing anticlimax, so save your money by sticking to two courses.

43 rue de Cîteaux, 12e (☎ 01/43-42-49-31). **Métro:** *Faidherbe-Chaligny. Keeping the St-Antoine hospital to your left, walk 1 block and turn left.* **Reservations:** *Not accepted.* **Prix-Fixe Menus:** *Lunch 66F ($12) and 85F ($15). MC, V.* **Open:** *Mon–Sat lunch and dinner.*

L'Epi Dupin
$$$. St-Germain-des-Prés (6e). TRADITIONAL BISTRO.
Right around the corner from the Bon Marché department store, this rustic bistro with half-timbered walls draws business folk by day and a chic Left Bank crowd by night. The attraction is excellent-value cooking from talented François Pasteau, whose market-driven menu focuses on tasty French classics like foie gras salad, confit of duckling with truffled potatoes, and lamb with ratatouille. Everything from the breads and pastries to the heavenly chocolate soufflé is homemade.

11 rue Dupin, 6e (☎ 01/42-22-64-56). **Métro:** *Sèvres-Babylone.* **Reservations:** *4 days ahead.* **Prix-Fixe Menus:** *Lunch 97F ($18); dinner 165F ($29). AE, MC, V.* **Open:** *Mon–Fri lunch and dinner, Sat dinner only. Closed first 3 weeks Aug.*

Les Fêtes Galantes
$$. Latin Quarter (5e). TRADITIONAL BISTRO.
This tropical-inspired bistro near the Pantheon is intimate (seats a max of 22 diners), friendly, and the home of some of the best-value menus in the city. Expect classic French dishes prepared with a bit of extra southern zest. Excellent main dishes include a succulent confit of duckling and roast chicken with spicy, tomatoey *sauce diable.* For dessert, the profiteroles and apple pie are both sure-fire winners.

17 rue de l'Ecole Polytechnique, 5e (☎ 01/43-26-10-40). **Métro:** *Cardinal Lemoine.* **Reservations:** *1 day ahead.* **Prix-Fixe Menus:** *Lunch 65F ($12); dinner 78F ($14), 100F ($18), and 159F ($28). MC, V.* **Open:** *Mon–Sat lunch and dinner.*

La Fontaine de Mars
$$$. Eiffel Tower & Invalides (7e). SOUTHWESTERN FRENCH.
The romantic and down-to-earth ambiance of lace curtains and checkered tablecloths, terrific bistro cooking, and a superbly priced 85F ($15) midday menu make this an exceptional lunch spot before or after visiting the Eiffel Tower. There's an animated dining room on the ground floor, but ask to sit upstairs in one of the two cozy rooms whose round tables, oil paintings, wainscoting, and parquet floors make you feel like you're in a private home. The cuisine comes from the Pyrénées and southwestern France, bearing rich heady flavors that go well with robust red wines—*piperade aux oeufs pochés* (a sauté of peppers, tomatoes, and onions with poached eggs), confit of duckling with parsley potatoes, *boudin* (blood sausage) with baked apples, fricassé of chicken with morel mushrooms in cream sauce, and red mullet with herb-flavored butter. For dessert, try the *tarte Tatin,* which comes capped with Calvados and cream.

129 rue Saint-Dominique, 7e (☎ 01/47-05-46-44). **Métro:** *Ecole-Militaire.* **Reservations:** *1 day ahead.* **Prix-Fixe Menus:** *Lunch 85F ($15). AE, MC, V.* **Open:** *Mon–Sat lunch and dinner.*

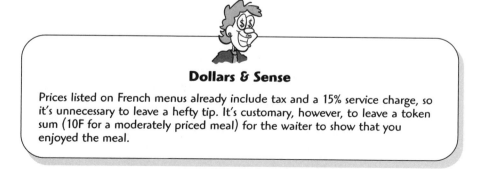

Dollars & Sense
Prices listed on French menus already include tax and a 15% service charge, so it's unnecessary to leave a hefty tip. It's customary, however, to leave a token sum (10F for a moderately priced meal) for the waiter to show that you enjoyed the meal.

Gros Minet
$$. Louvre (1er). TRADITIONAL BISTRO.
With terrific fixed-price menus and an endearingly cantankerous vintage ambiance, this place, between the Louvre and Les Halles, is a noticeable cut above the average budget bistro. Order from the *formule*, starting with one of the generous, freshly made salads. For your main course, try the mullet with basil or the excellent duck with bilberry sauce, which comes served with sautéed potatoes. Desserts tend toward the down-to-earth, like *crème brulée* and apple tart. This is a great bargain address to know, smack in the center of the city, but the tiny street is tricky to find without a good map. After exiting the Louvre-Rivoli métro (corner of rue du Louvre and rue de Rivoli), walk three blocks east on rue de Rivoli, turn left on rue des Roules, and cross rue St-Honoré.

1 rue des Prouvaires, 1er (☎ *01/42-33-02-62).* **Métro:** *Louvre-Rivoli.* **Reservations:** *Not necessary.* **Prix-Fixe Menus:** *Lunch 78F ($14); dinner 95F ($17). AE, DC, MC, V.* **Open:** *Tues–Fri lunch and dinner.*

Macéo
$$$. Louvre (1er). WINE BISTRO.
This lovely place near the Palais Royal is the third venture from Englishman Mark Williamson, who built his rep in Paris with two other congenial wine bistros, Willi's (see separate listing, below) and Juveniles (see chapter 11). Chef Jean-Paul Deyries's menu is sophisticated and globally influenced, like the Asian-inspired starter of giant shrimp on a bed of sautéed bean sprouts and an undeniably French wild-mushroom terrine. Main courses lean toward meat dishes that go well with red wine, perhaps sautéed nuggets of lamb wrapped around minced black olives or a beef filet with spicy red wine sauce. Unsurprisingly, the wine list is nothing short of fabulous.

15 rue des Petits-Champs, 1er (☎ *01/42-96-09-17).* **Métro:** *Palais Royal or Pyramides.* **Reservations:** *2 days ahead.* **Prix-Fixe Menus:** *Lunch 185F ($33). MC, V.* **Open:** *Mon–Sat lunch and dinner.*

Le Maquis
$$. Montmartre (18e). TRADITIONAL BISTRO.
If only every neighborhood bistro could be like this. Located on a tree-lined street on the residential, less-touristed side of Montmartre (but still just a 5-minute walk from the Sacré-Coeur), this much-loved, pink linen–draped spot is always packed at mealtimes with locals who come for the consistently good food and cheerful ambiance. The 159F ($28) fixed-price dinner menu is a rare no-surprises deal, comprising an aperitif, appetizer, main course, dessert, wine, *and* coffee. Come with an appetite, and prepare for some excellent comfort food. Begin with a salad of greens topped with foie gras or warm goat cheese and croutons, then savor the *contrefilet maître d'hôtel* (grilled steak topped with herb butter and served with scalloped potatoes). The desserts—from the fondant of chocolate to the crème brulée—are simple yet elegantly presented, the service friendly and helpful.

69 rue Caulaincourt, 18e (☎ *01/42-59-76-07*). **Métro:** *Lamarck-Caulaincourt.* **Reservations:** *Same day.* **Prix-Fixe Menus:** *Lunch 100F ($18); dinner 159F ($28). MC, V.* **Open:** *Mon–Sat lunch and dinner.*

Michel Rostang
$$$$$. Champs-Elysées (8e). HAUTE CUISINE.

Two-star chef Michel Rostang, the fifth generation of one of the most distinguished French "cooking families," has spread his name through a series of successful bistros abroad. But only in his elegant, four-room Paris restaurant does he tend the stove personally. Rostang changes his menu according to market availability and season, yet his flair with tastes and textures always shines through. Starters might include ravioli stuffed with seafood, roasted green asparagus with spiced crabmeat, or lobster nuggets with asparagus and baby artichokes. Main courses may run along the lines of roast Breton crayfish, brochette of prawns with rosemary, quail eggs with a *coque* of sea urchins, fricassée of sole, or Bresse chicken in a chervil sauce. Any dessert made from chocolate or apples is sensational, and the cheese tray and wine list are both copious.

20 rue Rennequin, 17e (☎ *01/47-63-40-77*). **Métro:** *Ternes.* **Reservations:** *4 weeks ahead. Jacket and tie advised.* **Prix-Fixe Menus:** *Lunch 325F ($58); dinner 595F ($106) and 795F ($142). AE, DC, MC, V.* **Open:** *Mon–Fri lunch and dinner, Sat dinner only. Closed first 2 weeks of Aug.*

Best-Value Lunch Menus

Au Bon Accueil:	120F ($22)	(Eiffel Tower & Invalides, $$)
Le Bouillon Racine:	78F ($14)	(St-Germain-des-Prés, $$)
Chez Alexandre:	49F ($9)	(Latin Quarter, $)
L'Ebauchoir:	66F, 85F ($12, $15)	(Bastille, $$)
L'Epi Dupin:	97F ($17)	(St-Germain-des-Prés, $$$)
Les Fêtes Galantes:	65F ($12)	(Latin Quarter, $$)
La Fontaine de Mars:	85F ($15)	(Eiffel Tower & Invalides, $$$)
Gros Minet	78F ($14)	(Louvre, $$)
Le Maquis:	100F ($18)	(Montmartre, $$)
Michel Rostang,	325F ($58)	(Champs-Elysées, $$$$$)
Polidor,	55F ($10)	(St-Germain-des-Prés, $)
Le Réconfort,	69F ($12)	(Le Marais, $$)
Au Trou Gascon,	190F ($34)	(Bastille, $$$$)

Le Moulin à Vins
$. Montmartre (18e). WINE BISTRO.

This unassuming little wine bistro with a 1930s decor is a favorite with the entire cross section of Montmartre locals, from bikers to ultrachic fashion mavens. It's a great place to come for a glass of Bordeaux or Côtes du Rhone and some old-fashioned bistro stalwarts at better-than-reasonable prices. Starters might include country terrine or quiche lorraine, followed by hot sausage with potato salad or rabbit in mustard sauce. Some terrific wines are available by the bottle or glass.

6 rue Burq, 18e (☎ *01/45-52-81-27).* **Métro:** *Abbesses.* **Reservations:** *Not necessary.* **Prix-Fixe Menus:** *None. MC, V.* **Open:** *Wed–Thurs lunch and dinner, Tues and Fri–Sat dinner only. (Call ahead for hours, which change often).*

L'O à la Bouche

$$. St-Germain-des-Prés (6e). MODERN BISTRO.
For proof that hard work and perseverance pay off, look no further than Franck Paquier. He opened this excellent-value eatery in early 1997 to rave reviews and has been wowing the hometown crowd ever since. Like every great bistro, there's always an agreeable crush of elbows and the din of diners having a good time. Expect modern dishes influenced by the globe-trotting bug, such as the excellent sesame-breaded shrimp that's fried and served with an Asian-inspired salad of greens and shoots. Mediterranean-style favorites include tart of tomato and mozzarella and fried sea bream with potatoes cooked in olive oil.

157 bd. du Montparnasse, 6e (☎ *01/47-83-70-09).* **Métro:** *Vavin.* **Reservations:** *3 days ahead.* **Prix-Fixe Menu:** *140F ($24) and 180F ($32).* **Open:** *Tues–Sat lunch and dinner. Closed the second week in Apr and the first 3 weeks in Aug.*

Best for Families

Androuët (Champs-Elysées, $$$)
Chartier (Opéra, $)
Chez Alexandre
  (Latin Quarter, $)
Polidor St-Germain-des-Prés, $)
Le Vieux Bistro (The Islands, $$$)

(See chapter 11 for more kid-friendly eateries.)

Les Olivades

$$$. Eiffel Tower & Invalides (7e). PROVENÇAL.
The 169F ($30) dinner menu at this engagingly upbeat restaurant is one of the city's great deals. While many Parisian chefs dabble in Provençal cooking, gifted young Flora Mikula hails from Nîmes and is the real McCoy. Located near the Champs de Mars, her two-room restaurant is decked out with a terra-cotta tile floor and bright floral fabrics that manage to evoke the southern sun even in midwinter. Mikula has an impressive resume, having trained with the three-star chef Alain Passard of Arpège and two-star chef Jean-Pierre Vigato of Apicius, and she's a wizard with Provence's rich, earthy bounty—from delicate goat cheese, meaty black olives, and sun-drenched tomatoes to grilled eggplant to batter-fried zucchini blossoms. The menu includes southern tempters such as quail confit with apples and pine nuts, goat cheese–stuffed ravioli in pesto

sauce, red mullet with tapenade, mouth-watering lamb with thyme, and roasted sea bass served with a hint of coriander. At the end of the meal, Mikula leaves the kitchen to greet her patrons—a gesture more of this city's chefs should make. Nice selection of well-priced Provençal wines.

41 av. de Ségur, 7e (☎ 01/47-83-70-09). **Métro:** *St-François-Xavier.* **Reservations:** *3 days ahead.* **Prix-Fixe Menus:** *Dinner 169F ($30). AE, MC, V.* **Open:** *Tues–Fri lunch and dinner, Mon and Sat dinner only. Closed Aug.*

L'Ostréa
$$. Louvre (1er). SEAFOOD.
Huge portions of fish and shellfish are the name of the game here, with an extensive and reasonably priced menu that's sure to make noncarnivores think they've died and gone to heaven. Starters run the gamut from jumbo shrimp salad to herrings in paprika, while main courses include sole meunière, bar flambé, monkfish in white wine sauce, and copious platters of mixed shellfish. The setting is casual and appropriately salty.

4 rue Sauval, 1er (☎ 01/40-26-08-07). **Métro:** *Louvre.* **Reservations:** *Not necessary.* **Prix-Fixe Menus:** *135F ($24). MC, V.* **Open:** *Mon–Fri lunch and dinner, Sat dinner only.*

Le Petit Niçois
$$. Eiffel Tower & Invalides (7e). PROVENÇAL/SEAFOOD.
If the white stucco walls and red tablecloths don't put you in a Mediterranean mood, the excellent, seafood-driven menu at this tiny sliver of Provence is just the ticket. The unmissable dish on the menu is an authentically garlicky, Niçoise-style bouillabaisse made with crayfish and lobster. There are also several paella and grilled fish dishes to choose from, all simply but thoughtfully prepared. For dessert, try the tarte Tatin topped with crème fraîche.

10 rue Amélie, 7e (☎ 01/45-51-83-65). **Métro:** *Latour-Maubourg.* **Reservations:** *1 day ahead.* **Prix-Fixe Menus:** *170F ($30). MC, V.* **Open:** *Tues–Sat lunch and dinner, Mon dinner only.*

Pierre Gagnaire
$$$$$. Champs-Elysées (8e). HAUTE CUISINE.
This is Paris's hottest three-star restaurant, inside which you'll find chef Pierre Gagnaire forever working his magic with unexpected tastes and textures. Every single dish served in his elegant blue-and-silver dining room is complex and jam-packed with sensory stimulation. You don't come here merely to fuel up; you

Meals after Midnight

Alcazar (St-Germain-des-Prés, $$$$)
Yvan Sur Seine (Louvre, $$)

(See chapter 11 for more late-night eateries.)

come to partake in a culinary odyssey that's audacious and artistic. Dishes might include foie gras and dried figs wrapped in a buckwheat galette raw black truffles and baby artichokes in Jerusalem artichoke cream; or a truffle-and-mozzarella lasagne. One of his most famous dishes is a tempura of prawns that's delicately fried and served with a cinnamon-infused beurre blanc. There's an extensive list of classy, delectable desserts ranging from tarts to sorbets to a chocolate soufflé so creamy that Gagnaire calls it a soup.

6 rue Balzac, 8e (☎ 01/44-35-18-25). **Métro:** *George V.* **Reservations:** *6 weeks ahead.* **Prix-Fixe Menus:** *Lunch 450F ($80); dinner 520F ($93) and 860F ($155). AE, DC, MC, V.* **Open:** *Mon–Fri lunch and dinner, Sun dinner only. Closed mid-July to mid-Aug.*

🌟Kids🌟 Polidor
$. St-Germain-des-Prés (6e). TRADITIONAL BISTRO.
Polidor is everyone's favorite budget bistro, a lace-curtained, 19th-century haunt where you can have a good meal with wine for under 125F ($22). The draws are good, honest cooking and a positively jolly atmosphere. Peer beyond the long, family-style tables and polished brass hat racks to see the pigeon holes where regular customers of bygone days used to keep their cloth napkins. Try the old-fashioned pumpkin soup or garlicky escargots followed by hearty portions of beef bourguignon, veal in white sauce, Basque-style chicken, or guinea fowl with cabbage. For dessert, the tarts—chocolate, raspberry, or lemon—are the best in all of Paris. Just be forewarned that the Turkish-style squat toilets are reached through the courtyard.

41 rue Monsieur-le-Prince, 6e (☎ 01/43-26-95-34). **Métro:** *Odéon.* **Reservations:** *Not accepted.* **Prix-Fixe Menus:** *Lunch 55F ($10); dinner 100F ($18). No credit cards.* **Open:** *Daily lunch and dinner.*

Le Réconfort
$$. Le Marais (3e). MODERN BISTRO.
Always abuzz with folks from the fashion and media worlds, this winningly laid-back Marais bistro is a hip place to be seen at lunch or dinner. The menu takes traditional bistro favorites and gives them a modern, cosmopolitan touch, as in starters such as basil-infused, stuffed mushrooms or the *compote de légumes*—a veggie cake flavored with Moroccan spices. Main dishes might include confit of duckling with crispy potatoes or cod grilled in balsamic vinaigrette. Friendly service, and a brief but well-priced wine list.

37 rue de Poitou, 3e (☎ 01/42-76-06-36). **Métro:** *Sébastien-Froissart.* **Reservations:** *3 days ahead.* **Prix-Fixe Menus:** *Lunch 69F ($12) and 89F ($16); dinner 179F ($32). MC, V.* **Open:** *Mon–Fri lunch and dinner, Sat dinner only.*

La Régalade
$$. Montparnasse (14e). SOUTHWESTERN FRENCH.
While the address is a bit off the tourist track, Parisians beat a path to the door of Yves Camdeborde, another gifted young chef to emerge from Christian Contant's stable (see review of Le Violon d'Ingres, below) who

148

performs miracles with his light and inventive touch. The ambiance in this bistro is downright convivial—think pleasantly harassed service and an enthusiastic clientele packed into Bordeaux-hued banquettes. The set menu features 10 choices for each course, featuring such down-home specialties as *beignets de légumes* (vegetable fritters), exotic mushrooms simmered in basil, panfried foie gras served with spice bread, and a wonderful *pot-au-feu* (beef stew). Other dishes—*hachis parmentier* made with rabbit, kidneys, and testicles? —Yikes—are strictly for the gutsy. You're definitely guaranteed a memorable—and *très* Parisian—dining experience, but be sure to book before leaving home. As you'd imagine, most of the wine list focuses on southwest France.

*49 av. Jean Moulin, 14e (☎ **01/45-45-68-58**). **Métro:** Alésia. **Reservations:** 2 weeks ahead. **Prix-Fixe Menus:** 175F ($31). MC, V. **Open:** Tues–Fri lunch and dinner, Sat dinner only.*

Restaurant du Palais-Royal
$$$. Louvre (1er). MODERN BISTRO.
In summertime, this romantic bistro has one of the prettiest al fresco settings in the city, tucked under the arcades in the northeastern corner of the Palais-Royal garden. The frequently changing menu is contemporary, featuring dishes like baby scallops and mushrooms in balsamic vinaigrette, roasted prawns in *ratatouille niçoise*, or sole with Languedoc-style garnish. For dessert, order one of the homemade ice creams or sorbets. The wine list is well chosen and reasonably priced.

*110 Galerie de Valois, 1er (☎ **01/40-20-00-27**). **Métro:** Palais-Royal. **Reservations:** 3 days ahead. **Prix-Fixe Menus:** None. AE, MC, V. **Open:** Mon–Fri lunch and dinner, Sat and Sun dinner only. Closed Sun Sept–May.*

Tante Louise
$$$. Champs-Elysées (8e). BURGUNDIAN.
This appealingly old-style haven of traditional Burgundian cooking arrived on the scene with a bang in the fall of 1998, with none other than three-star chef Bernard Loiseau (formerly of Saulieu) at the helm. This is a satisfying bastion of comfort food, pure and simple. Tried-and-true winners include sauté of mushrooms and snails, braised beef with caramelized carrots, or sole Tante Louise, which is served on a bed of *duxelle* mushrooms. The wine list is fittingly focused on Burgundian vintages.

*41 rue Boissy d'Anglas, 8e (☎ **01/42-65-06-85**). **Métro:** Concorde or Madeleine. **Reservations:** 10 days ahead. **Prix-Fixe Menus:** 190F ($34). AE, DC, MC, V. **Open:** Mon–Fri lunch and dinner.*

Au Trou Gascon
$$$$. Bastille (11e). SOUTHWESTERN FRENCH.
One of the most deservedly acclaimed chefs in Paris today, Alain Dutournier dazzles diners at this one-star restaurant with creative dishes from his native Gascony, a region in southwest France. The list of starters might include

fresh duck foie gras, oysters, warm foie gras-and-potato paté, warm paté of cèpe mushrooms and parsley, and Gascony cured ham cut from the bone. Main dishes include the best cassoulet served in Paris, succulent duck breast, and a superb roast Chalosse chicken.

40 rue Taine, 12e (☎ 01/43-44-34-26). **Métro:** *Daumesnil.* **Reservations:** *1 week ahead.* **Prix-Fixe Menus:** *Lunch 190F ($34); dinner 285F ($51). AE, DC, MC, V.* **Open:** *Mon–Fri lunch and dinner, Sat dinner only. Closed Aug and between Christmas and New Year.*

Ah, C'est Romantique!

L'Ambroisie (Le Marais, $$$$$)
La Bastide Odéon
(St-Germain-des-Prés, $$$)
Café de Vendôme (Louvre, $$$)
La Fontaine de Mars (Eiffel
Tower & Invalides, $$$)
Restaurant du Palais-Royal
(Louvre, $$$)

Trumilou
$. Le Marais. TRADITIONAL BISTRO.

One of the most deservedly popular budget haunts near Paris's Town Hall, Trumilou invites with a reassuringly rustic decor and a fantastic view of Notre Dame. The menu of hearty fare rarely changes, nor does it need to. Specialties include chicken Provençal, duckling with plums, stuffed cabbage, and a very good *blanquette* of veal in white sauce. Desserts are good and service is helpful.

84 quai de l'Hôtel-de-Ville, 4e (☎ 01/42-77-63-98). **Métro:** *Hôtel-de-Ville.* **Reservations:** *1 day ahead.* **Prix-Fixe Menus:** *65F ($12) and 80F ($14). MC, V. Open: Daily lunch and dinner.*

Kids Le Vieux Bistro
$$$. The Islands (4e). LYONNAIS.

Despite its touristy location in the shadow of Notre Dame, this lace-curtained old bistro still manages to preserve its good old-style cooking and authenticity. Bypass the dozen-or-so flanking souvenir stands, and then settle into one of two old-time dining rooms for flavorful stalwarts like sausage with potato salad, beef *bourguignon*, and a dessert of *tarte Tatin*, the celebrated upside-down caramelized apple pie.

14 rue du Cloître-Notre-Dame, 4e (☎ 01/43-54-18-95). **Métro:** *Cité.* **Reservations:** *Not necessary.* **Prix-Fixe Menus:** *200F ($36). MC, V.* **Open:** *Daily lunch and dinner.*

Le Violon d'Ingres
$$$$. Eiffel Tower & Invalides (7e). MODERN BISTRO.

Celebrity chef Christian Constant (formerly of Les Ambassadeurs restaurant at the Hôtel Crillon) created a sensation with gastronomes when he stepped out on his own. This comfortable and infinitely intimate restaurant is decked out with lots of warm, rose-colored wainscoting and elegant chintz fabrics patterned with old English tea roses. This eatery is truly a labor of love for Constant, who clearly throws his energies into every dish, be it elaborate fare or simple favorites like roast chicken with French fries. Dishes range from delicious roasts (veal in creamy milk sauce served with tender spring vegetables, mouthwatering leg of lamb with fresh garlic and thyme) to more elegant creations (lobster ravioli with crushed vine-ripened tomatoes). There's a copious and well-chosen selection of wine to accompany the meal, scrumptious desserts, and service that's charming and discreet. When Chef Constant leaves the kitchen at the end of the meal to greet diners, it's a chance to shake hands with one of France's best.

*135 rue St. Dominique, 7e (☎ 01/45-55-15-05). **Métro:** Ecole-Militaire or RER Pont de l'Alma. **Reservations:** 2 weeks ahead. **Prix-Fixe Menus:** Lunch 240F ($43); dinner 290F ($52) and 400F ($71). AE, MC, V. **Open:** Tues–Sat lunch and dinner. Closed Aug.*

Willi's Wine Bar
$$. Louvre (1er). WINE BISTRO.
An engaging hybrid between a wine bar and a bistro, Willi's is a *très* fashionable address owned by a pair of Brits who rank among the most knowledgeable oenophiles in Paris. Come for the warm ambiance and the modern bistro fare that's stylish without ever slipping to the merely faddish. The menu changes often, but you can expect dishes such as roast cod with eggplant marmalade, sautéed lamb with herbs, or terrine of guinea hen. The wines are, of course, excellent.

*13 rue des Petits-Champs, 1er (☎ 01/42-61-05-09). **Métro:** Pyramides. **Reservations:** 3 days ahead. **Prix-Fixe Menus:** Lunch 145F ($26); dinner 180F ($32) and 195F ($35). MC, V. **Open:** Mon–Sat lunch and dinner.*

Yvan Sur Seine
$$. Louvre (1er). TRADITIONAL BISTRO.
Celebrity chef Yvan's late-night bistro is a smashing success with in-vogue night owls in search of a meal. The food is satisfyingly hearty, the mood upbeat and party-minded. Try the stuffed eggplant or the steak with sautéed potatoes, which is served up against a lively disco soundtrack.

*26 quai du Louvre, 1er (☎ 01/42-36-49-52). **Métro:** Louvre Rivoli. **Reservations:** 1 day ahead. **Prix-Fixe Menus:** 140F ($24). MC, V. **Open:** Daily lunch and dinner, and late-night until 4am.*

Chapter 11

Light Bites & Munchies

Dining out in French restaurants is fabulously civilized, but there will be times when you just won't want to sit down to a full three-course meal or devote 2 hours to doing it. That's what makes this chapter so essential.

Nothing makes you feel more like an insider than knowing where to head for a quick bite—maybe just a salad, sandwich, or burger—or a snack to munch on while you stroll around. It's also extremely handy to know of a few fabulous cafes and wine bars, for when you want to kick back and indulge in the fine arts of conversation and people-watching. The establishments recommended here cover street food, fast food, and sit-down eateries where you can get in and out in under an hour (that's a lightning quick meal by French standards). And lastly, if you're blessed with fabulous weather, you've come to the right place—I'll tell you where to buy tasty picnic provisions.

Street Food in Paris

The quintessential French street food is the *crêpe*—a thin pancake served with just about any sweet filling you can imagine, from sugar to chocolate to cream to strawberries. Near most of the main sightseeing attractions and all along the rue de Rivoli between the Marais and place de la Concorde, you'll find street carts selling crêpes with sugar or whipped cream for about 7F each ($1.25). Some also sell sugared *gaufres*, or Belgian-style waffles.

If you buy a crêpe from a street vendor, the list of available fillings is often very limited. For more variety, grab a sit-down meal for under 40F ($7) at any of the city's ubiquitous crêperies. Aside from regular crêpes, the menu will also feature an assortment of *galettes*—buckwheat crêpes served with savory items like cheese or ham. Try *la forestière*—sautéed mushrooms, scrambled eggs, garlic, and chives. The city is full of good crêperies, but here are a few stand-outs:

Kids Amid the Latin Quarter's many tourist trap eateries, **Crêperie des Arts,** 27 rue St-André-des-Arts, 6e (☎ **01/45-44-89-39;** Métro: St-Michel), and **Crêperie de Cluny,** 20 rue Harpe, 5e (☎ **01/43-26-08-38;** Métro: St-Michel), both offer a wide selection of excellent crêpes and *galettes*.

Kids One of Montmartre's great budget addresses, **Lepic Assiette**, 35 rue Lepic, 18e (☎ **01/42-55-95-95;** Métro: Abbesses), offers a terrific-value two-course lunch menu for 55F ($10), featuring a salad, crêpes, and Breton cider.

Coming in a close second in the street-food popularity contest is the ***panini,*** a sandwich on Italian-style bread that's filled with mozzarella, basil, and sundried tomatoes—or another combination of Mediterranean ingredients—then flattened as it's grilled between two hot plates. Panini are cheap and usually very tasty and available *everywhere* in Paris.

Tourist Traps

The Latin Quarter between the river and Boulevard St-Germain could be called Little Athens, a pedestrian-friendly labyrinth of tiny *ruelles* chock-a-block with perpetually tanned men loudly heralding the merits of their kebabs. Rue de la Huchette and Rue de la Harpe, in particular, are thick with Greek joints, but bargain-hunters should think twice before entering for a sit-down meal. These eateries lure you with cheap menus, only to zap you later with overpriced beverages and other hidden extras. You're better off getting a kebab to go from one of the neighborhood's street vendors.

Quick Bites Near the Louvre

Hip minimalist-meets-Renaissance decor, voguish clientele, and an unparalleled view of I. M. Pei's glass pyramid are all reasons to head to the **Café Marly,** Cour Napoléon du Louvre (museum's courtyard), 1er (☎ **01/49-26-06-60;** Métro: Palais-Royal or Louvre-Rivoli). The quality of the international-inspired fare can be somewhat inconsistent, but you won't go wrong with the club sandwich or the excellent Caesar or warm goat cheese salads. Salads and main dishes: 50–85F ($9–$15). Nonmeal hours are best for nursing a coffee on the terrace and people-watching.

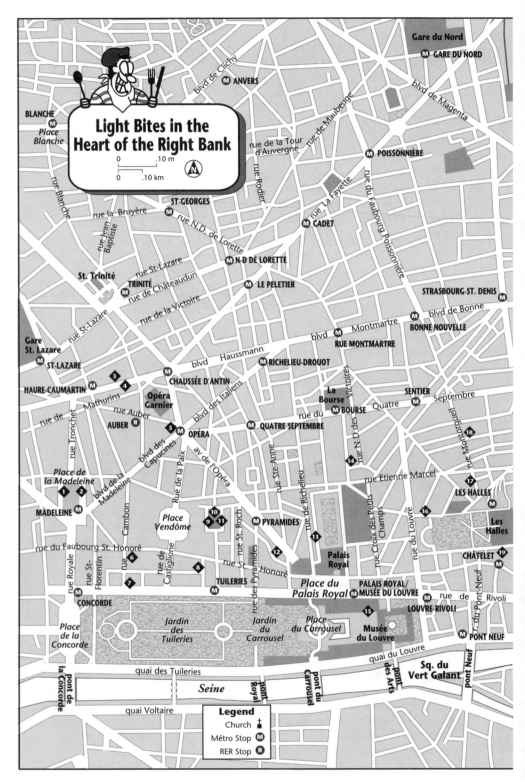

Light Bites in the
Heart of the Right Bank

0   .10 m
0   .10 km

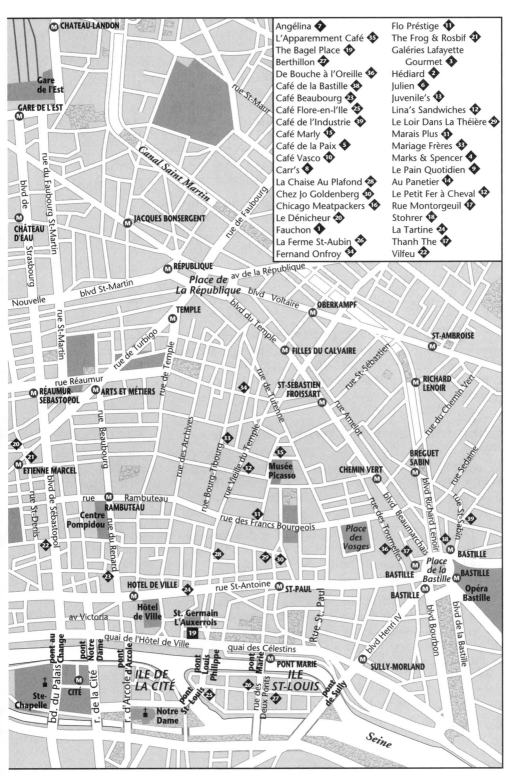

Angélina **7**
L'Apparement Café **35**
The Bagel Place **19**
Berthillon **27**
De Bouche à l'Oreille **36**
Café de la Bastille **38**
Café Beaubourg **23**
Café Flore-en-l'Ile **25**
Café de l'Industrie **39**
Café Marly **15**
Café de la Paix **5**
Café Vasco **10**
Carr's **8**
La Chaise Au Plafond **28**
Chez Jo Goldenberg **30**
Chicago Meatpackers **16**
Le Dénicheur **20**
Fauchon **1**
La Ferme St-Aubin **26**
Fernand Onfroy **34**

Flo Préstige **11**
The Frog & Rosbif **21**
Galéries Lafayette
   Gourmet **3**
Hédiard **2**
Julien **6**
Juvenile's **13**
Lina's Sandwiches **12**
Le Loir Dans La Théière **29**
Marais Plus **31**
Mariage Frères **33**
Marks & Spencer **4**
Le Pain Quotidien **9**
Au Panetier **14**
Le Petit Fer à Cheval **32**
Rue Montorgeuil **17**
Stohrer **18**
La Tartine **24**
Thanh The **37**
Vilfeu **22**

155

For delectably different fast food for under 35F ($6), head two blocks north of the Tuileries Gardens, to the place du Marché-St-Honoré, 1er (Métro: Tuileries). **Café Vasco,** at No. 38, (☎ **01/42-60-47-15**) serves delicious Basque-style sandwiches, salads, paella, *tortillas* (Spanish omelettes), and a heavenly foie gras sandwich. **Le Pain Quotidien,** at No. 18, (☎ **01/42-96-31-70**) is one of the city's best bakeries. At mealtimes you can order one of the yummy *tartines* (open-face sandwiches), made with combos like mountain ham and Gruyère cheese; beef, basil, and Parmesan; country terrine; goat cheese and honey; or fromage blanc, radishes, and onions.

Also just a stone's throw from the museum, **Lina's Sandwiches,** 7 av. de l'Opéra, 1er (☎ **01/47-03-30-29**; Métro: Palais-Royal) serves up made-to-order, deli-style sambos on a half dozen different kinds of breads. Ask for yours on a *pavé* (thick, whole grain pitalike square).

Kids A half-dozen blocks west of the Louvre, **The Bagel Place,** 6 place Ste-Opportune, 1er (☎ **01/40-28-96-40**; Métro: Châtelet) is a mecca for homesick Yankee expats, offering a dozen kinds of New York–style bagels and a blackboard full of yummy bagelwiches.

Kids With a model train that choo-choos above diners' heads and waiters who break periodically for line dancing, **Chicago Meatpackers,** 8 rue Coquillière, 1er (☎ **01/42-36-70-13**; Métro: Les Halles), is a fun place to come for spareribs and burgers worthy of the Windy City. Average main dish: 50F ($9).

Chomping on the Champs–Elysées

Kids Ensconced on the top floor of the Virgin Megastore, the **Virgin Café,** 52 av. Champs-Elysées, 8e (☎ **01/49-53-50-00**; Métro: Franklin D. Roosevelt), is a forever fashionable spot for lunch or a light afternoon snack. The menu is a trendy mix of salads, light pasta dishes, and elegant sandwiches, and there's a great view overlooking the avenue. Average dish: 50F ($9).

Kids Two branches of **Lina's Sandwiches** (see above) are located just off the Champs, at 8 rue Marbeuf, 8e (☎ **01/47-23-92-33**; Métro: Alma Marceau), and 105 rue du Faubourg St-Honoré, 8e (☎ **01/42-56-42-57**; Métro: St-Philippe-du-Roule).

Kids The avenue boasts a trio of Yankee-style burger joints serving main dishes that average 55F ($10): **Chesterfield Café,** 124 rue La Boétie, 8e (☎ **01/42-25-18-06**; Métro: Franklin D. Roosevelt), does decent renditions of Tex-Mex platters, burgers, and barbecued ribs. **Chili's,** 1 rue Washington, 8e (☎ **01/42-89-87-87**; Métro: George V), is good for burgers, salads, Tex-Mex dishes, and Philly steak sandwiches. And **Planet Hollywood,** 78 av. des Champs-Elysées, 8e (☎ **01/53-83-78-27**; Métro: George V), epitomizes the everything-but-the-kitchen-sink formula theme eatery, from Tex-Mex to pizza to a zillion incarnations of the burger.

Munch Time in the Marais

A few steps from the Musée Picasso, **L'Apparemment Café,** 18 rue des Coutures-St-Gervais, 3e (☎ **01/48-87-12-22;** Métro: Sébastien-Froissart), feels homey thanks to comfy leather armchairs, dim lights, and personable bric-a-brac. You can use the ingredients checklist on the lunch menu to concoct your own salad or choose from among the light *plats du jour.* Average dish: 50F ($9).

Thanh The, 24 rue des Tournelles, 4e (☎ **01/42-72-53-37;** Métro: Bastille), is a good-value Vietnamese joint known for its great noodle soups and *boulettes de porc,* tiny balls of minced pork that you roll in rice pancakes and dunk in peanut sauce. The set lunch menu is only 68F ($11). Closed for lunch Monday and all day Sunday.

Make Mine Kosher

Feel like noshing on some corned beef, pastrami, schmaltz herring, dill pickles, or bagels with a schmear? Head to **rue des Rosiers,** Paris's main hub of kosher eating, smack in the middle of the Marais (Métro: St-Paul). You can munch on deli fare as you roam, or pop into one of the eateries that offer sit-down meals, including **Chez Jo Goldenberg,** 7 rue des Rosiers, 4e (☎ **01/48-87-20-16**), where the *carpe farcie* (stuffed carp) is outstanding and the beef goulash a fine runner-up.

Snacking in St-Germain

Ever since it opened in the stunning Emporio Armani boutique, **Caffe Emporio Armani,** 149 bd. St-Germain, 6e (☎ **01/45-48-62-15;** Métro: St-Germain-des-Prés), has been a sensation with Left Bank fashionmongers. Dishes are Italian, minimalist, and delicious (mixed antipasti, four-cheese ravioli), if overpriced. Still, it's fun for a chic lunch break if you're hitting the St-Germain shops. Average main dish: 75F ($13). Open daily for lunch, except Sunday.

Also popular with the modish shopping crowd is **Guen Mai,** 2 bis rue de l'Abbaye, 6e (☎ **01/43-26-03-24;** Métro: St-Germain-des-Prés), an upmarket vegetarian delicatessen with a tiny restaurant in the back. Both serve the usual salads, quiches, and tofu dishes, as well as *tempura* and veggie fritters. Average dish: 80F ($14). Closed Sundays.

Kids A good spot for a relatively cheap, U.S.–style feed is **Coffee Parisian,** 4 rue Princesse, 6e (☎ **01/43-54-18-18;** Métro: Mabillon), which has a knack for cheeseburgers, omelettes, Italian-style sandwiches, and salads made with rocket, the leafy green *du jour.* Average main dish: 55F ($10).

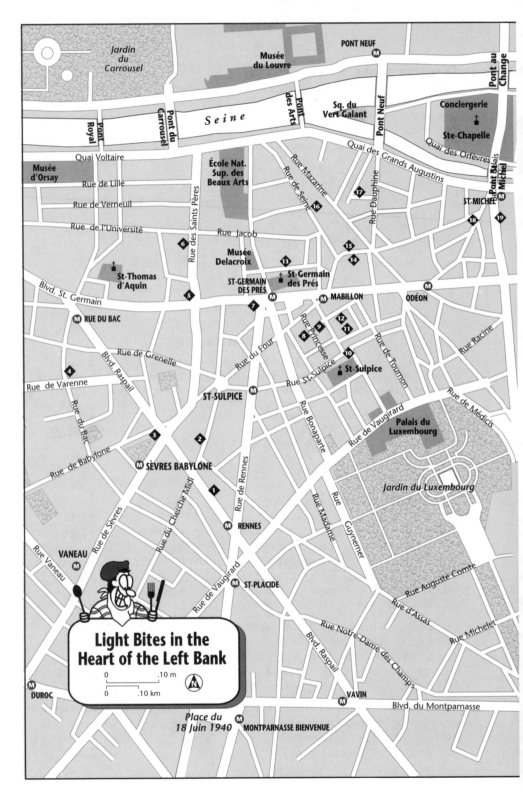

Light Bites in the
Heart of the Left Bank

0   .10 m
0   .10 km

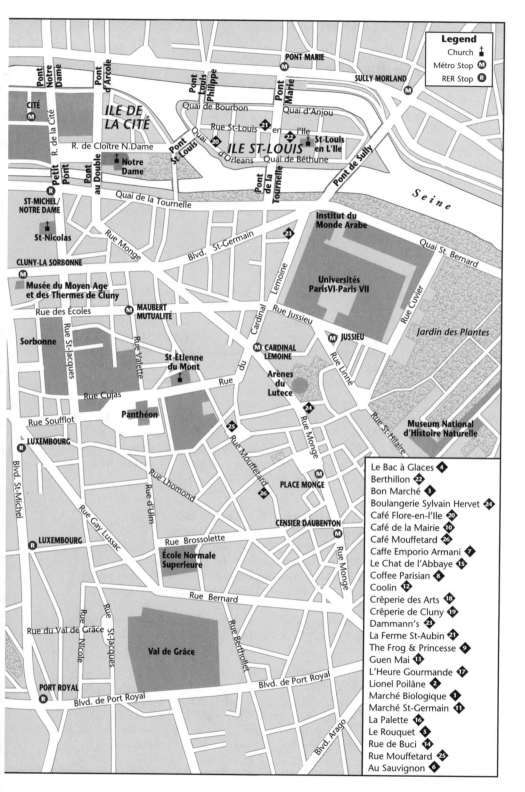

Legend
Church ✝
Métro Stop Ⓜ
RER Stop Ⓡ

PONT MARIE

SULLY MORLAND

Pont Notre Dame
Pont d'Arcole
CITÉ
Ⓜ
ILE DE LA CITÉ
R. de la Cité
Pont louis Philippe
Quai de Bourbon
Quai d'Anjou
Rue St-Louis **21** en l'Ile
22
St-Louis en L'Ile ✝
ILE ST-LOUIS
20
Quai d'Orleans
Quai de Béthune
Pont de Sully
Pont Louis
R. de Cloître N.Dame
Pont St-Louis
Pont au Double
Petit Pont
Notre Dame ✝
Pont de la Tournelle

ST-MICHEL/ NOTRE DAME
St-Nicolas ✝
Quai de la Tournelle
Seine

Rue Monge
Blvd. St-Germain
23
Institut du Monde Arabe
Quai St. Bernard

CLUNY-LA SORBONNE
Musée du Moyen Age et des Thermes de Cluny
Rue des Écoles
MAUBERT MUTUALITÉ Ⓜ
Lemoine
Rue Jussieu
Universités ParisVI-Paris VII
Rue Cuvier
Jardin des Plantes

Sorbonne
Rue St-Jacques
Rue Valette
St-Étienne du Mont ✝
CARDINAL LEMOINE Ⓜ
Rue du Cardinal
JUSSIEU Ⓜ
Rue Linné
Rue Cujas
Arènes du Lutece
Rue St-Hilaire
Museum National d'Histoire Naturelle
Panthéon
Rue Soufflot
24

LUXEMBOURG Ⓡ
25
Rue Mouffetard
PLACE MONGE Ⓜ
Rue Monge
Blvd. St-Michel
Rue Lhomond
Rue d'Ulm
26
CENSIER DAUBENTON Ⓜ
LUXEMBOURG Ⓡ
Rue Brossolette
École Normale Superieure
Rue Gay Lussac
Rue Bernard
Rue Nicole
Rue St-Jacques
Val de Grâce
Rue Berthollet
Rue Monge

PORT ROYAL Ⓡ
Rue du Val de Grâce
Blvd. de Port Royal
Blvd. de Port Royal
Blvd. Arago

Storming the Bastille

You gotta love a place named for a bathroom attendant. **La Dame Pipi,** 9 rue de Charonne, 11e (☎ **01/48-05-05-83;** Métro: Bastille) dishes out good-size salads and simple *plats du jour* (pastas, roast chicken) from 11am to 1am, backed by a blues soundtrack. Average dish: 50F ($9).

With its faux baroque interior crammed with original oil paintings, the hiply nostalgic **Café de l'Industrie,** 16 rue St-Sabin, 11e (☎ **01/47-00-13-53;** Métro: Bastille or Breguier-Sabin), is a hit with creative types in fashion and show biz. It's a great place to sample different wines, but if you're hungry, you can order one of the good *plats du jour*—perhaps beef bourguignon, fried haddock, or tagliatelle flavored with salmon, chives, and cream sauce. Dishes: 48–85F ($9–$15). Closed Saturdays.

Ab Fab Pub Grub

The Frog & Rosbif, 116 rue St-Denis, 2e (☎ **01/42-36-34-73;** Métro: Etienne-Marcel), and its Left Bank sister, **The Frog & Princess,** 9 rue Princesse, 6e (☎ **01/40-51-77-38;** Métro: Mabillon), are English-style micro-breweries serving good real ales (try the "Dark de Triomphe") as well as authentic pub grub like shepherd's pie and stuffed potato skins. On Sunday afternoons from August through May, you can catch English Premiership football matches live via satellite (ahem, that's soccer to the Yanks). Open daily 11am to 2am.

When you want to get your Irish up, **Carr's,** 1 rue du Mont-Thabor, 1er (☎ **01/42-60-60-26;** Métro: Concorde), and, on the Left Bank, **Coolín,** 15 rue Clément, 6e (☎ **01/44-07-00-92;** Métro: Mabillon), pull decent pints of Guinness and serve Hibernian treats like smoked salmon, lamb stew with mint, and fruit crumbles. Open daily noon to 2am.

A Cuppa Tea...And Yummy Cakes, Too

The Marais has two fabulous places to break for tea. The more elegant of the two is **Mariage Frères,** 30 rue Bourg-Tibourg, 4e (☎ **01/42-72-28-11;** Métro: Hôtel-de-Ville), an institution venerated by ladies-who-lunch that offers 500 blends of tea and a large array of classic French cakes and pastries. Decked out with deep armchairs, **Le Loir Dans La Théière,** 3 rue de Rosiers, 4e (☎ **01/42-72-90-61;** Métro: St-Paul), attracts the trendy, laid-back crowd. The menu is limited but includes scrumptious apple crumble, raspberry cheesecake, lemon pie, chocolate fondant, and pear charlotte. Closed Monday.

Set just a few blocks from the Champs-Elysées on one of the city's most luxurious shopping streets, **Dalloyau,** 101 rue du Faubourg St-Honoré, 8e (☎ **01/42-99-90-00;** Métro: St-Philippe-du-Roule), may be best known as the chocolatier and pastry shop that serves the nearby Elysée Palace and Rothschild mansions, but the upstairs tea room is a lovely place for an elegant snack. Specialties include the Mogador—a medley of chocolate cake, chocolate mousse, and a fine layer of raspberry jam.

Trendsetting Shops-n-Snacks

One phenomenon gaining steam in Paris is the emergence of *les restos-bazars*—great little boutiques that also serve fare that's elegant but inexpensive. They make particularly fun places to break from sightseeing or shopping.

➤ **Le Dénicheur,** 4 rue Tiquetonne, 2e (☎ **01/42-21-31-01;** Métro: Etienne Marcel), is a coffeehouse, secondhand clothing shop, library, and antiques dealer all rolled into one. Come for the petits plats like turkey with honey and hazelnut, homemade quiches, and a selection of excellent desserts.

➤ **Marais Plus,** 20 rue des Francs-Bourgeois, 4e (☎ **01/48-87-01-40;** Métro: Hôtel-de-Ville), is a colorful stationery shop-cum-toy-store-cum-tea-room that serves up tasty quiches (three cheese, salmon-and-spinach) and yummy desserts (cheesecakes, crumbles) for a pittance.

➤ **De Bouche à Oreille,** 15 rue des Tournelles, 4e (☎ **01/44-61-07-02;** Métro: St-Paul), is a secondhand Marais antiques shop. You can dine on light appetizers like foie gras salad or desserts such as hazelnut cake.

➤ **L'Entre-Pot,** 13 rue de Charonne, 11e (☎ **01/48-06-57-04;** Métro: Ledru-Rollin), is the sort of place that makes the Bastille district such a funky and fun neighborhood. Until 2am, you can eat (excellent pastas from 40F/$7), have a drink (try the Money Mint, made with scotch, mint, and honey), or rifle through racks of secondhand clothes (big on up-and-coming labels). But wait, there's more: On Wednesday and Friday, there are tarot card readings for 200F ($36); and on Wednesday and Saturday, you can have a manicure for 80F ($14), a haircut for 210F ($37), or a shiatsu facial massage for 150F ($27).

In bustling St-Germain-des-Prés, **L'Heure Gourmande,** 22 passage Dauphine, 6e (☎ **01/46-34-00-40;** Métro: Odéon), is a peaceful refuge that serves over 40 flavors of tea and delectable homemade desserts, from tarts to cakes to chocolates.

Kids You Scream, I Scream

No trip to the Ile St-Louis is complete without a visit to the no-doubt-about-it best ice cream parlor in Paris. **Berthillon,** 31 rue St-Louis-en-l'Ile, 4e (☎ **01/43-54-31-61;** Métro: Cité or Sully-Morland) still keeps up its artisanal quality despite an ever-increasing production. There are some 20 flavors, all of them endowed with the signature fine, creamy texture that brings aficionados to nirvana. On a warm Sunday afternoon, the lines can stretch around the block. Closed Monday and Tuesday.

Smack between the Pompidou Center and Les Halles, **Vilfeu,** 3 rue de la Cossonerie, 1er (☎ **01/40-26-36-40;** Métro: Les Halles) offers homemade *glace* in dozens of flavors ranging from the classic to the imaginative. For the kids, there's a flavor called "cowboy," a high-octane blend of toffee, peanut, popcorn, and cola.

In Montmartre, head to **La Butte Glacée,** 14 rue Norvins, 18e (☎ **01/42-23-91-58;** Métro: Lamarck-Caulaincourt), just off the Place du Tertre, for an Italian-inspired pick-me-up: espresso and a scoop of strawberry, licorice, or *stracciatella* (vanilla with chocolate flakes) 'scream.

When you're in the Latin Quarter, grab a seat on the outdoor terrace of **Dammann's,** 20 rue du Cardinal-Lemoine, 5e (☎ **01/46-33-61-30;** Métro: Cardinal-Lemoine), and cool off with a sundae that replicates an artist's palette using Italian ices of raspberry, mango, passion fruit, and black currant.

Just up the road from the Bon Marché department store on the Left Bank, **Le Bac à Glaces,** 109 rue du Bac, 7e (☎ **01/45-48-87-65;** Métro: Sèvres-Babylone), makes its ice cream with all-natural ingredients. Sit down for a sundae or take away a cone.

Where to Watch the World Go By

For many travelers, this is the most essential section of this entire book: where to people-watch, shoot the breeze, read a newspaper, write a few postcards, soak up the city's atmosphere, or just plain kick back. In spite of the general categories below, the line between cafes and wine bars is very nicely blurred, so you can order your beverage of choice at either type of establishment.

The Best Hot Chocolate in Paris

Kids The runner-up for the city's best cup of *chocolat chaud* is **Angélina,** 226 rue de Rivoli, 1er (☎ **01/42-60-82-00;** Métro: Concorde), a celebrated tearoom near the Louvre. But when only the very best will do, head to the **Café Flore-en-l'Ile,** 42 quai d'Orléans, 4e (☎ **01/43-29-88-27;** Métro: Cité or Sully-Morland), on the Ile St-Louis and its unbeatable view of Notre Dame's flying buttresses. The cafe's ultraaddictive hot chocolate arrives in two generous pots—one containing melted chocolate and the other frothy steamed milk—which you blend according to your own taste.

Cafes You Wish Would Move to Your Hometown

Overlooking the Pompidou Center's esplanade, **Café Beaubourg,** 100 rue St-Martin, 4e (☎ **01/48-87-63-96;** Métro: Rambuteau or Hôtel-de-Ville), has a chic minimalist decor by award-winning architect Christian de Portzamparc (just check out the bathrooms) and one of the best-positioned outdoor terraces in the city—an ideal place from which to watch the young and the restless pass by. Great coffee, soothing flavored teas, and tasty desserts.

The darling of the Latin Quarter is **Café Mouffetard,** 116 rue Mouffetard, 5e (☎ 01/43-31-42-50; Métro: Censier-Daubenton), on the lively market street of the same name. It's so popular that it recently expanded following its appearance in the film *Three Colors: Blue.*

Time-Savers

Cafes tend to hold long hours—usually from 8am to 1am—and wine bars generally open their doors from about noon to 2am.

In St-Germain-des-Prés, the vote is split between three lovely sidewalk cafes. **La Palette,** 43 rue de Seine, 6e (☎ 01/43-26-68-15; Métro: Mabillon), is a gorgeous turn-of-the-century artists' haunt with an exceptionally pretty outdoor terrace. It draws a winning mix of students, art dealers, and glamorous locals. **Café de la Mairie,** 8 place St-Sulpice, 6e (☎ 01/43-26-67-82; Métro: St-Sulpice), has an enviable terrace overlooking the lion-guarded fountain on the Place St-Sulpice and is a favorite meeting place for students, shoppers, and intellectuals. **Le Rouquet,** 188 bd. St-Germain, 7e (☎ 01/45-48-06-93; Métro: St-Germain-des-Prés), is less than 50 yards from the more celebrated, more touristed, and more expensive triumvirate of the Café de Flore, the Café aux Deux-Magots, and the Brasserie Lipp (see "Hemingway's Favorite Haunts," in chapter 14). The decor hasn't changed since a remodeling in 1954, so it still has a kitschy wavy ceiling, wacky wall sconces, and neon, but its ideally positioned sidewalk terrace makes for some of the best people-watching in the city.

The terrace at **Café de la Paix**, place de l'Opéra, 9e (☎ 01/40-07-30-20; Métro: Opéra), is so well placed that Parisians say if you sit here long enough, you'll see someone you know pass by. It's grandiose and fashionable, but service is sometimes brusque and the clientele is an anonymous mix of business folk and shoppers. Great coffee, but stay away from the overpriced food.

Café de la Bastille, 8 place de la Bastille, 12e (☎ 01/43-07-79-95; Métro: Bastille), is a 24-hour cafe whose front terrace is a great late-night perch for watching the constant parade of trendy young revelers pass through the place de la Bastille.

Undeniably Fab Wine Bars

The congenial duo of Brits that owns **Willi's Wine Bar** and **Macéo** (see chapter 10) also runs **Juveniles,** 47 rue Richelieu, 1er (☎ 01/42-97-46-49; Métro: Palais-Royal), a dapper place near the Louvre in which to hang out with a glass of good wine and to nibble on snacks. Closed Sundays.

When you're in the Marais, **La Chaise Au Plafond,** 10 rue du Trésor, 4e (☎ 01/42-76-03-22; Métro: Hôtel-de-Ville), and its older sister, **Le Petit Fer à Cheval**, 30 rue Vieille-du-Temple, 4e (☎ 01/42-72-47-47; Métro:

Hôtel-de-Ville), are both terrific spots for kicking back with a well-priced glass of wine and a taster plate of cheese or marinated olives. Nearby, **La Tartine,** 24 rue de Rivoli, 4e (☎ 01/42-72-76-85; Métro: Hôtel-de-Ville), has nicotine-stained walls, surly waitresses, Turkish toilets, and a blackboard menu where wines average 12F ($2) a glass. In other words, what's not to love? The place is caught in a time warp, which is why it appeals to elderly regulars, poverty-stricken students, and chic fashion plates alike.

The hippest wine bar in Montmartre is **Le Sancerre,** 35 rue des Abbesses, 18e (☎ 01/45-58-08-20; Métro: Abbesses). It has a mermaid on the ceiling and a band of cosmopolitan devotees who snatch up all the outside tables, the better to soak up the scene.

With a great address on a lively market street in the middle of the Left Bank, **Le Chai de l'Abbaye,** 28 rue de Buci, 6e (☎ 01/43-26-68-26; Métro: Odéon), is a convivial corner wine bar that draws a mixed crowd of locals and tourists. **Au Sauvignon,** 80 rue des St-Pères, 7e (☎ 01/45-48-49-02; Métro: Sèvres-Babylone), is strategically nestled in the midst of chic St-Germain designer shops and art galleries. The specialty of the house is its *tartines,* open-face sandwiches made with bread from the nearby Poîlane bakery. Near Les Invalides, **Café Thoumieux,** 4 rue de la Comète, 7e (☎ 01/45-51-50-40; Métro: Latour-Maubourg), is a sizzling, southern inspired setting for good wines and excellent tapas.

⭐Kids⭐ How to Pull Together a Parisian Picnic

A bottle of Bordeaux, a crusty baguette, some fresh fruit, a wedge of cheese, and a few delicious pastries to top it all off. Far from being a budget fallback, picnicking in Paris can be as fun and unforgettable as a meal in the finest restaurant—and for a fraction of the cost. Here's where to stock up on provisions:

Food Markets

Nowhere in Paris is far from a street market, which is by far the best place to find French produce and cheeses of excellent quality. No self-respecting foodie would miss out on either the food or this authentic reflection of Parisian society. Markets are generally open Tuesday to Saturday from 8am to 1pm and 4pm to 7pm, and on Sunday mornings. You can ask your hotel staff to direct you to the nearest *marché,* or hunt out these city highlights:

➤ **Rue Montorgeuil,** 1er (Métro: Châtelet). The numerous sidewalk cafes make this a great morning hangout.

➤ **Rue Mouffetard,** 5e (Métro: Monge). There's an accordion-led sing-along on Sunday mornings. Touristy but fun.

➤ **Rue de Buci,** 6e (Métro: Mabillon). Another wonderfully lively, if somewhat touristy, market.

➤ **Marché St-Germain,** 6e (Métro: Mabillon). In the center of this mini-mall, dominated by GAP, you'll find a terrific covered produce market.

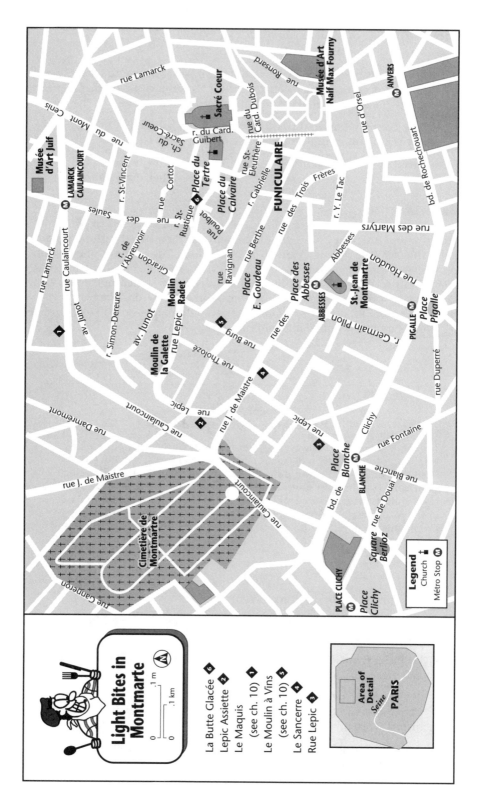

Light Bites in Montmartre

La Butte Glacée 6
Lepic Assiette 2
Le Maquis
  (see ch. 10) 1
Le Moulin à Vins
  (see ch. 10) 5
Le Sancerre 4
Rue Lepic 3

Legend
Church ✝
Métro Stop Ⓜ

Area of
Detail
Seine
PARIS

Musée d'Art
Naïf Max Fourny

ANVERS Ⓜ

Sacré Coeur

FUNICULAIRE

Place du
Tertre 6

Place du
Calvaire

Musée d'Art Juif

LAMARCK
CAULAINCOURT Ⓜ

Place des
Abbesses

ABBESSES Ⓜ

St.-Jean de
Montmartre

PIGALLE Ⓜ

Place
Pigalle

Moulin
Radet

Moulin de
la Galette

Place
E. Goudeau

Cimetière de
Montmartre

Place
Blanche

BLANCHE Ⓜ

Square
Berlioz

PLACE CLICHY Ⓜ

Place
Clichy

➤ **Marché Biologique,** boulevard Raspail between rue du Cherche-Midi and rue de Rennes, 6e (Métro: Rennes). An all-organic market featuring green grocers, winemakers, butchers, and bakers.

➤ **Rue Cler,** 7e (Métro: Ecole-Militaire). The most chi-chi market in the city is a haunt of diplomats' wives.

➤ **Rue Lepic,** 18e (Métro: Abbesses). This evocative, winding Montmartre street is lined with food shops rather than stalls.

Bakeries

In residential neighborhoods, you'll find a *boulangerie* (bakery) or *pâtisserie* (pastry shop) on every corner, but the quality of their bread varies considerably. The best bakeries are given away by the long line of locals queuing up on weekend mornings. You can get a sandwich or a slice of quiche to go, but be forewarned that, compared to American delis, the French make very plain sandwiches—often just a slice of meat and some cheese on a baguette with no lettuce, tomato, mayonnaise, or other accoutrement—so you might prefer to simply buy fresh ingredients and dress your own.

Branching Out, Bread-wise

The classic **baguette** is always a winner for sandwich-making, but a picnic is a great opportunity to try a delicious alternative: **fougasse,** a crusty flat loaf filled with onions and herbs; **pain de campagne** (a.k.a. **pain à l'ancienne, pain rustique,** or **pain paysanne**), a country-style, whole-wheat loaf with a thick crust; **pain aux six céréales,** multigrain bread; **pain de seigle,** a dense, small rye loaf; **pain d'épice,** spiced bread with honey; **pain au levain,** a chewy sourdough loaf; or **pain noir,** a dark-colored loaf made with rye and buckwheat.

Here are some of the best bakers in central Paris:

➤ **Julien,** 75 rue St-Honoré, 1er (Métro: Concorde). Open Monday through Saturday.

➤ **Le Pain Quotidien,** 18 place du Marché-St-Honoré, 1er (Métro: Tuileries). Also serves great sandwiches at mealtime. Open daily.

➤ **Stohrer,** 51 rue Montorgeuil, 1er (Métro: Châtelet). Opened by the pastry chef of Louis XV in 1730, with an interior classified as a national historic treasure. Open daily.

➤ **Au Panetier,** 10 place des Petits-Pères, 2e (Métro: Bourse). Open Monday through Friday.

➤ **Fernand Onfroy,** 34 rue de Saintonge, 3e (Métro: République). Open Monday through Friday and Saturday morning.

➤ **Boulangerie Sylvain Hervet,** 69 rue Monge, 5e (Métro: Monge). Great sourdough loaves and crusty *pain paillasse*. Open Tuesday through Sunday.

➤ **Lionel Poîlane,** 8 rue du Cherche-Midi, 6e (Métro: Sèvres-Babylone). France's most famous baker, known for his huge, round, coarse sourdough loaves. Open Monday through Saturday.

➤ **La Fontaine de Mars,** 112 rue St-Dominique, 7e (Métro: Ecole-Militaire). A traditional baker that still uses a wood oven, which produces bigger air holes in the bread. Open Monday through Saturday.

➤ **Jean-Luc Poujauran,** 20 rue Jean Nicot, 7e (Métro: RER Invalides). A great pioneer of organic bread. His delectable loaves are cooked with olives, thyme, figs, apricots, or anchovies. The mini loaves are especially picnic-friendly and portable. Open Tuesday through Saturday.

➤ **Réné Gérard St Ouen,** 111 bd. Haussmann, 8e (Métro: St-Augustin). His loaves are made from a secret recipe featuring flour from Chartres and olive oil from Provence. They make particularly great souvenirs, since they're baked in various shapes, from the Eiffel Tower to fish. Open Monday through Saturday.

Revenge of the Doughboys

The image of a Frenchman with a baguette under his arm isn't just a cliché. Just how seriously do the French take their bread? Injustice in the bread biz made national headlines when a 1997 law enforced a new order of French bread-makers. Up until then, the neighborhood *boulangerie* that baked its own bread was differentiated neither from the supermarket *boulangerie* that got its mass-produced baguettes from a factory nor from the black-sheep *boulangerie* that merely reheated—*mais non!*—frozen baguettes. Thousands of traditional bakers revolted, lawmakers listened, and now every French bakery has to deserve its title.

Before it can hang out the *boulangerie* shingle, a bakery must choose its own flour, make the dough, and bake the bread on the premises. This lets the public know what it's buying. One easy way to tell a homemade baguette from a frozen loaf: Homemade bread should be cream-colored with air holes that are uneven; frozen baguettes are often too white, with air holes that are suspiciously uniform. Also, a real *boulangerie artisanale* will have a plaque on the back wall verifying that it merits this title.

Deli-Style Food Shops

Look on storefront signs for the word *traiteur*, which designates a food shop with ready-made meat and pasta dishes and plenty of salads to go. The city's most famous *traiteurs* are the gourmet temples **Fauchon** and **Hédiard,** both at place de la Madeleine, 8e (Métro: Madeleine; see chapter 15). But every neighborhood has at least several good *traiteurs*, so keep your eyes peeled and ask your hotel staff for recommendations.

Flo Prestige, 42 place due Marché-St-Honoré, 1er (Métro: Pyramides), is a well-respected food shop and caterer offering everything you need for a fabulous feast, from foie gras and Norwegian smoked salmon to fancy breads to cheese to wine. Open daily.

On the Ile St-Louis, **La Ferme St-Aubin,** 76 rue St-Louis-en-L'Ile, 4e (Métro: Pont Marie), offers a fine selection of cheeses, foie gras, and champagne. Closed Sunday.

Rollet Pradier, 32 rue de Bourgogne, 6e (Métro: Assemblé Nationale), is a *traiteur*-cum-*boulangerie* with a fancy sandwich counter and a tearoom upstairs. Ask for the specialties of the house: the hand-rolled *flûte Rollet* and, on Fridays, the *boule de levain*, sourdough bread made with very little yeast and a 48-hour fermentation. Closed Sunday and Monday.

Some department stores have excellent *traiteurs*. Head to **Galéries Lafayette Gourmet,** 40 bd. Haussmann, 9e (Métro: Havre-Caumartin), and **Bon Marché,** 22 rue de Sèvres, 7e (Métro: Sèvres-Babylone; go to Ground Floor, Building 2), for wonderfully fresh produce, a huge selection of high-quality gourmet foods, large wine sections, and long *traiteur* counters with salads to go. Both stores are closed Sunday.

For ready-to-go picnic-makings like fresh sandwiches, packaged snacks, fresh fruit and veggies, and wine, make a beeline to the food section (*alimentation*) at either branch of the British department store **Marks & Spencer,** 35 bd. Haussmann, 9e (Métro: Havre-Caumartin), and 88 rue de Rivoli, 4e (Métro: Hôtel-de-Ville). This place is an enormous hit with Parisians. Closed Sunday.

Supermarkets & Dime Stores

All the French supermarket chains (Franprix, Champion, G-20) and dime stores (Prisunic, Monoprix) have branches throughout the city and are generally the cheapest places to pick up sliced deli-style meats, fruit, yogurt, cheese, bread, and other picnic makings. You'll find, however, that quality is higher at smaller, neighborhood produce markets, bakeries, and traiteurs. Supermarkets and dime stores are closed Sunday.

Part 5

Ready, Set, Go! Exploring Paris

Now that you've arrived, found a bed, and filled your belly, it's high time you saw the city. This section of the book is dedicated to helping you do just that.

There are so many tempting things to see in Paris that you'll never squeeze them all into one trip. Even lifetime residents haven't seen and done it all. So the first order of business is to prioritize sights and tailor your days to suit your interests.

First, toss aside that list of sights that "everyone's supposed to see." Life, not to mention your trip, is way too short to do what you're supposed to. Do what you want. Not interested in modern art? No problem—why waste your time traipsing around museums you don't like? Or maybe you love sculpture but hate Renaissance paintings. Or maybe all you really want to do is shop and eat. So be it; this city has something for everyone, so take advantage of what appeals to you.

Later in this section you'll find several recommended daylong itineraries that take in a number of major sights without being too regimented. If these plans don't suit your needs, the last chapter is a step-by-step guide to building your own itineraries.

Chapter 12

Should You Take a Guided Tour?

In This Chapter

➤ The lowdown on Paris orientation tours

➤ Walking tours

➤ In-depth art tours and lectures

➤ River cruises

➤ Two-wheeled tours: Paris by bike

Tours come in all shapes and sizes. At one end of the spectrum are the soup-to-nuts escorted group tours, such as those mentioned in chapter 3, where all the hassles (and decisions) are handled by someone else. But if you take pride in being an independent traveler, several alternatives are available.

There are many good reasons for spending a smaller part of your vacation time on a guided tour. A tour that only takes up an afternoon or day of your holiday is much less of a commitment, and thus less of a risk. If this is your first time in Paris, an orientation tour can help you quickly get a grip on the city's geography. And even if you've been coming to Paris for 25 years, a well-executed walking or architecture tour can introduce you to sides of the city you never knew existed.

The make-or-break factor in any guided tour is, of course, the guide. Some have an encyclopedic knowledge of their subject but drone on like school-marms, others are downright ill informed. But when you're lucky enough to be shown around by a resident whose enthusiasm makes the city come to life, it can be the high point of your entire trip.

Tourist Traps

Something to watch out for is a tour that's **too multilingual.** If a guide has to give her spiel in French, English, German, Japanese, Spanish, and Italian, she's going to be forced to speed–talk her way through a bare–bones commentary devoid of a single interesting anecdote. Whenever possible, stick to tours where the commentary is limited to just one or two languages.

Orientation Tours: Getting the Lay of the Land

Orientation tours show you around the city while pointing out various places of interest. The idea is to give you a sense of the city's layout, so it makes sense to take an orientation tour at the beginning of your trip—preferably on the first or second day. Wait later than that, and you'll probably already have seen a number of sights on the tour.

Minivan tours are intimate but not worth their hefty fares, which can run into the thousands of francs ($200 and up). The most popular and best-value orientation excursions are bus tours. The two biggest operators are **Paris Vision** (☎ 01/42-60-31-25), and **Cityrama** (☎ 01/44-55-61-00), both of whose tours cost 150F ($27) and cover all the main tourist sights in 2 hours, with recorded commentary in various languages. The downside for both of these tours is that you can't get off the bus.

Better than both is the **Paris Bus** (☎ 01/42-30-55-50), a London-style double-decker. A complete tour costs 125F ($22) and lasts 2 hours and 15 minutes with commentary in French and English (some tours have more languages, so choose carefully). You can pick up the bus at nine stops: Trocadéro, Eiffel Tower, Champ de Mars, Louvre, Notre Dame, Musée d'Orsay, Opéra Garnier, Arc de Triomphe/Champs Elysées, and Grand Palais. The beauty of the Paris Bus is that you can get off it as often as you like to see the sights, then reboard and continue the tour over a period of 2 days.

But best of all is the brand new **OpenTour** bus, an open-top double-decker that's especially fun in good weather. Like the Paris Bus, the whole tour lasts 2 hours and 15 minutes with commentary in French and English, and you can jump on and off as many times as you want within a 2-day period. The winning factor here is that there are more stops. You can buy your ticket from the bus driver: 135F ($24) for adults, 70F ($13) for kids 4 to 12, and free for under-4s. Pick up the OpenTour between 10am and 6pm at any of 16 stops in central Paris, including Place de la Madeleine, Palais Royal (3 avenue de l'Opéra), Louvre (Place du Carrousel), Notre Dame (6 rue de la Cité), Luxemburg Gardens (4 Place Edmond Rostand), Place St-Germain-des-Prés,

Musée d'Orsay, Place de la Concorde, three stops on the Champs-Elysées (at rue Marigny, rue de la Boétie, and avenue George V), Trocadéro (bottom of gardens), Eiffel Tower, and the esplanade in front of Les Invalides. The OpenTour bus is technically part of the public transit system, so for more information call the Paris Tourist Office (☎ **01/49-52-53-54**).

Walking Tours

The most comprehensive walking tours in Paris are given through **WICE**, 20 bd. du Montparnasse, 15e (☎ **01/45-66-75-50;** fax 01/40-65-96-53; e-mail wice@wice-paris.org) a nonprofit cultural association dedicated to Paris's English-speaking community. These are in-depth tours for travelers who want more than the usual skim-the-surface tour. In a recent month WICE's tours included "Archaeology at Work: Roman Paris," "Famous Women of the Left Bank," "The Royal Squares of Paris: From Place des Victoires to Place Vendôme," and "Marais Art Gallery Walk." Guides are experts in their fields and the commentary is always excellent.

The tours vary in length and cost but most run between 110F ($20) and 150F ($27) for a 2- or 3-hour tour. And while pricier than some other tours, WICE's walks have an unbeatable endorsement—they're so popular with Paris residents that you'll need to book a few weeks ahead if you want a place. The easiest way to peruse WICE's course offerings and reserve your place is by contacting the Web site at **www.wice-paris.org**.

Paris Walking Tours (☎ **01/48-09-21-40**) is a popular English-language outfit whose guided walks cost 60F ($11) a pop—about half as much as WICE's. Some tours concentrate on a single neighborhood (Montmartre, Le Marais), others are geared to a theme (art nouveau, Hemingway's Paris), and still others focus on a single sight (Les Invalides, the Panthéon, Sainte-Chapelle, Paris Sewers). There's at least one tour given every day of the week and you can just show up at the designated starting place without booking ahead.

Paris Contact (☎ **01/42-51-08-40**) also offers 2-hour guided walks built around themes (In Jefferson's Footsteps, The Origins of Paris) or neighborhoods (St-Germain-des-Prés, Le Marais, Montmartre). These preset tours cost 60F ($11) per person and don't have to be booked in advance—just call and ask for the full program to be faxed to your hotel. If you have a particular interest, this company can design a customized tour for you with 48 hours advance notice. The made-to-order tours have a two-person minimum and cost 80F ($14) per person.

In-Depth Art Tours & Lectures

Again, the best player in the field is **WICE** (see phone number above) for their in-depth coverage and expert speakers. Prices for WICE's 2-hour art tours are in line with the walking tours. In a recent month art tours included "Food and Its Symbolism at the Louvre," "Pompidou Collection at Musée d'Art Moderne," and "Discover the French Art Auction." Check out the Web site (**www.wice-paris.org**) for a program of courses to be offered when you'll be in town.

River Cruises

Nobody should leave Paris without seeing the city from the Seine. River cruises are orientation tours in the sense that you'll suffer through sketchy commentary but get an unparalleled look at the city's riverside buildings and monuments. The three largest companies that run boat trips are virtually interchangeable in terms of the length of their cruises (1 hour), the quality of their commentaries (mediocre), and their routes (passing all the same sights). The difference in price is also negligible, so you should just take the one with the handiest location.

Dollars & Sense

Don't opt for an overpriced lunch and dinner cruise, but do take a night cruise. The Seine is at its most dramatic when the street lamps reflect on the water and all the monuments are illuminated with spotlights.

Bateaux Parisiens, Pont d'Iéna, 7e (☎ **01/44-11-33-44**) departs from 9am to 10:30pm from the bridge right beneath the Eiffel Tower and charges 50F ($9) per person. **Vedettes du Pont Neuf,** Square du Vert Galant, 1er (☎ **01/46-33-98-38**) departs from 9am to 10:30pm from the Ile de la Cité and also charges 50F ($9). **Bateaux Mouches,** Pont de l'Alma, 8e (☎ **01/42-25-96-10**) departs from the Right Bank (at the end of avenue Montaigne) from 10am to 10:30pm and charges 40F ($7).

The Boat That Thinks It's a Bus

Another great way to see riverside Paris is aboard the **Bat-o-bus** (☎ **01/ 44-11-33-44**), a floating shuttle service without commentary. There are five stops: Trocadéro, Musée d'Orsay, Louvre, Notre Dame, and Hôtel de Ville. You can take it one stop for 12F ($2), but it's much more fun to buy a full-day ticket for 65F ($12) and jump on and off at whim.

Paris on Wheels

Paris has become more ecologically minded in recent years, and bike lanes are now ubiquitous throughout the city. **Paris à Vélo, C'est Sympa** (Paris By Bike, It's Nice), 37 bd. Bourdon, 4e (☎ **01/48-87-60-01**) runs 3-hour bicycle tours through various parts of the city with an English-language commentary rich in interesting anecdotes. Tours cost about 170F ($30) per person, including bike rental.

Bike 'n' Roller, 6 rue St-Julien-le-Pauvre, 5e (☎ **01/44-07-35-89**) rents out in-line skates at 25F ($4) per hour or 75F ($13) per day. Its affiliate, **Paris on Blades** (same address and phone number), meets at the store for blade-running guided tours of the Latin Quarter and St-Germain-des-Prés, given by a bilingual American former ice-skating champ.

Chapter 13

Paris's Top Sights A to Z

In This Chapter

➤ Attractions indexed by location and type

➤ Full write-ups of all the top attractions in town

➤ Your personal "greatest hits" list

➤ A worksheet for making your choices

This chapter starts off with indexes that list the city's top 20 sights by location and by type (museums, parks, churches, and so on). What follows is a succinct review of each sight, giving you the lowdown on when to go, how to get there, and why it's worth seeing in the first place.

Even after whittling down Paris's myriad attractions to only 20 sights, that's still probably more than you'll be able to do in a single trip. That's where the Complete Idiot's fool-proof system comes in. The first step: Grab a pen and, in the margin next to each review, rank each sight from 1 to 5 depending on your interest level. If you wouldn't be happy leaving Paris without seeing a sight, give it a 1. If another sight leaves you lukewarm, give it a 3. Put a 5 next to any sight in which you have no interest at all.

At the end of this chapter is a worksheet where you can plot your sights according to rank. Chapter 16 outlines six very doable itineraries, each of which takes in several top sights. And chapter 17 gives you pointers on how to create your own itineraries logically without ping-ponging all over the city.

Time–Savers

Use the location index to help you plan your itineraries. After visiting, say, the Musée d'Orsay, consult the index to find out what other major sights are nearby.

Quick Picks: Paris's Top Attraction at a Glance
Index by Location

The Right Bank

Louvre (1er)

Jardin du Palais-Royal

Jardin des Tuileries

Musée du Louvre

Le Marais & The Islands (3e, 4e)

Musée Picasso

Notre Dame

Place des Vosges

Sainte-Chapelle

Champs-Elysées (8e, 16e)

Arc de Triomphe

Champs-Elysées

Musée d'Art Moderne de la Ville de Paris

Musée Jacquemart-André

Further Afield

Montmartre (18e)

Père Lachaise Cemetery (20e)

Sacré-Coeur (18e)

The Left Bank

Latin Quarter (5e)

Panthéon

St-Germain-des-Prés (6e)

Jardin et Palais du Luxembourg

Eiffel Tower & Invalides (7e)

Eiffel Tower

Hôtel des Invalides (Napoléon's Tomb)

Musée d'Orsay

Musée Rodin

Index by Type of Attraction
Museums

Musée d'Art Moderne de la Ville de Paris

Musée Jacquemart-André

Musée du Louvre

Musée d'Orsay

Musée Picasso

Musée Rodin

Churches

Notre Dame

Sacré-Coeur

Sainte-Chapelle

Parks

Jardin du Palais-Royal

Jardin des Tuileries

Jardin et Palais du Luxembourg

Place des Vosges

Monuments & Architecture

Arc de Triomphe

Champs-Elysées

Eiffel Tower

Hôtel des Invalides (Napoléon's Tomb)

Panthéon

Neighborhoods

Montmartre

Cemeteries

Père-Lachaise

Dollars & Sense

If you're up for intensive sightseeing, the **Carte Musées et Monuments** is a terrific value. It gives you entry to 70 museums and monuments and—a real plus—lets you jump the lines. The cost is 80F ($14) for a one-day pass, 160F ($29) for a three-day pass, and 240F ($43) for a five-day pass. To find out if it'll save you money, add up the admissions fees for the museums you plan to see, and then compare prices. You can buy the card at participating museums, principal Métro and RER stations, and the Paris Tourist Office at 127 av. des Champs-Elysées.

The Top Sights

Kids Arc de Triomphe
Champs-Elysées (8e).

Sure, Napoléon's triumphal arch packs a big punch of French history. But the real thrill is the panoramic view from its 163-foot-high observation deck. Commissioned by the emperor in 1806 to commemorate his own victories, it now symbolizes both the thrill of victory and the agony of defeat. The memory of German troops marching under the arch in World War II still makes the French wince. Today the arch houses the Tomb of the Unknown Soldier. Allow an hour to visit.

Place Charles de Gaulle-Etoile, 8e. ☎ *01/43-80-31-31. Web site: www.smartweb.fr/visits/arcdetriomphe/index.html.* **Métro:** *Charles de Gaulle-Etoile.* **Bus:** *22, 30, 31, 52, 73, 92. Then take underground passage to arch.* **Open:** *Apr–Sept daily 9:30am–10pm; Oct–Mar daily 10am–10:30pm.* **Admission:** *35F ($6.25) adults, 23F ($4.10) ages 12–25, free for under-12s.*

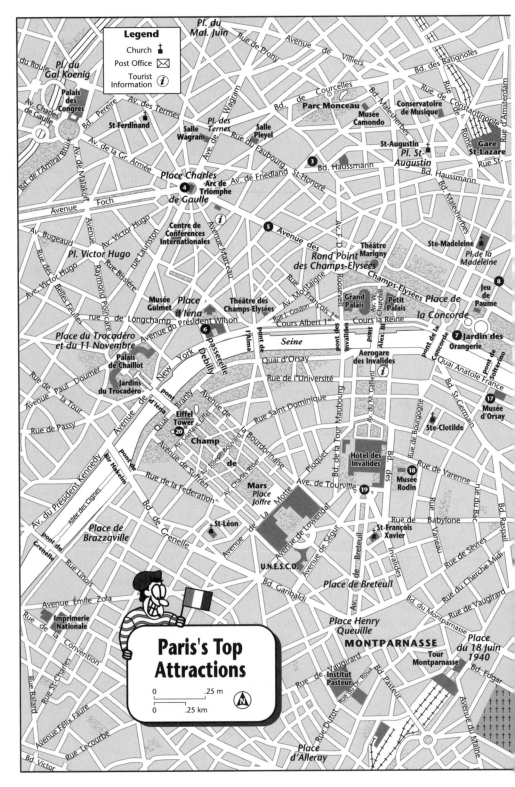

Paris's Top Attractions

0 .25 m
0 .25 km

Tourist Traps

When leaving the Métro to visit the Arc de Triomphe, don't even *think* about exiting to the street and confronting the kamikaze traffic at Place Charles-de-Gaulle. There's an underground passage that goes right to the Arc—use it and live to tell about it.

Kids Champs-Elysées

Champs-Elysées (8e).

If you were in Paris the night that France won the 1998 World Cup, you understand what the Champs-Elysées means to the French. As about one million singing, flag-waving Parisians spilled into the avenue, it was said that the country hadn't experienced such group euphoria since the heady days following the liberation in World War II. The scene is most vibrant on a Friday or Saturday night, with the masses lining up for the numerous cinemas and floodlights illuminating the Arc de Triomphe and Place de la Concorde at either end. Restaurants consist mainly of standard cafes and American-style burger joints (Planet Hollywood, Chili's, McDonald's), with the upscale Ladurée tearoom a notable exception. Shopping runs the full gamut from the very luxe (Louis Vuitton, Yves Saint Laurent) to chain stores you'd find in malls. For young kids, there's the ever-popular Disney Store. Most stores are closed on Sundays; an exception is the Virgin Megastore. Any day of the week, the avenue is a great place to see English-language films with French subtitles; just look for "V.O." (*version originale*) on movie posters and cinema schedules. Allow an hour to walk from top to bottom (or vice versa), longer if you want to shop, eat, or dawdle.

Runs from the Arc de Triomphe to the Place de la Concorde, 8e. **Métro:** *Concorde, Champs-Elysées Clémenceau, Franklin D. Roosevelt, George V, Charles de Gaulle-Etoile.* **Bus:** *Many lines cross it, but only the 73 travels its entire length.*

Kids Eiffel Tower

Eiffel Tower & Invalides (7e).

You could fill an entire page with fun trivia about Paris's most enduring symbol. For starters, it weighs 7,000 tons, soars 1,056 feet high, and is held together with 2.5 million rivets. And when Gustave Alexandre Eiffel designed the structure for the Exhibition of 1889, his plans spanned 6,000 square yards of paper. But forget the numbers. Just stand underneath the tower and look straight up through a funnel of steel lacework shooting into the sky. Or better yet, go to the top for a view that reaches 40 miles away on a clear day. Allow 2 hours: one to line up for the elevator and another to take in the panorama. Lines are shorter first thing in the morning, but the view is most magical at night.

What About the Pompidou Center?

Any other year and the **Pompidou,** France's National Museum of Modern Art would be right up there with these other top sights. But don't bother visiting until it reopens in January 2000, following extensive renovations. (The few parts of the museum still open aren't worth the Métro fare.) Until Y2K, you can catch the Pompidou's fabulous collection of 20th-century art at the **Musée d'Art Moderne de la Ville de Paris** (see below).

Champ-de-Mars, 7e. ☎ *01/44-11-23-23 or 01/44-11-23-45. Web site: www.smartweb.fr/visits/eiffel/index.html.* **Métro:** *Ecole-Militaire, Bir-Hakeim, RER Champ-de-Mars.* **Bus:** *42, 69, 82, 87.* **Open:** *Sept–May daily 9:30am–11pm; June–Aug daily 9am–midnight. In fall and winter the stairs are open only until 6:30pm.* **Admission:** *First landing 20F ($4), second landing 42F ($8), third landing 59F ($11). Stairs to second floor 14F ($3). Entry for kids ages 4–12 ranges from 11F ($2) to 30F ($5), free for under-4s.*

Memorial to a Princess

The August 1997 auto accident that killed Diana, Princess of Wales happened in a tunnel just under the **Place de l'Alma,** where a smaller replica of the Statue of Liberty's bronze flame stands. The flame was a 1987 gift to the city by the *International Herald Tribune* to honor Franco-American friendship. Many visitors still come to lay bouquets and messages around the flame, which has become a shrine to the Princess. Take the Métro to Alma-Marceau and you can't miss it.

Hôtel des Invalides (Napoléon's Tomb)
Eiffel Tower & Invalides (7e).
Louis XIV had this mammoth "invalids' hotel" built (1671–1676) as a military hospital and retirement home for soldiers who'd been injured in battle. After the Eiffel Tower, the gilded dome of Les Invalides is the second-tallest monument in Paris. Though much of the building now houses the Musée de l'Armée—a tediously comprehensive display of war paraphernalia through the centuries—the main attraction here is Napoléon's Tomb, displayed smack underneath the dome in the church (go past the museum to the rear of the building). First buried at St. Helena, Napoléon's remains were returned by the

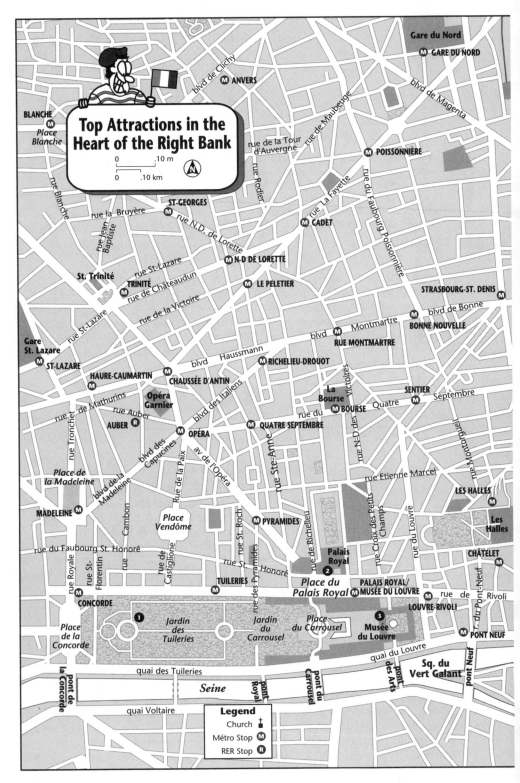

Top Attractions in the Heart of the Right Bank

0   .10 m

0   .10 km

Gare du Nord

Ⓜ GARE DU NORD

blvd de Magenta

blvd de Clichy

Ⓜ ANVERS

rue de Maubeuge

BLANCHE

Ⓜ

Place Blanche

rue de la Tour d'Auvergne

Ⓜ POISSONNIÈRE

rue de la Tour d'Auvergne

rue Rodier

rue La Fayette

rue du Faubourg Poissonnière

rue Blanche

ST-GEORGES

rue la Bruyère

Ⓜ

rue N.D. de Lorette

Ⓜ CADET

rue Jean Baptiste

rue St-Lazare

Ⓜ N-D DE LORETTE

STRASBOURG-ST. DENIS

St. Trinité

TRINITÉ

Ⓜ

rue de Châteaudun

Ⓜ LE PELETIER

Ⓜ

rue St-Lazare

rue de la Victoire

blvd de Bonne

Ⓜ

BONNE NOUVELLE

Gare St. Lazare

blvd Montmartre Ⓜ

Ⓜ ST-LAZARE

blvd Haussmann

RUE MONTMARTRE

Ⓜ RICHELIEU-DROUOT

HAURE-CAUMARTIN

Ⓜ

rue de Mathurins

CHAUSSÉE D'ANTIN

La Bourse

SENTIER

rue Auber

Opéra Garnier

blvd des Italiens

Ⓜ BOURSE

Quatre

Septembre

Ⓜ

rue N-D des Victoires

AUBER Ⓡ

blvd des Capucines

Ⓜ OPÉRA

Ⓜ QUATRE SEPTEMBRE

rue du Quatre

rue Tronchet

rue de la Paix

av de l'Opéra

rue Ste-Anne

rue Etienne Marcel

Place de la Madeleine

blvd de la Madeleine

rue Croix des Petits Champs

LES HALLES

Ⓜ

Cambon

Place Vendôme

Ⓜ PYRAMIDES

rue de Richelieu

Les Halles

MADELEINE Ⓜ

rue du Louvre

CHÂTELET

Ⓜ

rue du Faubourg St. Honoré

rue de Castiglione

rue St. Roch

rue St. Honoré

Palais Royal

②

Place du Palais Royal

LOUVRE-RIVOLI

rue Royale

rue St-Florentin

rue de Pyramides

TUILERIES

Ⓜ

PALAIS ROYAL/ MUSÉE DU LOUVRE Ⓜ

Ⓜ rue de Rivoli

rue du Pont-Neuf

CONCORDE

Ⓜ

①

Jardin des Tuileries

Jardin du Carrousel

Place du Carrousel

③

Musée du Louvre

Ⓜ **PONT NEUF**

Place de la Concorde

quai du Louvre

Sq. du Vert Galant

Pont Neuf

pont de la Concorde

quai des Tuileries

pont Royal

pont du Carrousel

pont des Arts

Seine

quai Voltaire

Legend

Church ⛪

Métro Stop Ⓜ

RER Stop Ⓡ

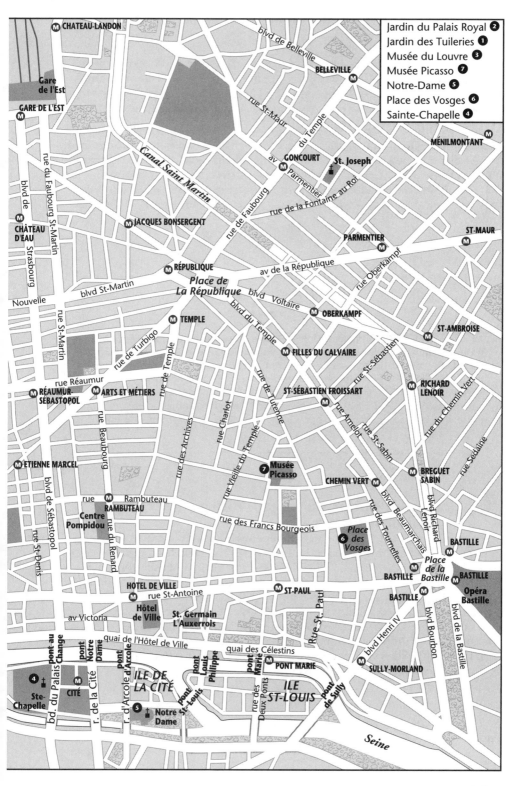

Jardin du Palais Royal ❷
Jardin des Tuileries ❶
Musée du Louvre ❸
Musée Picasso ❼
Notre-Dame ❺
Place des Vosges ❻
Sainte-Chapelle ❹

CHATEAU-LANDON

blvd de Belleville

BELLEVILLE

Gare
de l'Est

GARE DE L'EST

rue St-Maur

MÉNILMONTANT

Canal Saint Martin

rue du Faubourg St-Martin

blvd de Strasbourg

av GONCOURT
av Parmentier

St. Joseph

rue de la Fontaine au Roi

du Temple

CHÂTEAU
D'EAU

rue de Faubourg

JACQUES BONSERGENT

PARMENTIER

ST-MAUR

RÉPUBLIQUE

av de la République

rue Oberkampf

Place de
La République

blvd St-Martin

blvd Voltaire

OBERKAMPF

Nouvelle

rue St-Martin

TEMPLE

blvd du Temple

ST-AMBROISE

rue de Turbigo

FILLES DU CALVAIRE

rue Réaumur

rue de Temple

rue St-Sébastien

RÉAUMUR-
SÉBASTOPOL

ARTS ET MÉTIERS

ST-SÉBASTIEN FROISSART

RICHARD
LENOIR

rue Beaubourg

rue des Archives

rue Charlot

rue de Turenne

rue Amelot

rue St-Sabin

rue du Chemin Vert

blvd Richard Lenoir

rue Sédaine

ETIENNE MARCEL

Musée
Picasso ❼

BREGUET
SABIN

blvd de Sébastopol

rue St-Denis

rue Rambuteau RAMBUTEAU

rue Vieille du Temple

CHEMIN VERT

blvd Beaumarchais

Centre
Pompidou

rue du Renard

rue des Francs Bourgeois

Place
des
Vosges ❻

rue des Tournelles

BASTILLE

HOTEL DE VILLE

rue St-Antoine

ST-PAUL

Place
de la
Bastille

BASTILLE

BASTILLE

av Victoria

Hôtel
de Ville

St. Germain
L'Auxerrois

BASTILLE

Opéra
Bastille

quai de l'Hôtel de Ville

rue St-Paul

blvd Henri IV

blvd Bourbon

blvd de la Bastille

pont au Change

pont Notre Dame

quai des Célestins

pont Marie

PONT MARIE

SULLY-MORLAND

bd. du Palais

pont d'Arcole

pont Louis Philippe

ILE DE
LA CITÉ

Ste-
Chapelle ❹ †

CITÉ

r. de la Cité

r. d'Arcole

pont St-Louis

rue des Deux Ponts

ILE
ST-LOUIS

pont de Sully

Notre
Dame ❺ †

Seine

183

English in 1840 upon Louis-Philippe's request. The funeral procession befitted France's greatest military hero, passing under the Arc de Triomphe and down the Champs-Elysées before entering Les Invalides. Almost lampooning the small stature of the man, the tomb is done on a gargantuan scale.

Place des Invalides, 7e. ☎ *01/40-49-48-14. Web site: www.smartweb.fr/visits/ invalides/index.html.* **Métro:** *The closest stops are Latour-Maubourg, Varenne, and RER Invalides, but Champs-Elysées Clémenceau affords a more dramatic approach if you cross the gilded Alexander III bridge on foot.* **Bus:** *63, 83, 93.* **Open:** *Oct–Mar daily 10am–5pm; Apr–Sept daily 10am–6pm. Napoléon's Tomb is open until 7pm June–Sept.* **Admission:** *37F ($7) adults, 27F ($5) ages 12–18, free for under-12s.*

Tourist Traps

West of the city, in alignment with the Louvre, Champs-Elysées, and Arc de Triomphe, lies **La Défense,** the closest thing Paris has to a compact business district. The tourist board likes to bill it as a "futuristic showcase for architecture and engineering," which must be French for "a bunch of skyscrapers." Except for the view from the top of the *Grande Arche,* there's nothing to interest out-of-towners. Few Parisians live among the steel, glass, and concrete, and those who do come, come to work. Unless you've seen everything else first, give it a miss.

Kids Jardin et Palais du Luxembourg
St-Germain-des-Prés (6e).

With its elegant statues, abundance of benches, and formal gravel paths, this Left Bank haven is *the* quintessential Paris park. The French don't use their parks for rowdy recreation, so you won't see any ultimate Frisbee or touch football here—it's even forbidden to walk on the grass. If that turns you off, consider that there are also tennis courts, *pétanque* pitches, pony rides, puppet shows, and a hexagonal pool made expressly for sailing little toy boats that you can rent. Marie de Médicis ordered an Italianate palace built on the site in 1612 but didn't get to stay for long. She was forced into exile by her son, Louis XIII, when he discovered that she was plotting to overthrow him. The palace remained in royal hands until the 1789 revolution, and today it houses the French Senate.

Main entrance at corner of bd. St-Michel and rue de Médicis, 6e. **Métro:** *Odéon, RER Luxembourg, RER Port Royal.* **Bus:** *38, 82, 84, 85, 89.* **Open:** *daily, dawn to dusk.*

Jardin du Palais-Royal
Louvre (1er).
Cardinal Richelieu ordered the Royal Palace built in 1630 as his personal residence, complete with grounds landscaped by the royal gardener. Today the palace is no longer open to the public, but its statue-filled gardens remain one of the most restful public spaces in the city. The square is ringed by restaurants, art galleries, and specialty boutiques, and is also home to the Comédie Française.

*Place Palais-Royal, 1er. **Métro:** Palais-Royal. **Bus:** 21, 48, 72, 81, 95. **Open:** daily, dawn to dusk.*

◆Kids Jardin des Tuileries
Louvre (1er).
The city's most formal gardens originally ran between the Louvre and the Tuileries Palace, which was burnt down during the 1871 Paris Commune. In keeping with the French style of parks, trees are planted according to orderly design and the sandy paths are arrow straight. During the summer, a small fair features an enormous Ferris wheel (affording fabulous views), a splash-making flume and other rides, ice-cream stands, and arcade-style games. Kids of all ages love it. Come for a stroll before or after visiting the Louvre.

*Entrances on rue de Rivoli and Place de la Concorde, 1er. **Métro:** Concorde or Tuileries. **Bus:** 42, 69, 72, 73, 94. **Open:** daily, 7:30am–dusk.*

Montmartre
Right Bank, Further Afield (18e).
After visiting the Sacré-Coeur and the touristy-but-fun Place du Tertre, where mediocre artists set up their easels and hock their wares, wander down the hill and you'll stumble upon surprisingly unspoiled lanes, quiet squares, ivy-clad shuttered houses with gardens, and even Paris's only vineyard. Together, it all creates a sense of the rustic village still apart from the churning metropolis below. Take the Métro to Abbesses, and admire the evocative Place des Abbesses (a popular backdrop for movies) before taking the funicular to the top of the *butte*. Don't dine on the hilltop; the eating is better and cheaper just a few hundred yards downhill.

Time-Savers
If it's Tuesday, it must *not* be the Louvre. When planning your daily itineraries, keep in mind that most museums are closed either Monday or Tuesday. And remember that the vast majority of stores are closed on Sundays, with the exception of those in the Marais.

Musée d'Art Moderne de la Ville de Paris
Champs-Elysées (8e).
Normally this museum wouldn't be included among Paris's greatest hits, but this year is different. Most of the museum's regular collection has been temporarily replaced by the Pompidou Center's fabulous collection of modern art, whose breadth and quality is challenged only by MOMA in New York. Allow 2 hours to view the paintings and sculptures from 1905 to 1965, including key works by Matisse, Cézanne, Chagall, Picasso, Léger, Kandinsky, Derain, and Braque.

11 av. du Président Wilson, 16e. ☎ *01/53-67-40-00; Web site: www.musexpo.com/ english/amp/index.html.* **Métro:** *Alma-Marceau or Iéna.* **Bus:** *42, 63, 72, 80, 92.* **Open:** *Tues–Fri 10am–5:30pm, Sat–Sun 10am–6:45pm.* **Admission:** *27F ($5), 14F50 ($3) ages 18–25, free for under-18s.*

Art in a Nutshell

If you love...	Then don't miss...
Renaissance Art	Louvre
	Musée Jacquemart-André
Impressionism	Musée d'Orsay
	Musée de l'Orangerie (see chapter 14)
	Musée Marmottan (see chapter 14)
Modern Art	Musée d'Art Moderne de la Ville de Paris
	Musée Picasso
Sculpture	Musée Rodin
	Musée d'Orsay
	Louvre
	Père Lachaise cemetery

Musée Jacquemart-André
Champs-Elysées (8e).
This paradise for Renaissance art fans is worth visiting as much for a glimpse of how moneyed Parisians lived in the 19th century as for its Italian and Flemish masterpieces by Bellini, Botticelli, Carpaccio, Uccello, Rubens, Rembrandt, and van Eyck. The opulent townhouse and art collection belonged to Edouard André and his wife, Nélie Jacquemart, who scoured Europe amassing their now-priceless trove. Allow an hour to visit the museum, then take a break in what was Madame's lofty-ceilinged dining room, now a classy tearoom serving light lunches and snacks.

158 bd. Haussmann, 8e. ☎ *01/42-89-04-91. Web site: www.musexpo.com/english/ jacquemart/index.html.* **Métro:** *St-Philippe-du-Roule.* **Bus:** *28, 32, 49, 80.* **Open:** *daily, 10am–6pm.* **Admission:** *46F ($8), 33F ($6) ages 7–25, free for under-7s.*

Time-Savers

To make the most of your Louvre visit, go when the museum is quietest, first thing in the morning or during evening hours. Avoid the massive lines outside the pyramid by using the **rue de Rivoli/Carrousel du Louvre** entrance.

Musée du Louvre
Louvre (1er).

With a mind-boggling 30,000 works on display, the biggest danger you'll face at the Louvre is burnout—and we're talking the I'll-slit-my-wrist-if-I-see-another-painting kind. So pace yourself and don't try to do it all in a single visit. The sheer scale of the Louvre, organized in three wings—Richelieu, Sully, and Denon—makes it easy to get lost, so grab a map on you're way in. The best way to tame the beast is to take a guided tour. If you can dedicate an entire morning or afternoon to your visit, fork out 30F ($5) for an audio guide to 180 of the museum's key works— there's no need to follow a specific route so you can bypass collections that don't appeal to you. Or, for 20F ($4), you can also take a shorter, 90-minute tour in English with a walking, talking commentator (available 11am, 2pm, and 3:45pm, every day but Sunday). If you're in a hurry, do a quickie "best of the Louvre" tour, starting with Leonardo da Vinci's *Mona Lisa* (Denon wing, 1st floor). Nearby are two of the Louvre's most famous French paintings, Géricault's *The Raft of Medusa* and Delacroix's *Liberty Guiding the People* (both Denon wing, 1st floor). Next, visit the *Winged Victory* and Michelangelo's *Slaves* (both Denon wing, ground floor) before seeing the *Venus de Milo* (Sully wing, ground floor). After that, let your own interests guide you. Consider that only Florence's Uffizi Gallery rivals the Denon wing for its Italian Renaissance collection, which includes Raphael's *Portrait of Balthazar Castiglione* and Titian's *Man with a Glove*. And the revamped Egyptian antiquities department is one of the largest in the world. If it all seems never ending, consider that the huge palace evolved over several centuries, first opening as a museum in 1793. Relatively recent renovations have doubled its gallery space and added architect I. M. Pei's glass pyramid, now the main entrance to the museum.

99 rue de Rivoli, 1er. ☎ *01/40-20-50-50; recorded info line* ☎ *01/40-20-51-51. Web site: www.louvre.fr and www.smartweb.fr/louvre.* **Métro:** *Palais Royal-Musée du Louvre.* **Bus:** *21, 67, 69, 72, 76, 81.* **Open:** *Mon and Wed 9am–9:45pm, Thurs–Sun 9am–6pm.* **Admission:** *45F ($8) Mon and Wed–Sat until 3pm; 26F ($5) after 3pm and Sun, free under-18s. Tickets are valid all day and allow return visits. Admission is free the first Sun of the month, but be forewarned that crowds are enormous.*

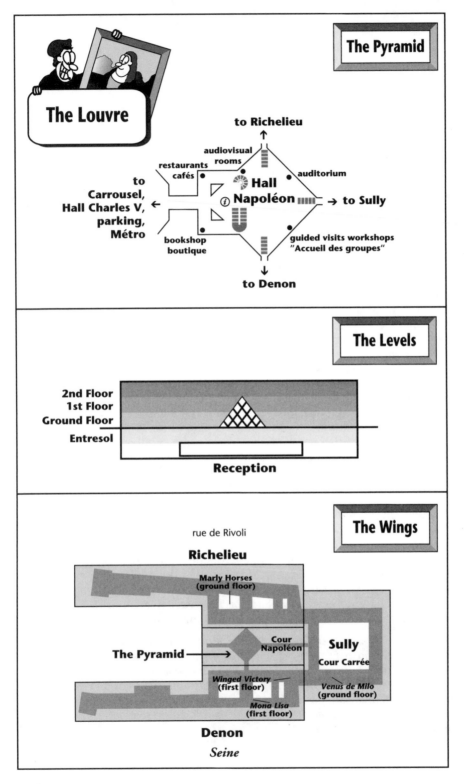

The Louvre

The Pyramid

to Richelieu

audiovisual rooms

restaurants cafés

auditorium

Hall Napoléon

to Carrousel, Hall Charles V, parking, Métro

→ to Sully

bookshop boutique

guided visits workshops "Accueil des groupes"

to Denon

The Levels

2nd Floor
1st Floor
Ground Floor
Entresol

Reception

The Wings

rue de Rivoli

Richelieu

Marly Horses (ground floor)

Cour Napoléon

Sully

Cour Carrée

The Pyramid →

Winged Victory (first floor)

Venus de Milo (ground floor)

Mona Lisa (first floor)

Denon

Seine

Musée d'Orsay
Eiffel Tower & Invalides (7e).

Before becoming president of France, one of Jacques Chirac's shining moments as mayor of Paris was taking the disued Orsay train station and turning it into one of the world's most brilliantly designed museums. To get a sense of this remarkable conversion, take a moment at the top of the central staircase to envision where the trains once pulled into the station under the curved roof. Architecture aside, the Musée d'Orsay's big claim to fame is its unsurpassed collection of Impressionist masterpieces. Don't visit the museum from bottom to top or by the time you get to the Impressionists, you'll be too weary to appreciate them. Instead, go directly to the top floor and work your way down after soaking up Monet, Renoir, Degas, Cézanne, Gauguin, van Gogh, and their contemporaries. Allow 90 minutes for the Impressionists, longer to see the whole museum. The Café des Hauteurs, which looks out toward the Right Bank through the train station's enormous clock, is a terrific place for a light lunch or snack.

1 rue de Bellechasse, 7e. ☎ *01/40-49-48-14. Web site: www.musee-orsay.fr and www.smartweb.fr/orsay/index.html. **Métro:** Solférino, RER Musée d'Orsay. **Bus:** 24, 68, 69, 73. **Open:** Tues, Wed, Fri, Sat 10am–6pm; Thurs 9am–9:45pm; Sun 9am–6pm. **Admission:** 40F ($7) Tues–Sat, 30F ($5) Sun; 30F ($5) ages 18–25, free for under-18s.*

These Attractions Are Better after Sundown

You can pop to the top of the **Arc de Triomphe** until 10pm any night... The **Champs-Elysées** is at its most lively on Friday and Saturday nights after 8pm... From September to May, the **Eiffel Tower** remains open until 11pm, and in summer until midnight... From 7pm to 9:45pm Monday and Wednesday nights at the **Musée du Louvre**, there are no crowds. No kidding... Thursdays from 7pm to 9:45pm, there's more room to admire the Impressionists at the **Musée d'Orsay**... The Seine is more bewitching at night on a floodlit **river cruise** (sailings nightly until 10:30pm).

Musée Picasso
Le Marais & The Islands (3e).

In 1973 the tax collector acquired the greatest collection of Picassos in the world in lieu of $50 million in death taxes. The French government knew a cash cow when it saw one: The Musée Picasso immediately became an enormous crowd pleaser and continues to be one of the city's most popular attractions. The collection is particularly compelling because it is the artist's personal trove—some 4,000 works he especially valued and kept for himself. Every phase of his innovative, 75-year career is represented here: The Blue,

Pink, and Cubist periods, humorous bathing scenes, eye-catching collages, sculpture and pottery, and a group of ribald paintings the artist turned out in his later years. The 17th-century mansion, with its gorgeous carved stairwell, is worth a trip in its own right.

Hôtel Salé, 5 rue de Thorigny, 3e. ☎ *01/42-71-25-21. Web site: www.musexpo.com/ english/picasso/index.html.* **Métro:** *St-Paul.* **Bus:** *29, 96.* **Open:** *Wed–Mon 9:30am–5:30pm.* **Admission:** *30F ($5) Mon and Wed–Sat, 20F ($4) Sun, 20F ($4) ages 18–25, free for under-18s.*

Musée Rodin
Eiffel Tower & Invalides (7e).
Auguste Rodin, often regarded as the greatest sculptor of all time, lived and worked in this elegant 18th-century mansion from 1908 until his death in 1917. It's worth a visit just to see the gardens, where some of the artist's most famous works—*The Thinker, The Gates of Hell, Balzac,* and *The Burghers of Calais*—stand among a whopping 2,000 rosebushes. The highlight of the indoor exhibits are *The Kiss* and *Eve.* Allow an hour to visit, longer if you want to break for coffee in the pretty garden cafe.

Hôtel Biron, 77 rue de Varenne, 7e. ☎ *01/47-05-01-34. Web site: www. musexpo.com/english/cluny/index.html.* **Métro:** *Varenne.* **Bus:** *69, 83.* **Open:** *Tues–Sun 9:30am–5:45pm.* **Admission:** *28F ($5), 18F ($3) ages 18–25, free for under-18s.*

⭐Kids Notre Dame
Les Marais & The Islands (4e).
Pope Alexander III laid the first stone of this Gothic masterpiece in 1163, but the cathedral wasn't completed until 1345. During the 1789 revolution, antiroyalists beheaded the statues of the 28 kings on the front facade, mistakenly believing they depicted the kings of France (in fact, they represented the kings of Judea). Before entering, walk around to the east end of the church to appreciate the spectacular flying buttresses. Visit on a sunny morning to catch the giant rose windows—which retain some of their 13th-century stained glass—in all their glory. The highlight for kids will undoubtedly be the 387-step climb to the bell tower for a fabulously Quasimodo view of the gargoyles and Paris. Allow 30 minutes to visit, longer if you visit the tower.

Place du Parvis-Notre Dame, 4e. ☎ *01,42-34-56-10.* **Métro:** *Cité.* **Bus:** *21, 38, 85, 96.* **Open:** *daily 8am–7pm (tower until 5pm).* **Admission:** *Free. Tower visits: 32F ($6), 21F ($4) ages 18–25, 15F ($2.50) ages 12–17, free for under-12s.*

Panthéon
Latin Quarter (5e).
The Panthéon is to France what Westminster Abbey is to England: a final resting place for the nation's great men of literature. Inside the domed church's barrel-vaulted crypt, you'll find the tombs of Voltaire, Rousseau, Hugo, Braille, and Zola. André Malraux became the newest member of the club in 1996.

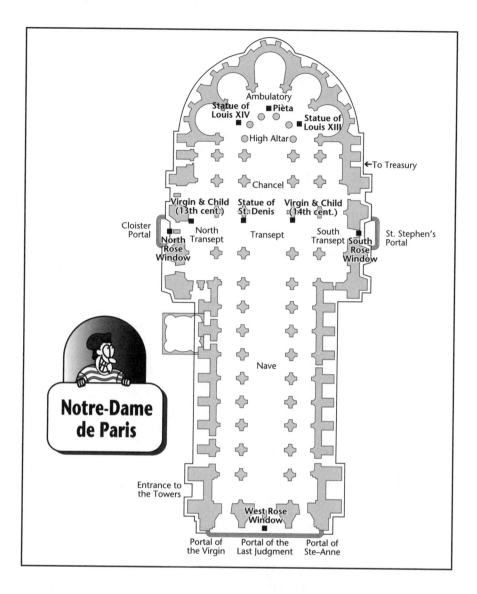

Ambulatory

Statue of Louis XIV ■ Pièta

Statue of Louis XIII ■

○ High Altar ○

← To Treasury

Chancel

Virgin & Child (13th cent.) ■ Statue of St. Denis ■ Virgin & Child (14th cent.) ■

Cloister Portal

North Transept

Transept

South Transept

St. Stephen's Portal

North Rose Window

South Rose Window

Nave

Notre-Dame de Paris

Entrance to the Towers

West Rose Window

Portal of the Virgin | Portal of the Last Judgment | Portal of Ste–Anne

Place du Panthéon, 5e. ☎ *01/44-32-18-00. **Métro:** RER Luxembourg, Cardinal Lemoine. **Bus:** 84, 85, 89. **Open:** Tues–Sat 10am–10:30pm, Sun–Mon 10am–6pm. **Admission:** 32F ($5), 21F ($4) ages 18–25, 15F ($3) ages 12–18, free for under-12s.*

Kids Père-Lachaise Cemetery
Right Bank, Further Afield (20e).

"When I feel myself flagging," Balzac once said, "I go cheer myself up in Père Lachaise...while seeking out the dead I see nothing but the living." There's little morbid about the world's most-visited cemetery, which is more an outdoor museum than a place of sadness. No wonder Parisians have always

Bet You Didn't Know

The perfect place to admire the facade of Notre Dame is the square directly in front of it, known to the French as *kilomètre zéro*. Considered dead-center Paris, it's the point from which all distances in France are measured.

come here to stroll and reflect; with its cobbled streets, park benches, and street signs, the 110-acre Père Lachaise is a minicity all its own. Many visitors leave flowers or notes scrawled on Métro tickets for their favorite celebrity residents, who include Jim Morrison, Isadora Duncan, Edith Piaf, Oscar Wilde, Chopin, Balzac, Max Ernst, Delacroix, Modigliani, Molière, Pissarro, Proust, Sarah Bernhardt, and Gertrude Stein. If for nothing else, go for the striking and often poignant statuary: the boy who seems to sit up in bed as if he'd heard a noise; the young woman who's frozen, mid-dance as if turned to stone without warning. You can obtain a free map from the gatekeeper at the main entrance, but the best guide of all is *Permanent Parisians* (1986, Chelsea Green Publishing), a book jammed with anecdotes and highly recommended walking tours. Allow at least 2 hours to visit.

Main entrance on bd. de Ménilmontant. ☎ *01/43-70-70-33.* **Métro:** *Père-Lachaise.* **Bus:** *61, 69.* **Open:** *9am–5:30pm daily.* **Admission:** *Free.*

Place des Vosges
Le Marais & The Islands (4e).
Right smack in the heart of the Marais, the most beautiful square in Paris was once the site of royal wedding celebrations and jousting tournaments. Its most impressive feature—apart from the fact that it's still marvelously intact after 400 years—is its symmetry: 36 townhouses, 9 on each side, built of brick and putty-colored stone with handsome slate roofs and dormer windows. At ground level is a lovely arcaded walkway that's now home to cafes, art galleries, antiques dealers, and smart boutiques. Allow 30 minutes to walk all the way around the square under the arcades.

Place des Vosges, 4e. **Métro:** *Bastille, St-Paul.* **Bus:** *69, 76, 96.*

🟊Kids Sacré-Coeur
Right Bank, Further Afield (18e).
The basilica dominates Paris's highest hill, the *butte* of Montmartre, and the best reason to come is the city-spanning views afforded from its dome. The Sacré-Coeur (Sacred Heart) was begun in 1875 as an act of penance for losing the Franco-Prussian War and was finally completed in 1914. Decide for yourself whether the mix-and-match Romanesque-Byzantine architecture is a hit or a miss. The star interior feature is the striking golden mosaic of Christ on

the chancel's ceiling, but it all pales after the nail-bitingly steep, corkscrew climb to the dome. The steps in front of the church come alive around dusk, when street musicians entertain the crowd that gathers to watch the city's lights come on.

35 rue du Chevalier-de-la-Barre, 18e. ☎ **01/53-41-89-00.** ***Métro:*** *Abbesses, then take the funicular (Métro tickets accepted) up to the church.* ***Bus:*** *The only bus that goes all the way to the top of the hill is the local Montmartrobus (Métro tickets accepted), which you can catch at the Jules-Joffrin Métro stop.* ***Open:*** *Church, daily 7am–11pm; dome/crypt, daily 9am–6pm.* ***Admission:*** *Church, free; Dome, 15F*

Bet You Didn't Know

Paris's most famous bridge is the **Pont Neuf,** which means "New Bridge." Its name hasn't changed since its erection in 1604 and today it's, ironically, the city's oldest bridge. In its day, the Pont Neuf was remarkable because it was paved and not flanked with houses and shops.

($3); Crypt, 15F ($3).

Kids Sainte-Chapelle
Le Marais & The Islands (3e, 4e).

Notre Dame and the Sacré-Coeur may be more famous, but the Sainte-Chapelle delivers a wow factor that the others don't. King Louis IX, better known as St. Louis, had this "Holy Chapel" built in 1248 to house what he believed was Christ's crown of thorns. The result has been hailed as one of the Western world's greatest architectural masterpieces. Servants and commoners worshipped in the lower chapel, while the upper level was reserved for the king and his family. There simply aren't enough superlatives to prepare you for the first time you set eyes on the royal chapel, entirely surrounded by stained-glass windows that soar 50 feet high to a star-studded vaulted ceiling. The windows form a pictorial Bible, depicting scenes from Genesis to the Apocalypse. Save this for a sunny day and it's guaranteed to blow your socks off—you'll think you've stepped inside a kaleidoscope. Allow 45 minutes to visit. Some evenings, when the upper chapel becomes a venue for classical-music concerts, the effect of chandelier lights dancing off the windows is magical.

4 bd. du Palais, 1er. Enter through the Palais du Justice (doorway is 50 yards to the left of the main gates) then go through the metal detector. The church is in the courtyard. ☎ **01/53-73-78-50,** *concert info* ☎ **01/44-07-12-38.** ***Métro:*** *Cité.* ***Bus:*** *21, 38, 85, 96.* ***Open:*** *daily Apr–Sept, 9:30am–6:30pm; Oct–Mar 10am–5pm.* ***Admission:*** *32F ($5), 21F ($4) ages 12–25, free for under-12s.*

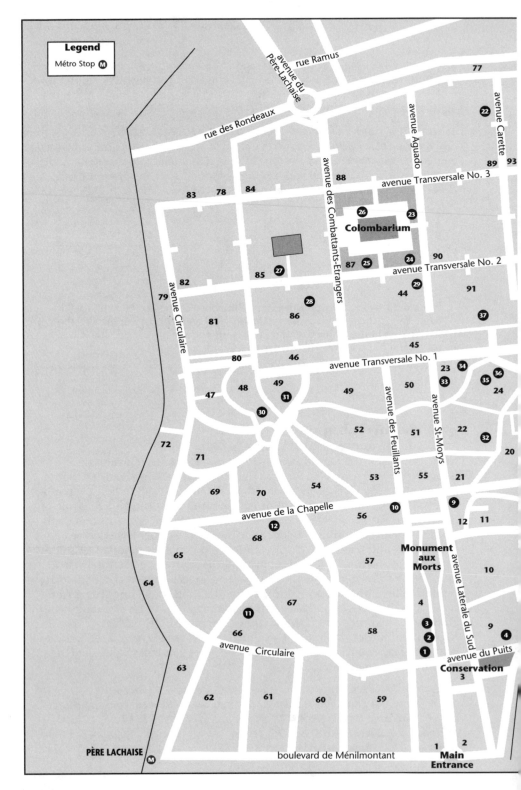

Legend

Métro Stop Ⓜ

rue Ramus

avenue du Père-Lachaise

rue des Rondeaux

avenue Aguado

avenue Carette

avenue Transversale No. 3

77

22

89   93

88

83   78   84

Colombarium

26   23

avenue des Combattants-Etrangers

85   27

87   25   24   90

avenue Transversale No. 2

82

79

28

44   29   91

86

37

81

45

80   46

avenue Transversale No. 1

avenue Circulaire

47   48   49

50   23   34

49

33   35   36

31

24

30

52   51   22   32

72   71

53   55   21   20

avenue des Feuillants

avenue St-Morys

69   70   54

10   9

56   12   11

avenue de la Chapelle

12   68

57

Monument aux Morts

65

64

avenue Laterale du Sud

10

67

4

11   66

58   3

2

9   4

avenue du Puits

63   Conservation

3

62   61   60   59

1   2

PÈRE LACHAISE Ⓜ

boulevard de Ménilmontant

Main Entrance

194

1 Sidonie Colette
2 Gioacchino Antonio Rossini
3 Alfred de Musset
4 Hans Bellmer
5 Rothschild family plot
6 Camille Pissaro
7 Abélard and Héloïse
8 Frédéric Chopin
9 Théodore Géricault
10 Jacques–Louis David
11 Georges–Pierre Seurat
12 Georges Bizet
13 Auguste Comte
14 Jim Morrison
15 Saint–Simon
16 Pierre–Auguste Beaumarchais
17 Edith Piaf
18 Amedeo Modigliani
19 Paul Éluard
20 Gertrude Stein
21 Alice B. Toklas
22 Oscar Wilde
23 Max Ernst
24 Richard Wright
25 Isadora Duncan
26 Maria Callas
27 Marcel Proust
28 Guillame Appollinaire
29 Simone Signoret/ Yves Montand
30 Honoré de Balzac
31 Eugène Delacroix
32 Gustave Doré
33 Jean-Auguste- Dominique Ingres
34 René Lalique
35 Jean-Baptiste- Camille Corot
36 Honoré Daumier
37 Sarah Bernhardt
38 Molière
39 Jean La Fontaine

The
Père-Lachaise
Cemetery

0   75 y
0   75 m

Worksheet: Your Must-See Attractions

Enter the attractions you most would like to visit to see how they'll fit into your schedule. Then use the date book below to plan your itinerary.

Attraction and location	Amount of time you expect to spend there	Best day and time to go

DAY 1

Morning:

Lunch:

Afternoon:

Dinner:

Evening:

DAY 2

Morning:

Lunch:

Afternoon:

Dinner:

Evening:

DAY 3

Morning:

Lunch:

Afternoon:

Dinner:

Evening:

DAY 4

Morning:

Lunch:

Afternoon:

Dinner:

Evening:

DAY 5

Morning:

Lunch:

Afternoon:

Dinner:

Evening:

Chapter 14

IO¢ PER RIDE

More Fun Things to Do

In This Chapter

➤ More sights and activities for art fans, literary buffs, history lovers, and others

➤ Quick lessons in French culture

➤ Where to bring your little munchkins

➤ Where to work out

If you have a particular interest—and who doesn't?—then the previous chapter's list of top sights may be too general for you. Here are some suggestions on how to dig a little deeper.

Don't Know Much About History

If you're looking for a way to digest Paris's past with only a minimum effort, **Paristoric,** 11 bis rue Scribe, 9e (☎ **01/42-66-62-06**), is a multimedia Cliff's Notes to the city's 2,000-year history, backed by a soundtrack of such varied musicians as Wagner and Edith Piaf. Maps, portraits, and scenes from dramatic times are projected on the large screen while you listen through headphones to a running commentary (available in 10 languages). Use it as a preview of what you want to see later, or stop in for a more in-depth look at what you've already visited. Either way, it's 45 minutes well spent. Take the Métro to Opéra. Rue Scribe is just to the left of the opera house (it intersects rue Auber). Open daily 9am to 6pm (until 9pm in summer). Admission: 50F ($9) adults, 30F ($5) students and under-18s.

^{Kids} The **Musée Carnavalet,** 23 rue de Sévigné, 3e (☎ **01/42-72-21-13;** Web site: www.musexpo.com/english/carnavalet/index.html), is great if you like history but are bored by textbooks. Inside two sumptuous Renaissance mansions, the history of Paris comes alive through an impressive selection of unique items, including the chessmen Louis XVI toyed with while waiting to go to the guillotine. One of history's most famous correspondents, Madame de Sévigné, moved here in 1677, pouring out nearly every detail of her life in letters that have proved invaluable to historians. Many salons depict events related to the revolution. The dauphin's homework notebook is a pathetic legacy he left the world before his mysterious disappearance. Here, too, is Napoléon's cradle and a replica of Marcel Proust's cork-lined bedroom, featuring his brass bed. The museum makes a very visual history lesson for kids 10 and older. Take the Métro to St-Paul. Walk one block east and turn left on rue de Sévigné. Open Tuesday to Sunday 10am to 5:40pm. Admission: 35F ($6) adults, 25F ($4) for students, free for under-18s.

One of the city's most charmingly intimate museums, the **Musée de Cluny,** 6 place Paul-Painlevé, 5e (☎ **01/53-73-78-00;** Web site: www.musexpo.com/ english/cluny/index.html) houses the national collection of medieval arts and artifacts. The Gothic mansion was built for the 14th-century abbot of Cluny atop the ruins of a Gallo-Roman baths complex. The star attractions are the celebrated "Lady and the Unicorn" tapestries and the Gallery of Kings, 21 stone heads of the Kings of Judea from Notre Dame's facade. You'll find the partly restored 3rd-century Roman baths on the lowest level. From the Cluny-La Sorbonne Métro stop, exit on boulevard St-Germain, then take a right on rue de Cluny, which brings you to place Paul-Painlevé. Open Wednesday to Monday 9:15am to 5:45pm. Admission: 30F ($5), 20F ($4) ages 18 to 25, free for under-18s.

^{Kids} If you found the Musée Carnavalet intriguing, you're ready for the **Musée de l'Histoire de France,** 60 rue des Francs-Bourgeois, 3e (☎ **01/ 40-27-61-78).** Here the entire history of France is brilliantly showcased— everything from King Dagobert to World War II and the occupation of Paris. On Napoléon's orders, this Renaissance mansion was made the official records depository of France. The archives contain documents that predate Charlemagne, and the letter collection contains writings of Marie Antoinette (a farewell note), Louis XVI (his will), Danton, Robespierre, Napoléon, and Joan of Arc. Even the jailer's keys to the old Bastille are here. From the Hôtel de Ville, walk four blocks north (away from the Seine) on rue des Archives and turn right. Open Monday and Wednesday to Friday noon to 5:45pm, Saturday and Sunday 1:45pm to 5:45pm. Admission: 15F ($3), 12F ($2) ages 18 to 25, free for under-18s.

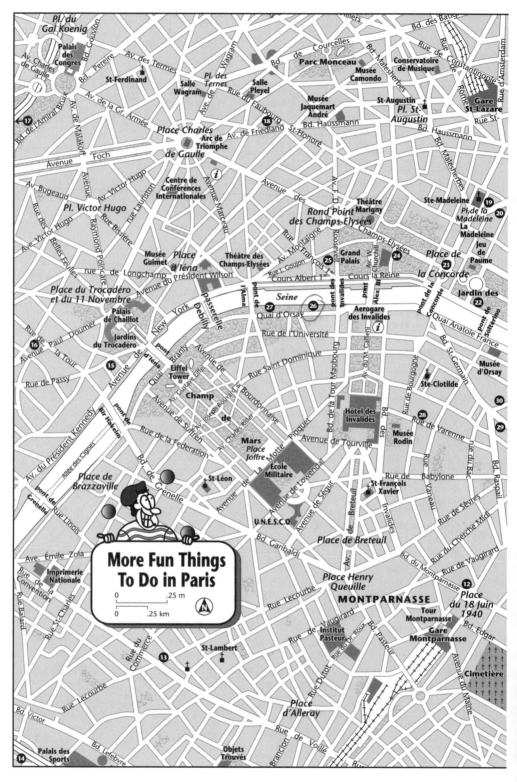

More Fun Things
To Do in Paris

0   .25 m
0   .25 km

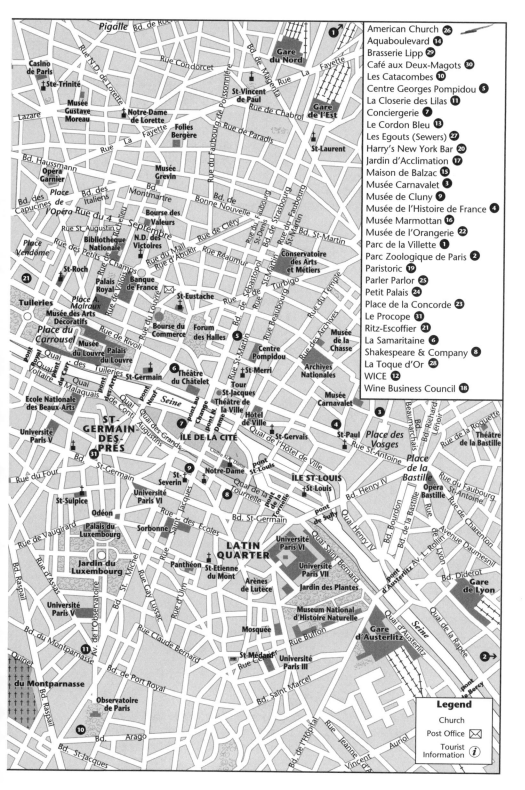

American Church ㉖
Aquaboulevard ⑭
Brasserie Lipp ㉙
Café aux Deux-Magots ㉚
Les Catacombes ⑩
Centre Georges Pompidou ⑤
La Closerie des Lilas ⑪
Conciergerie ⑦
Le Cordon Bleu ⑬
Les Egouts (Sewers) ㉗
Harry's New York Bar ⑳
Jardin d'Acclimation ⑰
Maison de Balzac ⑮
Musée Carnavalet ③
Musée de Cluny ⑨
Musée de l'Histoire de France ④
Musée Marmottan ⑯
Musée de l'Orangerie ㉒
Parc de la Villette ❶
Parc Zoologique de Paris ❷
Paristoric ⑲
Parler Parlor ㉕
Petit Palais ㉔
Place de la Concorde ㉓
Le Procope ㉛
Ritz-Escoffier ㉑
La Samaritaine ⑥
Shakespeare & Company ⑧
La Toque d'Or ㉘
WICE ⑫
Wine Business Council ⑱

Legend

Church †

Post Office ✉

Tourist Information ⓘ

205

Impressionist Nirvana

If the Musée d'Orsay merely whetted your appetite for Impressionism, you'll think the **Musée Marmottan,** 2 rue Louis-Boilly, 16e (☎ **01/42-24-07-02;** Web site: www.musexpo.com/english/marmottan/index.html), is a little slice of heaven. The highlight is its superb collection of 65 paintings by Claude Monet, including a series of his water lily canvases and *Impression-Sunrise,* whose title inspired the movement's name. In the early 1970s, Monet's son bequeathed part of the artist's personal art collection, including works by fellow Impressionists Renoir, Sisley, and Pissarro. This human-scaled 19th-century mansion is a welcome antidote to the city's huge museums. Take Métro line 9 to La Muette. As you exit the station, you'll see a small park to the left. Walk across it to avenue Raphaël, then turn onto rue Louis-Boilly. Open Tuesday to Sunday 10am to 5:30pm. Admission: 40F ($7), 25F ($4) ages 8 to 25, free for under-8s.

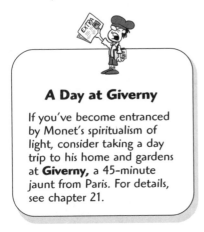

A Day at Giverny

If you've become entranced by Monet's spiritualism of light, consider taking a day trip to his home and gardens at **Giverny,** a 45-minute jaunt from Paris. For details, see chapter 21.

Everyone comes to the **Musée de l'Orangerie,** Jardin des Tuileries, 1er (☎ **01/42-97-48-16**) for Monet's water lilies, here beautifully bathed in natural light in the oval ground-floor rooms. But the former Tuileries Palace orangery also contains a sumptuous collection of French Impressionist masterpieces, including 14 Cézannes, 24 Renoirs, some early Picassos, and works by Matisse and Modigliani. Take Métro line 1 to Concorde. Open Wednesday to Sunday 9:45am to 5pm. Admission: 30F ($5) Wednesday to Saturday, 20F ($4) Sunday, 20F ($4) ages 18 to 25, free for under-18s.

Built for the 1900 exhibition, the **Petit Palais,** avenue Winston-Churchill, 8e (☎ **01/42-65-12-73**), holds works of art belonging to the city of Paris. As such, it is a hodgepodge that mainly interests the serious art aficionado with more than a few days to spend in Paris. Most visitors come here for the temporary exhibitions, but the permanent collections feature a number of rooms dedicated to 19th-century French painting, including works by Courbet, Corot, Delacroix, Manet, Sisley, Mary Cassatt (*Le Bain*), Maurice Denis, Odilon Redon, and Pierre Bonnard. Get off the Métro at Champs-Elysées Clémenceau and walk toward the river. The Petit Palais is on your left, facing the Grand Palais. Open Tuesday to Sunday 10am to 5:40pm. Admission: 27F ($4), 14.50F ($2) for under-25s, free on Sunday.

Hemingway's Favorite Haunts

Still going strong after all these years, **Harry's New York Bar,** 5 rue Daunou, 2e (☎ **01/42-61-71-14**), was so often a destination for Hemingway's and Fitzgerald's all-night benders that the place could have been renamed

Ernie and Scott's. Another claim to fame is that the Bloody Mary was invented here, or so they say. It's worth popping in for an after-dinner drink, but be aware that so many tourists come that the bar's ad campaign advises telling your cabbie to head to "Sank Roo Doe Noo", the phonetic equivalent of the street address. Forget the taxi. Take the Métro to Opéra, head down the rue de la Paix and take your first left. Open daily 10:30am to 4am.

Sorry to burst any bubbles, but **Shakespeare and Company,** 37 rue de la Bûcherie, 5e (☎ **01/43-26-96-50**), is merely an incarnation of the genuine article. Sylvia Beach's famous bookshop, beloved by Hemingway, Fitzgerald, and Joyce, opened in 1919 at 6 rue Dupuytren (take the Métro to Odéon, walk through the Carrefour de l'Odéon, and turn left). Then, two years later, Beach moved the shop to 12 rue de l'Odéon—the building is no longer standing, unfortunately—and stayed until the U.S. entry into World War II rendered her an enemy alien in German-occupied Paris.

Two of Papa's favorite hangouts were just across the street from each other on boulevard St-Germain-des-Prés—the **Brasserie Lipp** and the **Café aux Deux-Magots.** In *The Sun Also Rises*, Jake Barnes meets Lady Brett in the Deux-Magots. And in *A Moveable Feast*, Hemingway lovingly recalls downing beer and potato salad at the Lipp. Tourism has driven prices up, so go just for coffee or a glass of wine. Brasserie Lipp, 151 bd. St-Germain, 6e (☎ **01-45-48-53-91**), is open daily 9am to 1am. Café aux Deux-Magots, 170 bd. St-Germain, 6e (☎ **01/45-48-55-25**), is open daily 7:30am to 1:30am. Both cafes are less than 50 yards from the St-Germain-des-Prés Métro stop—you can't miss 'em.

It took Hemingway about 6 weeks to write *A Sun Also Rises* on the terrace of **La Closerie de Lilas,** 171 bd. du Montparnasse, 14e (☎ **01/43-26-70-50**), and much of the novel takes place there. In good weather, the author would sit under a lilac plant with his friend, John Dos Passos, and they'd read their favorite passages from the New Testament to each other. The place is more elegant and pricey than it was in the 1930s, but it's as packed now as it ever was then. You'll find it practically on top of the RER Port-Royal stop. Open daily 9:30am to 1am.

French Culture 101

Polish your rusty French at the **Parler Parlor,** Berlitz France, 35 av. Franklin D. Roosevelt, 8e (☎ **01/40-27-97-59;** e-mail leeds@wfi.fr). There are no textbooks, just free-form conversation with a mix of English- and French-speaking residents—it's a great way to get insider tips from Parisians. The parlor meets three times a week: Tuesday 6:30pm to 8pm; Thursday 3:30pm to 5pm; and Saturday 11am to 12:30pm. As a native English speaker, you get a 20% discount off membership (normally 350F for three months) and your first session is free. Visit the Web site at **www.wfi.fr/parler.**

If you want to learn more about French wines, several organizations offer brief oenology classes and wine tastings in English. First, contact the expats'

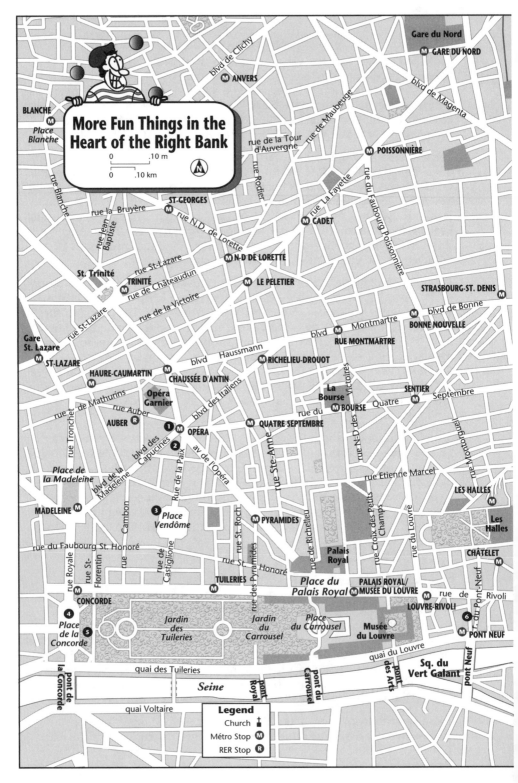

More Fun Things in the Heart of the Right Bank

0   .10 m

0   .10 km

Gare du Nord

Ⓜ GARE DU NORD

blvd de Clichy

blvd de Magenta

Ⓜ ANVERS

BLANCHE

Ⓜ

Place Blanche

rue de la Tour d'Auvergne

rue de Maubeuge

rue du Faubourg Poissonnière

rue de la Fayette

Ⓜ POISSONNIÈRE

rue Rodier

rue Blanche

rue Jean Baptiste

rue la Bruyère

ST-GEORGES

Ⓜ

rue N.D. de Lorette

Ⓜ CADET

rue St-Lazare

Ⓜ N-D DE LORETTE

St. Trinité

rue de Chateaudun

TRINITÉ

Ⓜ

Ⓜ LE PELETIER

STRASBOURG-ST. DENIS

rue de la Victoire

blvd de Bonne

Gare St. Lazare

rue St-Lazare

Ⓜ Montmartre

BONNE NOUVELLE

Ⓜ ST-LAZARE

blvd   Haussmann

blvd

RUE MONTMARTRE

Ⓜ RICHELIEU-DROUOT

HAURE-CAUMARTIN

Ⓜ

CHAUSSÉE D'ANTIN

Ⓜ

rue de Mathurins

Opéra Garnier

blvd des Italiens

La Bourse

SENTIER

Ⓜ

Septembre

rue Auber

Ⓜ BOURSE

Quatre

AUBER Ⓡ

❶

rue du

rue N-D des Victoires

rue Tronchet

Ⓜ OPÉRA

blvd des Capucines

❷

Ⓜ QUATRE SEPTEMBRE

rue Ste-Anne

rue Etienne Marcel

LES HALLES

Ⓜ

Place de la Madeleine

blvd de la Madeleine

av de l'Opéra

Rue de la Paix

rue Montorgueil

rue du Louvre

Les Halles

MADELEINE Ⓜ

Cambon

❸ Place Vendôme

Ⓜ PYRAMIDES

rue de Richelieu

rue Croix des Petits Champs

CHÂTELET

Ⓜ

rue du Faubourg St. Honoré

rue de Castiglione

rue St-Roch

Palais Royal

rue Royale

rue St-Florentin

rue des Pyramides

rue St-Honoré

PALAIS ROYAL/ MUSÉE DU LOUVRE

Ⓜ rue de Rivoli

Pont-Neuf

TUILERIES

Ⓜ

Place du Palais Royal Ⓜ

LOUVRE-RIVOLI

Ⓜ

❻

CONCORDE

Ⓜ

Place de la Concorde

❹

❺

Jardin des Tuileries

Jardin du Carrousel

Place du Carrousel

Musée du Louvre

Ⓜ PONT NEUF

quai du Louvre

Sq. du Vert Galant

Pont Neuf

pont de la Concorde

quai des Tuileries

pont du Carrousel

pont des Arts

Seine

pont Royal

quai Voltaire

Legend

Church ✝

Métro Stop Ⓜ

RER Stop Ⓡ

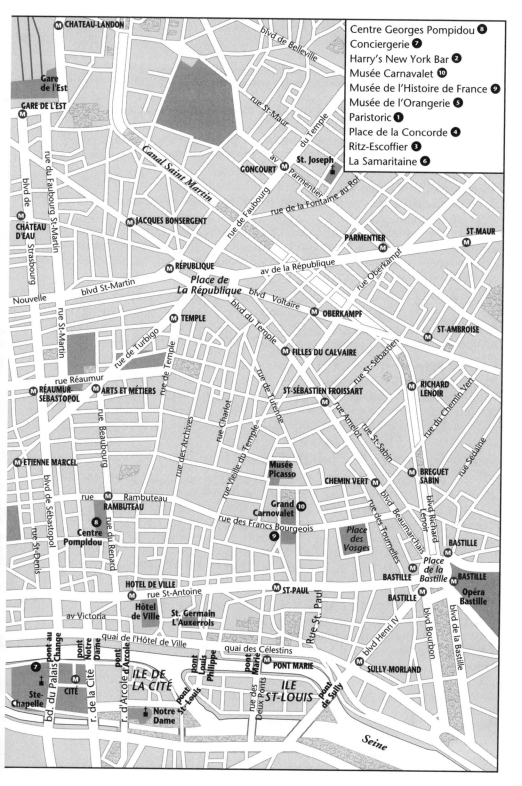

Centre Georges Pompidou **8**
Conciergerie **7**
Harry's New York Bar **2**
Musée Carnavalet **10**
Musée de l'Histoire de France **9**
Musée de l'Orangerie **5**
Paristoric **1**
Place de la Concorde **4**
Ritz-Escoffier **3**
La Samaritaine **6**

favorite cultural organization, **WICE,** 20 bd. du Montparnasse, 15e (☎ **01/45-66-75-50;** fax 01/40-65-96-53; e-mail wice@wice-paris.org; Web site: www.wice-paris.org) and ask for a brochure of its upcoming courses. If none suit your schedule, try the **Wine Business Conseil,** 138 rue du Faubourg St-Honoré, 8e (☎ **01/42-89-14-14;** fax 01/42-89-15-40), and **CIDD** (Centre d'Information de Documentation et de Dégustation), 30 rue de la Sablière, 14e (☎ **01/45-45-32-20;** fax 01/45-42-78-20).

Adventures in Gastronomy

At **La Toque d'Or,** 55 rue de Varenne, 7e (☎ **01/45-44-86-51;** fax 01/45-44-63-81; e-mail parisgourmet@multicable.fr), Cordon Bleu–trained Sue Young offers a number of short courses in French cuisine that take up only a morning or an afternoon. She also hosts a series of open-air market tours given by well-known Paris chefs. Request a brochure by fax or e-mail and book ahead for the courses.

Le Cordon Bleu, 8 rue Léon Delhomme, 15e (☎ **800/457-CHEF** in the U.S., or 01/53-68-22-50), has been the world's most famous French cooking school since it opened its doors in 1895. You'll need to enroll a few months in advance for one of its 3-hour demonstration classes, which costs 220F ($39).

Ritz-Escoffier Ecole de Gastronomie Française, 15 place Vendôme, 1er (☎ **800/966-5758** in the U.S., or 01/43-16-30-50), affiliated with the Hôtel Ritz, is another prestigious cooking school that offers afternoon bilingual demonstrations (in English and French) for 275F ($49). Call ahead for a program, and book well in advance.

Smile-Inducers for Small Fries

Kids The **Parc Zoologique de Paris,** Bois de Vincennes, 12e (☎ **01/44-75-20-00),** is vast enough to keep your brood occupied for an afternoon, with plenty of lions and tigers and bears, oh my! Most animals live in settings that closely resemble their natural habitats, so they don't have that depressed, caged-in look you see at some zoos. Unsurprisingly, the frolicking bears and seals steal the show. Get off the Métro at Porte Dorée or Château de Vincennes. Open daily 9am to 6pm. Admission: 40F ($7), 30F ($5) ages 4 to 25, free for under-4s.

Kids The **Jardin d'Acclimation,** Bois de Boulogne, 16e (☎ **01/40-67-90-82),** is a 25-acre amusement park on the northern side of the Bois de Boulogne that makes tykes under 8 squeal with joy. The park has an easy-to-follow layout—just follow the circular road in either direction and it will bring you around and back to where you started. En route is a house of mirrors, an archery range, a miniature-golf course, zoo animals, an American-style bowling alley, a playground, a hurdle-racing course, pony rides, paddle-boats, and a whole conglomerate of junior-scale rides, shooting galleries, and waffle stalls. Take Métro line 1 to Les Sablons. Or, from the Champs-Elysées, catch bus no. 73 heading west. Open daily 10am to 6pm. Admission: 12F ($2), free for under-3s.

Hot Sights for Cool Kids

Kids If you've brought kids 5 and older, head to the **Cité des Sciences et de l'Industrie,** Parc de la Villette, 30 av. Corentine-Cariou, 19e (☎ 08/40-05-12-12; Web site: www.cite-sciences.fr). In 1986 this vast learning minicity opened as the world's most expensive ($642 million) science complex designed to "modernize mentalities." The sheer dimensions of the place are awesome, with interactive exhibits on everything from outer space to genetically manipulated plants. Outside, the silver, 112-foot-high Géode sphere boasts a 3-D, IMAX cinema inside its curved walls. After the visit, let your kids run wild in the expansive, green Parc de la Villette. Take Métro line 7 to Porte de la Villette. Open Tuesday to Saturday 10am to 6pm, Sunday 10am to 7pm. Géode open Tuesday to Sunday 10am to 9pm. Admission: Cité Pass, Tuesday to Friday and Sunday 50F ($9), Saturday 35F ($6), 35F ($6) ages 7 to 25, free for under-7s; Cité/Géode, 92F ($16), 79F ages 7 to 25; Géode, 55F ($10), 44F ($8) ages 7 to 25. MasterCard and Visa accepted.

Kids It's dark and spooky, with a high gross-out factor. In other words, little monsters over 7 just love **Les Catacombes**, 1 place Denfert-Rochereau, 14e (☎ 01/43-22-47-63). Every year, some 50,000 visitors come to explore the 1,000 yards of dank tunnels lined with six million ghoulishly arranged skulls and skeletons. The place was a medieval quarry up until 1785, when the city started using it as a burial place for the surplus of bodies that overcrowded graveyards couldn't handle—

Bet You Didn't Know

In World War II, the Catacombs were HQ for the French Resistance.

thereby earning it the nickname place d'Enfer ("Hell Square"). Take Métro line 4 or 6, or the RER B line to Denfert-Rochereau. Open Tuesday to Sunday 2pm to 4pm; also weekends 9am to 11am. Admission: 27F ($5), 19F ($3) ages 7 to 18, free for under-7s.

Kids **Les Egouts,** the city's sewers, are laid out like an underground city, with streets clearly labeled and each branch pipe bearing the name of the building to which it's connected. Believe it or not, this sight is so popular that you sometimes have to wait as long as a half hour in line. The tour starts with a short film on the history of sewers, followed by a visit to a small museum, and finally a short trip through the maze. Don't worry, you won't trudge through anything vile, but the visit may leave your clothes smelling a bit ripe. Visit at the end of the day and wear something you don't mind not wearing again until it's washed. Get off Métro line 9 at Alma-Marceau, then walk across the bridge to the Left Bank. Or take RER C to Pont de l'Alma. The entrance is a stairway on the Seine side of the Quai d'Orsay, facing No. 93 (☎ 01/47-05-10-29). Open May through October Saturday to Wednesday 11am to 5pm; November through April Saturday to Wednesday 11am to 4pm. Closed 3 weeks in January for maintenance. Admission: 25F ($4), 20F ($4) ages 13 to 25, 15F ($3) ages 5 to 12, free for under-5s.

Wanna beat the summer heat? Water slides and wave machines make
Aquaboulevard, 4 rue Louis-Armand, 15e (☎ **01/40-60-15-15**), a fun substitute for the beach. This water world is open 9am to 11pm daily; admission
costs 68F ($12) on weekdays and 75F ($13) on weekends. Take the Métro to
Balard, head down avenue de la Porte de Sèvres. Just after you walk under
the overpass, you'll find Aquaboulevard straight ahead.

Catching a Flick, French or Otherwise

Kids Paris may be the best movie city in the world. On any given day, you can
choose between hundreds of old and new flicks or attend a film fest dedicated
to a single acclaimed director or actor. Most cinemas play films that have been
dubbed into French, indicated at the box office with the initials V.F. (*version
française*). Look for the initials V.O. (*version originale*), which means the film
has its original soundtrack and French subtitles. There are V.O. theaters all
along the Champs-Elysées and in the Forum des Halles underground mall, 1er
(Métro: Les Halles), whose three cinemas include a fabulous 25-theater complex called Ciné Cité. Consult the cinema section of *Pariscope* to find out
what's playing and where.

Views to Remember

Kids Most of the gallery space at the **Centre Georges Pompidou,** place
Beaubourg, 4e, is closed this year, but you can still ride the Habitrail-like
glass escalator to the top floor for free. From there, take in the terrific view
that skips across the Right Bank's Mansart rooftops. Take Métro line 11 to
Rambuteau, or line 1 to Hôtel de Ville. Open Monday and Wednesday to
Friday noon to 10pm; weekends 10am to 10pm.

Kids You can survey all of central Paris from the roof of **La Samaritaine**
department store, 19 rue de la Monnaie, 1er (☎ **01/40-41-20-20**). The
panoramic view is most magical at dusk, when the city's monuments
light up one by one like fireflies. In the summer, this means visiting on
a Thursday. Take Métro line 7 to Pont Neuf, or line 1 to Châtelet. Enter
Building 2 (there are five in all), take the elevator to the ninth floor, and
then the stairs to the observation deck. Open Monday to Wednesday, Friday,
and Saturday 9:30am to 7pm; Thursday 9:30am to 10pm.

More Literary Landmarks

Kids If you or your kids have read *The Hunchback of Notre-Dame* and *Les
Misérables*, you may want to visit the **Maison de Victor Hugo,** 6 place des
Vosges, 4e (☎ **01/42-72-10-16**). From 1832 to 1848 the novelist and poet
lived on the second floor of this townhouse, built in 1610. Mementos of his

work abound: samples of his handwriting, his inkwell, and first editions of his works. A painting of his funeral procession at the Arc de Triomphe in 1885 is on display, as are plentiful portraits and souvenirs of Hugo's family. The highlight is more than 450 of Hugo's drawings illustrating scenes from his own works. Take Métro line 1 to St-Paul. Open Tuesday to Sunday 10am to 5:40pm. Admission: 17F ($3), 9F ($2) ages 8 to 18, free for under-8s.

Where to Burn Off All That French Food

So you've downed a few too many chocolate eclairs on your trip? Keeping in shape can be easy if you choose a hotel near one of the city's larger parks, where the **best jogging routes** are. Unfortunately the most expansive city parks of all—the Bois de Boulogne and the Bois de Vincennes—are inconvenient if your hotel is in central Paris. On the Left Bank, try to stay near the **Jardin des Plantes** (5e), the **Luxemburg Gardens** (6e), or the **Champs de Mars** esplanade beneath the Eiffel Tower (7e). On the Right Bank, the only decent option in central Paris is the **Tuileries Gardens** (1er). A wonderful exception takes place every Sunday from 9am to 4pm, when the **Right Bank quays** are closed to traffic between the Pont d'Iéna (the bridge that links the Eiffel Tower to the Trocadéro) and the Pont de Sully (which connects the Ile St-Louis to the Marais). The whole strip becomes a mecca for joggers and bicyclists.

A cheap work-out option is the American-style **aerobics classes** at the American Church, 65 Quai d'Orsay, 7e (schedule info, ☎ **01/47-53-04-56**). For 45F ($8), you can take a 1-hour class in high- or low-impact aerobics, body sculpting, cardio funk, or step. Professional instructors give classes in English. The church is smack between RER Pont d'Alma and RER Invalides. From the Right Bank, take the Métro to Alma-Marceau, then walk across the bridge and head left on Quai d'Orsay.

If you absolutely need to work out in a **health club,** be prepared to pay through the nose. Gyms have popped up all over the city, but they're pricey for nonmembers. You can work out at the following clubs for a day rate of 150F ($27):

➤ **Gymnasium** has over 12 locations throughout city, including 129 bd. Haussmann, 8e. Métro: Miromesnil (☎ **01/42-89-89-14**).

➤ **Espace Vit'Halles**, 48 rue Rambuteau, 3e. Métro: Rambuteau (☎ **01/42-77-21-71**).

➤ **Gymnase Club** has over 15 locations throughout city, including 147 bis, rue St. Honoré, 1er. Métro: Louvre Rivoli (☎ **01/40-20-03-03**).

➤ The **Grand Hôtel Inter-Continental**, 2 rue Scribe, 9e, Métro: Opéra (☎ **01-40-07-32-32**), is the only hotel that allows nonguests to use its fitness center.

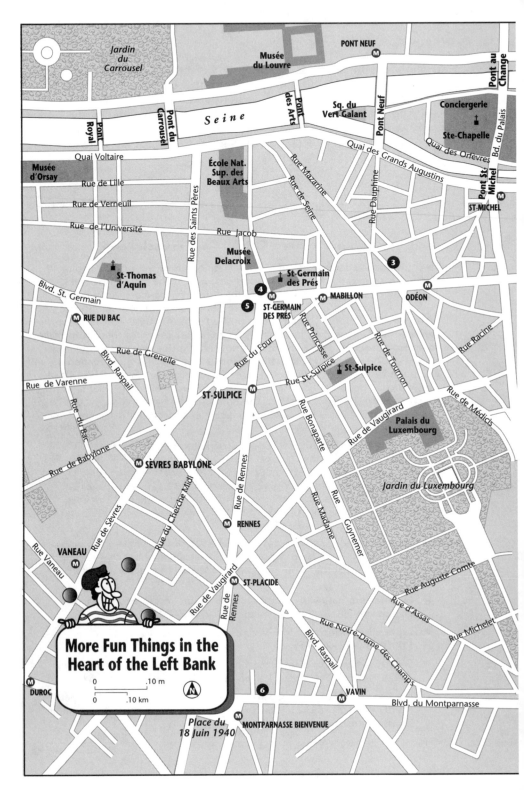

More Fun Things in the Heart of the Left Bank

0   .10 m
0   .10 km

Jardin du Carrousel

Musée du Louvre

PONT NEUF

Pont au Change

Pont des Arts

Sq. du Vert Galant

Pont Neuf

Conciergerie

Ste-Chapelle

Bd. du Palais

Quai des Orfèvres

Seine

Pont Royal

Pont du Carrousel

Quai Voltaire

Quai des Grands Augustins

Pont St. Michel

ST-MICHEL

Musée d'Orsay

Rue de Lille

École Nat. Sup. des Beaux Arts

Rue Mazarine

Rue de Seine

Rue Dauphine

Rue de Verneuil

Rue de l'Université

Rue des Saints Pères

Rue Jacob

Musée Delacroix

St-Germain des Prés

3

St-Thomas d'Aquin

Blvd. St. Germain

4

5

ST-GERMAIN DES PRÉS

MABILLON

ODÉON

RUE DU BAC

Rue de Grenelle

Blvd. Raspail

Rue du Four

Rue Princesse

Rue de Tournon

Rue Racine

Rue de Varenne

Rue du Bac

Rue St-Sulpice

St-Sulpice

ST-SULPICE

Rue de Médicis

Rue de Babylone

Rue de Sèvres

SÈVRES BABYLONE

Rue Bonaparte

Rue de Vaugirard

Palais du Luxembourg

Rue de Rennes

Jardin du Luxembourg

Rue du Cherche Midi

RENNES

Rue Madame

Rue Guynemer

VANEAU

Rue Vaneau

Rue de Vaugirard

ST-PLACIDE

Rue d'Assas

Rue Auguste Comte

DUROC

Rue de Rennes

Blvd. Raspail

Rue Notre-Dame des Champs

Rue Michelet

6

VAVIN

Blvd. du Montparnasse

Place du 18 Juin 1940

MONTPARNASSE BIENVENUE

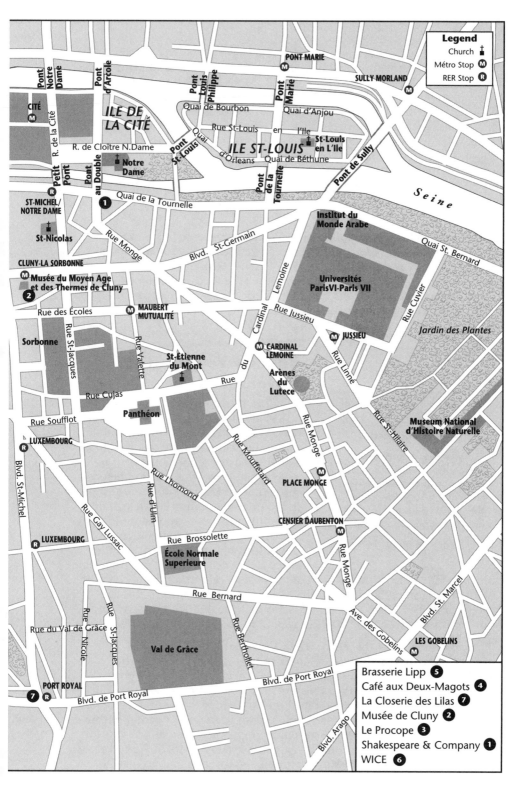

Legend
Church ✝
Métro Stop Ⓜ
RER Stop Ⓡ

PONT MARIE

SULLY MORLAND Ⓜ

Pont Notre Dame

Pont d'Arcole

CITÉ Ⓜ

R. de la Cité

ILE DE LA CITÉ

Pont Louis Philippe

Pont Marie

Quai de Bourbon

Quai d'Anjou

Rue St-Louis   en   l'Ile

St-Louis en L'Ile ✝

Pont Louis

R. de Cloître N.Dame

Quai St-Louis

ILE ST-LOUIS

Quai d'Orléans

Quai de Béthune

Petit Pont

Pont au Double

✝ Notre Dame

Pont St-Louis

Pont de la Tournelle

Pont de Sully

Seine

ST-MICHEL/ NOTRE DAME Ⓡ

❶ Quai de la Tournelle

St-Nicolas ✝

Rue Monge

Blvd. St-Germain

Institut du Monde Arabe

Quai St. Bernard

CLUNY-LA SORBONNE

Ⓜ Musée du Moyen Age et des Thermes de Cluny

❷

Rue des Écoles

MAUBERT MUTUALITÉ Ⓜ

Lemoine

Universités ParisVI-Paris VII

Rue Cuvier

Jardin des Plantes

Sorbonne

Rue St-Jacques

Rue Valette

Rue Jussieu

Cardinal

Rue du

JUSSIEU Ⓜ

CARDINAL LEMOINE Ⓜ

St-Étienne du Mont ✝

Rue Linné

Rue Cujas

Panthéon

Rue

Arènes du Lutèce

Rue St-Hilaire

Museum National d'Histoire Naturelle

Rue Soufflot

LUXEMBOURG Ⓡ

Blvd. St-Michel

Rue Lhomond

Rue Mouffetard

Rue Monge

PLACE MONGE Ⓜ

Rue Gay Lussac

Rue d'Ulm

CENSIER DAUBENTON Ⓜ

LUXEMBOURG Ⓡ

Rue Brossolette

École Normale Superieure

Rue Monge

Rue Bernard

Rue du Val de Grâce

Rue Nicole

Rue St-Jacques

Val de Grâce

Rue Berthollet

Ave. des Gobelins

Blvd. St. Marcel

LES GOBELINS Ⓜ

Blvd. de Port Royal

PORT ROYAL ❼ Ⓡ

Blvd. de Port Royal

Blvd. Arago

Brasserie Lipp ❺
Café aux Deux-Magots ❹
La Closerie des Lilas ❼
Musée de Cluny ❷
Le Procope ❸
Shakespeare & Company ❶
WICE ❻

215

In the *très* posh residential Passy neighborhood sits the modest **Maison de Balzac,** 47 rue Raynouard, 16e (☎ 01/42-24-56-38). The great Honoré de Balzac lived here from 1840 to 1847 under a false name to avoid his creditors, only allowing in those who knew a password. It was here that he wrote some of his most famous novels, including *La Cousine Bette*. You can imagine Balzac at his writing desk and chair, visit his library, and see the Limoges coffee pot (the novelist's initials are in mulberry pink) that his "screech-owl" kept hot throughout the night as he wrote *La Comédie Humaine*. Take Métro line 6 to Passy, walk one block away from the river and turn left onto rue Raynouard. Open Tuesday to Sunday 10am to 5:40pm. Closed in January. Admission: 17F ($3), 9F ($2) ages 8 to 18, free for under-8s.

Dating from 1686, **Le Procope,** 13 rue l'Ancienne-Comédie, 6e (☎ 01/40-46-79-00), is the oldest cafe in Paris. Statesmen such as Franklin and Jefferson, as well as the writers Diderot, Voltaire, George Sand, Balzac, Victor Hugo, and Oscar Wilde all stopped by in their days. Now its single drawback is that it's too famous. Food is typical brasserie fare, but the decor still has a satisfying patina of if-the-walls-could-speak nostalgia. Take the Métro to Odéon. Open daily 11:30am to 1am.

Dollars & Sense

Every Sunday afternoon there are free organ concerts in dozens of the city's old churches. Check *Pariscope,* the guide to entertainment events, for program details.

You Say You Want a Revolution?

The **Conciergerie,** 1 quai de l'Horloge, Ile de la Cité, 1er (☎ 01/53-73-78-50), is the most striking building along the Seine—it's the one that looks like it's wearing a dunce hat. During the revolution, it was the last stop before the guillotine for Marie Antoinette and some 1,300 other royals and royalists. And when the revolution turned on its own leaders, Danton and Robespierre also passed through here. These days the place is too well scrubbed to give a vivid glimpse of the horrors that occurred, but the old cells and torture chamber are interesting nonetheless. Take the Métro to Cité. Open April through September daily 9:30am to 6:30pm; October through March daily 10am to 5pm. Admission: 32F ($6), 21F ($4) ages 12 to 25, free for under-12s.

Everything about the **Place de la Concorde,** 8e (Web site: www.smartweb.fr/visits/concorde/index.html)—the site, the size, the elegance—combines to impress, but this square is most famous for the bloody role it played in France's history. It was here that, in 1793, revolutionaries erected a guillotine—dubbed the "nation's razor"—to execute King Louis XVI, and heads continued to roll for two years. In the center of the square stands a 75-foot, 3,300-year-old, hieroglyphic-covered obelisk from the temple at Luxor, a gift from the Egyptian viceroy in 1829. From the obelisk—take care when crossing the traffic—you get a fabulous view up the

Champs-Elysées to the Arc de Triomphe. The square is absolutely dazzling at night. Get off the Métro at Concorde.

Bet You Didn't Know

Trivia fans will love this one. In medieval times, the Conciergerie was the residence of the *Comte des Cierges* (Count of the Candles), who was the palace superintendent in charge of housing taxes. When the building's Gothic halls were transformed into a prison, the *comte* became the head jailer. Some 200 years later, what's the name of the professional association of hotel concierges? *La Clef d'Or*, which means "The Golden Key".

Chapter 15

Charge It!
A Shopper's
Guide to
Paris

In This Chapter

➤ The lowdown on TVA and credit cards

➤ The best shopping districts

➤ Department stores and flea markets

➤ What else to buy in Paris, and where

No other city embodies luxury and good living like Paris does. Your precon-
ceptions about Parisians being a civilized, well-turned-out, and chic lot will
almost certainly be borne out—at least in a general sense—during your visit.
And nothing demonstrates the average Parisian's *art de vivre* like his or her
shopping habits. Window-shopping, or what's known as *faire du lèche-vitrines*
(it literally means "licking the display windows"), rates just below dining on
the scale of life's great passions. The French look, touch, consider, scrutinize,
reconsider, and then buy—or maybe not. They're not into impulse buying
and reject the notion of a blow-out, hit-all-the-bases spree. Instead, they
tend to pick one neighborhood and shop it.

Once you consider that most of this city's residents still buy their food the
old-fashioned way—stepping into one specialty shop for bread, another for
wine, and yet a third for meat—you'll understand that here is a people willing to sacrifice convenience for personalized service and a higher quality of
merchandise. They're constantly seeking out good taste and craftsmanship.

Take a tip from residents and shop Paris by neighborhood, not item. This
chapter tells you where the best shopping *quartiers* are. Choose one and walk

it, staying alert for those irresistible, one-of-a-kind boutiques that make Paris an unparalleled shopping destination.

So, What Is TVA and How Do You Get It Back?

One reason that Paris is an expensive place to shop is that goods include a 20.6% sales tax. The inverse is the reason why Europeans think the United States is one gigantic bargain bin, so remember this the next time you hear a New Yorker whine about his paltry-in-comparison 8.25% sales tax. In France, this value-added tax (VAT) is called the TVA or *dètaxe*.

If you live outside the European Union, you can get a good hunk of this tax back. But there's a catch: To reclaim the TVA, you have to spend at least 1200F ($214) in the same store in a single day. The amount of the refund varies from store to store but is generally between 13% and 17%. Big depart-ment stores have special *dètaxe* desks where clerks prepare your *bordereaux* (sales invoices). But small shops don't always have the necessary paperwork, so ask first before making any large purchases.

Paying with a credit card will help you get reimbursed faster. If you pay with cash, the red tape is longer because the government has to cut you a refund check. One day when you're old and gray, your long-awaited check will arrive in the mail and it'll be made out in French francs—another reason to pay with plastic.

The last step is to present your *bordereaux* to French customs on your way out of the country. You may be required to produce the purchased goods and their sales tags, so keep that in mind when packing for home.

It's a Plastic City

You'll have no problem using credit cards in France; even the corner tobacconist will accept plastic for purchases over 100F ($18). But again, there's a caveat: Virtually every card-toting Frenchman carries a **Carte Bleue,** the Gallic equivalent of **Visa.** Your MasterCard will also be wel-come in virtually every French establish-ment, but American Express, Discover, Diner's Club, and JCB are not widely accepted in small shops. As you'd expect, higher-end hotels, upscale restaurants, and large international stores will let you pay with practically any brand of plastic.

Dollars & Sense

Most Paris shops, including all the swankiest luxury bou-tiques, have major twice-annual sales in January and July. Follow the signs indi-cating *soldes* and you can typically save 30% and 50% off normal retail prices.

Destination Shopping: The Big Four

While every neighborhood in Paris has its own selection of tempting bou-tiques, four areas stand out as true shopping magnets. Each has a very differ-ent character, so there's bound to be one that appeals to your shopping style.

Shopping Dos and Don'ts

➤ Don't believe what you've heard about the French being rude—it's just another cliché based on cultural misunderstandings. In reality the French have such a well-developed code of politeness that they'd be considered overly formal in your country.

➤ Do make an effort to use five basic French phrases of good manners: *Bonjour* (hello); *S'il vous plaît* (please); *Excusez-moi* (excuse me); *Merci* (thank you); and *Au revoir* (good-bye). These few words will completely change the way you'll be treated. Honest.

➤ Do greet the shopkeeper with *"Bonjour, Madame"* (or *"Monsieur"*) as you enter a boutique. Using the "Madame" tag may feel strange at first, but in France it's a sign of being *bien élevé*, or well bred.

➤ Do start every question with *"Excusez-moi, Monsieur"* (or *"Madame"*), even if the next words out of your mouth are in English. It's considered rude to begin a conversation without first excusing yourself.

➤ Do say *"Merci, au revoir"* on your way out of a small boutique, even if you don't buy anything. Again, it's the minimum in French politeness.

➤ Don't take it personally when shopkeepers don't automatically return your smile. The French simply aren't a smiley bunch, and it's got nothing to do with you.

Fantasy Land: The 8th

If you want to see where Paris gets its reputation as a bastion of over-the-top luxury, head for the 8th *arrondissement* on the Right Bank. Practically every one of the elite French designers is based in the 8th. If there are two streets that positively breathe *haute couture*, they are **avenue Montaigne** (Métro: Alma-Marceau, Franklin D. Roosevelt) and **rue du Faubourg St-Honoré** (Métro: Concorde). There are *Parisiennes* who shop exclusively on these two streets and, as you'd expect, the snob quotient is sky-high. But even if you don't have a platinum card, you can have a helluva good time window-shopping here.

While avenue Montaigne and rue du Faubourg St-Honoré boast some of the same big designer names, they are completely different in temperament. Avenue Montaigne is wide, graceful, and lined with chestnut trees. Once upon a time it was filled strictly with French designers, but thanks to an influx of international names it's become undeniably hip. Beginning at the Pont de l'Alma end, there's Dolce & Gabbana at No. 2 (☎ 01/47-20-42-43), Prada at No. 10 (☎ 01/53-23-99-40), Inès de la Fressange at No. 14 (☎ 01/47-23-08-94), Joseph at No. 16 (☎ 01/47-20-39-55), Valentino at No. 19 (☎ 01/47-23-64-61), Christian Lacroix at No. 26 (☎ 01/47-20-68-95),

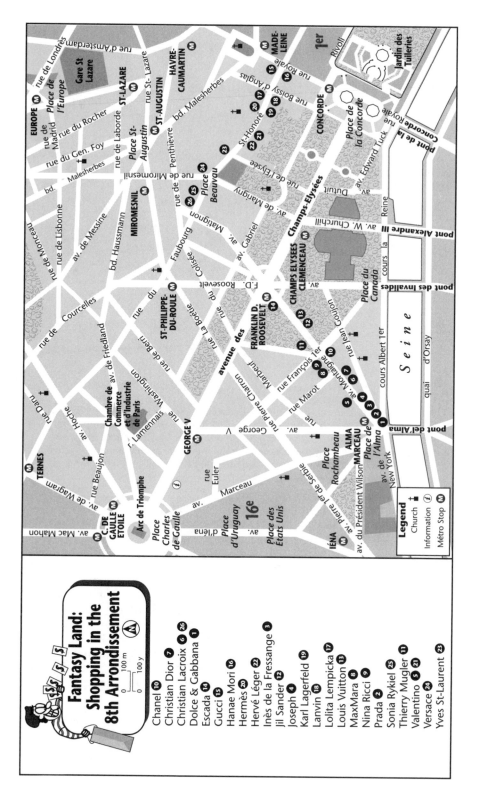

Fantasy Land:
Shopping in the
8th Arrondissement

0   100 m
0   100 y

Chanel **10**
Christian Dior **7**
Christian Lacroix **6** **26**
Dolce & Gabbana **1**
Escada **14**
Gucci **15**
Hanae Mori **16**
Hermès **20**
Hervé Léger **22**
Inès de la Fressange **3**
Jil Sander **12**
Joseph **4**
Karl Lagerfeld **19**
Lanvin **18**
Lolita Lempicka **17**
Louis Vuitton **13**
MaxMara **8**
Nina Ricci **9**
Prada **2**
Sonia Rykiel **25**
Thierry Mugler **11**
Valentino **5** **21**
Versace **24**
Yves St-Laurent **23**

Christian Dior at No. 30 (☎ 01/40-73-54-44), MaxMara at No. 31 (☎ 01/47-20-61-13), Nina Ricci at No. 39 (☎ 01/49-52-56-00), Chanel at No. 42 (☎ 01/47-23-74-12), Thierry Mugler at No. 49 (☎ 01/47-23-37-62), Jil Sander at No. 50 (☎ 01/44-95-06-70), Louis Vuitton at No. 54 (☎ 01/45-62-47-00), and Escada at No. 57 (☎ 01/42-89-83-45).

Rue du Faubourg St-Honoré is narrower with small sidewalks, and it's always jammed with shoppers. If you begin at the rue Royale intersection and head west, you'll come across Gucci at No. 2 (☎ 01/53-05-11-11), Hanae Mori at No. 9 (☎ 01/47-42-76-68), Lolita Lempicka at No. 14 (☎ 01/49-24-94-01), Lanvin at No. 15 (☎ 01/44-71-33-33), Karl Lagerfeld at No. 19 (☎ 01/42-66-64-64), Hermès (pronounced "Air-mess") at No. 24 (☎ 01/40-17-47-17), Valentino at No. 27 (☎ 01/42-66-95-94), Hervé Léger at No. 29 (☎ 01/44-51-62-36), Yves Saint Laurent at No. 38 (☎ 01/42-65-74-59), Versace at No. 62 (☎ 01/ 47-42-88-02), Sonia Rykiel at No. 70 (☎ 01/42-65-20-81), and Christian Lacroix at No. 72 (☎ 01/42-68-79-00).

The Hot Kid on the Block

A few blocks east of rue Royale is **Colette**, 213 rue St-Honoré, 1er (**☎ 01/ 55-35-33-90**), a must-stop for eagle-eyed trend watchers. The emporium showcases all that's hip and now in home design, beauty products, art, and fashion accessories, with prices ranging from the very reasonable to the astronomical. Downstairs is a high-tech cafe with light fare and over 40 brands of bottled water on offer.

Rarefied Chic: The 6th

Every once in a while one neighborhood gets an infusion of shopping karma and emerges as the darling of Parisian retail. Right now that place is the 6th. It's the perfect destination if you've only allotted a morning or an afternoon for shopping. The 6th has always been a magical *quartier* brimming with tiny one-of-a-kind boutiques, antiques dealers, art galleries, interior decorators, ivy-covered courtyards, and cafes in which you could happily spend the rest of your life. What's new is that the luxe big boys from the Right Bank have been moving in. Louis Vuitton, Dior, Armani, Gucci, Hermès, and Cartier have already opened branches here, and others are close behind. Still, it's the tiny, one-of-a-kind specialty shops that make this neighborhood such a pleasure.

The area's best specialty boutiques are disproportionately clustered on and around place St-Germain-des-Prés (Métro: St-Germain-des-Prés), place d'Acadie (Métro: Mabillon), and place St-Sulpice (Métro: St-Sulpice). But the best way to do the 6th is to simply wander its streets, keeping an eye peeled for serendipitous discoveries. Below are just a few highlights.

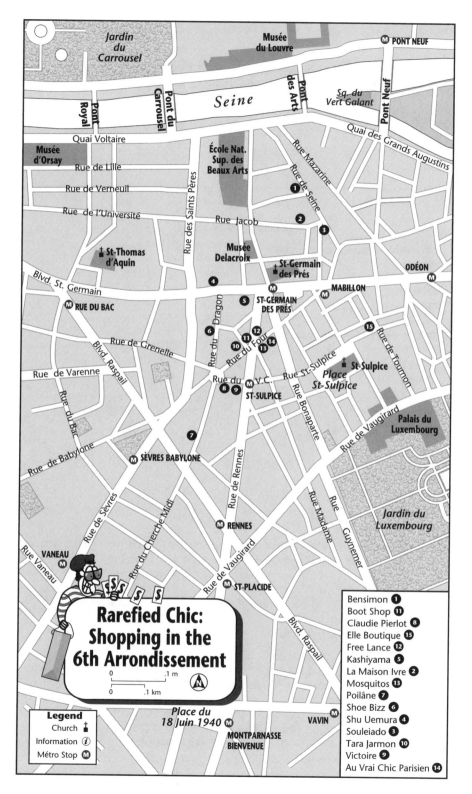

Jardin du Carrousel

Musée du Louvre

M PONT NEUF

Pont des Arts

Pont Royal

Pont du Carrousel

Seine

Sq. du Vert Galant

Pont Neuf

Quai Voltaire

Quai des Grands Augustins

Musée d'Orsay

Rue de Lille

École Nat. Sup. des Beaux Arts

Rue Mazarine

Rue de Verneuil

Rue de l'Université

Rue des Saints Pères

Rue Jacob

Rue de Seine

① Bensimon

② La Maison Ivre

③ Souleiado

✝ **St-Thomas d'Aquin**

Musée Delacroix

✝ **St-Germain des Prés**

ODÉON **M**

Blvd. St. Germain

④

M **ST-GERMAIN DES PRÉS**

M **MABILLON**

M RUE DU BAC

⑤ Kashiyama

⑮

Rue de Tournon

Rue du Dragon

⑥

Rue de Four

⑪ ⑫

⑭

⑬

⑩

Rue St-Sulpice

Rue de Grenelle

Rue de Varenne

Blvd. Raspail

Rue du Bac

⑧ ⑨

M V.C.

Rue du **ST-SULPICE**

Rue Bonaparte

✝ **St-Sulpice**

Place St-Sulpice

Palais du Luxembourg

Rue de Vaugirard

⑦

Rue de Babylone

M SÈVRES BABYLONE

Rue de Rennes

Rue Madame

Rue Guynemer

Jardin du Luxembourg

Rue de Sèvres

Rue du Cherche-Midi

M RENNES

Rue Vaneau

VANEAU

M

Rue de Vaugirard

M ST-PLACIDE

Blvd. Raspail

💲 💲 💲 💲

Rarefied Chic: Shopping in the 6th Arrondissement

0 ———— .1 m
0 ———— .1 km

Ⓝ

VAVIN **M**

Legend

Church ✝
Information ⓘ
Métro Stop **M**

Place du 18 Juin 1940 **M**

MONTPARNASSE BIENVENUE

Bensimon	①
Boot Shop	⑪
Claudie Pierlot	⑧
Elle Boutique	⑮
Free Lance	⑫
Kashiyama	⑤
La Maison Ivre	②
Mosquitos	⑬
Poilâne	⑦
Shoe Bizz	⑥
Shu Uemura	④
Souleiado	③
Tara Jarmon	⑩
Victoire	⑨
Au Vrai Chic Parisien	⑭

➤ **Boulevard Saint-Germain** is the Left Bank's main drag, with a suitably tempting array of shops. Head to **Shu Uemura** at No. 176 (☎ 01/45-48-02-55) for voguish cosmetics that come in a zillion shades, and to **Kashiyama** at No. 147 (☎ 01/46-34-11-50) for a look at what the world's most trendsetting designers are turning out these days.

What's Your Size?

Women's dresses, coats, skirts:

American	6	8	10	12	14	16	18
British	8	10	12	14	16	18	20
French	36	38	40	42	44	46	48

Women's shoes:

American	5	6	7	8	9	10	
British	3	4	5	6	7	8	
French	36	37	38	39	40	41	

Men's suits:

American/British	34	36	38	40	42	44	46	48
French	44	46	48	50	52	54	56	58

Men's shirts:

American/British	14	15	15½	16	16½	17	17½	18
French	36	38	39	41	42	43	44	45

Men's shoes:

American	7	7½	8	8½	9½	10½	11	11½
British	6	7	7½	8	9	10	11	12
French	39	40	41	42	43	44	45	46

➤ **Rue de Seine** is fabulous for quintessential French items. **Bensimon** at No. 54 (☎ 01/43-54-64-47) stocks the sort of striped Breton mariner tops that grace every French girl's vacation wardrobe. **Souleiado** at No. 78 (☎ 01/43-54-62-25) is *the* name for scarves, bags, and linens in traditional Provençal patterns. And **La Maison Ivre**, half a block away at 38 rue Jacob (☎ 01/42-60-01-85), sells pottery from all over France.

➤ **Rue du Four** has two don't-miss women's shops, **Tara Jarmon** at No. 18 (☎ 01/46-33-26-60), for chic, understated streetwear and **Au Vrai Chic Parisien** at No. 47 (☎ 01/45-44-77-00), for retro French styles. Also worth checking out are the fun and funky shoes at **Boot Shop** at No. 20 (☎ 01/43-54-96-28), **Mosquitos** at No. 25 (☎ 01/43-25-25-16), and **Free Lance** at No. 30 (☎ 01/45-48-14-78). **Shoe Bizz**, nearby at 42 rue du Dragon (☎ 01/45-44-91-70), replicates the latest footwear styles for 30% cheaper than you'll find elsewhere.

➤ **Rue du Vieux Colombier** is where to come for that seemingly effortless, chic Parisian look. Try **Victoire** at No. 15 (☎ 01/45-44-28-02) for smart weekend menswear and **Claudie Pierlot** at No. 23 (☎ 01/45-48-11-96) for fabulous womenswear that simmers between retro and classic. Just on the other side of the place St-Sulpice, the **Elle Boutique,** 30 rue St-Sulpice (☎ 01/43-26-46-10), a spin-off of the famous women's magazine, is where Left Bank girls shop for classic separates.

Artsy Ecclecticism: The 4th

The Marais (4e) is an idyllic, picture-postcard setting crammed with artists' studios, secret courtyards, magnificent Renaissance mansions, and some of the most original shops in the city.

Rue des Francs-Bourgeois is the neighborhood's main artery, chock-a-block with jewel box–size shops of every ilk. And don't miss **rue des Rosiers,** a fashion destination in its own right with its white-hot designers standing shoulder-to-shoulder with Jewish delis. Everything is really close in the Marais, so don't be afraid to ramble down the tiniest lane whenever whim dictates. Part of the fun of this neighborhood is that it's such a mixed shopping bag.

A Taste of Paris

While knocking around in St-Germain-des-Prés, pop into **Poilâne**, 8 rue du Cherche-Midi (☎ 01/45-48-42-59) for some of the most famous bread in the world. The yummy sourdough loaves grace Paris's best tables and are even express delivered to eateries in the United States and Japan.

Marais highlights include **Paule Ka,** 20 rue Mahler (☎ 01/45-44-92-60), for the sort of timeless womenswear Grace Kelly and Audrey Hepburn used to wear; **Argenterie des Francs-Bourgeois,** 17 rue des Francs-Bourgeois (☎ 01/42-72-04-00), for inexpensive bracelets made from Victorian-era silverware; **L'Eclaireur,** 3 ter rue des Rosiers (☎ 01/48-87-10-22), for cutting-edge designerwear that draws a faithful celebrity following; **Anne Séverine Liotard,** 7 rue St-Merri (☎ 01/48-04-00-38), for candles that double as *objets d'art* and burn forever; **Lunettes Beausoleil,** 28 rue Roi du Sicile (☎ 01/42-77-28-29), for glamorous sunglasses that flatter any face; **Extrem Origin,** 10 rue Ferdinand Duval (☎ 01/42-72-70-10), for ultrachic interior design that uses only natural elements; and **Shamballa,** 30 rue de Sévigné (☎ 01/42-78-69-76), for eye-catching contemporary jewelry for men and women.

Time-Savers

Save the Marais for a Sunday afternoon. While the rest of the city is virtually shuttered up, this enchanting enclave of cobbled streets and funky boutiques remains wonderfully animated.

225

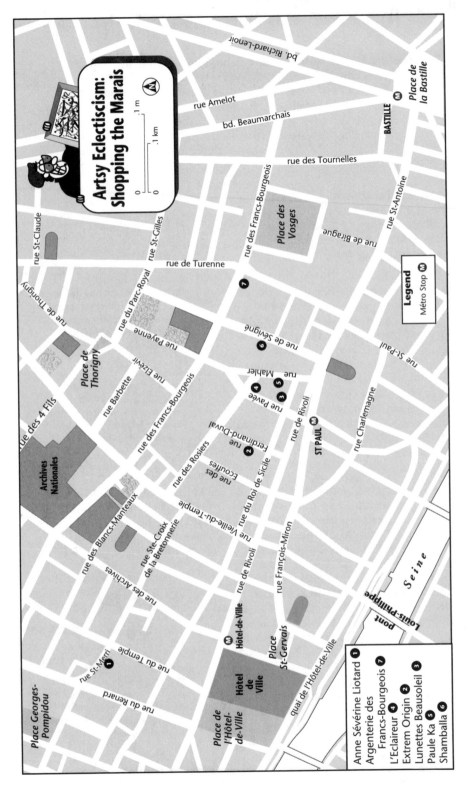

Artsy Eclecticism: Shopping the Marais

Legend
Ⓜ Métro Stop

Anne Sévérine Liotard ❶
Argenterie des
Francs-Bourgeois ❼
L'Éclaireur ❹
Extrem Origin ❷
Lunettes Beausoleil ❸
Paule Ka ❺
Shamballa ❻

Cheap & Cheerful Souvenirs

Ain't got tons of leftover cash but want to return home with a nifty memento? Try the **Seine-side booksellers** for frame-worthy vintage French ads from old magazines. The interior stalls at **St-Ouen flea market,** 18e (Métro: Clignancourt, open Saturday to Monday 9am to 6pm) sell charming postcards of Paris, circa 1900 to 1940. Either of France's two ubiquitous dime stores, **Monoprix** and **Prisunic,** are the place to go for inexpensive Bourjois cosmetics (made in the Chanel factories). Stop by a **pharmacy** for Roger & Gallet perfumed bath gels, pure-vegetable *savons de Marseille* (soaps), and Klorane hair products. **La Vaissellerie,** 332 rue St.-Honoré, 1er (☎ **01/42-60-64-50**), sells those huge bowl-shaped breakfast mugs that are quintessentially French. **Louis Vuitton** (see "Fantasy Land: The 8th," above), makes a *carnet de voyage* ($30), a scrapbook filled with watercolors of Paris sights and plenty of room to jot down your vacation memories. And finally, for lovers of kitschy keepsakes, you can pick up that miniature Eiffel Tower or World Cup '98 T-shirt (now priced to sell) in any of the souvenir shops on **rue de Rivoli,** 1er (Métro: Tuileries, Palais-Royal, or Louvre-Rivoli).

Young & Trendy: The 2nd

While it lacks the atmosphere of St-Germain-des-Prés and the Marais, the 2nd *arrondissement* is where young, hip Parisians with more dash than cash head for this season's trendiest looks. With the noteworthy exception of Place des Victoires, a hub of pricey designerwear, all the best shopping in the 2nd happens in an area called the **Sentier.** This is Paris's garment district, which bleeds into corners of the 1st and 3rd. The name of the game here is exploiting trends cheaply—a concept that may make *haute couturiers* grimace, but certainly one that makes fashion more democratic.

Many of the best shops are found within a square formed on the south by **rue Rambuteau,** on the west by **rue du Louvre,** on the north by **rue Réaumur,** and on the east by **rue St-Martin.** This ragtag pocket of the city is absolutely fabulous for hip secondhand clothes, funky clubwear, and "stock boutiques" selling last season's designerwear at a discount.

Don't miss **Mon Amie Pierlot,** 3 rue Montmartre, 1er (☎ **01/40-28-45-55**), for Claudie Pierlot's (see "The Rarified Chic: The 6th," above) less-expensive, casual line; **Agnès b.,** 3-6 rue du Jour, 1er (☎ **01/45-08-56-56**), for timelessly chic basics for men and women; **Kiliwatch,** 64 rue Tiquetonne, 2e (☎ **01/42-21-17-37**), for supercool retro looks that'll be on next year's runways (designers come here for inspiration); **Le Shop,** 3 rue d'Argout, 2e (☎ **01/40-28-95-94**), for two floors of clubwear by France's hottest young designers; **Orb,** 39 rue Etienne Marcel, 1er (☎ **01/40-28-09-33**), for wild-'n-chunky urban footwear; **Et Vous Stock,** 15 rue de Turbigo,

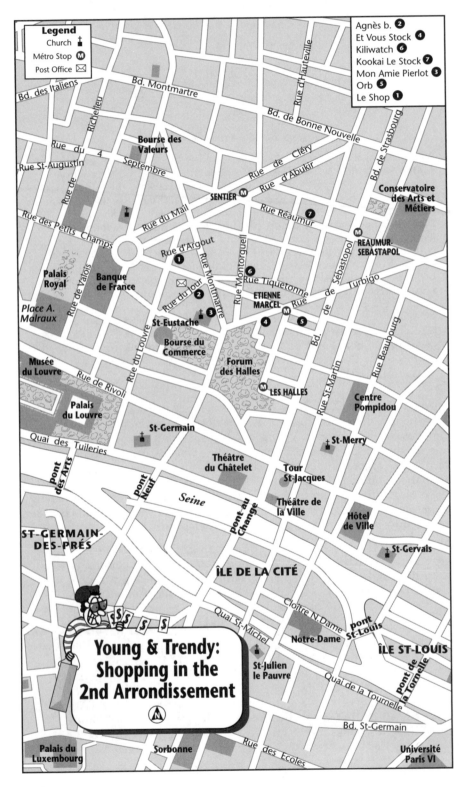

Young & Trendy:
Shopping in the
2nd Arrondissement

2e (☎ **01/40-13-04-12**), for last year's unsold Et Vous styles at half price; **Kookaï Le Stock,** 82 rue Réaumur, 2e (☎ **01/45-08-93-69**), for massive reductions on Kookaï clothes.

Dollars & Sense

Itching for a bargain? **Rue Alésia,** 14e (Métro: Alésia), is chock-a-block with French designer discount outlets selling last year's surplus at up to 70% below retail prices. These "stock boutiques" are more downscale than their sister shops, so prepare to rifle through racks to find the gems. Designers with outlets here include **Chevignon** at No. 12, **Sonia Rykiel** at No. 64, and **Cacharel** at No. 114. French childrenswear lines include **Sergent Major** at No. 82, **Tout Compte Fait** at No. 101, and **Jacadi** at No. 116.

Department Stores

Though a lot less fun than shopping in boutiques, department stores are great if you want everything under one roof. You'll get the biggest hit on boulevard Haussmann, 9e (Métro: Chaussée d'Antin or Havre-Caumartin). Here, side by side, sit two venerable shopping institutions, **Galéries Lafayette** at No. 40 (☎ **01/42-82-34-56**) and **Au Printemps** at No. 64 (☎ **01/42-82-50-00**). Both stock a huge array of big-name, international labels and have enormous perfumeries.

Try as they might, the Right Bank's two other department stores never quite managed to acquire the same stature. But **La Samaritaine,** 19 rue de la Monnaie, 1er, Métro: Pont Neuf or Châtelet (☎ **01/40-41-20-20**), and the **Bazar de l'Hôtel de Ville** (known as **BHV**), 52 rue de Rivoli, 4e, Métro: Hôtel de Ville (☎ **01/42-74-90-00**), are good if you're near the Seine and in a hurry. On the Left Bank, your only, but excellent, choice is the wonderfully revamped **Bon Marché**, 22 rue de Sèvres, 7e, Métro: Sèvres-Babylone (☎ **01/44-39-80-00**).

Flea Markets

Paris's most famous market by a long shot is the **Marché aux Puces St-Ouen** (a.k.a. the Marché Clignancourt), 18e (Métro: Porte de Clignancourt)—some 3,000 stalls and shops rolled into one indoor-outdoor emporium. It's open weekends and Mondays from about 9am to 6pm. Within its labyrinthine innards you'll find everything from valuable antiques to kitschy art to wartime memorabilia to vintage clothing to bona fide junk. It's one of the few places in the city where it's okay to dicker.

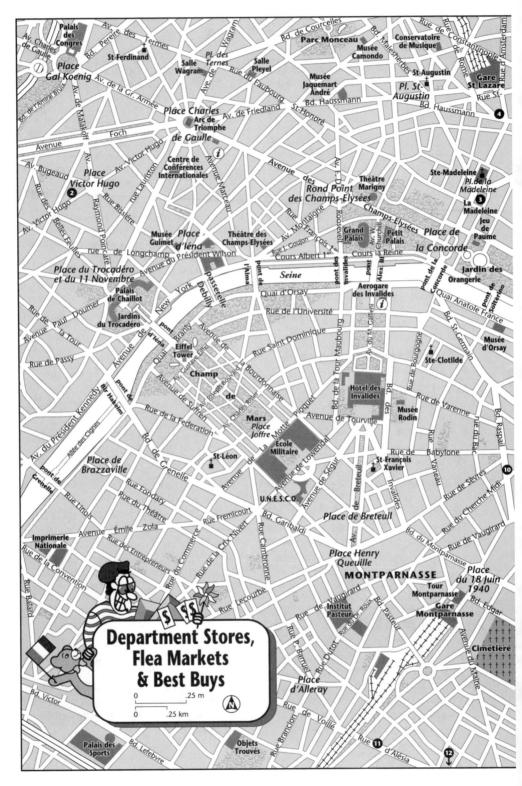

Department Stores,
Flea Markets
& Best Buys

$ $$

0   .25 m

0   .25 km

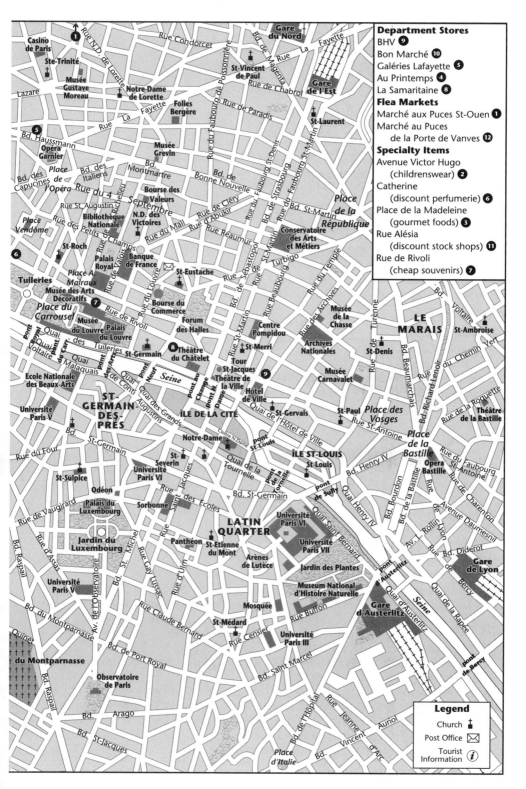

Department Stores
BHV **9**
Bon Marché **10**
Galéries Lafayette **5**
Au Printemps **4**
La Samaritaine **8**

Flea Markets
Marché aux Puces St-Ouen **1**
Marché au Puces
de la Porte de Vanves **12**

Specialty Items
Avenue Victor Hugo
(childrenswear) **2**
Catherine
(discount perfumerie) **6**
Place de la Madeleine
(gourmet foods) **3**
Rue Alésia
(discount stock shops) **11**
Rue de Rivoli
(cheap souvenirs) **7**

Legend
Church ✝
Post Office ✉
Tourist
Information ⓘ

231

Tourist Traps

Browsing at **Marché aux Puces St-Ouen** can be a lot of fun, as long as you realize that, like any crowded market, this one has its share of pickpockets, pea-under-the-shell conmen, and pushy vendors.

Meanwhile, on the other side of town, the **Marché aux Puces de la Porte de Vanves,** 14e (Métro: Porte de Vanves) is open on weekends from 6:30am to 4:30pm. It looks like a big old yard sale, but dealers swear by it. Among the clutter you may find collectibles like silverware from French estates, vintage Hermès scarves, and old-fashioned toys. Haggle, because asking prices are often high.

Best Buys in Paris

If you're coming to shop with a particular item in mind, it's a good idea to do a price check before you leave home. Without the French TVA included, the same product might be cheaper at your local mall. Here are some items that are almost always better buys in Paris:

Perfume

You'll run across many duty-free perfumeries all over central Paris, and they're always a better deal than airport duty-free. Better yet, go to one of the discount perfumeries that sell beauty products at 20% to 30% below retail. One of the best is **Catherine**, 5 rue Castiglione, 1er, Métro: Concorde (☎ **01/42-61-02-89**). On top of the discount, you can reclaim the TVA if you spend more than 1600F ($285).

🌟Kids Children's Clothing

If you love the quality and creativity that goes into French childrenswear, make your way to **Avenue Victor Hugo,** 16e (Métro: Victor Hugo). Here, on one of the city's most chi-chi shopping drags, you'll find four boutiques selling stylish, colorful, and fun clothes that are also wearable, washable, and affordable: **Petit Bateau** at No. 72 (☎ **01/45-00-13-95**), has been around for generations and is a staple in French kids' wardrobes; **Du Pareil Au Même** at No. 97 (☎ **01/40-49-00-33**), sells well-made cotton separates for babies to preteenagers (a few doors down at No. 111, its sister store, **Du Pareil Au Même Maison** focuses on irresistibly cute layette items for newborns). **Sergent Major** at No. 109 (☎ **01/53-65-12-17**), and **Tout Compte Fait** at No. 115 (☎ **01/47-55-63-36**), sell fashionable clothes for babies to school-age children. All four boutiques are part of chains with locations throughout the city, but these branches have better selections than most.

Gourmet French Foods

For foodies, heaven is a shopping binge on place de la Madeleine, 8e (Métro: Madeleine). Here you'll find France's two most famous gourmet shops, **Fauchon** at No. 26 (☎ **01/47-42-60-11**), and **Hédiard** at No. 21 (☎ **01/42-66-44-36**). The French consider Fauchon the more prestigious of the two, but both have been in business since the 1800s and are synonymous with high-quality, delectable eats. You can buy foie gras, pâté, cassoulet, truffles, cookies, chocolates, mustards, honeys, jams, and hundreds of other addictions either individually or packed in gorgeous gift baskets.

Most items are packed so that they can be brought legally into the United States, but there are limitations. Meat products, including foie gras and cassoulets, and mushrooms, such as truffles, must be shelf-stable without refrigeration, and either vacuum-sealed or canned. Cheeses must be fully cured. If you're not sure, it's best not to try to bring it home. For more information on food products that can be brought into the United States, visit the USDA's Web site at www.aphis.usda.gov/oa/travel.html.

Chapter 16

Battle Plans for Seeing Paris: Six Great Itineraries

In This Chapter

➤ Six itineraries to show you the best of Paris

There are a zillion ways to see Paris, and no two travelers do it exactly the same. First timers may hit all the major sights but see little else, while veteran visitors might blow off museums altogether and spend all their time shopping and hanging out in cafes. It's very likely that you fall somewhere in between. How much you can accomplish will depend largely on how many days you'll be in the city and what pace you want to set. To make the most of your time, it's always a good idea to avoid the ricocheting pinball technique—bouncing across town to see one attraction and then back again for another. If you only have a few days, think about lowering your ambitions and choosing only a handful of sights. You might also want to begin with one of the better orientation bus tours mentioned in chapter 12.

This chapter proposes six itineraries, each of which will show you several of the top sights. Every itinerary is meant to wind up around nightfall, leaving you in a place where you can easily hop on a Métro back to your hotel or to one of the nightlife options listed in chapters 18 to 20. Shopping, when included, is left for the end of the afternoon so you won't be trudging around town with shopping bags. For more information on each attraction, please refer to chapters 13 and 14.

Itinerary 1—The Louvre & Champs-Elysées

This itinerary covers the city's most celebrated stretch and is loaded with don't-miss sights: the Louvre, the Tuileries Garden, the place de la Concorde, the Champs-Elysées, and the Arc de Triomphe. **Best days:** Monday or Wednesday through Friday. **Worst days:** The Louvre is closed on Tuesday, and weekends draw maddening crowds.

1. **The Louvre.** Plan to arrive around 9am, just as the museum is opening. Arriving early is a good idea because the museum gets more crowded as the day progresses. Remember to use the rue de Rivoli entrance to avoid the long lines at the pyramid. Begin with the *Mona Lisa* and other "best of" highlights (see chapter 13), so you can enjoy them before elbow room becomes scarce. Allow a minimum of 3 hours for your visit.

2. **Lunchtime.** The Louvre has two great lunch options. You can either grab something quick and cheap at the **food court** inside the Carrousel du Louvre underground mall or hang out with the hip crowd at the chic **Café Marly** (see chapter 11) whose terrace looks out over the museum's courtyard and I. M. Pei's pyramid. It's on the Richelieu wing, entered via the courtyard.

3a. **Jardin du Tuileries.** Take a stroll down the center of the gardens for a view that sweeps all the way up the Champs-Elysées to the Arc de Triomphe. Nab one of the benches (the most-coveted are alongside the reflecting pools) if you're feeling a bit tired. In summertime, families may want to spend an hour at the little fairground, where there's a fab view of the city from the Ferris wheel.

3b. **Jardin du Palais-Royal.** You can relax and admire the statues in these peaceful gardens or peruse the elegant shops and galleries that line the square.

4. **Musée de l'Orangerie.** If you're up to contemplating more art, pop into the old Tuileries orangery for a look at Monet's water lilies.

5. **Champs-Elysées.** Starting on the place de la Concorde, take a leisurely walk up what the French call "the most beautiful avenue in the world." If your feet aren't too tired, take a detour down avenue Montaigne, one of the world's most luxurious shopping drags, then return to the Champs and continue on your way.

6. **Arc de Triomphe.** Be sure to use the pedestrian tunnel instead of attempting to cross the city's biggest traffic circle on foot. Then ride the elevator to the top and savor the view.

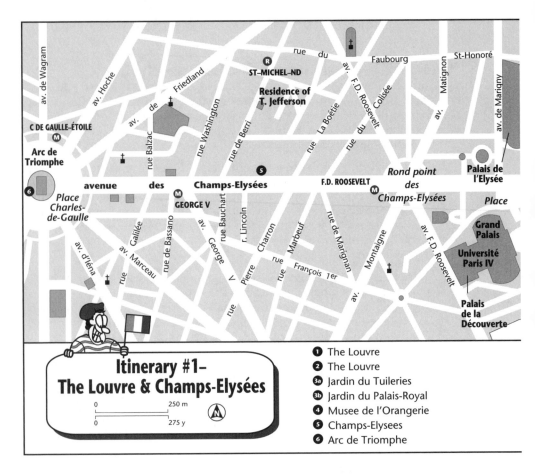

Itinerary #1–
The Louvre & Champs-Elysées

0   250 m
0   275 y

❶ The Louvre
❷ The Louvre
❸a Jardin du Tuileries
❸b Jardin du Palais-Royal
❹ Musee de l'Orangerie
❺ Champs-Elysees
❻ Arc de Triomphe

Itinerary 2—Champs-Elysées & the River

This route takes in a handful of the city's top sights—Arc de Triomphe, Champs-Elysées, Musée d'Art Moderne de la Ville de Paris, and Eiffel Tower—and ends with a river cruise. If you choose the late-lunch option, remember that you need to book a few days in advance. **Best days:** Tuesday to Saturday. **Worst days:** Much of the Champs-Elysées is shut down on Sunday, and the modern art museum is closed on Monday.

1. **Arc de Triomphe.** Use the pedestrian tunnel instead of trying to cross the traffic circle on foot. The arch opens at 9:30am April to September, and at 10am the rest of the year—prime time for watching the city wake up.

2. **Champs-Elysées/Avenue Montaigne.** Make your way down the upper half of the avenue at your own pace, then turn right down avenue Montaigne for window-shopping at the elegant haute couture shops.

3. **Princess Diana's Memorial.** Once you get to the riverside end of avenue Montaigne, you'll see the replica of the Statue of Liberty's bronze torch (see chapter 13) at the far side of the place de l'Alma. If you'd like to pay your respects, spend a few moments here.

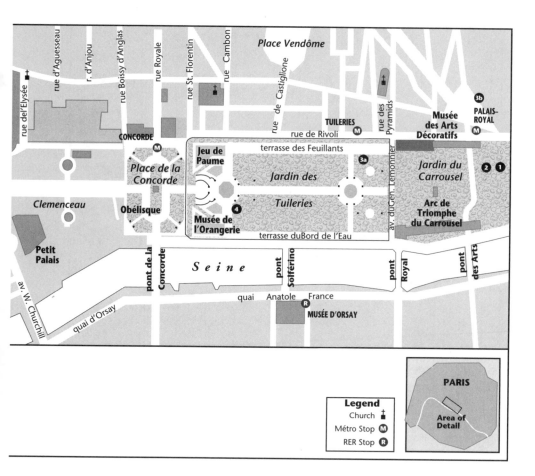

4a. Early Lunch. If you're hungry now, **Lina's Sandwiches**, 8 rue Marbeuf, is an inexpensive option in this tony neighborhood. (From place de l'Alma, head up avenue George V and take your second right). See chapter 11 for details.

4b. Late Lunch. If you can hold out a few hours until after you've visited the modern art museum, wait to lunch at **Au Bon Accueil** (see chapter 10) and order from the excellent, daily-changing market menu. From place de l'Alma, walk across the bridge to the Left Bank and head down avenue Rapp. Take the third right, onto rue de Monttessuy. Remember to book ahead—the last seating is at 2pm.

5. Musée d'Art Moderne de la Ville de Paris. The attraction here is the Pompidou Center's magnificent collection of modern art (see chapter 13). Allow 2 hours for your visit.

6. Eiffel Tower. If you're coming from the modern art museum, walk along the river toward the tower, then cross the Pont d'Iéna to the Left Bank and you're there. If you're coming from Au Bon Accueil, you're already within spitting distance. Walk to the end of rue de Monttessuy (going in the opposite direction from which you came), and look up.

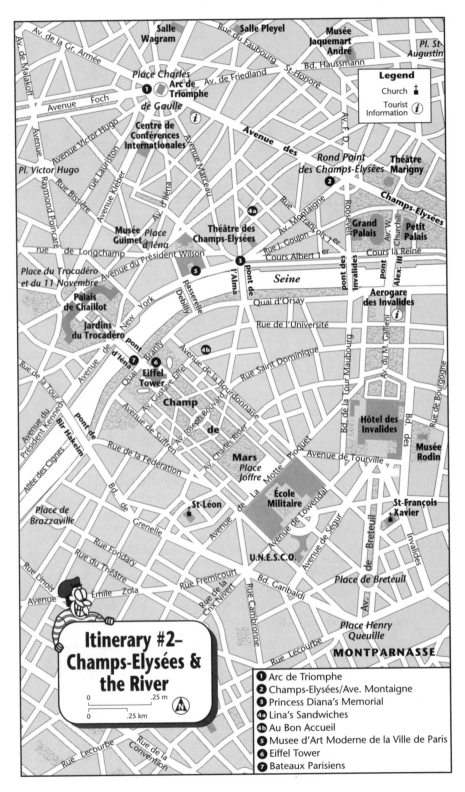

Itinerary #2–
Champs-Elysées &
the River

0   .25 m
0   .25 km

❶ Arc de Triomphe
❷ Champs-Elysées/Ave. Montaigne
❸ Princess Diana's Memorial
❹ⓐ Lina's Sandwiches
❹ⓑ Au Bon Accueil
❺ Musee d'Art Moderne de la Ville de Paris
❻ Eiffel Tower
❼ Bateaux Parisiens

238

7. **River Cruise.** At the base of the Eiffel Tower, look along the river's quay for the **Bateaux Parisiens** embarking point (see chapter 12). The cruise takes an hour.

Itinerary 3—The Marais

Since this itinerary is dedicated to one of the city's most captivating pockets, it has a leisurely pace with plenty of free time for rambling and discovering. It includes the Musée Picasso, lunch on place des Vosges, and an afternoon of window-shopping. **Best day:** Sunday, when the Marais is the only neighborhood in the city where the stores don't shut down. **Worst days:** Monday and Tuesday, when museums are closed.

1. **Musée Picasso.** Try to get to the museum as it opens, around 9:30am. Allow 2 hours for your visit.

2. **Place des Vosges.** Enjoy a promenade under the arcade surrounding this gorgeous square, taking time to browse in antiques shops, art galleries, and designer boutiques.

3. **Maison de Victor Hugo.** If you're interested in seeing where one of France's greatest writers lived, spend a half hour in his former home at No. 6 (see chapter 14).

4. **Lunchtime.** There are two great lunch spots on place des Vosges: **Ma Bourgogne** at No. 19 and **La Chope des Vosges** at No. 22. Both serve very good salads and bistro fare at reasonable prices and have delightful arch-covered terraces. Try for an outside table at Ma Bourgogne first. If none are available, go to La Chope. (Ma Bourgogne doesn't take credit cards, but there are ATMs nearby on rue de Rivoli.)

5. **Musée Carnavalet.** If you're in the mood to learn about Paris's fascinating history (see chapter 14), spend 60 to 90 minutes here before shopping.

6. **Shopping.** Spend the rest of the afternoon browsing in the neighborhood's terrific boutiques (see chapter 15 for shopping highlights).

7. **Tea Break.** If you need to take the weight off your feet, stop at one of the Marais's great tearooms (see chapter 10): **Le Mariage Frères** is the more elegant and expensive of the two, with over 500 kinds of tea and a clientele of ladies-who-lunch; **Le Loir dans la Théière** is more relaxed and hip, with lots of comfy armchairs and low tables. Both serve scrumptious *pâtisseries*.

Itinerary 4—Latin Quarter & the Islands

This itinerary dedicates the morning to the Latin Quarter and the afternoon to the islands. It's not nearly as taxing as the 11 steps suggest because many sights require less than an hour. The route features some of the most enchanting corners of the city and includes the Panthéon, Musée de Cluny, Notre Dame, Sainte-Chapelle, and Conciergerie. **Best days:** Wednesday to

239

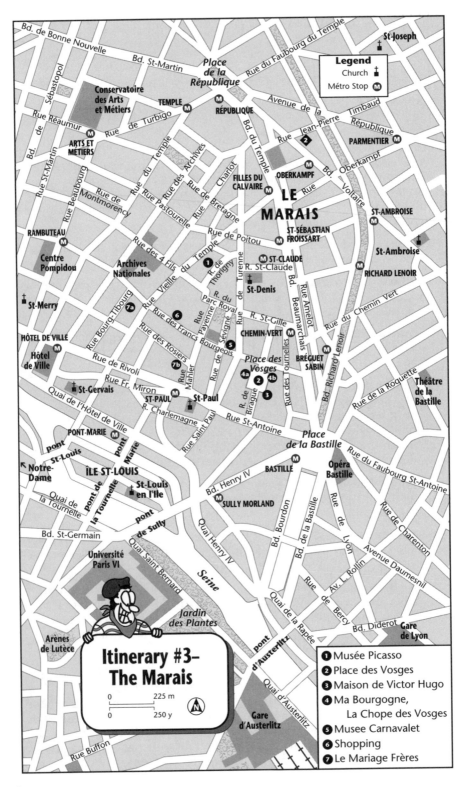

Legend

Church †
Métro Stop Ⓜ

LE MARAIS

**Itinerary #3–
The Marais**

0   225 m
0   250 y

❶ Musée Picasso
❷ Place des Vosges
❸ Maison de Victor Hugo
❹ Ma Bourgogne,
   La Chope des Vosges
❺ Musee Carnavalet
❻ Shopping
❼ Le Mariage Frères

Sunday. **Worst days:** The Mouffetard market is closed on Mondays, the Musée de Cluny is closed on Tuesdays, and Berthillon is closed both days.

1a. Musée de Cluny. Try to get to the museum as it opens, at 9:15am. Allow an hour to visit the medieval collections and the Roman baths (see chapter 14).

1b. Jardin du Luxembourg. If you're not interested in seeing a museum first thing in the morning, head instead to the park and share a bench with Left Bank nannies and their charges. If you've got young kids, rent a toy boat and sail it on the reflecting pond.

2. Panthéon. Leaving the Musée de Cluny, head straight ahead on rue de la Sorbonne (the big building you'll pass on your left is the university), take a left on rue Soufflot and the Panthéon will be right in front of you. If you're coming from the park, exit at boulevard St-Michel and the Panthéon is 3 blocks east. Allow a half hour to visit.

3. Rue Mouffetard. Join the locals at this wonderfully colorful open-air market (open 8am to 1pm), but don't be suckered into any of its restaurants. Their fixed-price menus may appear inexpensive, but there's usually a catch—like outrageously priced beverages or desserts.

4. Lunchtime. In a neighborhood packed with touristy eateries, there are two notable exceptions (see chapter 10): **Chez Alexandre** and **Les Fêtes Galantes**. Both offer delicious and affordable fixed-price lunch menus.

5. Notre Dame. Head to the river and cross over to the Ile de la Cité. After viewing the cathedral's interior, burn off lunch by climbing to the church's tower.

6. Ile St-Louis. Cross the footbridge to the magical Ile St-Louis, allowing an hour to window-shop and stroll along its tree-lined quays.

7. Taste-of-Paris Break. Before leaving Ile St-Louis, visit **Berthillon** (see chapter 11) for the most delectable ice cream in France. If you've come during the winter, stop into the **Café Flore-en-l'Ile** (see chapter 11) for what may be the world's best hot chocolate and a fabulous view of Notre Dame's flying buttresses.

8. Sainte-Chapelle. If you're thinking of dropping a sight from today's itinerary, don't let it be this one. Buy a ticket to both the lower and upper chapels, then prepare yourself for something magical. You may have to wait in line for about a half hour, then allow another 30 minutes for your visit. Remember to enter through the Palais de Justice's courtyard (see chapter 13).

9. Conciergerie. If you're up to seeing one more sight today, spend a half hour in the prison that held guillotine-destined royalty and royalists (see chapter 14).

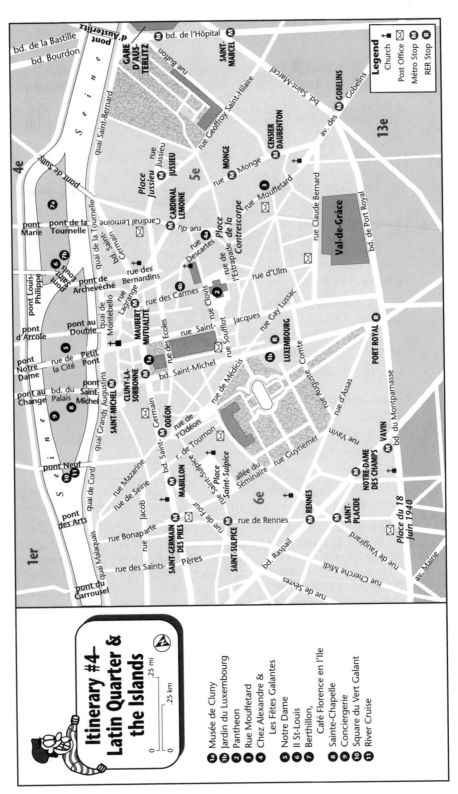

Itinerary #4—
Latin Quarter &
the Islands

0 .25 mi
0 .25 km

① Musée de Cluny
⑪ Jardin du Luxembourg
② Pantheon
③ Rue Mouffetard
④ Chez Alexandre &
   Les Fêtes Galantes
⑤ Notre Dame
⑥ Il St-Louis
⑦ Berthillon,
   Café Florence en l'Ile
⑧ Sainte-Chapelle
⑨ Conciergerie
⑩ Square du Vert Galant
⑪ River Cruise

10. **Square du Vert Galant.** Hemingway said that standing on this little triangle of green felt like being at the prow of a boat. Jutting into the Seine with wonderful views of the Louvre and both riverbanks, it's a magical place to watch the sun set.

11. **River cruise.** If you haven't already done it on Itinerary 2, take a 1-hour cruise with **Vedettes du Pont Neuf** (see chapter 12).

Itinerary 5—Musée d'Orsay & St-Germain-des-Prés

The day's highlights are the Musée d'Orsay's Impressionist collection and shopping in St-Germain-des-Prés. **Best days:** Tuesday to Saturday. **Worst days:** The shops in St-Germain-des-Prés are closed on Sunday. The Rodin and Orsay museums are closed on Monday.

1. **Hôtel des Invalides (Napoléon's Tomb).** For the most dramatic approach, get off the Métro at Champs-Elysées Clémenceau, then cross the Pont Alexandre III on foot. Plan to arrive for the 10am opening time. Bypass the army museum and head straight to the Eglise du Dôme to visit Napoléon's tomb. Allow 20 to 30 minutes.

2. **Musée Rodin.** After exiting Les Invalides' church, turn left onto boulevard des Invalides, then right on rue de Varenne. Spend an hour visiting the sculptor's home and gardens.

3. **Matignon.** Regardless of whether you're coming from Les Invalides or the Rodin museum, continue east down rue de Varenne to sneak a peek past the guards to the residence of Lionel Jospin, the French Prime Minister.

4. **Lunch at the Musée d'Orsay.** From Matignon, follow rue de Bellechasse all the way to the river, alongside which sits the museum. Head directly to the top floor and have an early lunch in the **Café des Hauteurs** (see chapter 13). It's smart to eat before 1pm, when long lines form.

5. **Musée d'Orsay.** Stay on the top floor and allow 90 minutes for viewing the Impressionist collection. If you're not too tired, visit the ground floor's collection of sculpture before leaving.

6. **Shopping.** After exiting the museum, turn left on rue de Bellechasse. Walk 3 blocks, turn left, and follow boulevard Saint Germain to the Café aux Deux-Magots and the St-Germain-des-Prés church. Spend the rest of the afternoon shopping in Paris's chicest neighborhood (see chapter 15 for shopping highlights).

7. **Coffee Break.** When you've made your way to place St-Sulpice, grab an outside table at the **Café de la Mairie** (see chapter 11) and have a café crème while gazing at the lion-guarded fountain.

8. **Quick Hit of Art.** Before leaving place St-Sulpice, pop into the neo-classical St-Sulpice church for a brief look at the paintings by Delacroix in the first chapel on the right.

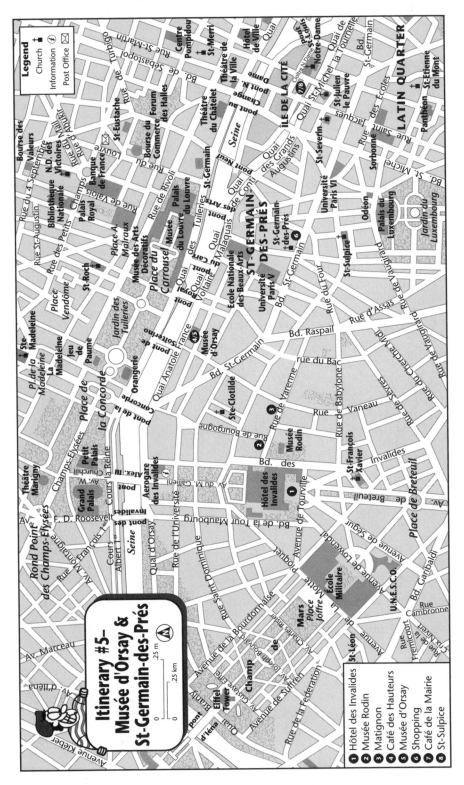

Legend
✝ Church
ℹ Information
☒ Post Office

Itinerary #5–
Musée d'Orsay &
St-Germain-des-Prés

0 —— .25 km
0 —— .25 m

1 Hôtel des Invalides
2 Musée Rodin
3 Matignon
4 Café des Hauteurs
5 Musée d'Orsay
6 Shopping
7 Café de la Mairie
8 St-Sulpice

LATIN QUARTER

ÎLE DE LA CITÉ

ST-GERMAIN-
DES-PRÉS

244

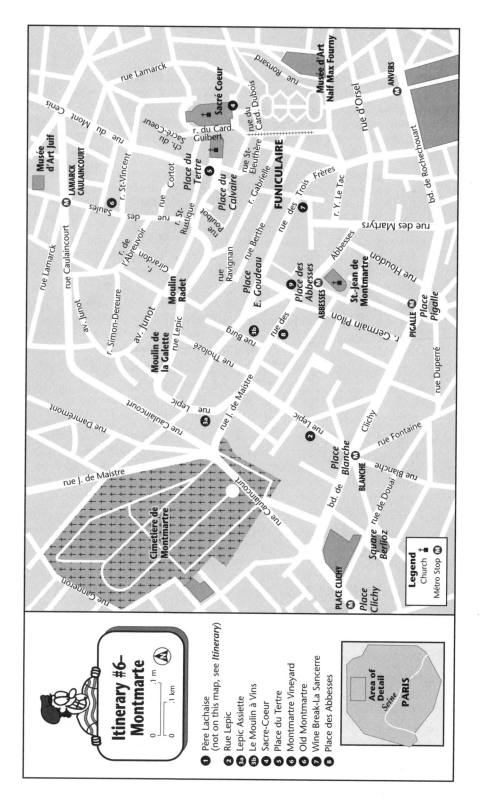

Itinerary #6–
Montmarte

0 ─── .1 m
0 ─── .1 km

1 Père Lachaise
   (not on this map, see *Itinerary*)
2 Rue Lepic
3a Lepic Assiette
3b Le Moulin à Vins
4 Sacre-Coeur
5 Place du Tertre
6 Montmartre Vineyard
6 Old Montmartre
7 Wine Break-La Sancerre
8 Place des Abbesses

PARIS
Area of
Detail
Seine

Itinerary 6—Père-Lachaise & Montmartre

This itinerary combines two of the most popular and enjoyable sights outside of central Paris: the Père Lachaise cemetery and Montmartre. The day entails a lot of walking, so be sure to wear comfortable shoes. **Best days:** Tuesday to Saturday. **Worst days:** Most shops and restaurants in Montmartre are closed on Sunday, and the rue Lepic market is closed on Monday.

1. **Père-Lachaise.** Try to get to the cemetery before 10am (it opens at 9am). Enter through the main gate, and don't forget to get a free map from the gatekeeper (or use the one in chapter 13). Plan to leave around noon.

2. **Rue Lepic.** Take Métro line 6 to Blanche, then walk up the winding rue Lepic to catch the last half hour of the outdoor market's buzz before purveyors start closing up shop, around 1pm. The market is liveliest on weekends.

3. **Lunchtime.** So stay near the place des Abbesses and join the locals for inexpensive crêpes and cider at **Lepic Assiette** or light bistro fare at **Le Moulin à Vins** (see chapter 10). Note that Lepic Assiette is closed on Sunday and Le Moulin à Vins is closed on Monday.

4. **Sacré-Coeur.** From place des Abbesses, walk past the post office on rue Yvonne le Tac, and continue down rue Tardieu to the base of the Sacré-Coeur's gardens. Take the funicular to the top, then spend 15 to 20 minutes inside the church before climbing to the dome.

5. **Place du Tertre.** Artists have been setting up their easels and hawking their paintings in this colorful square since the 19th century. Some of them can be a tad pushy, but if you don't want your portrait done, just say "non, merci" and keep walking. The cafes that line the square make this an evocative place to stop for coffee or a glass of wine, though prices are slightly higher than elsewhere.

6. **Montmartre Vineyard.** Leave the square via rue Norvins, then take a right and walk downhill on rue des Saules. On your right you'll come across the city's only surviving vineyard. One of Paris's most famous cabarets, Au Lapin Agile, sits opposite the vineyard on the corner of rue des Saules and rue St-Vincent.

7. **Old Montmartre.** Head back up rue des Saules, pass the place du Tertre on your left, and continue down the opposite side of the hill via the old twisting streets. Rue des Trois Frères, rue Yvonne le Tac, and rue des Abbesses are lined with fun boutiques.

8. **Wine break.** If you feel like ending the day with a glass of wine, take one of the outside tables at **Le Sancerre** (see chapter 11) and watch the world go by.

9. **Place des Abbesses.** Before leaving this pretty square—a favorite backdrop for movies—stop to admire the entrance to the Métro station. It's one of very few left in Paris that still has its art nouveau wrought-iron arches.

Designing Your Own Itinerary

The itineraries in chapter 16 might need a tuck here or some extra room there to match your schedule and taste—or they might not suit your needs at all. You'll need to design your own itineraries for at least some of the days you'll be in Paris. The trick is getting organized. The disorganized traveler wastes a lot of time in Paris. She shows up at the Louvre on the day it's closed and leaves shopping in St-Germain-des-Prés for a Sunday.

First, you have some prioritizing to do. There simply aren't enough hours in the day—or at least in your visit—for you to do everything that has caught your attention so far. If you've been paying attention, there are check marks and numbers all over the margins of the five previous chapters. Those mark-ups form the pattern for your customized itinerary. The worksheets in this chapter will help you make the most of the hours you do have.

Back to the Drawing Board: Your Top Attractions

Begin with any activities you've booked ahead—perhaps a walking tour (see chapter 12) or a cooking class (see chapter 14)—and plot them on their designated days.

Next, turn to chapter 13, where you and your fellow travelers assigned a number (from 1 to 5) to your top attractions and listed them on the worksheet. Enter them here according to number.

#1 Picks

➤ _____

➤ _____

➤ _____

➤ _____

➤ _____

➤ _____

➤ _____

➤ _____

➤ _____

➤ _____

#2 Picks

➤ _____

➤ _____

➤ _____

➤ _____

➤ _____

➤ _____

➤ _____

➤ _____

➤ _____

➤ _____

#3 Picks

➤ _____

➤ _____

➤ _____

➤ _____

➤ _____

#4 Picks

➤ _____

➤ _____

➤ _____

➤ _____

➤ _____

➤ _____

Now go back to chapter 14 and find the other activities and attractions that fit your interests. Assign each one a number, and add them to the lists above. Then flip through chapters 12 and 15, and add anything else that's littered with check marks to the appropriate list. (You're probably wondering why there are no spaces for #5s. If you're a typical visitor, you've already listed a week's worth of activities without including them, that's why.)

Suppose your #1 list says "Louvre, Shopping in St-Germain-des-Prés, Musée d'Orsay, river cruise, walking tour in the Marais, Eiffel Tower, Sainte-Chapelle." That would easily fill 2 days to the overflowing point. You might start the first day at the Louvre, have lunch in the Marais (before your walking tour, perhaps), visit the Sainte-Chapelle, and cap off the day with a river cruise with Vedettes du Pont Neuf (which embarks on the Ile St-Louis). The next day, you'd concentrate on the Left Bank, starting with the Eiffel Tower, spending mid-morning to mid-afternoon at the Musée d'Orsay (including lunch at the museum's Café des Hauteurs), and then leaving the rest of the afternoon for shopping in St-Germain-des-Prés.

Notice that the sample itinerary didn't include the Champs-Elysées or Notre Dame, and the world didn't immediately come to an end. Remember, the cardinal rule is: *See what you want to see, not what you think you should see.*

Budgeting Your Time

Most sights take 60 to 90 minutes to visit. Some, like Notre Dame and the Place des Vosges, will probably take less; others, such as the Louvre and Père Lachaise Cemetery, take longer. Add travel and meal time, plus some down time to relax and reflect, and that means you'll have time for three to four sights per day.

Time-Savers

If all this planning seems like a drag, remember that you can cannibalize the itineraries in chapter 16. Use them as a template, but feel free to mix and match, work backward, or substitute activities in the same neighborhood while keeping the same basic structure.

Add the number of entries on your #1 and #2 lists, and divide by the number of full days in your trip. (Don't include days earmarked for out-of-town trips, no matter how organized you think you are.) If your resulting number is larger than four, you have a bit of a time-management dilemma.

Of course, it's theoretically possible to see six or eight sights in a day. But like a lot of other things that are theoretically possible, that's a terrible idea. You're better off reducing the number of sights per day, but how?

➤ **Lengthen your visit.** Although this may not be possible.

➤ **Split up.** If you and your travel companions don't share identical lists of #1s, this may be the only way to make everybody happy. Spending half a day or even a day apart will ensure fewer compromises.

➤ **Skip the #3s.** You'll have more fun and make better use of your hard-earned money if you concentrate on your list of unmissables. Immerse yourself in fewer experiences and enjoy them more.

Time-Savers

If you're coming to Paris in the wintertime, be sure you're prepared for damp-ness and rain. If the weather is particularly bleak one day, have a Plan B itinerary full of indoor activities handy.

Getting All Your Ducks in a Row

Visualize, visualize, visualize. Grab a map and mark your must-see attractions, then mark your hotel. Now find activities that naturally group together, and plan to visit them on the same day. Most of Paris's attractions are centrally located, but stick-ing to one neighborhood at a time will lead to less backtracking. Think strategical-ly.

Fill-ins

These are things you squeeze in between your "must dos." Shopping and hanging out in cafes are naturals; go back to chapters 11 and 15 and pick out the spots you especially want to visit. List them here.

Shopping

➤ _____

➤ _____

➤ _____

➤ _____

➤ _____

➤ _____

➤ _____

➤ _____

➤ _____

➤ _____

Cafes

➤ _____

➤ _____

➤ _____

➤ _____

➤ _____

➤ _____

➤ _____

➤ _____

➤ _____

➤ _____

Plot these on the map, and match them with your unmissable sights. Be realistic about time—storming the Marais will take a lot longer than window-shopping in the luxury boutiques on avenue Montaigne.

Dining is another fill-in. For now, don't worry about dinner. If there are specific places where you want to have lunch, plot them on the map and note them here. If nothing jumps out at you, look through chapters 10 and 11 for places that are in the same neck of the woods as your other attractions. Note those below.

Lunch

➤ _____

➤ _____

➤ _____

➤ _____

➤ _____

➤ _____

➤ _____

➤ _____

➤ _____

➤ _____

Sketching Out Your Itineraries

Finally, you're ready to outline some itineraries. A basic one should go something like this:

Breakfast at (*hotel/place/neighborhood*). See (*attraction*) in the morning. Lunch at (*place/neighborhood*) or (*alternate place*). Walk or take the Métro to (*attraction*) and spend the afternoon.

Don't forget to include other attractions and shopping: "Pass through the Luxemburg Gardens on the way to the Panthéon"; "stop at Colette after the Louvre."

Itinerary #1

➤ _____

➤ _____

➤ _____

➤ _____

➤ _____

Itinerary #2

➤ _____

➤ _____

➤ _____

➤ _____

➤ _____

Itinerary #3

➤ _____

➤ _____

➤ _____

➤ _____

➤ _____

Itinerary #4

➤ _____

➤ _____

➤ _____

➤ _____

➤ _____

Part 6

On the Town: Nightlife & Entertainment

The City of Light shines brightest at night. Smoky jazz clubs, gilded opera and dance halls, comedy clubs, rock concerts in baroque auditoriums, risqué cabarets, understatedly chic wine bars, techno dance clubs—whatever your preference, you can be sure that Paris has got it in spades. Entertainment can be found in every district of the city—some of it expensive, and some of it free. You may have already booked tickets to a concert or show (see chapter 4), but probably have left a few evenings free for spontaneous fun. At least let's hope so. Chapters 18 to 20 give you a selection of what's out there and how to make the most of it.

Chapter 18

The Sound of Music

In This Chapter

➤ How to find out what's playing

➤ Where to hear your kind of music

➤ How to get tickets

Stevie Wonder was right: Music *is* a language we all understand. And Paris offers up just about every kind of music you can imagine—from classical orchestras and chamber music to rock and blues to jazz to *chanson*. This chapter will tell you how to find out what's going on when you're in town.

How to Find Out What's on

If you've been organized, you already have a good idea of what's going on in Paris from surfing the Web sites mentioned in chapters 1 and 4. But even if you arrive in town clueless, it's a snap to get up to speed. Obviously, that's much easier if you speak French, since you can learn a lot from the local newspapers. The Wednesday edition of *Le Figaro* includes *Figaroscope*, a supplement with a copious rundown of the week's entertainment offerings. *Libération*'s weekend arts section is the best around, especially for music.

But if you speak only English, fear not. Your best resource is the digest-size culture Bible, *Pariscope*. It comes out on Wednesday and is available at any newsstand for just 3F (50¢). In its back pages, you'll find a "TimeOut Paris" section in English with quickie reviews under headings such as "Music: Classical & Opera" and "Music: Rock, Roots & Jazz." These give the highlights of concerts happening that week.

Then there are the freebie publications—the monthly *Paris Free Voice* and the quarterly *TimeOut Paris Free Guide*—that you'll find stacked in all the city's English-language bookstores (see "News Media" in Appendix A), expat eateries, and Anglophone bars. But if you're really serious about finding out who's in town, you should peruse the posted schedules in the *billetterie* (ticket office) at FNAC or Virgin Megastore, the two biggest ticket dispensers in Paris (see below for details).

Where to Rock, Pop, or Groove Your World

Aside from two stadium-size venues large enough to host superstar bands (Palais Omnisport de Bercy, Stade de France), Paris's concert halls are generally midsize to small. The most centrally located venues are the **Grand Rex**, 1 bd. Poissonière, 2e (☎ 01/40-28-08-55; Métro: Bonne-Nouvelle); the **Olympia**, 28 bd. des Capucines, 9e (☎ 01/47-42-25-49; Métro: Opéra) and **Casino de Paris,** 16 rue de Clichy, 9e (☎ 01/42-85-26-27; Métro: Trinité). Three more of the main sites are clustered in Pigalle and lower Montmartre: **La Cigale,** 120 bd. Rochechouart, 18e (☎ 01/49-25-89-99; Métro: Pigalle); the **Elysée Montmartre,** 72 bd. Rochechouart, 18e (☎ 01/44-02-45-42; Métro: Anvers); and the **Divan du Monde,** 75 rue des Martyrs, 18e (☎ 01/44-92-77-66; Métro: Abbesses). **La Bataclan,** 50 bd. Voltaire, 11e (☎ 01/47-00-30-12; Métro: Oberkampf), is north of the Bastille in heart of the hip Oberkampf *quartier*. And last but not least, the **Zénith**, 211 av. Jean Jaurès, 19e (no box office; Métro: Porte de Pantin), is on the city's fringe in the Parc de la Villette.

That's the Ticket

If you want to go to a rock gig while you're in town, don't bother calling the box office directly. Some venues, like the Zénith, don't even have box offices; others don't accept credit cards. And paying by credit card over the phone has never really taken off in France, so you'll probably be told to come in person to buy your tickets anyway. It's far more convenient to simply go to a centrally located music store with a general *billetterie* (ticket office). You can get tickets to virtually every non-sold-out concert at:

➤ **Virgin Megastore,** basement ticket office at 52 av. des Champs-Elysées, 8e (☎ 01/44-68-44-08; Métro: George V), and Carrousel du Louvre, 99 rue de Rivoli, 1er (☎ 01/49-53-52-90; Métro: Palais Royal–Musée du Louvre).

➤ **FNAC,** 3rd level down at Forum des Halles, 1 rue Pierre Lescot, 1er (☎ 01/40-41-40-00; Métro: Les Halles); 136 rue de Rennes, 6e (☎ 01/49-54-30-00; Métro: St-Placide); and 74 av. des Champs-Elysées, 8e (☎ 01/53-53-64-64; Métro: George V).

Expect to pay anywhere from 90F to 300F ($16 to $54) per ticket, depending on the band and venue, plus a 20F ($4) per-ticket handling fee.

Live Music on Tap

If you like your music live but don't have the time or money for procuring concert tickets, head to a bar known for great live gigs. **The Chesterfield Café**, 124 rue La Boétie, 8e (☎ **01/42-25-18-06**; Métro: Franklin D. Roosevelt), is much more than just a Tex-Mex place off the Champs-Elysées. It's a mecca for up-and-coming or just-arrived rock and blues bands, with an occasional blast from the past thrown into the mix. Alanis Morissette, The Spin Doctors, Eagle Eye Cherry, Dogstar (Keanu Reeves's band), and John McEnroe have all played here. Free concerts start at 11:30pm Tuesday to Saturday.

The Horses Mouth, 120 rue Montmartre, 2e (☎ **01/40-39-93-66;** Métro: Rue Montmartre), is an unpretentious English-style pub that hosts free concerts almost nightly, from French blues and *chanson* to reggae, raï, or funk. Call ahead to see what's the flavor *du jour.*

The cavernous space at **La Réservoir,** 16 rue de la Forge-Royale, 11e (☎ **01/43-56-39-60;** Métro: Faidherbe-Chaligny), has become a magnet for music industry moguls and impromptu star turns (like Jewel). Thursdays focus on young talent, Saturdays on groove. Other nights are a mixed bag of comedy (in French), videos, and art shows.

Live from Paris, It's MCM Café

Is it a watering hole or a TV studio? Cyber cafe or a video arcade? Whatever you want to call it, the new **MCM Café**, 92 bd. de Clichy, 18e (☎ **01/ 42-64-39-22;** Métro: Blanche), is the largest and most daring music bar/club/cafe in Paris. The place is the brainchild of the French cable music channel MCM, which broadcasts *en direct* (live) from the all-day, all-night venue with musical acts, chart shows (*à la* the BBC's "Top of the Pops"), and interviews. On Thursday and Friday, you're likely to see established Gallic and international acts, while Monday and Tuesday are dedicated to sniffing out fresh, unsigned talent. The interactive atmosphere doesn't stop at the door; passersby can watch the show from boulevard de Clichy as it's projected on the studio's glass facade. Open daily from 9am to 5am.

All That Jazz

Paris's love affair with jazz continues. The extremely lively local scene is bolstered by a constant barrage of guest appearances from top international talent. In the clubs, American singers and musicians enjoy elite status (expat success stories include Dee Dee Bridgewater), though several Frenchmen and -women have also broken through.

Many good jazz clubs are concentrated on the Left Bank and around Les Halles in the 1st *arrondissement*. All the local acts tend to play the same clubs, so check the specialty publications *Jazz Hot* or *Jazz Magazine* (both available at newsstands) to see who's playing where.

The *crème de la crème* of jazz clubs are **New Morning,** 7 rue des Petites-Ecuries, 10e (☎ **01/45-23-51-41;** Métro: Château d'Eau), and **Jazz Club Lionel Hampton,** Hôtel Méridien Etoile, 81 bd. Gouvion-St-Cyr, 17e (☎ **01/40-68-30-42;** Métro: Porte Maillot). At both clubs, most acts come straight from New Orleans and Harlem.

On the Left Bank, favorite haunts include **Le Bilboquet,** 13 rue St-Benoit, 6e (☎ **01/45-48-81-84;** Métro: St-Germain-des-Prés); **Birdland,** 20 rue Princesse, 6e (☎ **01/43-26-97-59;** Métro: Mabillon); **La Villa,** 29 rue Jacob, 6e (☎ **01/43-26-60-00,** Métro: St-Germain-des-Prés); and **Le Petit Journal,** 71 bd. St-Michel, 5e (☎ **01/43-26-28-59;** Métro: RER Luxembourg).

Near Les Halles, **Le Petit Opportun,** 15 rue des Lavandières-Ste-Opportun (☎ **01/42-36-01-36;** Métro: Châtelet), sometimes draws top-flight American talent. **Au Duc des Lombards,** 42 rue des Lombards, 1er (☎ **01/42-33-22-88;** Métro: Les Halles), and **Le Sunset,** 60 rue des Lombards, 1er (☎ **01/40-26-46-60;** Métro: Les Halles), are just up the street from each other.

That's the Ticket: The good news about jazz clubs is (a) you rarely need to buy your ticket in advance (though showing up early for the marquis gigs is a smart idea); and (b) many clubs offer free admission. The bad news is that they zap you later with exorbitant prices for alcoholic beverages. When a club does charge admission, it can vary wildly from 40F ($7) to over 130F ($24), depending on the popularity of the performer. Note that shows rarely get started before 10pm.

Where Classical Is King

For classical music aficionados, Paris is a paradise of never-ending, inexpensive lunchtime and evening concerts. They're held in many of the city's most evocative churches (Ste-Chapelle, Notre Dame, St-Germain-des-Prés) and museums (Louvre, Musée d'Orsay, Musée Cluny), and range in styles from chamber music to orchestral works to choral performances. Check *Pariscope* for weekly listings.

Web Sites for Gig Info

Musi–Cal   http://concerts.calendar.com.

JazzNet   www.culturekiosque.com

Jazz en France   www.jazzfrance.com

For big-name classical artists, the top three venues are all in the 8th *arrondissement*. The most illustrious out-of-towners (Kiri Te Kanawa, Jessye Norman, Vienna Philharmonic) tend to perform at either the sumptuous **Théâtre des Champs-Elysées,** 15 av. Montaigne, 8e (☎ **01/49-52-50-50;** Métro: Alma-Marceau), or the **Salle Pleyel,**

252 rue du Faubourg St-Honoré, 8e (☎ 01/45-61-53-00; Métro: Ternes), where the Orchestre de Paris also appears regularly. Nearby, the **Salle Gaveau,** rue de la Boétie, 8e (☎ 01/49-53-05-07; Métro: Miromesnil), is an old-world setting for chamber music and vocal recitals.

That's the Ticket: Since the most prestigious classical concerts sell out way in advance, consider using a stateside ticket broker. **Edwards and Edwards (☎ 800/223-6108)** will give you a rundown of who'll be performing during your stay and have your tickets delivered to your home or to your hotel. There's a handling surcharge of 10% to 20%. You can also order tickets by phoning the box office directly, but you risk running into an operator who doesn't speak English.

Once you're in town, you can buy tickets to many recitals and concerts at the ticket office in **FNAC** (see above), which charges a 20F ($3) per-ticket fee. For discounts of up to 50% on unsold tickets of same-day performances, go in person to the **Kiosque Théâtre,** 15 place de la Madeleine, 8e (no phone; Métro: Madeleine). Tickets are sold Tuesday to Friday from 12:30pm to 7:30pm and Saturday from 2pm to 8pm.

The Best Concerts in Life Are Free

If your taste runs more toward Mozart than Madonna or Morrissey, you may not need much of an entertainment budget. Paris offers a bounty of free classical music, often in splendid settings.

Maison de la Radio, 116 av. du Président Kennedy, 16e (☎ 01/42-30-15-16; Métro: RER Kennedy–Radio France), the home of top classical radio station France Musique, regularly hosts free concerts and public recordings of young classical musicians. Many other concerts, including world music and jazz, can be attended for just 30F ($5).

Conservatoire de Musique et de Dance de Paris, 209 av. Jean-Jars, 19e (☎ 01/40-40-46-46; Métro: Porte de Pantin), is a very prestigious music-and-dance school at Parc de la Villette that opens its doors to the public during many rehearsals and classes. The pupils are some of the best classical musicians in France, and the conductors are often world famous.

Concerts du Midi et Demi, Salle Cortot, 78 rue Cardinet, 17e (☎ 01/47-63-07-96; Métro: Courcelles), offers a winter program of free concerts by promising young musicians.

Eglise St-Merri, 78 rue de la Verrerie, 4e (☎ 01/42-71-40-75; Métro: Hôtel-de-Ville), an 18th-century church in the Marais, is a venue for free chamber music concerts Saturdays at 9pm and Sundays at 4:30pm, featuring different ensembles each week.

Eglise St-Medard, place St-Medard, 5e (☎ 01/42-71-40-75; Métro: Censier-Daubenton), is a Latin Quarter church with an incredibly popular program of occasional orchestral concerts (check *Pariscope* for dates). Go early.

Frère Jacques, Frère Jacques...The Cabaret Scene

There are two breeds of cabaret in Paris—the kind with scantily-clad show-girls and the kind that specializes in the art of *chanson* (literally, "song"). The latter includes French folk songs, old army ditties, sappy love ballads, music-hall numbers, and many an improvised tune about current events (often inspired by the "disaster of the day"). The city's best *chansonniers* gather at **Au Lapin Agile,** 22 rue des Saules, 18e (☎ **01/46-06-85-87;** Métro: Lamarck-Caulaincourt), a dimly lit cottage near Montmartre's vineyard where Picasso and Utrillo used to hang out. A satisfyingly rustic aura is intact, thanks to wooden tables and random memorabilia, and everyone is expected to sing along, even if it's just the *"oui, oui, oui, non, non, non"* refrain of "Les Chevaliers de la Table Ronde." It can be crowded with tourists (though less so in the off-season), but nonetheless good for a laugh. The 110F ($20) cover charge includes your first drink.

Chapter 19

Performing Arts in Paris

> ### In This Chapter
>
> ➤ How to get plugged into the cultural scene
>
> ➤ Opera, dance, cabaret, comedy, and more
>
> ➤ How and where to get tickets

Paris is a terrific town for cultural pursuits. If you love opera, theater, or dance—or if you just like to have a good laugh—this chapter will steer you toward what's going on. Remember that many popular performances are likely to sell out in advance, so book as early as possible.

Finding Out What's on

If you speak French, your best resource for cultural events is the Parisian newspapers: Check the Wednesday edition of *Le Figaro* for its weekly entertainment listings supplement, or the weekend arts section of *Libération*. If you speak only English, look in the back pages of the weekly entertainment digest, *Pariscope,* for its English-language section, "TimeOut Paris." You can buy *Pariscope* at any newsstand for 3F (50¢). Highlights of the week's performances are listed under headings such as "Dance & Theatre" and "Music: Classical & Opera."

A Night at the Opera

For opera lovers, Paris has an embarrassment of riches. The city's prestigious opera company, the Opéra de Paris, makes its home at the ultramodern **Opéra Bastille,** place de la Bastille, 12e (☎ **08/36-73-13-00;** Métro: Bastille). The setting can feel unnervingly high-tech at times, but all 2,700 seats have a good view of the stage. And although it's primarily a dance venue, the *trés* opulent **Opéra Garnier**, place de l'Opéra, 9e (☎ 08/36-69-78-68; Métro: Opéra) still stages the occasional opera.

Web-Footed Culture Vultures

Paris Free Voice (**http://parisvoice.com**) features an events calendar and reviews of current opera, dance, and theater offerings. **Culture Kiosque** (**www.culturekiosque.com**) contains excellent magazine-style sites about opera and dance, replete with schedules of upcoming events, reviews of on-going productions, and phone numbers for ordering tickets.

Lightweight operas and musical comedies are performed at the **Opéra Comique** (Salle Favart), 5 rue Favart, 2e (☎ 01/42-96-12-20; Métro: Richelieu-Druout), and opera also is a big part of the programming at the sumptuous **Théâtre des Champs-Elysées,** 15 av. Montaigne, 8e (☎ 01/49-52-50-50; Métro: Alma-Marceau), and at the **Théâtre du Châtelet,** 2 rue Edouard-Colonne, 1er (☎ 01/40-28-28-40; Métro: Châtelet). Opera ticket prices can range from 50F to 640F ($9 to $114), depending on venue, seat, and performance.

Dance Fever

Due to France's arts policy of decentralization, many of the country's best dance companies are located outside the capital. But they frequently visit Paris, as do great companies from around the world. The **Opéra Garnier**, place de l'Opéra, 9e (☎ 08/36-69-78-68; Métro: Opéra), is the residence of one of the world's best classical dance companies, the Ballet de l'Opéra de Paris. Celebrated modern dance companies (Merce Cunningham, Twyla Tharp, Martha Graham, Paul Taylor, Alvin Ailey) also frequently perform there. Tickets cost from 30F to 350F ($5 to $63), depending on the seat and performance.

Though more famous for its classical music program, the elegant **Théâtre des Champs-Elysées** (see "A Night at the Opera") has been known to welcome such diverse hoofers as Mikhail Baryshnikov, Mark Morris, the American Harlem Dance Company, and London's Royal Ballet. Expect to pay between 40F and 400F ($7 to $70) for your ticket.

After the Opéra Garnier, the city's most important venue for modern dance is the **Théâtre de la Ville** (once run by Sarah Bernhardt), 2 place du Châtelet, 1er (☎ 01/42-74-22-77; Métro: Châtelet), a state-subsidized venue that has given international clout to choreographers such as Jean-Claude Gallotta and Regine Chopinot. You're likely to run across younger, more experimental troupes at the **Théâtre de la Bastille,** 76 rue Roquette, 11e (☎ **01/43-57-42-14;** Métro: Bastille). Tickets at these venues typically cost between 60F and 180F ($11 to $33).

The Inside-Outfit Scoop

The lament is always the same: what to wear, what to wear? For most cultural performances, smart casual dress is fine (sports jackets for men, dresses or pants suits for women). These days, dressy evening clothes are only worn to gala events at the Opéra Garnier or to the premiere of an important play at the Comédie-Française.

Getting Opera & Dance Tickets

You can usually reserve tickets with a credit card if you phone the box office directly, but you may encounter an operator who doesn't speak English. Also, you'll probably have to arrive early to pick up your tickets, or risk them being sold to someone else at the last minute. You can also show up in person at the venue's box office to see if tickets are still available. If the show is sold out, a favorite Parisian tactic is to stand at the entrance with a sign that reads *"Cherche une place"* (or *"deux places"* if they need two tickets). It's surprising how often this works.

But if you've got your heart set on seeing one of the most prestigious performances, your safest bet is using a U.S.–based ticket broker like **Edwards and Edwards (☎ 800/223-6108** in the U.S.). You can have your tickets delivered to your home or to your hotel. There's a handling surcharge of 10% to 20%.

Another proven strategy is to enlist the help of your **hotel concierge.** Don't wait until you arrive in Paris. As soon as you've booked your room, contact the concierge and let him know which performances you'd like to see, your preferred dates, and how much you're willing to spend on tickets. When you arrive in town, don't forget to tip him for his help. Plan on a tip of 100F ($18) for most services, but you may go as high as 500F ($90) if it's a sold-out performance.

The Play's the Thing

Theater is flourishing in Paris, but this is a moot point for the English-speaking visitor. Naturally, hallowed venues such as the **Comédie-Française**, 2 rue de Richelieu, 1er (☎ **01/44-58-15-15;** Métro: Palais-Royal), put on their plays in Molière's language, as do smaller classical and experimental theaters.

The only Paris venue devoted to English-language productions is the **Théâtre de Nesle,** 8 rue de Nesle, 6e (☎ 01/46-34-61-04; Métro: Odéon). Tickets can usually be obtained the day of the performance and typically cost 85F to 100F ($16 to $18).

Dollars & Sense

Half-price tickets for same-day theater, opera, and ballet performances are available to non-sold-out shows at the **Kiosque Théâtre,** across from 15 place de la Madeleine, 8e (no phone; Métro: Madeleine). Tickets are sold Tuesday to Friday from 12:30pm to 7:30pm and Saturday from 2pm to 8pm. Credit cards are not accepted. Expect a line.

Life Is a Cabaret, Old Chum

Even before Josephine Baker showed us her bananas, Paris's cabarets had a reputation for sensual naughtiness. And in today's Parisian revue shows, you can still expect to see a lot of breasts and butts peek-a-booing from behind boas and g-strings. Tourists love 'em, Parisians shun 'em, and none are suitable for children.

Most cabarets offer a menu of ticket options. Prices typically range from 200F ($36) for the show plus one drink to 750F ($134) for the show and dinner. Five hundred francs ($89) usually buys you a seat and a half-bottle of champagne. There are dozens of cabarets in Paris, but these are among the best known.

The 1,100-seat **Lido,** 116 av. des Champs-Elysées, 8e (☎ 01/40-76-56-10; Métro: George V), is the biggest cabaret. Its evening show, *"C'est Magique"* is pure Vegas, complete with lasers, pyrotechnics, and 60 sequin-clad dancers called the Bluebell Girls. The **Crazy Horse,** 12 av. George V, 8e (☎ 01/47-23-32-32; Métro: Alma-Marceau), which claims to be "the most beautiful nude show in the world," is a striptease joint masquerading as a cabaret. The show at the **Moulin Rouge,** 82 bd. de Clichy, 18e (☎ 01/46-06-16-04; Métro: Blanche), is mixed bag, running the gamut from a risqué sexual fantasy sequence to a coquettish can-can line with nods to Piaf and Chevalier. If you're looking for something tamer, try the **Paradis Latin,** 28 rue du Cardinal Lemoine, 5e (☎ 01/43-25-28-28; Métro: Cardinal Lemoine), the most Parisian of the big cabarets, which features an emcee that jokes with the audience in 12 languages.

Movies by Moonlight

If you're visiting between mid-July and late-August, join cinephile Parisians at the **Cinéma en Plein Air,** an annual outdoor film festival at Parc de la Villette, 19e (Métro: Porte de Pantin). Every night, a different film is projected onto an enormous, inflated screen as spectators watch from the lawn. Sound quality is excellent and **entry is free.** To find out what's playing, keep an eye peeled for Métro posters or pick up a program at the main Paris Tourist Office at 127 av. des Champs-Elysées. Films are shown in their original language with French subtitles, so be sure to choose an English–language movie. The show starts around 10pm, but arrive early and rent a lawn chair for 30F ($5). Come laden with blankets and picnic goodies, like the Parisians do.

Ha Ha! Hee Hee! A Comedy Club to Tickle Your Funny Bone

A fabulous new addition to the capital's nightlife scene is **Laughing Matters,** a company that has turned one of the city's best-loved buildings, the historic Hôtel du Nord, 102 quai de Jemmapes (on the Canal St-Martin), 10e (Métro: Jacques Bonsergent), into a thriving comedy club for Paris's English-speaking community. The line-ups are always terrific, featuring award-winning stand-up comics from the United States, the United Kingdom, Ireland, and Australia. Shows start at 8:30pm; admission costs 100F ($18) at the door. For a program of upcoming performers, call ☎ **01/ 48-06-01-20,** fax 01/40-21-86-33, or e-mail matters@altern.org.

Chapter 20

Hitting the
Bars & Clubs

In This Chapter

➤ Where the beautiful people hang out

➤ Where to dance to your kind of music

➤ A rundown of pubs, bars, and cocktail lounges

➤ The best gay bars and clubs

Whether you want to spend the evening chatting over martinis, rubbernecking for models and actors, or dancing till you drop, Paris has a bar or club for you. The French capital may not rival New York for the "city that never sleeps" title, but you can still manage to paint the town a very vivid shade of *rouge*. Bars tend to close around 2am, but clubs keep humming until 5am. Always check the "TimeOut Paris" section in *Pariscope* to find out which clubs are hosting special theme nights.

On the Trail of *le Beau Monde*

If you're looking for wall-to-wall leggy models, the obvious choice is the **Buddha Bar,** 8 rue Boissy d'Anglas, 8e (☎ **01/53-05-90-00;** Métro: Concorde), a restaurant-bar with a chic, Asian-influenced decor and a 30-foot fiberglass Buddha in lotus position. **Barfly,** 49 av. George V, 8e (☎ **01/53-67-84-60;** Métro: George V), is an icon on the see-and-be-seen scene, best known as the place where George Clooney met his French girlfriend (she was working as a hostess at the time). The same owners also run **Le Débarcadère,** 11 rue de Débarcadère, 17e (☎ **01/53-81-95-95;** Métro: Porte Maillot), which attracts a similar crowd of fashionable Parisians and celebrity out-of-towners.

In the wee hours, the glitterati slides over to **Niel's,** 27 av. Ternes, 17e (☎ 01/47-66-45-00; Métro: Ternes), a nightclub that offers a bit of everything—rap, disco, and techno. The ultramod, industrial look is in at **Le Bash,** 67 rue Pierre-Charron, 8e (☎ 01/45-62-95-70; Métro: Franklin D. Roosevelt), which is thick with Armani-clad, Rolex-wearing, jet-setting fashion and media folk from midnight until sunup. **Les Bains,** 7 rue du Bourg-l'Abbé, 3e (☎ 01/48-87-01-80; Métro: Etienne-Marcel), is a staple stop with celebrities and is notoriously difficult to get into. It helps to wear black, look like a model, or have a reservation in the restaurant.

Oberkampf, the Hub of Hip

Five years ago, the center of ultravogue Paris nightlife was indisputably the Bastille. But now the action has migrated due north to neighboring *quartiers* known as Oberkampf and Menilmontant. If you want to drop yourself right in the lap of Paris's hippest hangouts, head to rue Oberkampf, 11e (Métro: Parmentier). **La Cithéa,** at No. 114 (☎ 01/40-21-70-59), is credited with igniting the neighborhood's meteoric rise to übercool. The place gets steamy on Friday and Saturday nights, when a free live band kicks off at 10pm (jazz, groove, and world music predominate); in the wee hours, a DJ takes over to hold the crowds. From Sunday to Tuesday, it's DJ only. Across the street at No. 109, **Café Charbon** (☎ 01/43-57-55-13), is a turn-of-the-century dance hall with a faded opulence and a constant crowd of cosmopolitan, trendy, gorgeous, young things. Expect mellow jazz before 10pm, and then a DJ enters and livens things up. Up the road at No. 131, **La Favela Chic** (☎ 01/43-57-15-47) is a cool, Brazilian-style bar where fashion-conscious Parisians chill out to Latin tunes and sip *caïpirinhas.*

Paris, Straight Up or on the Rocks

If you're looking for someplace classy to have a cocktail, the city's most elegant (and perhaps priciest) watering hole is the **Bar Vendôme,** just inside the entrance of the Hôtel Ritz, 15 place Vendôme, 1er (☎ 01/42-60-38-30; Métro: Concorde). Higher in nostalgia is the Ritz's woodsy **Hemingway Bar,** which the writer "liberated" in World War II while Nazi tanks retreated. Speaking of Papa's hangouts, **Harry's Bar,** 5 rue Daunou, 2e (☎ 01/42-61-71-14; Métro: Opéra), may be the birthplace of the Bloody Mary, but the bartenders will concoct anything under the sun. The house drink, *le Pétrifiant,* (rum, vodka, Cointreau, cognac, Calvados, bitters, and ginger ale), is as lethal as it sounds. Every night, there's a pianist and singer performing a medley of well-known, international standards in the panelled, clubby **Bar Anglais** in the Plaza Athénée hotel, 25 av. Montaigne, 8e (☎ 01/53-67-66-65; Métro: Alma-Marceau).

If you're visiting in chilly weather, sink into one of the cushy fireside armchairs (preferably with a snifter of Armagnac in your hand) at **Le Normandy,** in the hotel of the same name, 7 rue de l'Echelle, 1er (☎ 01/42-60-30-21; Métro: Palais Royal). And for unabashed romanticism, it's hard to beat **Le Bélier,** the theatrically overdecorated bar at the eccentric,

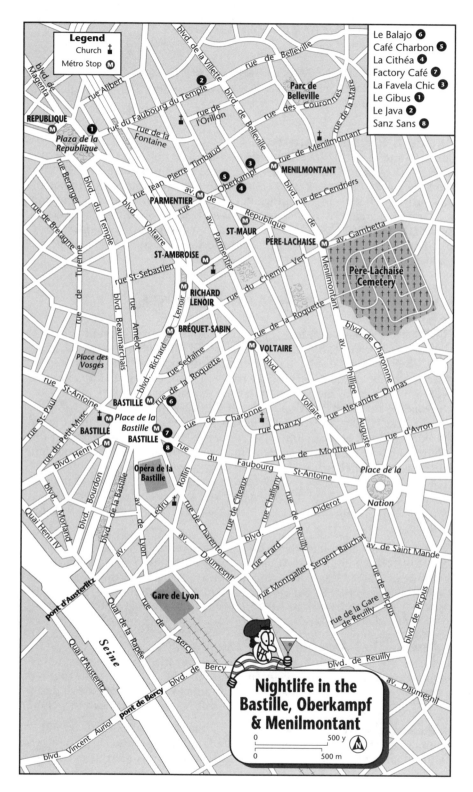

Nightlife in the
Bastille, Oberkampf
& Menilmontant

exclusive L'Hôtel, 13 rue des Beaux-Arts, 6e (☎ **01/43-25-27-22**; Métro: St-Germain-des-Prés), where Oscar Wilde lived and died ("I am dying beyond my means").

Fancy a Pint of Guinness?

Some 40-and-counting Irish pubs ensure that Guinness does a booming trade in Paris. There are many pretenders out there, but **Tigh Johnny's,** 55 rue Montmartre, 2e (☎ **01/42-33-91-33**; Métro: Rue Montmartre), is the genuine article; it boasts an authentically Hibernian vibe and barmen who know how to pull a great pint. Likewise, **The Quiet Man,** 5 rue des Haudriettes, 3e (☎ **01/48-04-02-77**; Métro: Rambuteau), feels like a tiny country pub that jumped out of County Cork. The downstairs bar is a favorite venue for traditional Irish music sessions.

Out & About: Gay Bars in the Marais & Elsewhere

The Marais is ground zero for Paris's homosexual community and has the gay bars to prove it. **Cox's Café,** 15 rue des Archives, 4e (☎ **01/42-72-08-00**; Métro: Hôtel-de-Ville), is the coolest of the lot because it eschews the disco fever vibe of most Parisian gay bars—in favor of house music, Blonde beer on tap, and Internet access. Also virtually free of gym boys is **Le Duplex,** 25 rue Michel-le-Comte, 3e (☎ **01/42-72-80-86**; Métro: Rambuteau), whose eclectic, creative crowd comes for the changing contemporary-art exhibits. **Le Quetzal,** 10 rue de la Verrerie, 4e (☎ **01/48-87-99-07**; Métro: Hôtel-de-Ville), is a contemporary, laid-back place made for mingling. For early morning dancing, the city's best gay club is **Le Queen,** 102 av. des Champs-Elysées, 8e (☎ **01/53-89-08-90**; Métro: George V). Expect huge lines for Monday's "Disco Inferno" party and Wednesday's "Respect" (the easiest night for women to get in). Other nights, expect a crowd of wall-to-wall drag queens.

Paris's hippest lesbian hangout is **Les Scandaleuses,** 8 rue des Ecouffes, 4e (☎ **01/48-87-39-26**; Métro: St-Paul), which only allows men if they are accompanied by a "scandalous woman." In the wee hours, the all-girl scene leaves the Marais for the red-velvet, faded coziness of **Le Pulp!,** 25 bd. Poissonière, 2e (☎ **01/40-26-01-93**; Métro: Rue Montmartre).

I Am a DJ, I Am What I Play

These days, a bar just ain't hot if there's no DJ in the house at least a few nights a week. The comparatively small size of DJ bars can be either a pro or a con, depending on your mood. But the 2am closing time requires a decision: Is it time for bed or simply time to shift up a gear and head to a club?

In the Marais, **Café du Trésor,** 5 rue du Trésor, 4e (☎ **01/44-78-06-60**; Métro: Hôtel-de-Ville), has nightly guest DJs spinning house, funk, new jack, and acid jazz. Nearby at the **Lizard Lounge,** 18 rue du Bourg-Tibourg, 4e

(☎ **01/42-72-81-34;** Métro: Hôtel-de-Ville), the basement cellar bar heats up nightly to house and techno. **Le Web Bar,** 32 rue de Picardi, 3e (☎ **01/42-72-57-47;** Métro: République), is where technology, art, and music collide. There's Internet access for cybersurfers, plus a huge program of events (poetry readings, short films, fashion shows) and some of the best DJ parties in Paris. Be there Monday by 10pm sharp for "Salsa du Web": salsa class, followed by a Latin party with a DJ.

Bet You Didn't Know

DJ bars are a lower-keyed alternative to the club scene—less hassle at the door, less pressure to be cool, and much more affordably priced drinks.

A bit farther west, in the Bastille neighborhood, **Sanz Sans,** 49 rue du Faubourg St-Antoine, 12e (☎ **01/44-75-78-78;** Métro: Bastille), has a resident DJ and a hypertrendy clientele permabopping to R&B, Latin, and 70s soul. On the same street, **Factory Café,** 20 rue du Faubourg St-Antoine, 12e (☎ **01/44-74-61-42;** Métro: Bastille), sports the currently in-vogue industrialized look and some of the capital's best rap, hip-hop, and groove. After 2am, the crowd shifts to nearby **Bartók,** 64 rue de Charenton, 12e (☎ **01/43-45-25-53;** Métro: Ledru-Rollin), where the hip-hop, house, and jungle goes strong until 4am from Wednesday to Sunday.

Cruising the Club Scene

Paris's clubs cater to all musical tastes, from hip-hop and Latino to drum 'n bass to house. Most clubs are open Wednesday to Sunday, from midnight until at least 5am.

Extra! Extra!

Two rules to know before you hit the clubs: Don't bother showing up in a club before 1am, and come with loads of cash. Drinks are exorbitantly priced once you finish the one that's usually included in the cover charge, which typically hovers between 50F and 100F ($9 to $18), depending on the night and theme. Credit cards are usually accepted only at the bar and not for entry.

Rex Club, 5 bd. Poissonière, 2e (☎ **01/42-36-10-96;** Métro: Bonne Nouvelle), has the best sound system in Paris and resident DJ spinning house, deep house, and techno. **Le Balajo,** 9 rue de Lappe, 11e (☎ **01/47-00-07-87;** Métro: Bastille), focuses on disco from Thursday to Saturday, with smidgens of rap, salsa, and techno thrown in for good measure.

Wednesday at **Le Gibus,** 18 rue du Faubourg du Temple, 11e (☎ **01/47-00-78-88;** Métro: République), is great for techno and trance, while other nights are predominately gay, featuring A-list, Channel-hopping DJs from London. Tuesday night at **Le Java,** 105 rue du Faubourg du Temple, 10e (☎ **01/42-02-20-52;** Métro: Belleville), is dedicated to *ethno-techno,* a mélange of techno and world music. On Thursday and Friday, there are Latin jam sessions. **Divan du Monde,** 75 rue des Martyrs, 18e (☎ **01/44-92-77-66;** Métro: Pigalle), has the most eclectic musical program of all, ranging from Breton to Brazilian to house to gay *bals* (literally translated as a ball, though not as dressy as the name would indicate).

Part 7

Get Outta Town: Easy Excursions from Paris

Two of France's most glorious virtues are diversity and accessibility. High-speed train travel makes it possible to get from Paris to anywhere in l'Héxagone, as the French call their country, in fewer than 6 hours. Moreover, you can be in Brussels in 90 minutes or London in a zippy 3 hours. But much closer than that, right at Paris's doorstep, lie the magnificent châteaux of kings and aristocrats, medieval villages, glorious Gothic cathedrals, and adorable little country inns. Together, they turn Paris's hinterland into a multifaceted paradise for travelers.

For most of us, the difficulty is choosing where to go. The 5 day trips suggested in this chapter barely nick the surface of possibilities for single-day jaunts. They are merely the most popular expeditions for travelers with just a day or two to spare. For a more extensive list of excursions, consult Frommer's France '99.

Chapter 21

Day-trippin':
Five Great
Escapes

In This Chapter

➤ Sumptuous excess in the palace at Versailles

➤ Monet's Gardens at Giverny

➤ Fun with Mickey at Disneyland Paris

➤ The magical cathedral at Chartres

➤ The royal forest at Fontainebleau

With all there is to see and do in Paris, why trek beyond the city limits? Because, quite simply, each of the sights reviewed in this chapter are mini destinations in themselves and might just turn out to be your trip's most memorable experience. One free day (or in some cases, just an afternoon) is all you need.

The Royal Palace at Versailles

Go because there's nothing else like it. The over-the-top opulence of Versailles (☎ **01/30-84-74-00**) is an enduring symbol for the excessiveness of Louis XIV's reign. The Sun King hired the country's best architects (Louis Le Vau and Jules Hardouin-Mansart), the best interior decorator (Charles Le Brun), and the best landscaper (André Le Nôtre) to create the largest, most stupendous palace in Europe. In its heyday, it housed more than 10,000 people—including royal family members, their servants, advisers, and confidants, 400 gardeners, and a 2,000-strong kitchen staff.

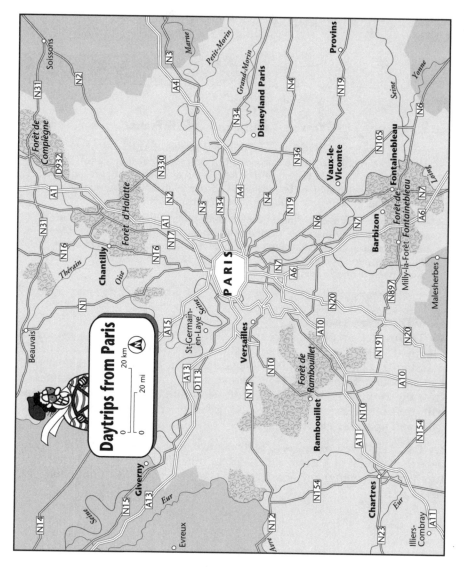

Daytrips from Paris

Versailles Essentials

Admission to the palace is 45F ($8) for adults; 35F ($6.30) ages 18 to 25; it's free for under-18s and over-60s. Entry to just the gardens is free. Versailles is open Tuesday through Sunday, except public holidays; from May to September, hours are 9am to 6:30pm; from October to April, from 9am to 5:30pm. For more information, try the Web site: **www.chateauversailles.fr** or **www.smartweb.fr/versailles/index.html.**

If You're Taking the SNCF Train...

If you're traveling by SNCF train (as opposed to the RER) to one of the destinations in this chapter, there's no need to book your seat in advance. Just buy your ticket in the train station, either from a ticket window or coin-operated automatic ticket machine. To locate the correct platform (*quai*), look for your train number (it's on your ticket) on the departures board.

Important: Before boarding, you must time-punch your ticket in the bright orange *composteur* machine located at the head of the platform. Insert your ticket face up into the machine's slot. Inspectors regularly check tickets on SNCF trains, and you can be fined up to 200F ($36) on the spot if your ticket hasn't been properly *composté*.

How Do I Get There?

By Train: Pick up RER line C5 at any of these Left Bank RER stations: Javel, Champ de Mars, Pont de l'Alma, Invalides, Musée d'Orsay, St-Michel, or Gare d'Austerlitz. Take it to Versailles-Rive Gauche. The one-way trip takes about half an hour and costs 21F ($4). As you exit the train station at Versailles, cross the avenue and turn right. Continue about 200 yards, and the château will come into view on your left. Then it's another 500 yards through the gates and up to the château.

By Car: Head west on the A13 highway from Porte d'Auteuil toward Rouen. Take the Versailles-Château exit, about 14 miles from Paris. Park in the visitors' carpark (paying) at Place d'Armes. The drive takes a half hour, longer in heavy traffic.

Tourist Traps

Both **Cityrama**, 2 rue des Pyramides, 1er (☎ **01/44-55-61-30**; Métro: Palais-Royale), and **Paris Vision**, 214 rue de Rivoli, 1er (☎ **01/42-60-30-01**; Métro: Tuileries), run half-day "tours" for 195F ($35). You ride to Versailles by tour bus, listening to a recorded commentary about the palace and gardens. But once you get to Versailles, you're on your own (entry ticket included). **The upshot:** you're paying through the nose for a glorified taxi ride to the palace. For a half-day tour of the State Apartments, the Hall of Mirrors, and the Queen's Bedroom, with a live, qualified guide, you'll pay 295F ($52) at Paris Vision or 320F ($57) at Cityrama. **A better bet:** Travel by RER and take a tour with an audioguide and/or lecturer from the Château.

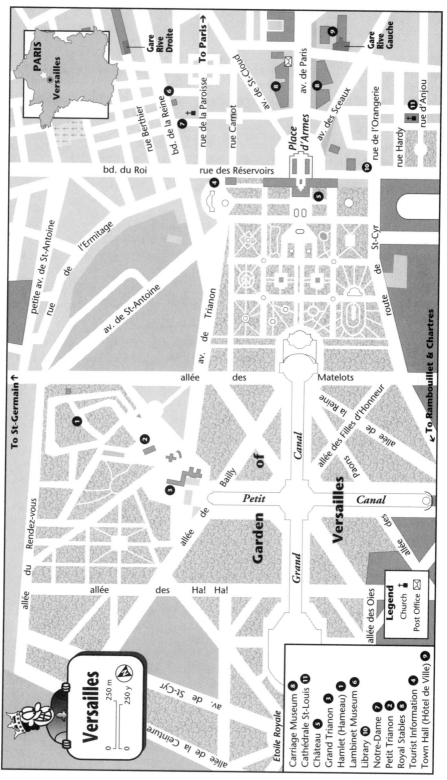

Versailles

0 — 250 m
0 — 250 y

← To St-Germain

To Paris →

PARIS
Versailles

Gare Rive Droite

rue Berthier

bd. de la Reine

rue de la Paroisse

rue Carnot

av. de St-Cloud

To Paris →

av. de Paris

av. des Sceaux

Gare Rive Gauche

rue de l'Orangerie

rue Hardy

rue d'Anjou

bd. du Roi

rue des Réservoirs

Place d'Armes

de St-Cyr

route

l'Ermitage

petite av. de St-Antoine

rue de

av. de St-Antoine

av. de Trianon

allée des Matelots

allée de la Reine

allée des Filles d'Honneur

allée de

Garden

of

Versailles

Petit Canal

Bailly

allée de

Grand Canal

allée des

allée des Oies

← To Rambouillet & Chartres

Rendez-vous

du

allée

allée des Ha! Ha!

av. de St-Cyr

allée de la Ceinture

Étoile Royale

Legend
✝ Church
☒ Post Office

Carriage Museum ❽
Cathédrale St-Louis ⓫
Château ❺
Grand Trianon ❸
Hamlet (Hameau) ❶
Lambinet Museum ❻
Library ❿
Notre-Dame ❼
Petit Trianon ❷
Royal Stables ❽
Tourist Information ❹
Town Hall (Hôtel de Ville) ❾

How to See Versailles

Get an early start from Paris; you'll need an entire day to see Versailles. The sheer size of the palace, the crowds, and the choice of tours can be totally overwhelming, so it's a good idea to pick up an orientation brochure/map from the information booth. Start your visit with the **Château,** entering through the Cour de Chapelle (Entrance A). You can visit the State Apartments (where court life took place), the Royal Chapel, and the Hall of Mirrors (where the Treaty of Versailles was signed) without a guide, but if you want to understand what you're seeing, an audioguide is indispensable. The commentary is rich in fascinating anecdotes and well worth its 25F ($4.50) rental fee.

To see the private apartments of the king and queen (re-enter the Château at Entrance C), you need to take a separate tour, either by audioguide or lecturer, for a supplement of 25F ($4.50).

After you've seen the Château, plan to spend at least an hour strolling through the **Formal Gardens.** This is the epitome of French landscaping: geometric paths and box-hedged shrubs interrupted with fountains, sparkling pools, grandiose stairways, and hundreds of marble statues.

Due to the big crowds and long lines, most visitors are content to visit only the Château and Gardens, but there's much more to see at Versailles if you've got the stamina. The most important of the remaining sights are the **Grand Trianon** and **Petit Trianon,** both opulent love nests constructed for kings' mistresses. The combined entry fee for both trianons is 30F ($5.50).

The High-Living Highlights: What Not to Miss

➤ The Château

➤ Royal Chapel

➤ Salon de Venus

➤ Hall of Mirrors

➤ King's and Queen's Apartments

➤ Formal Gardens

Lunchtime at Versailles

The town of Versailles has no shortage of places where you can break for lunch, but once you're on the palace grounds, it's infinitely more convenient to just stay put—otherwise you'll have to hike into town and back out to the palace again. Consider bringing a sandwich or snack with you in your day pack, or try one of these in-situ options. In the Château, there's a **cafeteria** just off the Cour de la Chapelle. In the Formal Gardens, there's an informal **restaurant,** La Flotille, on Petite Venise. (To get there from the Château, walk directly back through the Gardens to where the canal starts. You'll see Petite Venise and the restaurant to your right.) And lastly, there are several **snack bars** located in the Gardens near the Quinconce du Midi and the Grand Trianon.

 **Giverny**

If you're a fan of Impressionism or even a gardening buff, visiting Claude Monet's home at Giverny (☎ **01/32-51-28-21**) is a must. Obsessed with light and color, Monet poured endless time, money, and energy into his voluptuous garden—complete with artificial lily pond and exotic plants—which served as the subject of so many of his paintings. The artist painted his water lily canvasses from a barge he set up on the pond. The country-style house, with its apricot-colored roughcast exterior and green shutters, contains much of the artist's furniture and belongings. Plan to spend half a day at Giverny, longer if you break for lunch.

Giverny Essentials

For adults, admission to the house and garden is 35F ($6); for the garden only, 25F ($5). It's 20F ($3) for kids ages 7 to 12, and free for under-7s. Giverny is open from April to October, Tuesday through Sunday from 10am to 6pm. For more information, call up the Web site at **http://giverny.org/index.htm**.

How Do I Get There?

By Train: Take the SNCF train from Gare St-Lazare to Vernon. A round-trip ticket costs 68F ($12). Once in Vernon, a shuttle bus will take you the remaining 3 miles to Giverny. You can buy the 19F ($3) round-trip ticket on board from the driver.

The Best Time to Go...And the Worst

Giverny's gardens are at their most spectacular in **late April and early May,** but they remain pretty all the way through to early October thanks to an end-less rotation of flowering plants.

To avoid mammoth crowds, the **best day to visit is Friday.** Giverny is closed Monday. Most tour groups come on Tuesday and Thursday afternoons. French schoolkids habitually take their field trips on Wednesday (only a problem during the school year). And weekend afternoons get packed with French week-end warriors.

By Car: Head west on the A13 highway from Porte d'Auteuil toward Rouen. Get off the highway at Exit 14, at Bonnières, and follow signs for Vernon. Once in Vernon, cross the bridge over the Seine and follow signs on D5 to Giverny. The whole trip takes about an hour.

Where to Grab Lunch

Your entry ticket is no longer valid once you leave Monet's home, so think ahead about whether you'll eat lunch before or after your visit. Most people arrive in early afternoon, so crowds are slightly lighter in the mornings.

The square directly across from Monet's house, as well as the adjacent street, has many little cafes and crêperies. But if you're in the mood for more substantial fare, take a 5-minute walk to the **Auberge du Vieux Moulin**, 21 rue de la Falaise (☎ **02/32-51-46-15**), where cozy dining rooms make a great backdrop for very good, honest Norman cooking—escargot in puff pastry with garlic butter, guinea fowl braised in cider, or perhaps escalope of salmon with sorrel sauce. For dessert, try the *tarte Normande*—a.k.a. apple pie spiked with Calvados. The three-course, prix-fixe menu at 98F ($18) is the best deal in the house. The restaurant is open for lunch Tuesday to Sunday from 12pm to 3pm. Visa and MasterCard are accepted.

Kids Disneyland Paris

If you've brought the family, it's very difficult not to come to this kid magnet. Disneyland Paris (☎ **01/60-30-60-30**), is a smaller version of the Disney resorts in Orlando and Anaheim, but new attractions are being added every year.

Forget what you've heard about French resistance to Mickey, Donald, and the gang. Disneyland Paris is France's No. 1 tourist attraction, with 50 million annual visitors. That's right, it's bigger than the Eiffel Tower and the Louvre, a status that sparked one French newspaper to run the headline, *Monsieur Mickey Triumphs!* Forty percent of the visitors are French, and half of those are Parisian.

Disneyland Paris Essentials

One-day admission to the park is 160F to 200F ($29 to $36) for adults, 130F to 155F ($23 to $28) for ages 3 to 12, and free for under-3s (prices vary by season). Two-day admission is 305F to 380F ($55 to $68) for adults, 250F to 295F ($45 to $53) for ages 3 to 12, and free for under-3s. Disneyland Paris is open from September to June, Monday through Friday, 10am to 6pm, and Saturday and Sunday 10am to 8pm. In July and August it's open daily from 9am to 11pm. Peak season is from mid-June to mid-September, as well as Christmas and Easter weeks. For more information, consult the Web site at **www.disneylandparis.com**.

Set on 1,500 acres in the suburb of Marne-la-Vallée, the park looks, tastes, and feels like its siblings in California and Florida—except perhaps for the cheeseburgers *"avec pommes frites"* and the availability of wine on restaurant menus. Allow a full day to see Disneyland Paris.

When to Do Disney

Unfortunately, Disneyland Paris is as crowded as its American predecessors, and you can expect to have to line up for an hour for some attractions. The best way to steer clear of the enormous crowds? Come **outside of the peak periods** (Easter, July, August, and Christmas) and **avoid weekends** at all cost.

How Do I Get There?
By Train: Pick up the RER line A4 at any of these Right Bank RER stations: Charles-de-Gaulle-Etoile, Auber, Les Halles, Gare de Lyon, or Nation. Take it to its terminus at Marne-la-Vallée/Chessy, and you'll get off at the park's doorstep. The round-trip fare from central Paris costs 76F ($14). Trains run every 10 to 20 minutes, depending on the time of day, and the journey takes about 40 minutes.

By Car: Head east on highway A4 from Porte de Bercy toward Reims and Nancy. Get off at Exit 14, and follow signs to Parc Disneyland Paris. The drive takes about a half hour in normal traffic. There are thousands of parking spaces, each available for 40F ($7) per day. Parking is free if you're staying at any of the hotels in the resort. A network of moving sidewalks speeds up pedestrian transit from the parking areas to the theme park's entrance.

Destination Disney
Like all the Disney resorts, this one was designed as a vacation destination in itself. For most visitors, the highlight is the theme park with its five different entertainment "lands" (Main Street U.S.A., Frontierland, Adventureland, Fantasyland, Discoveryland) and their rides and attractions. But there are also six large hotels, a campground, a nightlife center (Village Disney), a 27-hole golf course, and scores of restaurants, shows, and shops.

Disney after Dark
With twice-nightly performances (at 6:30 and 9:30pm), **Buffalo Bill's Wild West Show** (☎ **01/60-45-71-00**) is the premier theatrical venue of Disneyland Paris. The show is a copy of the one that once traveled the West with Buffalo Bill and Annie Oakley. You dine at tables that ring, amphitheater-style, a rodeo ground where sharpshooters, runaway stage coaches, and dozens of horses and Indians ride very fast and perform some alarmingly

realistic acrobatics. The show includes a Texas-style barbecue buffet and costs 325F ($58) for adults, 195F ($35) for kids ages 3 to 11. You can receive a 10% discount if you book through the concierge of your Disneyland Paris hotel.

Hi-ho, Hi-ho Highlights

Best for Kids Under 7:
➤ Main Street, U.S.A.

➤ Parade held every afternoon and some evenings

➤ Fantasyland

➤ Sleeping Beauty's Castle

Best for Kids 7 to 12:
➤ Frontierland

➤ Phantom Manor ghost house

➤ Big Thunder Mountain roller coaster

➤ Adventureland

➤ Indiana Jones and the Temple of Doom roller coaster

➤ Pirates of the Caribbean ride

Best for Teens:
➤ Discoveryland

➤ Space Mountain roller coaster

➤ Star Tours simulated spacecraft ride

Village Disney, located just outside the park's boundary, is where to head when you want to escape the munchkins for a while. The pedestrianized street is lined with dance clubs, snack bars, theme restaurants, souvenir shops, and bars with a surprisingly good lineup of live music. Unlike the park, admission to Village Disney is free.

Where to Stay

It's very possible to visit most of Disneyland Paris in a single day, but if you want to stay longer, there are plenty of hotels at different price levels inside the park. You can book via the park's Web site (**www.disneylandparis. com**) or by calling ☎ **407/W-DISNEY** (407/934-7639) in North America, or 0171/753-2900 in the United Kingdom. For information in France, contact the **Central Reservations Office,** Euro Disney Resort, S.C.A., B.P. 105, F-77777 Marne-la-Vallée Cedex 4 (☎ **01/60-30-60-30**). All of Disney's hotels accept all major credit cards (AE, DC, DISC, MC, V). From most expensive to least expensive, here are the accommodations options:

Helpful Tips for Families

➤ Coin-operated lockers can be rented for 10F ($1.80) per use, and larger bags can also be stored for 15F ($2.70) per day.

➤ Children's strollers and wheelchairs can be rented for 30F ($5.40) per day, with a 20F ($3.60) deposit.

➤ Baby-sitting is available at all of the resort's hotels with 24–hour notice.

The 500-room **Disneyland Hotel** is faux Victorian in style, with red-tile turrets and jutting balconies. The decor is tastefully conservative and plush. There are three restaurants, a health club with indoor/outdoor pool, whirlpool, sauna, room service, laundry, and baby-sitting. On the "Castle Club" floor, there are free newspapers, all-day beverages, and access to a well-equipped private lounge.

☎ *01/60-45-65-00. Fax 01/60-45-65-33.* **Rates:** *1550–2250F ($279–$405) for 1 to 4 persons; from 3850F ($693) suite.*

Inspired by the Big Apple, the **Hotel New York** is a nine-story central "skyscraper" flanked by the Gramercy Park Wing and the Brownstones Wing, which resemble New York terrace houses. The bedrooms are comfortably appointed with art deco accessories and New York–inspired memorabilia. There's a diner, a restaurant, two bars, an indoor/outdoor pool, two outdoor tennis courts, a health club, room service, laundry, and baby-sitting.

☎ *01/60-45-73-00. Fax 01/60-45-73-33.* **Rates:** *1000–1620F ($180–$292) for 1 to 4 persons; from 2900F ($522) suite.*

The blue-and-cream **Newport Bay Club** is reminiscent of a harborfront New England hotel, with nautically inspired bedrooms. There are two restaurants, a lakeside promenade, a glassed-in pool pavilion, an outdoor pool, and a health club.

☎ *01/60-45-55-00. Fax 01/60-45-55-33.* **Rates:** *830–1180F ($149–$212) for 1 to 4 persons; from 1600F ($288) suite.*

Built of gray stone and rough-hewn wood, the **Sequoia Lodge** evokes a remote inn in the Rocky Mountains. Rooms are comfortably appointed and are decked out in a rustic decor. There are two restaurants, an indoor pool, and a health club.

☎ *01/60-45-51-00. Fax 01/60-45-51-33.* **Rates:** *705–1060F ($127–$191) for 1 to 4 persons; from 1500F ($270) suite.*

Located right next to one another, the **Hotel Cheyenne** and **Hotel Santa Fé** are the least expensive hotels at the resort and both conjure up the Old

281

West. Each has its own restaurant and rooms that are tastefully decorated, if more basic than at the park's other hotels. In the summer heat, the biggest disadvantages are the lack of air-conditioning and a swimming pool.

Hotel Cheyenne. ☎ **01/60-45-62-00.** *Fax 01/60-45-62-33.* **Rates:** *535–925F ($96–$166), for 1 to 4 persons.*

Hotel Santa Fé. ☎ **01/60-45-78-00.** *Fax 01/60-45-78-33.* **Rates:** *435–780F ($78–$140) for 1 to 4 persons.*

Dining at Disneyland

Wherever you are at Disneyland Paris, it's never a problem finding somewhere to eat. The park has 45-and-counting eateries, ranging from fast-food joints, cafeterias, and snack bars to five more upscale, full-service restaurants—one in each "land." Since the cuisine tends to correspond to the "land," you can expect barbecue fare in Frontierland, exotic and spicy meals and snacks in Adventureland, and so on. The five full-service restaurants are the only eateries in the park that serve wine and beer, and also the only ones to accept credit cards.

Chartres

Most visitors come to Chartres to see its magnificent cathedral, but the town itself is one of the prettiest in France and well worth exploring in its own right. Rodin called it the French Acropolis, and surely the **Cathédrale Notre-Dame de Chartres,** 16 Cloître Notre-Dame (☎ **02/37-21-56-33**), is one of the world's most glorious medieval architectural achievements. Come to see its soaring, High Gothic ceilings, magnificent sculpture, and, above all, its glorious stained glass, which gave the world a new color, Chartres blue. The dearth of good accommodations in Chartres makes this best as a day trip.

Chartres Essentials

The **Chartres Tourist Office** is located on Place de la Cathédrale (☎ **02/ 37-21-50-00**). Admission to the cathedral is free. Admission to the tower is 28F ($5) for adults, 15F ($2.70) for students. The cathedral is open Easter through October, daily from 7:30am to 7:30pm; and November to Easter, daily from 7:30am to 7pm. (The tower is closed between noon and 2pm every day.) For more information, try **www.chartres.com**.

How Do I Get There?

By Train: Pick up one of the hourly SNCF trains from Gare Montparnasse to Chartres. A round-trip ticket costs 71F ($13). The journey takes less than an hour and passes through a sea of wheat fields.

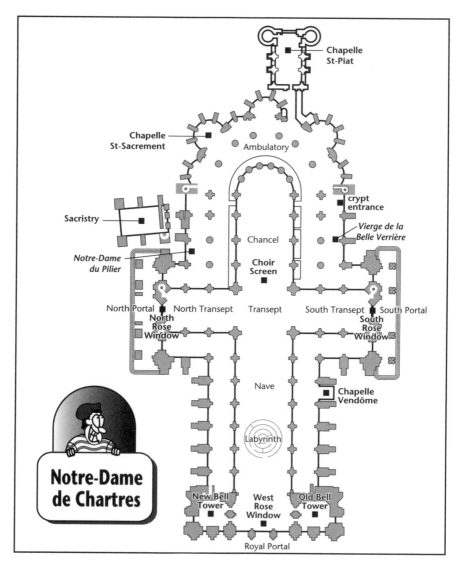

Notre-Dame de Chartres

By Car: Take the A10/A11 highway from Porte d'Orléans and follow the signs to Le Mans and Chartres. The drive takes about 75 minutes.

By Tour Bus: Cityrama, 2 rue des Pyramides, 1er (☎ **01/44-55-61-30;** Métro: Palais-Royale) offers 5-hour excursions departing from Paris every Tuesday and Saturday afternoon, which cost 275F ($49) and feature a tour of the cathedral with a qualified guide.

Going Gothic

Book ahead for the sell-out tours conducted by Malcolm Miller (☎ **02/37-28-15-58;** fax 02/37-28-33-03), an Englishman who has spent three decades studying the cathedral and sharing his knowledge with visitors. His blend of scholarship, enthusiasm, and humor will help you understand and appreciate the cathedral. Miller's 75-minute tours begin at 12pm and 2:45pm, Monday to Saturday, and cost 30F ($5) per person.

When to Go

Consider saving Chartres Cathedral for a Sunday afternoon (most of Paris is dead then, anyway), when free organ concerts (4:45pm to 5:45pm) and the filtered light upon the western stained-glass windows conspire to make the church come thrillingly alive.

The cathedral you see today dates principally from the 13th century and was the first to use flying buttresses. The **Royal Portal** (Doorway) features appealingly elongated bodies, the women with dangling braids and long flowing robes. Most of the **stained glass** you see is original, dating from the 12th and 13th centuries. It was spared in both World Wars because of a decision to remove it painstakingly piece by piece.

Around the chancel, there is a celebrated **choir screen;** work on it began in the 16th century and lasted until 1714. The 40 niches contain statues illustrating scenes from the life of Christ.

The **nave,** the widest in France, still contains its ancient floor-maze, which formed a mobile channel of contemplation for monks.

An arduous climb up the narrow, spiral staircase of the **New Tower** rewards with exceptional views of flying buttresses, gargoyles, and the town below. Note, however, that the tower is closed between noon and 2pm.

An Insider Tip

The vast amount of stained glass—some 3,000 square yards of it—makes the cathedral's interior mysteriously dim. **Bring a pair of binoculars** to truly appreciate the painstaking details, like the expulsion of the red-faced devils or a cobbler threading laces into a shoe.

Exploring the Old Town

If you have extra time, spend it exploring the medieval cobbled streets of the Old Town. At the foot of the cathedral are lanes with gabled houses and humped bridges spanning the Eure River. Try to find **rue Chantault,** which boasts houses with colorful facades, one of which dates back eight centuries.

The **Musée des Beaux-Arts de Chartres,** 29 Cloître Notre-Dame (☎ 02/ 37-36-41-39), features paintings from mainly the 17th to 19th centuries, including such old masters as Zurbarán, Watteau, and Brosamer. Of particular interest is David Ténier's *Le Concert.* The museum is open Wednesday to Monday, from 10am to 12pm and from 2pm to 5pm. Entry costs 10F ($2).

Dining à la Chartres
Set in a 300-year-old house just a stone's throw from the cathedral, **Le Buisson Ardent,** 10 rue au Lait (☎ **02/37-34-04-66**), serves up well-prepared fare made with farm-fresh ingredients in a quaint, wood-beamed dining room. Favorite dishes include an escalope of warm foie gras prepared with apples and Calvados, and roast pigeon with lemon juice, served with potato pancakes and fresh vegetables. For dessert, try the crispy hot apples with sorbet and Calvados-flavored butter sauce. There are three fixed-price menus, at 128F, 168F, and 228F ($23, $30, and $41). The restaurant is open daily for lunch, and Monday through Saturday for dinner only. MasterCard and Visa are accepted.

Fontainebleau
Deep within the vestiges of the Fontainebleau Forest, early French kings used **Fontainebleau** (☎ 01/60-71-50-70), as a hunting lodge and found recreation in its magnificent forest. But that all changed with King François I, the cultured French contemporary to England's uncouth-by-comparison Henry VIII. A huge fan of Italian Renaissance style, François I turned the lodge into a royal palace with the help of several Italian artists, including Benvenuto Cellini, Il Rosso (a protégé of Michelangelo), and Primaticcio. Napoléon had a particular affection for the Château de Fontainebleau, and it was here that he bade farewell to his sobbing soldiers before departing for his exile on Elba.

Fontainebleau Essentials
The **Fontainebleau Tourist Office** is at 4 rue Royale (☎ **01/60–74–99–99**). Admission to the Grands Appartements, Napoléon's Apartments, and Chinese Museum is 35F ($6) for adults, 23F ($4) for ages 18 to 25, and free for under-18s. The château is open September to June, Wednesday to Monday, 9:30am to 12:30pm and 2pm to 5pm. In July and August hours are Wednesday through Monday, 9:30am to 6pm.

Of the five excursions recommended in this chapter, this is the only one where a car really comes in handy, so that after visiting the château, you can explore the lovely artists' town of Barbizon. If you only visit Fontainebleau, plan to spend a half day. If you visit both Fontainebleau and Barbizon, spend the whole day and have lunch in Barbizon.

When to Go

The best days to visit Fontainebleau are Monday, Thursday, and Saturday. The Château is closed on Tuesday. If you're arriving by train, the shuttle bus service is slower on Sunday. Wednesday, Friday, and Sunday are the big days for tour groups.

How Do I Get There?

By Train: Take the SNCF train from Gare de Lyon to Fontainebleau-Avon. A round-trip ticket costs 94F ($17), and the journey takes 35 to 60 minutes, depending on time of day. From the station, a shuttle bus makes the 2-mile trip to the château every 10 to 15 minutes Monday to Saturday (every 30 minutes on Sunday). A one-way bus ticket costs 9F ($1.60). Unfortunately, there's no easy way to see both Fontainebleau and Barbizon if you go by train.

By Car: Take the A6 highway southeast from Porte d'Orléans toward Lyon. Get off at the Fontainebleau exit, then follow N7 into town. Barbizon is 5 miles northwest of Fontainebleau and well signposted on N7.

A Château Checklist: Things Not to Miss

➤ Horseshoe Staircase (Staircase of the Farewells)

➤ Napoléon's Apartments

➤ Gallery of François I

➤ The Queen's Boudoir (designed for Marie-Antoinette)

➤ Ballroom

➤ Château Gardens and the Forest of Fontainebleau

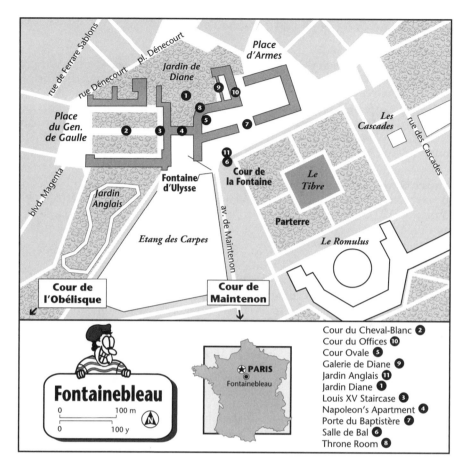

By Tour Bus: Both **Cityrama**, 2 rue des Pyramides, 1er (☎ 01/44-55-61-30; Métro: Palais-Royale), and **Paris Vision**, 214 rue de Rivoli, 1er (☎ 01/42-60-30-01; Métro: Tuileries), offer 5-hour excursions that combine both Fontainebleau and Barbizon. Both companies charge 330F ($59) per person. Cityrama's tours leave Wednesday and Sunday at 1:45pm, and Paris Vision's tours leave Wednesday and Friday at 1pm.

Exploring the Château

Napoléon's affection for the château was understandable. You can wander around much of the palace on your own, visiting sites that evoke his 19th-century imperial heyday. They include the **throne room** where he abdicated his rule of France, his **offices,** his monumental **bedroom,** and his **bathroom.** Some of the smaller Napoleonic rooms, especially those containing his personal mementos and artifacts, are accessible by guided tour only.

Other highlights include the 210-foot long **Gallery of François I,** with stucco-framed panels that depict such scenes as *The Rape of Europa* and the eponymous monarch holding a pomegranate (a symbol of unity). When ascending the rich, elegant **Louis XV Staircase,** look for the Italian fresco that portrays the queen of the Amazons climbing into Alexander the Great's bed. Sometimes called the Gallery of Henri II, the **Ballroom** displays the interlaced initials "H&D," referring to Henri and his mistress, Diane de Poitiers. Competing with this illicit tandem are the initials "H&C," symbolizing Henri and his ho-hum wife, Catherine de Médicis. Above the wainscoting is a series of frescoes, painted between 1550 and 1558, which depict such mythological subjects as *The Feast of Bacchus.*

Lunchtime: BYO vs. Barbizon

If you're arriving by train and only plan to visit Fontainebleau, consider bringing your own lunch from Paris. In fine weather, the Château's gardens and the nearby forest beckon—no, make that scream—for a **picnic.** But if you've got a car, save your appetite for Barbizon.

On the western edge of France's finest forest, the 62,000-acre *Forêt de Fontainebleau*, lies the village of **Barbizon.** In the mid–19th century, Barbizon was home to a number of noted landscape artists—Corot, Millet, Rousseau, and Daumier, among others—whose breakaway from studio painting and love of the great outdoors greatly inspired the Impressionists. The colorful town has a lively mix of good restaurants, boutiques, and antiques shops—the perfect place to while away an afternoon.

For lunch, try the **Relais de Barbizon,** 2 av. Charles-de-Gaulle (☎) **01/60-66-40-28**), whose five-course, 140F ($25) lunch menu features hearty, home-style dishes such as duckling in wild cherry sauce or braised lamb with thyme. The restaurant has a fine terrace where meals are served in warm weather. Closed for dinner Tuesday, and for lunch and dinner Wednesday. MasterCard and Visa are accepted.

Paris A to Z: Facts at Your Fingertips

Airport Info: Charles-de-Gaulle (☎ **01/48-62-22-80;** flight info ☎ 08/36-68-15-15); Orly (☎ **01/49-75-15-15**).

Airport Transportation: Airport Shuttle (☎ **01/45-38-55-72**). Door-to-door service from hotel to airport, with English-speaking operator.

American Express: 11 rue Scribe, 9e (☎ **01/47-77-79-50**). Open Mon–Fri 9am–7pm, Sat 9am–5:30pm, Sun 10am–5pm.

Baby-Sitters: Baby-sitting Service (☎ **01/46-37-51-24;** fax 01/42-66-52-45), AAA Baby-Sitting Express (☎ **01/42-86-54-22**), and Good Morning Europe (☎ **01/44-87-01-22;** fax 01/44-87-01-42) provide English-speaking sitters.

Baby Equipment Rental: Eurobaby (☎ **01/60-61-81-79**) rents out cribs, strollers, and other baby essentials.

Cell Phone Rentals: Rent-A-Cell Express (116 bis, av. des Champs-Elysées, 8e (☎ **01/53-93-78-00;** fax 01/53-93-78-09) delivers in a half hour or less.

Computer Repair: Micro-King (☎ **01/53-06-65-10** or 06/03-70-31-99) will make on-site calls.

Consulates/Embassies: American Consulate, 2 rue St.-Florentin, 8e (☎ **01/43-12-22-22**); American Embassy, 2 av. Gabriel, 8e (☎ **01/42-96-12-02**); Australian Embassy and Consulate, 4 rue Jean-Rey, 15e (☎ **01/40-59-33-00**); British Consulate, 16 rue d'Anjou, 8e (☎ **01/42-66-38-10**); British Embassy, 35 rue du Fbg St-Honoré, 8e (☎ **01/44-51-31-00**); Canadian Embassy, 35 av. Montaigne, 8e (☎ **01/44-43-29-00**); Irish Embassy and Consulate, 12 av. Foche, 16e (☎ **01/44-17-67-00**); New Zealand Embassy, 7 rue Léonard-de-Vinci, 16e (☎ **01/45-00-24-11**); South African Embassy, 59 quai d'Orsay, 7e (☎ **01/53-59-23-23**).

Dentists: See chapter 4 for recommended dentists. SOS Dentistes (☎ **01/43-37-51-00**) is an English-speaking referral service.

Doctors: See chapter 4 for recommended doctors. SOS Medecins (☎ **01/ 47-07-77-77**) is an English-speaking referral service.

Electrical Current: The French electric system operates on 220 volt, 50 cycles with a plug bearing two cylindrical prongs. To use standard American 110 volt, 60 cycle appliances, you will need both a transformer and a plug adapter. Most new laptop computers have built-in transformers, but some still do not, so beware. Attempting to use only a plug adapter is a sure way to fry your appliance or, worse, cause a fire. To use standard British 250 volt, 60 cycle appliances, you'll need only a plug adapter. You can buy plug adapters and transformers at most department stores and electronics shops, but the Bazar de l'Hôtel de Ville, better known as BHV, (52-64 rue de Rivoli, 4e; ☎ **01/42-74-90-00**) has a special department for adapting foreign fax machines, computers, and office equipment.

Emergencies: Ambulance: dial **15**; Police: dial **17**; Fire: dial **18.**

Hair Salons: Michele & Heinz Coiffeurs, 4 rue de la Trémoille, 8e (☎ **01/ 47-23-75-55; ask for Susan**).

Hospitals: American Hospital in Paris, 63 bd. Victor Hugo, Neuilly-sur-Seine (☎ **01/46-41-25-25**); Hertford British Hospital, 3 rue Barbès, Levallois-Perret (☎ **01/46-39-22-22**).

Hotlines: S.O.S. Help (☎ **01/47-23-80-80**) is France's only English-speaking crisis line, open daily 3–11pm. FACTS-Line (☎ **01/44-93-16-69**) offers HIV/AIDS support in English, Mon, Wed, Fri 6–10pm. The Paris branch of Alcoholics Anonymous can be reached via the American Church (☎ **01/ 46-34-59-65**).

Information for Tourists: Paris Tourist Office, 127 av. des Champs-Elysées, 8e (☎ **01/49-52-53-54**); 24-hour recording in English (☎ **01/ 49-52-53-56**).

Internet: Local access numbers are: CompuServe (☎ **01/41-30-20-10**); America Online (☎ **08/36-06-13-10**).

Mail Delivery, Overnight: DHL (☎ **01/48-63-70-00**); Federal Express (☎ **01/47-99-39-00**).

Maps: The best city maps are pocket-size guides available at bookshops and newsagents (look for "Presse" signs) and cost about 35F ($6). Look for *Paris Classique-l'Indispensable, Paris Par Arrondissement,* or *Paris Eclair.* All three have alphabetized street-name indexes and are clearly organized by *arrondissement.*

MasterCard: (☎ **08/00-90-13-87**). To report a lost or stolen card, or to find the nearest cash machine.

News Media: The *International Herald Tribune* is available at larger newsstands, as are British newspapers such as *London Times, London Independent, Observer,* and *The Guardian.* The British bookstore W. H. Smith, 248 rue de Rivoli, 1er (☎ **01/44-77-88-99**) has an extensive English-language newspaper and magazine section. Brentano's, 37 av. de l'Opéra, 2e (☎ **01/42-61-52-50**) has a smaller, albeit good selection. International all-news television channels such as CNN International, BBC News, and Sky News are widely available in most hotels with three or more stars. The French channel Canal Plus broadcasts the *ABC Evening News* weekday mornings at 7am. With a short- or medium-wave radio, you can pick up the BBC World Service at 650 AM on your dial.

Pharmacies (24-hour): Pharmacie des Champs, 84 av. Champs-Elysées, 8e (☎ **01/45-62-02-41**).

Pharmacies (English-speaking): Anglo-American Pharmacy, 6 rue de Castiglione, 1er (☎ **01/42-60-72-96**); British Pharmacy, 62 av. des Champs-Elysées, 8e (☎ **01/43-59-22-52**); British and American Pharmacy, 1 rue Auber, 9e (☎ **01/47-42-49-40**).

Rest Rooms: Coin-operated porta-toilets are scattered throughout the city, if you're daring. If you're squeamish, you're better off trying department stores; McDonald's, Pizza Hut, and other American-style restaurants; The Virgin Megastore on the Champs-Elysées (top floor, behind the cafe); museums; and cafes. Be forewarned that in the oldest neighborhoods (Latin Quarter, Marais, Montmartre), Turkish toilets are prevalent.

Safety: Paris is a relatively safe city, and violent crime is rare. Your biggest riska are pickpockets and purse snatchers, so be particularly attentive on the Métro and on crowded buses, in museum lines, and around tourist attractions.

Taxis: Alpha Taxis (☎ **01/45-85-85-85**); Artaxi (☎ **01/42-41-50-50**); Taxis Bleus (☎ **01/49-36-10-10**). All are reliable services, with switchboard operators who can usually speak English. Be aware that the meter starts running as soon as the call is made, so they're more expensive than regular cabs.

Telephone Calling Cards: The access numbers for using calling cards to dial from France are: MCI (☎ **08/00-99-00-19**); AT&T (☎ **08/00-99-00-11**); Sprint (☎ **08/00-99-00-87**).

Time Zone: Eastern Standard Time +6 hours; Greenwich Mean Time +1 hour. So when it's 9am in New York and 2pm in London, it's 3pm in Paris. France uses the 24-hour clock, so 08h00 is 8am but 20h00 is 8pm.

Transit Info: The English-language line of the RATP is ☎ **08/36-68-41-14.**

Toll-Free Numbers for Airlines, Car-Rental Agencies, & Hotel Chains

Airlines and Car-Rental Companies

Major North American Carriers
For the latest on airline Web sites, check http://airline-online.com or http://www.itn.com.

Air Canada
☎ 800/776-3000 in the U.S.
☎ 800/555-1212 in Canada for local number
www.aircanada.ca

American Airlines
☎ 800/433-7300
www.americanair.com

Canadian Airlines
☎ 800/426-7000 in U.S.
☎ 800/665-1177 in Canada
www.cdnair.ca

Continental Airlines
☎ 800/231-0856
www.flycontinental.com

Delta Airlines
☎ 800/241-4141
www.delta-air.com

Northwest Airlines
☎ 800/447-4747
www.nwa.com

Tower Air
☎ 800/221-2500
www.towerair.com

TWA
☎ 800/892-4141
www.twa.com

US Airways
☎ 800/622-1015
www.usairways.com

European Carriers (National and Country-Affiliated Airlines)

Aer Lingus (Ireland)
☎ 800/223-6537
www.aerlingus.ie

Air France
☎ 800/237-2747
www.airfrance.com

Alitalia (Italy)
☎ 800/223-5730
www.alitalia.it

Austrian Airlines
☎ 800/843-0002
www.aua.com

British Airways
☎ 800/247-9297
www.british-airways.com

Finnair (Finland)
☎ 800/950-5000
www.us.finair.com

Iberia (Spain)
☎ 800/772-4642
www.iberia.com

Icelandair (Iceland)
☎ 800/223-5500
www.centrum.is/icelandair/front.html

KLM (Royal Dutch Airlines)
☎ 800/374-7747
www.klm.nl

Lufthansa (Germany)
☎ 800/645-3880
www.lufthansa.com

Olympic Airways (Greece)
☎ 800/223-1226
agn.hol.gr/info/olympic1.htm

SAS (Scandinavian Airlines)
☎ 800/221-2350
www.flysas.com

Swissair
☎ 800/221-4750
www.swissair.com

TAP Air Portugal
☎ 800/221-7370
www.TAP-AirPortugal.pt

Virgin Atlantic Airways (British)
☎ 800/862-8621
www.fly.virgin.com

Major International Car-Rental Agencies

Avis
☎ 800/331-1212
www.avis.com

Budget
☎ 800/527-0700
www.budgetrentacar.com

Dollar (Eurodollar)
☎ 800/800-6000
www.dollarcar.com

Hertz
☎ 800/654-3131
www.hertz.com

Thrifty
☎ 800/367-2277
www.thrifty.com

The following companies specialize in Europe:

Auto-Europe
☎ 800/223-5555
www.autoeurope.com

Europe by Car
☎ 800/223-1516
☎ 800/252-9401 in California
☎ 212/581-3040 in NYC
www.europebycar.com

Kemwell
☎ 800/678-0678
www.kemwell.com

Major Hotel Chains in Paris

Best Western International
☎ 800/528-1234
www.bestwestern.com

Hilton Hotels
☎ 800/HILTONS
www.hilton.com

Holiday Inn
☎ 800/HOLIDAY
www.holiday-inn.com

Hyatt Hotels & Resorts
☎ 800/228-9000
www.hyatt.com

ITT Sheraton
☎ 800/325-3535
www.sheraton.com

Marriott Hotels
☎ 800/228-9290
www.marriott.com

Radisson Hotels International
☎ 800/333-3333
www.radisson.com

Glossary of French Words & Phrases

French	English	Pronunciation
Basics		
Oui/Non	Yes/No	Wee/Nohn
D'accord	Okay; it's agreed	DAK-kor
Ça va	That's fine	Sah-vah
Parlez-vous Anglais?	Do you speak English?	PAHR-lay VOO zahn-GLAY?
Je ne parle pas Français.	I don't speak French.	Zhuhn pahrl pah frahn-SAY.
Je ne comprends pas.	I don't understand.	Zhuhn cohm-PRAHN pah.
In an Emergency		
Au secours!	Help!	Oh suh-COOR
Arrêtez!	Stop!	Ah-RET-tay
Appelez une ambulance!	Call an ambulance!	AP-puh-LAY oon ahm-boo-lahnzz
Greetings & Pleasantries		
S'il vous plaît	Please	SEE voo PLAY
Merci	Thank you	Mayr SEE
Je vous en prie	You're welcome	Zhuh VOO zahn PREE
Excusez-moi	I'm sorry	Ex-COO-zay mwah
Pardon	Excuse me	Pah-DOHN
Bonjour	Hello	Bohn-ZHOOR
Bonsoir	Good evening	Bohn-SWAH
Au revoir	Good-bye	Ohr VWAH
Comment allez-vous?	How are you?	Koh-MAHN tal-lay VOO
Très bien, merci	Very well, thanks	Tray bee-EN, mayr SEE
Enchanté	Nice to meet you	Ahn shahnt-AY

Getting Around

Je cherche...	I'm looking for...	Zhuh shayrsh
...une banque	...a bank	...Oon Bahnk
...une cabine téléphonique	...a phone booth	...Oon ka-BEEN tay-LAY-foh-NEEK
...un supermarché	...a supermarket	...Uh SOO-payr-mar-SHAY
...une pharmacie	...a drugstore/chemist	...Oon far-ma-SEE
...l'ascenseur	...the elevator	...Lah-sahn-SUHR
...la sortie	...the exit	...Lah Sohr-TEE
Où est...?	Where is...?	Oo way
...le Métro	...the subway	...Luh May-troh
...l'arrêt d'autobus	...the bus stop	...Lah-REH Doh-Toh-BOOS
...la gare	...the train station	...Lah gar
Un billet s'il vous plait	A ticket, please	Uh bee-YAY, SEE voo PLAY
Billet aller-simple	One-way ticket	Bee-YAY AL-lay SAMP-luh
Billet aller-retour	Round-trip ticket	Bee-YAY AL-lay ruh-TOOR

Necessities

Je voudrais...	I would like...	Zhuh voo-DRAY
...une carte postale	...a postcard	...Oon Kart poh-STAL
...un timbre	...a stamp	...Uh TAM-bruh
...une carte téléphonique	..a phonecard	...Oon kart tay-LAY-foh-NEEK

Shopping

C'est combien?	How much does it cost?	Say Cohm-bee-YEN?
Je regardes, merci	I'm just looking, thanks	Zhuh ruh-GAR, mayr-SEE
Je voudrais...	I would like...	Zhuh voo-DRAY
...mon taille	...my size	...mohn TIE
...de l'essayer	...to try it on	...duh LAY-say-YAY
Salon d'essayage	Changing room	Sa-LOHN DAY-say-YAHZH
Où est la caisse?	Where's the cash register?	Oo way lah kess?
Je paie en espèces	I'm paying in cash	Zhuh pay on es-SPESS
Acceptez-vous...?	Do you accept...?	Ak-sep-tay VOO...
...des cartes de crédit?	...credit cards?	...day kart duh cray-DEE
...des chèques de voyage?	...travelers' checks?	...day shek duh voy-YAHZH

Index

Page numbers in *italics* refer to maps.

A

Abbesses, place des, 245, 246

Accommodations, 47–84. *See also specific accommodations*
  aparthotels, 21–22, 58–59
  bathrooms in, 57
  best bets
    for dining, 70
    for families, 73
    for gay travelers, 80
    for Internet access, 76
    panoramic views, 74
    for romantic interludes, 78
    trendy hotels, 75
  booking tips, 56
  budget, 56–57
  budgeting for, 19
  for disabled travelers, 59, 69
  Disneyland Paris, 280–82
  hotel chains, major, 293–94
  Left Bank, 51–53, 64
  location, 49–53, 61, 64
  money-saving tips, 21–22, 53
  price index, 64–65
  pricing, 53, 54–56
  reservations, 57–58, 59
  Right Bank, 49–51, 61, 64
  room size, 54
  worksheet, 82–83

Airfares, 29–30
  worksheet, 33–35

Airlines, 30
  package tours, 28–29
  Web sites and phone numbers, 292–93

Airports, 30–31, 86–90
  information, 289
  transportation to/from, 9, 38, 87–90, 289

Air travel tips, 31–32, 43–44

Alcazar, 130

Alma, place de l', 181, 236, *238*

American Church, *205*, 213, 290

American Consulate, 39

American Embassy, 289

American Express, 16, 18, 28, 289

American Hospital, 40, 290

Americans in Paris, 206–7, 266. *See also* Hemingway, Ernest

America Online, 76, 290

Amusement parks, 210
  Disneyland Paris, 278–82

Androuët, 134, 136

Angélina, 162

Aparthotels, 21–22, 58–59

Appollinaire, Guillame, 141, 195

Aquaboulevard, *205*, 212

Arc de Triomphe, 177, 180, 189, 235, 236, *236*, *238*

Army Museum, 181

Arriving in Paris, 86–90

Arrondissements, 91, 94–97

Art. *See also* Art museums; Impressionism; *and specific artists and artworks*
  Bazart, 5–6
  tours and lectures, 172–73

Art galleries, 225

Art museums, 186

Musée d'Art Moderne de la Ville de Paris, 181, 186, 237, *238*

Musée de Cluny, 203, *205*, 241

Musée de l'Orangerie, *205*, 206, *209*, 235, *236*

Musée des Beaux-Arts de Chartres, 285

Musée du Louvre, 185, 187, 189, 235, *236*

Musée d'Orsay, 189, 206, 243, *244*

Musée Jacquemart-André, 186

Musée Marmottan, *205*, 206

Musée Picasso, 189–90, 239, *240*

Musée Rodin, 190, 243, *244*

Petit Palais, *205*, 206

Astier, 136

Atelier Montparnasse, 68

ATM machines, 16–17, 90

Attractions. *See* Sightseeing; *and specific attractions*

Auberge du Vieux Moulin (Giverny), 278

Au Bon Accueil, 139, 237

Au C'Amelot, 140

Au Lapin Agile, 245, 259

Au Printemps, 229

Au Trou Gascon, 149–50

Avenue Montaigne, 51, 96, 220, 236, *238*

B

Baby bistros, 108–9

Baby equipment rental, 289

299

301